Modelling Reality and Personal Modelling

Contributions to Management Science

Ulrich A. W. Tetzlaff
Optimal Design of Flexible Manufacturing Systems
1990. 190 pages. Softcover DM 69,-
ISBN 3-7908-0516-5

Fred von Gunten
Competition in the Swiss Plastics Manufacturing Industry
1991. 408 pages. Softcover DM 120,-
ISBN 3-7908-0541-6

HaraldDyckhoff/Ute Finke
Cutting and Packing in Production and Distribution
1992. 248 pages. Hardcover DM 120,-
ISBN 3-7908-0630-7

Hagen K. C. Pfeiffer
The Diffusion of Electronic Data Interchange
1992. 257 pages. Softcover DM 85,-
ISBN 3-7908-0631-5

Evert Jan Stokking / Giovanni Zambruno (Eds.)
Recent Research in Financial Modelling
1993. 174 pages. Softcover DM 90,-
ISBN 3-7908-0683-8

Richard Flavell (Ed.)

Modelling Reality and Personal Modelling

With 26 Figures

Physica-Verlag
A Springer-Verlag Company

Series Editors
Werner A. Müller
Peter Schuster

Editor
Dr. Richard Flavell
The Management School
Imperial College
53 Prince's Gate
Exhibition Road
London SW7 2PG
United Kingdom

ISBN 978-3-7908-0682-3 ISBN 978-3-642-95900-4 (eBook)
DOI 10.1007/978-3-642-95900-4

CIP-Kurztitelaufnahme der Deutschen Bibliothek
Modelling reality and personal modelling / Richard Flavell
(ed.). - Heidelberg : Physica-Verl., 1993
(Contributions to management science)
ISBN 978-3-7908-0682-3

NE: Flavell, Richard [Hrsg.]

2100/7130-543210 – Printed on acid-free paper

CONTENTS

MODELLING REALITY

Financial modelling takes many forms, as evidenced by the wide spread of topics covered in this volume. All the papers published herein were presented at either the 9th meeting, in Curaçao, or the 10th meeting, in London, of the EURO Working Group and subsequently independently refereed and in many cases revised. I would like to express my gratitude to all the referees for their work. I would especially like to thank Robin Hewins for co-organising the London meeting with me, and for helping in the production of this volume. The topics range from the simulation of a pension fund to the management of a swaps portfolio; from inventory evaluation to the pricing of contingent claim securities; from the behaviour of traders to the inclusion of subjective beliefs in forecasting.

Given this wide range, what are the common elements? They all start from the concept of a model, a representation of the real world or what we might call "reality". Whilst a model is defined by the Oxford Dictionary as a "representation in three dimensions of a proposed structure", systems such as economic, astrophysical or financial do not possess easy physical representations and mathematical descriptions are used. With the advent of computers, such models have become increasingly common, even replacing earlier physical models in many areas of technology as it is of course far easier to manipulate a computer-based model than a physical one.

What constitutes a "good" model of reality? People operate all the time with models, albeit mental ones, of reality [1]. Because every individual is unique, their perception of the world is unique and hence their models are unique. The mental models may be thought of as interacting with "external" mathematical models in the following way. Suppose we initially characterise a mental model of mine as representing 100% of (some limited aspect of) reality. However, some parts of this mental model are computationally very demanding, others require the manipulation of a lot of data, and yet other parts are clearly structured. External models are created to handle some or all of these parts, rather like subroutines in a computer program. My mental model now represents some X% of reality, with (100-X)% being handled by the external models. The results from the external models then slot into my reduced mental model for my own use. The level of X is my decision, based upon my perception of reality. Obviously different people would want to set different levels, and hence require different external models.

So it would seem that "goodness" could be defined in two very distinct ways. First a traditional way which regards a mathematical model as an end in itself. For example, does it provide a close statistical fit to past behaviour, does it provide accurate predictions of the future, does it provide additional inter-relations or insights between different observable parts of reality, and so on. But a second and equally valid way would be to examine how well the outputs from the external models fit into one's mental model.

To illustrate this second way of assessment, consider the following piece of history. Modern financial modelling probably started with the spread of corporate mainframe computers in the 60's and 70's. Complex models of entire organisations were constructed at the cost of several man-years. The idea being that strategic and tactical plans could be simulated under a range of future scenarios. But such models were seldom used despite the large expenditures and the considerable efforts to ensure completeness and accuracy.

The reasons generally suggested are the following. The models were (had to be) developed and in many cases run by modelling "experts" and not by the ultimate "users"[1], due to both hardware and software constraints. This meant that they had to be build using the expert's mental model of the user's mental model of reality. Unfortunately expert modellers tend to have a different style of mental model to that of users [2] and in practice the expert's prevailed. Therefore the models inherently did not provide the users with the required information, and were rejected. In terms

---

[1] The term "user" incorporates the idea of a decision-maker or manager.

of above, the experts' objective seemed to be to minimise X!

In the mid 80's Michel Schlosser [3] and I coined the phrase "personal modelling" to try to explain the rise in popularity of the computerised spreadsheet. In our opinion, this was because the software had developed so that the users themselves were able to create the models, eliminating the experts. The fact that such models may be incomplete, inaccurate, unauditable was less important than they modelled the relevant aspects of reality as perceived by the users. There were of course still obstacles, not least imposed by the physical 2-dimensional layout. We also used the phrase "communicable" to represent models that were to be shared with other people, and therefore had to meet certain external quality conditions. Another development that has helped users is "visual interactive modelling" or VIM [4]. This is the concept that users should be able to "see" inside a model, to "see" it working, and to "see" and play around with the results. VIM creates an environment around a model which is tailored for the user.

So, to me, a good model should be assessed on two levels. Is it a good representation of a very restrictive part of the real world? And does it provide the information required by the users? The reader of this volume will have to use his or her own judgement to rate each model.

References

1. Anthony Sanford, Models, Mind and Man, Pressgang, 1983
2. Paul Finlay, Mathematical Modelling, Croom Helm, 1985
3. Michel Schlosser, Corporate Finance, Prentice Hall, 1989
4. Peter Bell, VIM as an OR technique, Interfaces, 15(4), July-August 1985, pp26-33

Richard Flavell

Economic Policy Determinants: Sensitivity Testing Based on the Mahalanobis Distance Statistic

Dirk-Emma Baestaens
Erasmus University Rotterdam
Dept. of Finance (H14-1)
PO.Box 1738 3000 DR Rotterdam, The Netherlands

1. Introduction

The objective of this paper is to argue for, and to demonstrate, the use of multivariate statistical modelling in order to detect potential periods of unusual behaviour by the unit under examination (for instance, a company). Apparently, exceptional periods as detected by this purely empirical test, may then be investigated using more specifically economic concepts. This paper mainly avoids the latter task.

The approach is empirical and relatively atheoretical, if viewed from the standpoint of traditional econometrics. Econometrics has traditionally estimated numerous equations and variables based on a-priori models of the structure of economic decision behaviour. However the performance of econometric models has sometimes been disappointing (Leamer,1982;Fildes,1985).

The fundamental source of such problems was identified by Malinvaud(1989), namely that empirical economic data sets normally contain too few degrees of freedom to estimate the models that economic theory seems to require. To alleviate the scarce degrees of freedom problem, Time Series modellers have used the few available degrees of freedom to fit statistically well specified models, but to one or two variables (VAR models). In ex ante forecasting, Time Series models are often as good as econometric ones but they suffer from the disadvantage that variables and relationships of economic interest are ignored, so they often lack any implications for economic policy(Sims,1980;Fildes,1985).

We argue that although the problem of scarce degrees of freedom is by its nature insoluble, our proposed method of multivariate distributional modelling is a new way to allocate the scarce degrees of freedom, intermediate between the extremes of Time Series and Econometric modelling. This may on occasion generate useful insights. By including large numbers of variables, in addition to specifications based on alternative theories, we can incorporate the full detail used in economic theory. Yet at the same time, by fitting only static distributions and bivariate correlations, we conserve degrees of freedom for estimating the bivariate relationships and for inferring (though not conclusively estimating) the presence of more dynamic phenomena.

Our basic method is to apply the Mahalanobis Distance statistic (d^2) in order to detect points which are the most extreme values within a (fitted) multivariate normal distribution. Some of these points may fall within a confidence interval set for the assumed distribution, others are outliers which violate it. Our present approach on the contrary may be somewhat novel in the sense that outliers are treated as the major information source (Ezzamel and Mar-Molinero,1990; Howell,1989). As the presence of outliers may cause non normality, the conventional statistical approach has always been to identify such outliers with a view to deleting or separating them from the rest of the data under study (Karels and Prakash,1987). We assume that events in which either individual variables or the relationships between variables take unusual values or are distorted into unusual levels (as measured by statistical criteria) may reflect strain in or upon the economy, respectively the individual firm. This strain may or may not endure after the stress is removed. Here we are interested in extreme states in their own right, though we accept that some of them will be due to spurious observations or chance events.

2. The Mahalanobis Distance Test (d^2)

2.1. Presentation

Where there are many variables, as here, multivariate methods are well developed only for the normal distribution, as discussed by Bacon-Shone and Fung (1987), and this paper uses the Mahalanobis distance (d^2) and Hotelling's T^2 as representative of such methods. Although d^2 assumes either a multivariate normal or elliptical distribution (Mitchell and

Krzanowski,1985), we are hoping that our data are not jointly normally distributed since we are actively seeking outliers from such a distribution. In this sense, we believe we are among the first to apply the Mahalanobis distance in its own right to the issue of measuring corporate fitness.

The joint distribution of normally distributed individual variables is often multivariate normal. Figure 1 shows a resulting ellipse of uniform probability density for two such variables X and Y, standardised to equal standard deviations. A joint confidence region for X and Y is elliptical. This region is not the intersection of the two univariate confidence levels at the same significance level (circle in Figure 1). We call this circle an "uncorrelated" confidence region and points outside it "uncorrelated" outliers. Points in Regions I and II are respectively outliers and inliers for both the ellipse and the circle, whilst points in the Regions III are inliers to the ellipse but outliers to the square. Points in Regions IV are outliers to the ellipse but inliers to the square.

Conventional regression analysis does not yield confidence regions equivalent to the ellipse - projection into the X space makes predictions of Y conditional on X rather than absolute, so that the confidence region is hyperbolic and unbounded before X is observed, and "unusual" states of X are not recognised on observation. In general, the absence of a theoretical framework disallow researchers to give any particular set of X variables special status as independents.

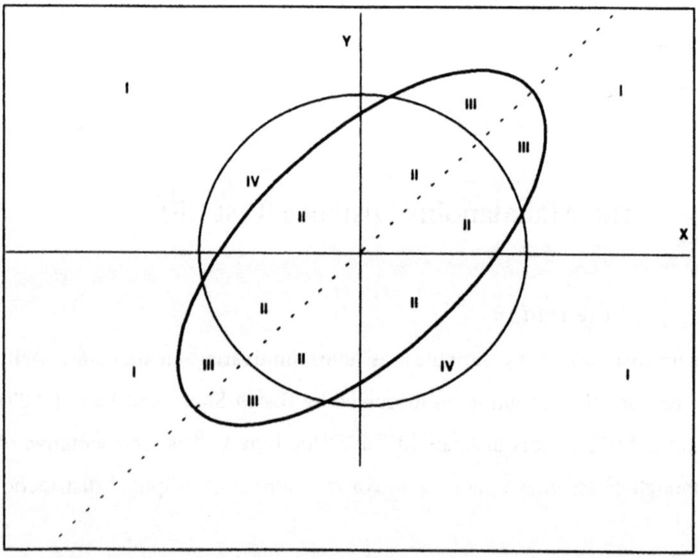

Figure 1: *Possible Confidence Regions using Uncorrelated and Correlated Multivariate Criteria.*

To deal with this we note that points on the ellipse in share not ony the same probability density, but also the same Mahalanobis Distance from the mean observation. The Mahalanobis Distance of a single multivariate observation from the mean observation of a sample of n observations can be estimated using:

$$d^2 = \sum_{i=1}^{p} \sum_{j=1}^{p} (x_i - \overline{x}_i) c^{ij} (x_j - \overline{x}_j) \tag{1}$$

where

$\overline{x}_i$ is the mean of the ith variable

and c^{ij} is the element in the ith row and jth column of the inverse of the variance-covariance matrix C^{-1}.

d^2 follows a Chi Squared distribution with p degrees of freedom (Manly,1986). Figure 1 suggests that in correlated data sets this test will be the most useful and is likely to detect a set of outliers distinct from uncorrelated outliers. A chosen cut off value of the Mahalanobis Distance separates observations between Mahalanobis Outliers (Regions I plus IV in Figure 1) and Mahalanobis Inliers (Regions II plus III). We assume temporarily that a d^2 value has been chosen so as to give these regions convenient relative probabilities, and interpret them as follows. Points in Regions III are events where at least one variable is outside its individual confidence interval, but the joint value is not. Such events we call "structure preserving" in the sense that the expected correlation structure is preserved. In contrast, points in Regions IV we call "structure violating", because although neither variable is outside its individual confidence interval, the expected correlation of the two variables is violated. Events in Region I may or may not violate correlation structures.

2.2. *Decomposition of the Mahalanobis Distance*

In a p dimensional observation each of the p(p-1)/2 pairs of variates may show either structure violating or structure preserving behaviour. It is desirable to have a means of inspecting this behaviour directly, and one which does not make use of an arbitrary d^2 to discriminate between Structure Violation and Structure Preservation.

We can express d^2 in equation (1) as the sum of all the elements of a (pxp) matrix **F** where ,in deviation form (Kendall and Stuart,1983)

$$F_{ij} = x_i x_j C_{ij}^{-1} \tag{2}$$

so that

$$d^2 = \sum_{ij} F_{ij} \tag{3}$$

Diagonal elements of **F** represent a weighting of a single squared deviation of the ith element (i.e. variable) from its mean, and off-diagonal elements represent a weighting of the product of the deviations of the ith and jth variables from their respective means. Since **F** is symmetrical we can conveniently combine off diagonal F_{ij} and F_{ji} in a single cell by defining **T** (pxp) such that

for i = j	$T_{ii} = F_{ii}$	
for i < j	$T_{ii} = 2F_{ii}$	(4)
for i > j	$T_{ii} = 0$	

Diagonal elements of **T** show the contribution to d^2 of the individual deviation of each variable in isolation, while subdiagonal elements show the specific contribution to d^2 from each variable's interaction with each single other variable. Diagonal elements in **T** and **F** are by definition positive, but off diagonal elements can take either sign.

A negative element T_{ij} for i<j indicates that the joint deviations of x_i and x_j in this observation are less unlikely than the diagonal elements (their individual unlikelihoods) would suggest, and the fact that they are varying in the expected joint direction is "Structure Preserving". Such terms reflect the fraction of the joint variation of x_i and x_j that can be predicted from their correlation, and is akin to the "sum of squares explained" in ANOVA. They may correspond to events in Regions II and III of for the x_i and x_j concerned. Conversely a positive value for T_{ij} for i<j indicates that an expected positive or negative correlation has been reversed, and this unexpected joint state of x_i and x_j we can call "Structure Violating". It can correspond to an event in Regions IV or I (for variables x_i and x_j only).

A zero value of T_{ij} can occur for i<j if x_i and x_j are uncorrelated in the sample as a whole ($T_{ij} = F_{ij} = 0$ for i not equal to j), or if standardised x_i or x_j or both are close to zero in this observation. Such observations are Structurally Neutral, or Uninformative.

2.3. *Matrix Simplification of* F *and* T *to* $\mathbf{F_s}$ *and* $\mathbf{T_s}$

So far, the triangular matrix **T** represents nothing more than a rearrangement of the full contribution matrix **F**. The value for d^2 was not at all affected. As matrices **F** and **T** in section above contain p(p-1)/2 different entries per observation, we attempted to simplify these matrices by setting to zero all elements in **F** (**T**) whose absolute value was smaller than a filter value *s*. The resulting matrix can be called $\mathbf{F_S}$ ($\mathbf{T_S}$) , and the approximated Mahalanobis Distance is d_s^2 , where

$$d^2 \approx d_s^2 = \sum_{i,j=1}^{p} F_{(s)ij} \tag{5}$$

$$d^2 \approx d_s^2 = \sum_{i,j=1}^{p} T_{(s)ij} \tag{6}$$

We used no theory to set s but investigated the sensitivity of d_s^2 to s, and selected the largest value of s for which d_s^2 seemed a close and stable approximation to d^2. This simplified interpretation as well as providing a heuristic to avoid over interpreting the large noise content of a p dimensional observation.

2.4. *Classification of Entries in* $\mathbf{F_s}$

Given the simplest acceptable $\mathbf{F_S}$ (or $\mathbf{T_S}$), we sorted the variables in descending order of the joint net contributions to d_s^2 (that is, the column, respectively row, totals of **F**). This partitioned $\mathbf{F_S}$ into three regions: Block **A**, where all totals were positive, Block **B** where the sums were zero and Block **C** where all aggregates were negative. We call all variables with nonzero diagonal entries Main Variables, since they matter in their own right.

Block **A** variables contribute positively to d^2 and are therefore acting in a Structure Violating way. These variables can be observed to reinforce d^2 in their own right (diagonal entry larger than zero resulting in the classification of this variable as Main Variable) and/or in interaction with other variables (off-diagonal entries larger than zero). The contribution of Block **B** variables remains neutral or uninformative as all diagonal and off-diagonal elements are set to zero. While the net contribution by Block **C** variables can be classified as structure preserving (i.e. distance reducing), their individual contributions are never negative (diagonal elements are weighted squared deviations from respective means) implying that the variable interactions must more than offset these individual excursions. Again a nonzero positive deviation results in a classification as a Main Variable.

2.5. *Hotelling's T^2 to Search for Longer Lasting Outlier Episodes*

Mahalanobis outliers for large enough d^2 are rare in the sample. They may at times be caused by chance events, or invalid measurements, or valid measurements of relationships that have no substantive economic importance. However they may also reflect important structural effects. For example the observed overall correlation may be due to forces that tend to suppress certain joint states of the variables. If the system is driven suddenly into a "non favoured" state by some shock or stress, and the corrective forces do not take full effect within a single sampling interval lagged effects may occur.

If such lagged effects are present, some Mahalanobis outliers will form part of extended episodes, in which extreme states in p space are only gradually approached and/or gradually departed from. While the squared Mahalanobis Distance was convenient for testing individual outlier observations, we used the Hotelling's T^2 to test whether the mean of a group of p dimensional observations differs from the mean of a second group (the remaining observations) assumed to have the same covariance matrix. For a null hypothesis of equal sample means the relevant test statistic reduces to an F distribution with p and (n-p-1) degrees of freedom, in the notation of equation (7) below (Manley,19-86; Krzanowski,1988).

$$T^2 = n_1 n_2 / n_1 + n_2 \sum_{i,j=1}^{p} (\overline{x}_{1i} - \overline{x}_{2i}) c^{ij} (\overline{x}_{1i} - \overline{x}_{2i}) \tag{7}$$

where

$\overline{x}_{1i}$ = the mean of the ith variable for group 1

p = number of variables

n = pooled sample size or ($n_1 + n_2$), and

c^{ij} = the element in the ith row and jth column of the inverse of the pooled within group covariance matrix

In order to avoid bias by each outlier itself, the latter should be omitted it from each putative episode. A search for subsets of the total sample, contiguous with but not including the outlier(s), which differ significantly from the total sample, can then be conducted by trial and error. Clearly there is some risk of "Data Mining" in such a search, and we have not attempted to derive an exact correction for it. Explicitly dynamic methods were not used because of the scarcity of degrees of freedom, and because uniform simple dynamics may not be present throughout the sample.

3. Summary of Hypotheses

1. The Mahalanobis distance will readily identify extreme points in data sets which are wholly or mainly multivariate normal in their distribution . For convenience, these points are called Mahalanobis outliers regardless of whether they are outliers under any specific combination of formal tests and assumed distribution.

2. Sets of Mahalanobis outliers will differ from those identified by tests which ignore mutual correlation, such as the Euclidean and Penrose distance measures. Outlier detection methods based on a count of a significant number of variables reaching a significance level as indicated by, for instance, the Kolmogorov-Smirnov and Shapiro-Wilks tests, will perform even weaker because of their inherently univariate nature.

3. Mahalanobis Distances of outliers (or inliers) can be decomposed to show the contributions made by each individual variable and by each pair of variables. The latter can in turn be divided into "Structure Preserving", "Structure Violating" and "Structurally Neutral" behaviour. No specific predictions are made, but the structure of actual outliers is assumed to be of interest to economic modellers (for instance, public utility regulators).

4. Mahalanobis Outliers will sometimes be a part of longer Dynamic episodes, in which either the approach to or the retreat from an outlier value in Mahalanobis space spreads over several sampling intervals. Such outliers may be followed by "rebounds", or outliers in the opposite direction in space, such that the average of the two outliers does not differ significantly from the mean observation as measured by Hotelling's T^2.

5. Some outliers may not be associated either with extended episodes nor rebounds. Such "solitary" outliers may be due to data errors, but may also be due to extreme shocks to the system. In the latter case, they may be followed by extreme values for single variables.

6. Multivariate distributions of data on an economy will not be static, but will show, in addition to outliers, signs of sustained structural change (perhaps corresponding to intuitively identifiable periods of economic history). Such secular changes will increase the scatter of a fitted static distribution, and so reduce the power of tests for outliers, but Mahalanobis extreme values will still occur, and outliers strong enough to be detectable in these conditions may have substantive meaning.

To demonstrate the potential of the Mahalanobis distance approach, this paper will address hypotheses one and three by means of a simple application . The aim is to improve our understanding of corporate health (however defined) and to get a feel of the firm's sensitivity to interventions by interested parties such as fiscal authorities, managers or stockholders.

4. Application: Categorizing Corporate Fitness

An investigation into the condition of a particular company usually degenerates into the question whether or not the firm faces the prospect of failure. Most attempts to quantify the failure process, which is ,incidentally, not accounted for by a solid theoretical framework, make use of the multiple discriminant analysis (MDA). In theory, the use of MDA requires the prevalence of at least two easily identifiable and mutually exclusive groups of observations, multivariate normality of the cases under study, specification of the a priori probabilities of occurrence of each group and dispersion matrices' equality in case of linear discriminant analysis (LDA). We assert that, because of the restrictive nature of these requirements, the MDA method may not be the most appropriate method to describe and predict failure. Distributional analysis is argued to alleviate these constraints and represents therefore a viable alternative to MDA.

We selected a sample of 13 companies listed on the LSE and for which the FT provides daily financial coverage under the heading Newspapers & Publishers. Our sample constitutes about 34% of the total industry with strong emphasis (about 60%) on the newspapers & periodicals segment. The companies are given in table 1.

1	Black (A.& C.)	BLAC
2	Maxwell Comms.Corp.	MAXC
3	Pearson	PSON
4	Trinity Int Hld.	TRIN
5	Utd.Newspapers	UNWS
6	News Int Spec.Div.	NEWS
7	Portsm'th & Sund	PSUN
8	Reed International	REED
9	Haynes Pub	HYNES
10	Bristol Eve.Post	BRTL
11	EMAP	EMAP
12	News Corp	NEWSC
13	Daily Mail "A"	DMGT

Table 1: Selected Companies and Code

Annual data from 1984 to 1989 (and where possible 1990) were compiled from Datastream. The Printing & Publishing industry was selected because of its alleged homogeneity in terms of cost structure and of the press coverage some industry members were/are receiving. The small number of companies (in absolute sense) excluded every attempt to restrict the sample to only those companies with the same year end. We agree with Gonedes (1973) that such restriction may be viewed as a sample stratification in the sense that the selected companies may share some characteristics that differ from those companies with different year ends.

Since we are interested in the health (or vulnerability) of individual firms over time relative to the industry considered, we pooled the cross-sectional data on individual firms resulting in 82 observations.

Raw data were collected in seasonally adjusted form and where appropriate differenced to remove time trends. Table 2 lists the variables and codes. It can also be seen that most variables depart from a normal distribution on the Lilliefors test (1967), a variant on the Kolmogorov-Smirnov test when the population parameters are unknown, at the 5% significance level.

CATEGORY		VARIABLE	CODE	K-S TEST
1 COMPANY SPECIFIC				
1	PROFITABILITY	OPERATING MARGIN	PROFMAR	YES
2	CAPITAL STRUCTURE	BORROWING RATIO	BORRAT	NO
3	LIQUIDITY	CASH / CUR LIABILITIES	CASHCUR	NO
4	UTILIZATION RATE	SALES / NET CUR ASSETS	TURNCUAS	NO
5	FISCAL CLIMATE	TAX / PRETAX PROFIT	TAXRAT	YES
2 PRINTING & PUBLISHING INDUSTRY RELATED				
6	EARNINGS INDEX	AVG EARNINGS EMPLOYEES P&P INDUSTRY TO AVG EARNINGS MANUFACTURING INDUSTRY	EARNRAT	NO
7	TRADE TERMS	PPI OUTPUT OF PAPER PRODUCTS TO PPI MATERIALS PURCHASED	TRADET	NO
8	PRODUCTIVITY INDEX	OUTPUT INDUSTRY/OUTPUT MANUF IND IN VOLUME TERMS	RELOUTP	NO
3 ECONOMY WIDE				
9	MARKET CONFIDENCE	SP / FT ALL SHARE INDEX	SPFTA	NO
10	NATIONAL OUTPUT	GDP (SA)	GDP	YES
		PERCENTAGE CHANGE	GDP	YES

Table 2: Selected variables

The bad results on the normality tests , while not very encouraging, must not be dramatised.

First, a non normal distribution represents a well known property of most financial ratios (Karels and Prakash,1987). Following Barnes (1982) we did therefore not attempt to apply standard Box and Cox transformations for right skewed data using the logarithm, square roots and cubic roots. Negative data values prevented the use of these transformations. Of course we could have added a constant where necessary or we could have applied the reciprocal transformation but we feared that too much data manipulation might have destroyed the ratios' informational content. The univariate non normality, of course, may have an adverse impact on the presence of multivariate outliers implying the need to consider the them with great caution, although univariate normality by itself does not guarantee multivariate normality.

Second, assuming the homogeneity of our sample, it may be argued that for a large sample such as ours a small violation of the normality assumption is sufficient for it to be rejected.

Unlike most multiple discriminant analysis studies , we attempted to incorporate three possible determinants of corporate well-being and their interaction effects in one dataset. A firm's financial health can be viewed as a function of firm specific, industry related and/or economy wide elements. Obviously, each of these components could be emulated by numerous variables and ratios. In order to select a meaningful variable set for each component, factor analysis (PCA) may be called for to reduce the number of relevant variables. Here, we selected the variables on the basis of their perceived popularity in the literature. The TAXRAT variable can be interpreted as management's ability in minimising taxes paid by incorporating the idea of tax relief on new investment. Consequently, more money will be available for productive uses.

4.1. Presence of Mahalanobis Outliers

Table 3 shows the set of five outliers all at 1% significance. On the null hypothesis one might expect one or two such outliers in a sample of 82 observations.

Case #	CODE	d^2	d
62	585	79.34	8.91
68	1085	57.33	7.57
67	1385	49.16	7.01
76	684	31.53	5.62
64	785	26.61	5.16
79	984	20.99	4.58
66	985	20.11	4.48
70	1285	17.24	4.15
69	1185	17.06	4.13
72	284	16.2	4.02

Table 3: Mahalanobis Outliers

Key to Code:

Last two digits refer to year

first two digits refer to company number in Table 1

Cut-off value at the 1%: 23.11 $(X^2_{0.01;10})$

All significant outliers (and for that matter the first ten outliers) refer to either 1984 or 1985. The nonuniform distribution of the outliers over time may indicate that the industry or parts thereof was under severe strain during that period. It would be useful to check the evidence of this assumed strain by examination of the relevant annual reports of the identified firms. Figure 2 illustrates that the Printing & Publishing industry employees earned relatively more than employees in other sectors of the manufacturing industry, hereby weaking their industry's attractiveness to investors. Moreover, the producer price index (PPI) of paper products' output dropped relative to the PPI of materials purchased by the publishing industry. The industry's outlook for 1984-85 looked gloomly which may have been a contributory factor to the high d^2 values for that period. Furthermore , it appears to confirm our expectation of a nonstationary mean for the Mahalanobis model implying a structural break within the economy or industry under investigation. To the extent the break does not alter the estimated dispersion matrix, the model's validity remains safeguarded.

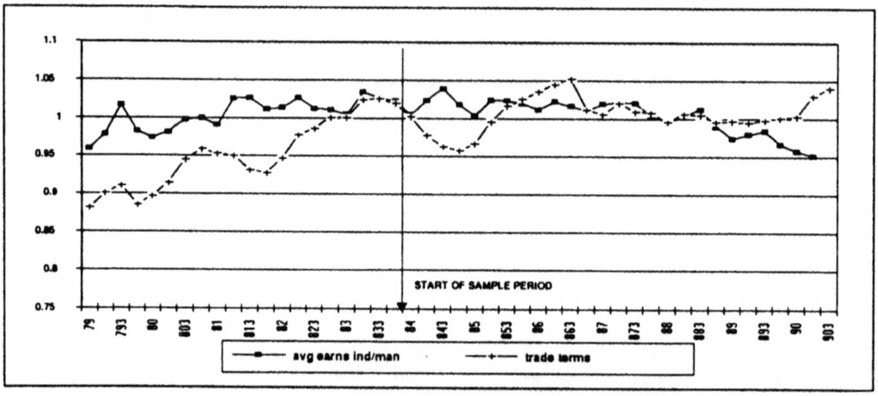

Figure 2: Competitive Position of Printing & Publishing Industry

Figures 3 and 4 show all outliers over time ranked by firm. It can be seen that the outlier for firm 7 (PSUN) appears to be part of a longer dynamic episode in which both the approach to and the retreat from the outlier value spreads over several sampling intervals. In contrast, the values for firms 10 (BRTL) and 13 (DMGT) seem to belong to an episode in which the approach to, respectively the retreat from the outlier marks a rather abrupt process.

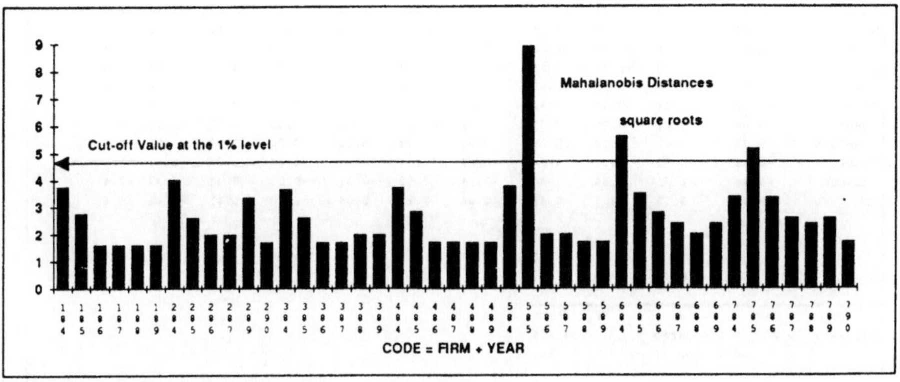

Figure2: Distances Firms 1 (BLAC) to 7 (PSUN)

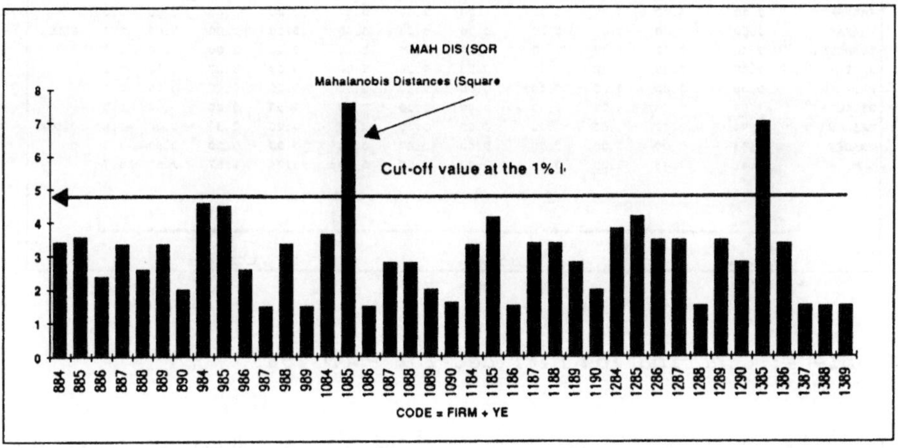

Figure 3: Distances Firms 8 (REED) to 13 (DMGT)

4.2. Decomposition of Outliers

We now decompose the d^2 values by rearranging the variables in such a way that we gain insight in their individual and joint behaviour.

Since our variable set is not very large (p=10), the 45 pairs can be evaluated without necessarily simplifying the contribution matrix (**F**). Table 4 shows contribution matrices

CODE 785: PORTSM'TH & SUNDERLAND 1985

UNSIMPLIFIED SORTED CONTRIBUTION MATRIX F

	TAXRAT	GDP	PROFMAR	RELOUTP	SPFTA	EARNRAT	BORRAT	TURNCUAS	TRADET	CASHCUR	SUM
TAXRAT	30.63	4.83	1.87	-7.57	-0.31	-0.99	0.04	0.02	-2.55	-3.94	22.0
GDP	4.83	2.62	0.56	0.18	-0.08	-0.34	0.01	0.01	-0.50	-1.21	6.1
PROFMAR	1.87	0.56	1.57	-1.26	-0.52	-0.44	0.00	0.00	0.01	-0.64	1.2
RELOUTP	-7.57	0.18	-1.26	7.53	0.69	0.30	0.01	0.01	0.04	0.64	0.6
SPFTA	-0.31	-0.08	-0.52	0.69	0.66	0.22	0.01	0.00	-0.19	-0.14	0.3
EARNRAT	-0.99	-0.34	-0.44	0.30	0.22	1.03	-0.01	0.00	0.34	0.10	0.2
BORRAT	0.04	0.01	0.00	0.01	0.01	-0.01	0.00	0.00	-0.01	-0.01	0.0
TURNCUAS	0.02	0.01	0.00	0.01	0.00	0.00	0.00	0.00	0.00	-0.01	0.0
TRADET	-2.55	-0.50	0.01	0.04	-0.19	0.34	-0.01	0.00	1.05	0.41	-1.4
CASHCUR	-3.94	-1.21	-0.64	0.64	-0.14	0.10	-0.01	-0.01	0.41	2.37	-2.4
SUM	22.04	6.08	1.15	0.55	0.34	0.21	0.04	0.03	-1.41	-2.44	26.6

SIMPLIFIED SORTED CONTRIBUTION MATRIX T

FILTER s = 2 D Squared 26.608
D Simplified 24.696

	TAXRAT	GDP	EARNRAT	BORRAT	TURNCUAS	SPFTA	PROFMAR	RELOUTP	CASHCUR	TRADET	SUM	
TAXRAT	30.63	4.83	0.00	0.00	0.00	0.00	0.00	-7.57	-3.94	-2.55	21.4	BLOCK
GDP	4.83	2.62	0.00	0.00	0.00	0.00	0.00	0.00	0.00	0.00	7.5	A
EARNRAT	0.00	0.00	0.00	0.00	0.00	0.00	0.00	0.00	0.00	0.00	0.0	
BORRAT	0.00	0.00	0.00	0.00	0.00	0.00	0.00	0.00	0.00	0.00	0.0	BLOCK
TURNCUAS	0.00	0.00	0.00	0.00	0.00	0.00	0.00	0.00	0.00	0.00	0.0	B
SPFTA	0.00	0.00	0.00	0.00	0.00	0.00	0.00	0.00	0.00	0.00	0.0	
PROFMAR	0.00	0.00	0.00	0.00	0.00	0.00	0.00	0.00	0.00	0.00	0.0	
RELOUTP	-7.57	0.00	0.00	0.00	0.00	0.00	0.00	7.53	0.00	0.00	0.0	
CASHCUR	-3.94	0.00	0.00	0.00	0.00	0.00	0.00	0.00	2.37	0.00	-1.6	BLOCK
TRADET	-2.55	0.00	0.00	0.00	0.00	0.00	0.00	0.00	0.00	0.00	-2.5	C
SUM	21.41	7.45	0.00	0.00	0.00	0.00	0.00	-0.04	-1.57	-2.55	24.7	

BLOCK A BLOCK B BLOCK C

Table 4: Contribution Matrices for PSUN 1985

ranked by the net variable contribution to d^2 and d_s^2 (ie. column, respectively row, labelled sum) for firm 7 (PSUN) for 1985.

The d^2 contribution matrix shows that all variables are active, that is display nonzero entries. This finding which was confirmed by the analysis of all **F** matrices supports our claim that it is dangerous to rely on univariate criteria when assessing corporate vulnerability. Moreover, the finding demonstrates the weakness of those techniques such as MDA that attempt to identify failure trigger points by the sole use of internal, company specific factors. External (industry and economy) factors are not to be omitted from the analysis.

It can be seen that d^2 appears to be driven (Block **A**) by the solitary contribution of the tax ratio variable and the joint contributions of the GDP variable. Structure preserving behaviour (Block **C**) is displayed by the trade terms, turnover to net current assets and liquidity ratios. The remaining variables do not contribute in any way to d^2 and are therefore classified as Block **B** variables.

All Block **A** variables are Main variables, i.e. important in their own right whereas one Block **C** variable (Trade terms) figures as a nonmain variable (i.e. unimportant in its own right).

Sensitivity Analysis

The decomposed contribution matrix **F** could be used as input for the selection of appropriate "policy variables" by regulatory authorities or industry watchdogs. To understand the variables joint behaviour within the system, estimated variance and covariances could be altered to quantify the effects (that is, changes in d^2) of potential policy changes. The aim would then be to minimise d^2 or to bring it below some agreed reference value. To exemplify, we doubled the variance of the TAXRAT variable mentioned in Table 4 (authorities indirectly control this variable through the tax rate). The outcome of this intervention can be judged from Table 5.

	TAXRAT	RELOUTP	GDP	EARNRAT	SPFTA	PROFMAR	TURNCUAS	BORRAT	TRADET	CASHCUR	SUM
TAXRAT	7.84	-1.94	1.24	-0.25	-0.08	0.48	0.01	0.01	-0.65	-1.01	5.64
RELOUTP	-1.94	6.14	1.07	0.12	0.63	-0.91	0.01	0.01	-0.43	-0.09	4.60
GDP	1.24	1.07	2.05	-0.22	-0.04	0.34	0.01	0.01	-0.20	-0.75	3.49
EARNRAT	-0.25	0.12	-0.22	1.00	0.21	-0.39	0.00	-0.01	0.28	0.01	0.74
SPFTA	-0.08	0.63	-0.04	0.21	0.66	-0.50	0.00	0.01	-0.21	-0.17	0.51
PROFMAR	0.48	-0.91	0.34	-0.39	-0.50	1.49	0.00	0.00	0.12	-0.46	0.16
TURNCUAS	0.01	0.01	0.01	0.00	0.00	0.00	0.00	0.00	0.00	-0.01	0.02
BORRAT	0.01	0.01	0.01	-0.01	0.01	0.00	0.00	0.00	-0.01	-0.01	0.01
TRADET	-0.65	-0.43	-0.20	0.28	-0.21	0.12	0.00	-0.01	0.89	0.17	-0.04
CASHCUR	-1.01	-0.09	-0.75	0.01	-0.17	-0.46	-0.01	-0.01	0.17	1.99	-0.33
SUM	5.64	4.60	3.49	0.74	0.51	0.16	0.02	0.01	-0.04	-0.33	14.81

Table 5: Impact of Fiscal Intervention on Mahalanobis Distance

Due to the intervention, this observation has become an inlier. Note that the TAXRAT variable is still the most important Main variable. Obviously, to fully assess the impact of government's intervention, it is necessary to compute all d^2 values again to ascertain whether or not outliers have become inliers or vice versa. We hope our simplified example has demonstrated the model's potential usefulness in identifying target, intermediary and policy variables without having recourse to monetarist or post-keynesian theories.

5. Conclusions

An important task for regulatory authorities is to identify times when the economy is behaving unusually. Relatively little attention in a statistical sense has been paid to the criteria for classifying economic behaviour as unusual. This paper argues that traditional outlier detection methods have usually been an extension of univariate analysis and therefore not statistically efficient since the fact is ignored that economic variables are highly mutually correlated . The advocated approach , the Mahalanobis distance d^2, is empirical and relatively atheoretical. In this sense it is closely related to other "model free" approaches such as neural nets. But even when neural nets are used, the way the data are defined and transformed has implications in economic theory. It can be observed that our model identifies and analyzes the actual distortions rather than its origins. Indeed, it would be futile to try to isolate causal factors because a dynamic economic system behaves very much like a nonrecursive model in which the variables cannot be arranged in any hierarchical order. Consequently, no single variable can be picked as the sole or determining cause of the state of the system afterwards.

The d^2 method which we call distributional analysis seems to be logically intermediate between the traditional extremes of econometric regression and time series analysis. Given an endemic shortage of degrees of freedom, it may for certain phenomena be the most effective method for collecting evidence or identifying new areas for investigation.

We applied distributional analysis to account for companies' performance as measured by a set of accounting and financial ratios. The analysis may then be viewed as an alternative model to the classic multiple discriminant technique (MDA). A comparative analysis of the contribution matrices (**F**) to the distance d^2 may yield valuable insights into the corporate health issue and could eventually contribute to a more systematic approach of the corporate collapse question. Furthermore, the Mahalanobis model is argued to assist industry regulators in the selection of "policy" variables and testing of various competing economic theories.

The Mahalanobis technique incorporates some advantages over the MDA. First, there is no need to worry about the conceptualisation of the categories the observations fall into and to resort to ad hoc criteria. Second, as the Mahalanobis model actively hunts for outliers, deviations from multivariate normality are tolerated. Lastly, contrary to most MDA analyses, we see no need to restrict the variables to those endogeneous, that is accounting or financial, components. External factors, such as industry and economy effects, need incorporated into the analysis.

The Mahalanobis model is, of course, not without its defects. We assumed a stable variance-covariance matrix. Our empirical test showed the presence of a nonstationary mean so the manifestation of an equally nonuniform variance cannot be dismissed. Furthermore, the predictive ability of the Mahalanobis model is restricted to those outliers that form part of longer lasting episodes. Unexpected or sudden outliers cannot be forecasted, but then how good is MDA at anticipating sudden corporate fragility ?

6. References

Bacon-Shone,J. and Fung,W.K. (1987) "A new graphical method for Detecting Single and Multiple Outliers in Univariate and Multivariate Data" Applied Statistics, 36:2,153-162

Baestaens,D.J.E.(1990),The Market Impact of Regulation on Financial Institutions, Ph.D. Thesis, Manchester Business School

Barnes,P.(1982),"Methodological Implications of Non-Normally Distributed Financial ratios",Journal of Business Finance & Accounting, 9:1, 51-62

Ezzamel,M. and Mar-Molinero,C.(1990),"The Distributional Properties of Financial Ratios in UK Manufacturing Companies",Journal of Business Finance & Accounting, 17:1,1-29

Fildes,R.(1985), "Quantitative Forecasting-The State of the Art: Econometric Models", J.O.R.S., 36:7, 549-580

Gonedes,N.J.(1973),"Properties of Accounting Numbers: Models and Tests",Journal of Accounting Research, 212-237

Hotelling,H. (1931)," The generalisation of Student's ratio", Ann. Math. Stat.,Vol 2,360-78

Howell S.D. (1989) "Quantitative Forecasting: Issues and Methods " in Ashton D. and Hopper T. (eds) Readings for Accounting pratice, London: Philip Allen

Karels,G.V. and Prakash,A.J. (1987),"Multivariate Normality and Forecasting of Business Bankruptcy",Journal of Business Finance & Accounting,14:4, 573-593

Leamer,E.E.(1982),"Let's Take the Con out of Economics", Am.Economic.Rev., 73:1,31-43

Lilliefors,H.W.(1967),"On the Kolmogorov-Smirnov Test for Normality with Mean and Variance Unknown",Journal of the American Statistical Association,62,399-402

Mahalanobis,P.C. (1930), "On Tests and Measures of Group Divergence", Jounal of the Asiatic Society of Bengal,vol 26,541-88

Mahalanobis,P.C.(1936)," On the Generalised Distance in Statistics", Proceedings National Institute of Sciences of India, vol 2,49-55

Mahalanobis,P.C.(1948)," Historical Note on the Dý-Statistic", Sankhya,vol 9, 237-40

Malinvaud,E.(1989),"Observation in Macroeconomic Theory Building", European Economic Review, 33,205-223

Manly,B.F.J. (1988), Mutivariate Statistical Methods.A Primer, London: Chapman and Hall

Martikainen,T. and Ankelo,T.(1990),"On the Instability of Financial Paterns in Failed Firms and the Predictability of Corporate failure", Proceedings of the University of Vaasa, Discussion Papers 113,Vaasa:Finland

Mitchell A.F.S.and Krzanowski,W.J.(1985) "The Mahalanobis Distance and Elliptic Distributions", Biometrika,72:2, 464-7

Richardson,F.M. and Davidson,L.F.(1983),"An Exploration into Bankruptcy Discriminant Model Sensitivity",Journal of Business Finance & Accounting,10:2,195-207

Sims,C.A.(1980),"Macroeconomics and Reality",Econometrica, 48:1,1-48

Time Dominance and I.R.R.

Francesca Beccacece and Erio Castagnoli
Università Commerciale L. Bocconi, Milano, Italy

Abstract

Time dominance among cash flows leads, in a very simple way, to state inequalities among their present values evaluated with generic discount factors.

In particular it is shown how some well known theorems concerning the uniqueness of a non-negative I.R.R. represent special cases, requiring no proof, of the above argument.

I Introduction

Time dominance of various orders, first introduced by Ekern [5] in 1981, is a unifying and powerful tool for many financial problems. In our opinion, it is still scarcely used: in any case considerably less than its natural counterpart represented by stochastic dominance. The present paper does not aim to present new results, but only to show how some classical conditions for the internal rate of return (I.R.R.) of a financial project (Norstrøm [7], de Faro [4], Bernhard [1], and others) can be simply obtained arguing by time dominance of cash flows.

There are two main advantages in this line of reasoning: the first one is simplicity, the second one is that the arguments are kept entirely on a financial ground, through a very clear and close link with time dominance that is with quite general preference orderings among cash flows. Moreover, it is possible to cover not only the particular case of exponential (i.e. compound) discount factors, but also the general case of arbitrary discount factors.

A (non random and discrete) financial project is described in the usual way by a set of maturities and a set of money amounts. For mathematical convenience, in the first part of the paper (sec. II and III) we consider only countable sets. Following this approach the cash flow of a finite project has to be completed (by adding zeroes at arbitrary maturities) to cover an infinite horizon: this may appear cumbersome but it simplifies formal deduction of results.

In the last section of the paper, to complete the derivation of classical results in a simplified way, we will deal with finite sets of maturities (sec. IV) and, in order to capture negative I.R.R.'s, with increasing discount factors (sec. IV).

II Preliminaries

Definition and results of this section, with some slight modifications, are particularizations of Ekern's ones to the discrete case.

Let $\mathbf{T}$ be a countable set of maturities $0 \leq t_0 < t_1 < t_2 < ... < t_s < ...$ having no finite accumulation point and x be a countable cash flow $x_0, x_1, x_2, ..., x_s, ...$

Using a discount factor $\varphi : \mathbf{T} \to [0, +\infty)$ with $\varphi(0) = 1$, the present value of x is:

$$V_x[\varphi] = \sum_{s=0}^{+\infty} x_s \varphi_s \tag{1}$$

where $\varphi_s = \varphi(t_s)$.

Throughout the paper we will confine our attention to the class $\mathcal{X}(\mathbf{T})$ of all financial projects having the same set of maturities $\mathbf{T}$ and a cash flow which is definitely (i.e. a part from a finite number of terms) of constant sign or zero.

Under the stated assumptions, $V_x[\varphi]$ exists (finite or infinite) for all $x \in \mathcal{X}(\mathbf{T})$.

Let $x \in \mathcal{X}(\mathbf{T})$. Its cumulative cash flow will be denoted by $\overline{x}^{(1)}$; $\overline{x}^{(2)}$ will indicate the cumulative of $\overline{x}^{(1)}$ and so on:

$$\overline{x}_s^{(k)} = \sum_{r=0}^{s} \overline{x}_r^{(k-1)} \qquad k = 1, 2, \ldots.$$

with $\overline{x}^{(0)} = x$.

Remark. Setting $x_i = 0$ for negative i's, we have:

$$\overline{x}_s^{(k)} = \sum_{r=0}^{s} \binom{k+r-1}{r} x_{s-r} \tag{2}$$

Definition 1 Let $x, y \in \mathcal{X}(\mathbf{T})$. We will say that there is *time dominance of order* k of x on y, briefly that x *k-dominates* y, written $x \succeq_k y$ or $y \preceq_k x$, if:

$$\overline{x}^{(k)} \geqq \overline{y}^{(k)} \qquad k = 0, 1, 2, \ldots.$$

Remark. If $x \succeq_k y$, then $x \succeq_h y$ for any integer $h > k$.

In the sequel $\Delta^k \varphi_s$ will stand for the k-th difference of φ_s:

$$\Delta^k \varphi_s = \sum_{r=0}^{k} (-1)^{k-r} \binom{k}{r} \varphi_{s+r}.$$

For $k \in \mathbf{N}_0$, we will denote by Φ_k the class of discount factors such that $(-1)^h \Delta^h \varphi_s \geq 0$ for any s and for $h = 0, 1, 2, \ldots, k$. Φ_∞ stands for $\bigcap_{k=0}^{+\infty} \Phi_k$. Obviously:

$$\Phi_0 \supset \Phi_1 \supset \Phi_2 \supset \cdots \supset \Phi_\infty.$$

In particular:

Φ_0 is the class of all (non negative) discount factors;

Φ_1 is the class of decreasing discount factors;

Φ_2 is the class of decreasing and "convex" discount factors[1].

Exponential discount factors ($\varphi(t) = e^{-\delta t}, \delta \geq 0, t \geq 0$) belong to[2] Φ_∞.

Summing by parts, (1) can be rewritten:

$$V_x[\varphi] = \sum_{s=0}^{+\infty} x_s \varphi_s = (-1)^k \sum_{s=0}^{+\infty} \overline{x}_s^{(k)} \Delta^k \varphi_s. \tag{3}$$

We can give the following:

Theorem 2 *Let $x, y, x - y \in \mathcal{X}(\mathrm{T})$. If $x \succeq_k y$, then $V_x[\varphi] \geq V_y[\varphi] \quad \forall \varphi \in \Phi_k$.*

Proof: It suffices to apply (3) to $x - y$. □

Denoting by **0** the zero cash flow, the following general property is an obvious consequence of Theorem 2.

Theorem 3 *If $x \succeq_k \mathbf{0}$ (or $x \preceq_k \mathbf{0}$), that is $\overline{x}^{(k)} \geqq 0$ (or $\overline{x}^{(k)} \leqq 0$), then $V_x[\varphi] \geq V_{\mathbf{0}}[\varphi] = 0$ (or $V_x[\varphi] \leq 0$) $\forall \varphi \in \Phi_k$.*

Theorem 3 can be used to discuss painlessly the existence of the IRR for a financial project[3]. For instance, if the cumulative vector $\overline{x}^{(k)}$ is non negative for some k, Theorem 3 guarantees that the present value of x is non negative for any interest rate and thus no IRR exists.

Since the exponential discount factors belong to Φ_∞, we can consider any sequence $\overline{x}^{(k)}$ when discussing the I.R.R. of x.

III Non-negative I.R.R.: existence and uniqueness

In this section we will consider exponential discount factors with (constant) non-negative instantaneous interest rate: $\varphi(t) = e^{-\delta t}$, $\delta \geq 0$.

Let:

$$V_x(\delta) = \sum_{s=0}^{+\infty} x_s e^{-\delta t_s} \qquad x \in \mathcal{X}(\mathrm{T})$$

be the present value in this case. A value $\delta^* \geq 0$ is intended an I.R.R. if $V_x(\delta^*) = 0$ and the graph of $V_x(\delta)$ crosses the horizontal axis.

Without any serious loss of generality, we can suppose equidistance of maturities: $t_s = as, a > 0$ (it suffices to insert some maturities with null payments). It is:

$$\Delta^k \varphi_s = \Delta^k e^{-\delta as} = e^{-\delta as}(e^{-\delta a} - 1)^k.$$

Hence the present value of x is:

$$V_x(\delta) = \sum_{s=0}^{+\infty} x_s e^{-\delta as} = (-1)^k \sum_{s=0}^{+\infty} \overline{x}_s^{(k)} \Delta^k e^{-\delta as} =$$

$$= (1 - e^{-\delta a})^k \sum_{s=0}^{+\infty} \overline{x}_s^{(k)} e^{-\delta as} = (1 - e^{-\delta a})^k V_{\overline{x}^{(k)}}(\delta).$$

Excluding $\delta = 0$, all the equations $V_{\overline{x}^{(k)}}(\delta) = 0$, $k = 0, 1, 2, \ldots$, have the same roots. Thus: $\delta^* > 0$ is an I.R.R. for x if and only if it is an I.R.R. for any $\overline{x}^{(k)}$ as well. Notice that the exclusion of $\delta = 0$ is costless: indeed, this case is trivially equivalent to

$$\sum_{s=0}^{+\infty} x_s = lim_{s \to +\infty} \overline{x}_s^{(1)} = \overline{x}_\infty^{(1)} = 0.$$

Since all the equations $V_{\overline{x}^{(k)}}(\delta) = 0$ are of algebric type in $e^{-\delta a}$, the number of positive roots of any of them (and a *fortiori* the number of positive I.R.R.'s) cannot exceed the number of sign changes in any sequence $\overline{x}^{(k)}$. In conclusion: let x be a financial project with $\overline{x}_\infty^{(1)} \neq 0$ and q be the minimum number of sign changes in all the sequences $\overline{x}^{(k)}$, $k = 0, 1, 2, \ldots$. Then project x has at most q positive I.R.R.'s.

In particular:

(i) If $q = 0$ (at least one sequence $\overline{x}^{(k)}$ shows no sign changes) there are no positive I.R.R.'s.

(*ii*) If $q = 1$ (all the sequences $\overline{x}^{(k)}$ show sign changes and at least one of them presents only one sign change) there is exactly one positive I.R.R.. The previous argument shows that there is at most one positive I.R.R.; the fact that $\overline{x}_0^{(k)}$ and $\overline{x}_\infty^{(k)}$ have different signs[4] guarantees that there is at least one positive I.R.R..

The above property is de Faro's Theorem[5], containing as special cases Norstrøm's result [7] (only sequence $\overline{x}^{(1)}$ is considered) and de Faro's test ξ [4] (only sequence $\overline{x}^{(2)}$ is considered).

Examples (on Sections II and III). Let T={0,1,2,...}.

1. Consider the project $x = \{-1, 5, -7, 0, 0, ...\}$. Sequences $\overline{x}^{(k)}$ show sign changes for $k = 0, 1, 2, ..., 12$, while $\overline{x}^{(13)} < 0$. Thus $V_x[\varphi] \leq 0 \quad \forall \varphi \in \Phi_{13}$: in particular no positive I.R.R. exists. But, taking for instance $\varphi_0 = 1$, $\varphi_1 = \frac{3}{5}$, $\varphi_2 = \frac{2}{7}$, (notice that such φ belongs to Φ_2), $V_x[\varphi] = 0$.

2. Consider the project $x = \{-1, 5, -6, 0, 0, ...\}$. All the sequences $\overline{x}^{(k)}$ show two sign changes and thus $V_x[\varphi]$ is not of constant sign for any $\varphi \in \Phi_\infty$. It is easy to check that, in effect, the project has two positive I.R.R.'s.

3. Consider the project $x = \{-2, 5, -2, 0, 0, ...\}$. All the sequences $\overline{x}^{(k)}$, $k = 1, 2, ...$, show one sign change and thus $V_x[\varphi]$ is not of constant sign $\forall \varphi \in \Phi_\infty$: the project has in fact one positive I.R.R..

4. Consider the following four project x, y, z, w (Castagnoli [2]). All of them have inflows of amount 10 at maturities $1, 2, ..., 24$ and outflows:

(*i*) for x: -1 at time 0, -40 at time 4, -186.5 at time 12.

(*ii*) for y: -1 at time 0, -40 at time 4, -187 at time 12.

(*iii*) for z: -40 at time 4, -187.5 at time 12.

(*iv*) for w: -0.5 at time 0, -40 at time 2, -187 at time 12.

The four projects are very close each other. Nevertheless x has one positive I.R.R., y three, z none and w five[6].

This is shown also by cumulative cash flows: $\overline{y}^{(k)}$ exhibits three sign changes for $k \geq 2$, $\overline{w}^{(k)}$ five sign changes for any k while, definitely, $\overline{z}^{(k)}$ is positive and $\overline{x}^{(k)}$ presents one sign change.

IV The finite case. Negative IRR's

The previous approach leads in any case to consider infinite sequences. For finite financial projects it appears rather unnatural, but it is possible to introduce a slight modification in order to maintain the finiteness of the problem.

Let now **T** be a finite set of maturities $0 = t_0 < t_1 < t_2 < ... < t_n$ and x a cash flow $x_0, x_1, x_2, ... x_n$. The present value of x:

$$V_x[\varphi] = \sum_{s=0}^{n} x_s \varphi_s$$

can be rewritten as:

$$V_x[\varphi] = -\sum_{s=0}^{n-1} \overline{x}_s^{(1)} \Delta\varphi_s + x_n \varphi_n$$

or:

$$V_x[\varphi] = \sum_{s=0}^{n-2} \overline{x}_s^{(2)} \Delta^2 \varphi_s - \overline{x}_{n-1}^{(1)} \Delta\varphi_{n-1} + x_n \varphi_n$$

or, after $n+1$ steps:

$$V_x[\varphi] = \sum_{r=0}^{n} (-1)^r \overline{x}_{n-r}^{(r)} \Delta^r \varphi_{n-r}.$$

Denoting by x^* the finite sequence $x_n, \overline{x}_{n-1}^{(1)}, \overline{x}_{n-2}^{(2)}, \cdots, \overline{x}_0^{(n)}$, we have:

Theorem 4 $V_x[\varphi] \geq 0 \quad \forall \varphi \in \Phi_n$ *if and only if* $x^* \geqq 0$.

Let us consider, in particular, the case in which an exponential discount factor is used. As in sec. III, we assume equidistance of maturities ($t_s = as$) so that:

$$(-1)^r \Delta^r \varphi_{n-r} = (1 - e^{-\delta a})^r e^{-\delta a(n-r)}.$$

Hence:

$$V_x(\delta) = \sum_{s=0}^{n} x_s e^{-\delta a s} = \sum_{r=0}^{n} \overline{x}_{n-r}^{(r)} (1 - e^{\delta a})^r e^{-\delta a(n-r)} =$$

$$= \sum_{r=0}^{n} \overline{x}_r^{(n-r)} (1 - e^{-\delta a})^{n-r} e^{-\delta a r} = V_{x^{**}}(\delta)$$

where x^{**} is the sequence with elements $\bar{x}_r^{(n-r)}(1-e^{-\delta a})^{n-r}$, $r = 0, 1, 2, \cdots, n$ and we can conclude that x and x^{**} have the same I.R.R.'s[7]. Notice that for $\delta > 0$, x^{**} and x^* show the same sign changes so that the number of positive I.R.R.'s for x cannot exceed the number of sign changes in x^* (or x^{**}). In particular, if x^* has no sign changes, x has no positive I.R.R., while if x^* has one sign change, x has exactly one positive I.R.R.. The above property is de Faro's diagonal method [4] that coincides with Bernhard's result [1].

When looking for negative I.R.R.'s, the exponential discount factor $\varphi(t) = e^{-\delta t}, \delta < 0$, turns out to be increasing. Let us consider briefly this possibility from a general viewpoint. Let x be a finite project and φ an increasing discount factor.

Denoting by $\psi_{n-s} = \varphi_s / \varphi_n$:

$$V_x[\varphi] = \sum_{s=0}^{n} x_s \varphi_s = \varphi_n \sum_{s=0}^{n} x_s \psi_{n-s} = \varphi_n \sum_{s=0}^{n} x_{n-s} \psi_s = \varphi_n V_{\hat{x}}[\psi]$$

where $\hat{x}$ stands for x in reversed order. Since ψ is decreasing, it suffices to discuss "ordinary" present value of the reversed financial project. In particular, the above argument applies to negative I.R.R.'s (de Faro [4]).

Example. Reconsider examples **1**, **2** and **3** at the end of sec. III. The first two present a negative reversed cumulative and thus no negative I.R.R. exists. For the third one, $x = \hat{x}$ and hence it has one negative I.R.R..

V Conclusions

For simplicity, we have discussed above only the discrete case but it is not difficult to extend our arguments to the continuous case.

A natural development is represented by time-stochastic dominance, to cover the case of random cash flows.

In any case, since present value is a linear functional of cash flow, the formal problem is to garantee that this functional preserves a given order (time dominance and/or stochastic dominance of given orders).

Endnotes

1. Assuming discount factors defined for any $t \geq 0$ and belonging to $\mathbf{C}^k$, the characterization of Φ_k is amenable to the signs of the derivatives:

$$\Phi_k = \{\varphi : (-1)^h \varphi^{(h)}(t) \geq 0 \qquad \forall t \geq 0, h = 0, 1, 2, ..., k\}.$$

2. Exponential discount factors do not exhaust Φ_∞: f.i., $\varphi = (1+it)^{-1}, i \geq 0$, are members of Φ_∞ as well.

3. It allows to discuss the more general question of the existence of Internal Financial Laws (for definition and results [6] [8]).

4. That is: $\overline{x}_0^{(k-1)}$ and $\sum_{s=0}^{+\infty} \overline{x}_s^{(k-1)}$ have different signs, so that $V_{\overline{x}^{(k-1)}}(\delta)$ has different signs for $\delta \to +\infty$ and for $\delta \to 0^+$.

5. Formula (2), in particular, is the same considered in [4], footnote 5.

6. Annual internal rates are :

   997.25% for x

   4.876%, 6.559% and 997.24% for y

   2.997%, 19.468%, 56.5%, 188.76% and 1542.6% for w.

7. Since x^{**} depends on δ, the assertion is circular. However the dependence is irrevelant since we are interested only in the sign changes of x^{**}, not affected by δ.

References

[1] R. H. Bernhard (1979): "A More General Sufficient Condition for a Unique Nonnegative Internal Rate of Return", *Journal of Financial and Quantitative Analysis*, **14**, 2, pp. 337-341.

[2] E. Castagnoli (1983): "Quasi una fiaba sul tasso di rendimento", *Il Risparmio*, **XXXI**, 2, pp. 261-282.

[3] E. Castagnoli (1990):"Funzioni che preservano un ordinamento e problemi di decisione", *Scritti in omaggio a Luciano Daboni*, Lint, Trieste, pp. 53-65.

[4] C. de Faro (1978): "A Sufficient Condition for a Unique Non-negative Internal Rate of Return: Further Comments", *Journal of Financial and Quantitative Analysis*, **13**, 3, pp. 577-584.

[5] S. Ekern (1981): "Time Dominance Efficiency Analysis", *Journal of Finance*, **XXXVI**, 5, pp. 1023-1034.

[6] P. Manca (1989): "The splitting up of a financial project into uniperiodic consecutive projects", *Rivista di Matematica per le Scienze Economiche e Sociali*, **12**, 1, pp. 107-118.

[7] C. J. Norstrøm (1972): "A Sufficient Condition for a Unique Nonnegative Internal Rate of Return", *Journal of Financial and Quantitative Analysis*, **7**, 2, pp. 1835-1839.

[8] L. Peccati (1989): "Multiperiod Analysis of a Levered Portfolio", *Rivista di Matematica per le Scienze Economiche e Sociali*, **12**, 1, pp. 157-167.

LINEAR GEARS FOR ASSET PRICING[1]

Erio CASTAGNOLI
Istituto di Metodi Quantitativi
Università Bocconi

Marco LI CALZI
Istituto di Matematica Finanziaria
Università di Torino

1 Introduction

The purpose of this paper is to use a few simple results of linear algebra to derive some properties of a general asset pricing model. Since one can apply essentially the same techniques in both cases, we start by considering a traditional asset pricing model and then show how to extend the reasoning to a more general model. In order to present our results, we need to state several assumptions that are customarily made in the studies of finance. Unless explicit mention is made, we maintain these assumptions throughout this work although some of them could be relaxed with little effort.

The setup is as usual. There are $n \geq 2$ different investment opportunities providing random returns which are called *securities*. Any linear combination of securities having a positive market value is called *portfolio*. All investors who have access to the market are assumed to be greedy: their preferences are increasing in wealth. Thus, they trade securities on the market to build portfolios which maximize their wealth.

This setup is endowed with a structure stemming from a few other assumptions which are standard in the study of asset pricing models. Following Merton [2], we state them as follows.

Price taking behavior: Any investor believes that his actions cannot affect the probability distribution of returns on the available securities. Hence, the probability distribution of returns on a portfolio depends only on the weights that it attributes to the securities entering it.

Frictionless markets: There are no transaction costs or taxes. All securities are perfectly divisible and transactions take place continuously. There are no costs for information processing or for operating the markets.

Absence of institutional restrictions: Short-sales of all securities, with full use of proceeds, is allowed without restrictions. If there exists a riskless security, then the borrowing rate equals the lending rate.

Absence of arbitrage opportunities: All riskless portfolios must have the same instantaneous rate of return.

The condition of absence of arbitrage opportunities can be deduced by the assumption of greedy investors in combination with the other assumptions. Nevertheless, we state it explicitly because of its importance in the following discussion. Remark also that we do not assume the existence of a riskless security; in fact, we show in the following that this is unnecessary since under our assumptions there exists a riskless portfolio which can be used as a riskless security.

Suppose that the underlying uncertainty in the economy is captured by $m+1$ state variables, one of which is usually taken to be time. We assume that these state variables are semimartingales arranged in a time-dependent vector $\mathbf{Z}_t$ and normalized so that $\mathbf{Z}_0 = 0$. Since the set of semimartingales is a vector space, we can combine several state variables into one by adding them. Therefore, coalescing state variables if necessary, we can assume without loss of generality that $m+1 \leq n$.

2 A traditional asset pricing model

In the traditional asset pricing model, we add to this set of hypotheses three other assumptions. The first one is that the first state variable is time and the other m are given by the components of a standard m–dimensional Wiener process $(Z^1 \ \dots \ Z^m)$. The second assumption is that there exists a riskless asset R among the n originary securities which has zero diffusion coefficients and an instantaneous rate of return r_t depending only on time. For simplicity, we assume that $R = X^1$.

The third additional assumption is that the dynamics of the rates of return for the n distinct securities X^i $(i = 1, \dots, n)$ as a function of the $(m+1)$ state variables $(t\ Z^1\ \ldots\ Z^m)$ $(m < n)$ is described by

$$\frac{dX_t^i}{X_t^i} = \mu^i(X^i,t)dt + \sum_{j=1}^{m}\sigma_j^i(X^i,t)dZ_t^j \qquad i = 1,\ldots,n \tag{1}$$

where μ^i and σ_j^i $(i = 1,\ldots,n; j = 1,\ldots,m)$ are assumed to be Lipschitz functions in order to guarantee the existence of a solution for this system of stochastic differential equations and its uniqueness (up to indistinguishable versions) in the class of n-dimensional adapted càdlàg processes $\mathbf{D}^n$. Remark that (1) implies that $X_t^i \neq 0$ a.s. for every $t > 0$ and all $i = 1,\ldots,n$. Moreover, by the assumption on the existence of a riskless asset, the first equation in (1) can be simply written as $dX_t^1 = r_t X_t^1 dt$.

Under these assumptions, the rate of return on each available security X^i (hence, the dynamics of its price) is completely characterized by a (not constant) $(m+1)$-dimensional vector. More briefly, then, we can identify security X^i with an $(m+1)$-dimensional vector of functions[2]

$$X^i = [\mu^i\ \sigma_1^i\ \ldots\ \sigma_m^i]$$

which reduces, at each fixed time t, to a vector of scalars.

More generally, we can consider a portfolio $P(h_t) = \sum_{i=1}^{n} h_t^i X_t^i$. This is a linear combination with weights $h_t = [h_t^1\ \ldots\ h^n]$ of the n available securities. Representing these as vectors, one sees immediately that at any time t the portfolio itself can be represented as a vector in $\mathbf{R}^{m+1}$. Thus, we take this to be the space of available portfolios at any time t. If we assume that the first $m+1$ securities (when represented as vectors) are linearly independent for all t, they span the space of all available portfolios: thus, any portfolio $P(h)$ can be replicated by some n-dimensional weights vector $h = (h^1\ \ldots\ h^{m+1}\ 0\ \ldots\ 0) \in \mathbf{D}^n$ whose last $(n-m-1)$ components are zero. Hence, we will assume that portfolios are built out of the first $(m+1)$ securities using the weights described by one of such weights processes h and, for simplicity, we will omit the last $(n-m-1)$ zero components.

By the standard (and natural) assumption of no arbitrage opportunities, it follows immediately that there is only one riskless asset which

[2] For typographical convenience, we write vectors indifferently as row or column vectors. However, all the vectors introduced in this work should be considered column vectors.

is actually traded on the market. This surviving security is called the efficient riskless asset and for simplicity we will denote it by $[r\ 0\ \dots\ 0]$. Quite obviously, the instantaneous rate of return of the efficient riskless asset defines the instantaneous riskless rate of return of the market.

Remark that if a weights process is multiple of another weights process, the associated portfolios have the same rate of return dynamics and thus yield the same instantaneous rate of return. By the price taking assumption, investors are interested only in the rates of return and these portfolios are indistinguishable. Hence, we can partition the set of available portfolios into equivalence classes $\{P(h_t) : P(h_t) = \alpha P_t, \text{ for all } t \geq 0,\ \alpha \neq 0\}$. Each class can be represented by a dynamic portfolio P_t with weights process normalized so that $\sum_{i=1}^{m+1} h_t^i = 1$ for all $t \geq 0$. From now on, therefore, we restrict attention to normalized portfolios. This assumption implies that from the viewpoint of trades the space $\mathbf{R}^{m+1}$ of available portfolios loses one dimension and reduces to the space $\mathbf{R}^m$ of portfolios expressible as a linear combination of $X^1, \dots, X^{m+1}$ with weights process $h = (h^1\ \dots\ h^{m+1})$ such that $\sum_{i=1}^{m+1} h_t^i = 1$ for all $t \geq 0$. We call these portfolios *efficient*.

Under our assumptions, in order to build up the (efficient) portfolio corresponding to the vector of functions $[\mu\ \sigma^1\ \dots\ \sigma^m]$ we need to find for any $t > 0$ a non-zero solution for the system of linear equations

$$\sum_{i=1}^{m+1} h_t^i \begin{bmatrix} \mu^i \\ \sigma_1^i \\ \vdots \\ \sigma_m^i \end{bmatrix}_t = \begin{bmatrix} \mu \\ \sigma^1 \\ \vdots \\ \sigma^m \end{bmatrix}_t$$

under the constraint $\sum_{i=1}^{m+1} h_t^i = 1$. This is equivalent to the system

$$\sum_{i=1}^{m+1} h_t^i \begin{bmatrix} \mu^i - \mu \\ \sigma_1^i - \sigma^1 \\ \vdots \\ \sigma_m^i - \sigma^m \end{bmatrix}_t = \begin{bmatrix} 0 \\ 0 \\ \vdots \\ 0 \end{bmatrix} \qquad \forall t > 0$$

which has a non-zero solution if and only if the coefficient matrix of the system is singular for all $t > 0$. Therefore, there must exist a non-null vector of processes $\lambda = [\lambda^0\ \lambda^1\ \dots\ \lambda^m]$ such that

$$\lambda^0(\mu^i - \mu) = \sum_{j=1}^{m} \lambda^j(\sigma_j^i - \sigma^j) \qquad i = 1, \dots, m+1 \tag{2}$$

Thus, if a portfolio is efficient, its coefficients lie on the hyperplane described by (2). We call the subset of portfolios satisfying (2) the *efficient region* of the market. If we further assume a regularity condition stating that the submatrix $[\sigma^j_i - \sigma^i]$ (for $i = 1, \ldots, m$; $j = 1, \ldots, m+1$) has rank m for all $t > 0$, we can normalize $\lambda^0 = 1$ in (2) and obtain the hyperplane describing the *regular efficient region* of the market

$$\mu^i - \mu = \sum_{j=1}^{m} \lambda^j (\sigma^i_j - \sigma^j) \qquad i = 1, \ldots, m+1 \tag{3}$$

From now on, we restrict attention to such region. By the assumption that the riskless asset is efficient, we obtain by (3)

$$\mu^i - r = \sum_{j=1}^{m} \lambda^j \sigma^i_j \qquad i = 1, \ldots, m+1 \tag{4}$$

and subtracting (3) from (4) the equation of the regular efficient region for any portfolio $P = [\mu \; \sigma_1 \; \ldots \; \sigma_m]$ becomes

$$\mu - r = \sum_{j=1}^{m} \lambda^j \sigma^j \tag{5}$$

Equation (5) has the same formal structure of the A.P.T. model. However, whereas in Ross' A.P.T. model the λ^j's are read as (static) regression coefficients, in this setting they represent the dynamically changing coefficients of a stochastic differential equation. It is simply a matter of how we choose to dress the linear skeleton.

Equation (5) can also be interpreted as an additive decomposition of the market price of risk for a portfolio P into the sum of the market prices for its m risk components. Under this interpretation, λ^j is read as the market price of risk for the j-th component of the Wiener process representing the underlying uncertainty of the economy.

Together with Ito's formula, Equation (5) can also be used to price derivative securities. Assume that the state variables are time and the (independent) components of a standardized m-dimensional Wiener process. Suppose that the coefficient defining the rate of return dynamics for a security $X = [\mu \; \sigma^1 \; \ldots \; \sigma^m]$ are continuous functions and let $f : \mathbf{R}^2 \to \mathbf{R}^+$ be a function of class C^2. Consider the derivative security $Y = f(X_t, t)$. By Ito's formula, we obtain

$$dY_t = \frac{\partial f}{\partial t}(X_t, t)\, dt + \frac{\partial f}{\partial x}(X_t, t)\, dX_t + \frac{1}{2}\frac{\partial^2 f}{\partial x^2}(X_t, t)\, d[X, X]_t$$

Using continuity of X and bilinearity of the quadratic variation process, and substituting from (1) gives

$$dY_t = \left(\frac{\partial f}{\partial t} + \mu X_t \frac{\partial f}{\partial x} + \frac{1}{2}\sum_{j=1}^{m}(\sigma^j)^2 X_t^2 \frac{\partial^2 f}{\partial x^2}\right)(X_t, t)\, dt +$$

$$+ \sum_{j=1}^{m} \sigma^j X_t \frac{\partial f}{\partial x}(X_t, t)\, dZ_t^j$$

Since $Y \neq 0$ a.s., a suitable relabelling of the coefficients gives us the rates of return dynamics

$$\frac{dY_t}{Y_t} = q^0 dt + \sum_{j=1}^{m} q^j dZ_t^j$$

from which it is immediately seen that a derivative security Y can be replicated by some portfolio whose price is also the price of Y. In particular, an efficient derivative security must also satisfy (5). Up to minor technicalities, it is not particularly difficulties to extend this kind of argument from the case of a derivative security based only on time and one underlying security to more complex financial instruments depending also on other securities.

Finally, we remark that in the derivation above we have neglected the possibility of derivative cash flows originating from the securities. Examples of such possibility are dividends on equities, interests on currencies, storage costs on goods or taxes. Their consideration amounts to a partial relaxation of the assumption of frictionless markets. If such derivative cash flows depend only on time and the uncertainty sources, they can be included in the model by suitably modifying the coefficients in (1). In the more general case where they may also depend on other elements, we might add these as new sources of risk.

3 An extended asset pricing model

In this section, we formalize and discuss an asset pricing model which extends the traditional one by relaxing to different degrees its three characterizing assumptions. In particular, we suppose that the state variables are semimartingales, there does not necessarily exist a riskless security and the rate of return dynamics may depend also on the past history of prices of all securities. The extension of the model is made while preserving its intrinsic linear structure and this guarantees that an analog of (5) still holds, although other attractive properties of the traditional model may be lost.

As above, we suppose that there are $m+1$ state variables represented by semimartingales arranged in a vector $\mathbf{Z}_t$ and normalized so that $\mathbf{Z}_0 = 0$ and that the set of $n \geq m+1$ available securities is denoted by the vector $\mathbf{X} = [X^1 \ \ldots \ X^n]$. Generalizing (1), we suppose now that their rates of return dynamics is described by

$$\frac{dX_t^i}{X_{t-}^i} = G_0^i(\mathbf{X})_{t-}dZ_t^0 + \sum_{j=1}^{m} G_j^i(\mathbf{X})_{t-}dZ_t^j \qquad i = 1, \ldots, m \tag{6}$$

where G_j^i is a non-random functional Lipschitz operator for all $i = 1, \ldots, n$ and $j = 0, 1, \ldots, m$. By Theorem 5.7 in Protter [3], this system of stochastic differential equations has a unique solution in $\mathbf{D}^n$ which we take to represent the dynamics of the rates of return.

For the moment, we assume that the semimartingale Z^0 represents time and thus $Z_t^0 = t$. Thus, we say that G_0^i is the *drift* and the G_j^i's $(j = 1, \ldots, m)$ are the *diffusion coefficients* of the process X^i. For ease of reference, we will continue to refer to G_0^i as the drift and to the G_j^i's as the diffusion coefficients of X^i even after removing the assumption that $Z_t^0 = t$.

The dynamics in (6) makes the rate of return on a security explicitly dependent both on time and on the past history of the prices of all securities. Hence, it embodies the traditional assumption of weak efficiency of financial markets better than the traditional model, where drift and diffusion coefficients of a security depend at most on time and its current price. Moreover, since the operators G_j^i are non-random, agents can still estimate them and henceforth learn about the dynamics of the rates of return. Hence, we assume that all drifts and diffusion coefficients in (6) are known to the investors.

Similarly to the above, when the dynamics is given by (6), $X^i \neq 0$ a.s. for all $i = 1, \ldots, n$ and we can represent any security by the vector of its drift and diffusion coefficients. Therefore, we will denote security X^i by the vector $[G_0^i \ G_1^i \ \ldots \ G_m^i]$. Now, let $P(h) = \sum_{i=1}^n h^i X^i$ be a generic portfolio of securities with weights process $h_t = [h_t^1 \ \ldots \ h_t^n]$. By analogy, we are led to think of $P(h_t)$ as the dynamically changing vector corresponding to the linear combination of the vectors X^i with weights h^i. This gives the dynamic portfolio

$$\begin{aligned} P_t &= [G_0^p(\mathbf{X})\ G_1^p(\mathbf{X})\ \dots\ G_n^p(\mathbf{X})]_{t-} = \\ &= \left[\sum_{i=1}^{n} h_t^i G_0^i(\mathbf{X})\ \sum_{i=1}^{n} h_t^i G_1^i(\mathbf{X})\ \dots\ \sum_{i=1}^{n} h_t^i G_n^i(\mathbf{X})\right]_{t-} \end{aligned} \tag{7}$$

This informal derivation can be shown to be correct by the following reasoning. From (6) it follows that, if it exists, the dynamics of the rate of return on this portfolio satisfies the stochastic differential equation

$$\frac{dP_t}{P_{t-}} = \sum_{i=1}^{n} h_t^i G_0^i(\mathbf{X})_{t-} dZ_t^0 + \sum_{i=1}^{n}\sum_{j=1}^{m} h_t^i G_j^i(\mathbf{X})_{t-} dZ_t^j$$

However, since the sum of functional Lipschitz operators is still a functional Lipschitz operator, Theorem 3 guarantees that this equation has a unique solution in $\mathbf{D}^1$. Hence, there actually exists a portfolio $P(h_t)$ corresponding to the vector described in (7). This observation guarantees that we can still use essentially the same linear gears as above: the model maintains a linear structure and allows to reduce some questions of asset pricing to simple problems in linear algebra.

The last assumption we need is purely technical. We assume that for any $t > 0$ and any realization of $\mathbf{X}$ up to t there exists a subset (possibly depending on t and $\mathbf{X}_{0<s\leq t}$) of $m+1$ securities out of the originary n such t hat the square matrix G obtained by juxtaposing the vectors representing them is a.s. not singular. If a certain subset of $m+1$ securities satisfies this condition at some t, we say that it *covers* the dynamics in t. For simplicity, we assume without loss of generality that for all $t > 0$ the dynamics is covered always by the subset $(X^1 \dots X^{m+1})$ and call this the *covering assumption.* In other words, the covering assumption states that

$$G = \begin{bmatrix} G_0^1 & G_0^2 & \dots & G_0^{m+1} \\ G_1^1 & G_1^2 & \dots & G_1^{m+1} \\ G_2^1 & G_2^2 & \dots & G_2^{m+1} \\ \dots & \dots & \dots & \dots \\ G_m^1 & G_m^2 & \dots & G_m^{m+1} \end{bmatrix}_{t-} \tag{8}$$

is a.s. not singular for all $t > 0$.

3.1 All efficient portfolios still lie on the same hyperplane

In this section, we assume that $Z_t^0 = t$ and show that (5) still holds for the extended model. The proof is mostly a simple matter of linear algebra. We show first that there is no loss of generality in assuming that a riskless asset may not exist because under the covering assumption there always exists a riskless portfolio which can be used in its place. For completeness, we show also how to derive the condition of no arbitrage opportunities implying that all traded riskless portfolios are equivalent. This amounts to say that there is essentially a unique riskless efficient portfolio.

Proposition 1 *If the covering assumption holds, there exists a riskless portfolio $R = [G^r\ 0\ \ldots\ 0]$. In equilibrium, any traded riskless portfolio has the same instantaneous rate of return.*

Proof: The key observation is that under the covering assumption the matrix G in (8) is invertible for all $t > 0$. Thus, given any dynamic portfolio $P_t = [G_0^p\ G_1^p\ \ldots\ G_m^p]_{t-}$, we can replicate it using only the first $m+1$ securities by choosing at each instant t the vector of weights h_t which solves the linear system $G(\mathbf{X})_{t-}h_t = P(\mathbf{X})_{t-}$. Remark that this implies that we adjust dynamically the weights of the replicating portfolio depending on t and the realization of $\mathbf{X}$ up to t. If $Z_t^0 = t$, in particular, any riskless portfolio $R_t = [G^r(\mathbf{X})_{t-}\ 0\ \ldots\ 0]$ can be built by using the weights process $h_t = G^{-1}(\mathbf{X})_{t-}R_{t-}$. Hence, we can build a riskless portfolio with any arbitrary instantaneous rate of return G^r.

However, there cannot be two traded riskless portfolios with distinct instantaneous rates of return, because at any time $t \geq 0$ all investors prefer to hold only the portfolio with the highest instantaneous rate of return in t. Therefore, the prices of all riskless portfolios adjust instantaneously to keep all the instantaneuos rates of returns at the same level. □

Proposition 2 *If the covering assumption holds, there exists a non-null vector $\lambda = [\lambda^0\ \lambda^1\ \ldots\ \lambda^m]$ of adapted processes such that for any traded portfolio $P_t = [G_0^p\ G_1^p\ \ldots\ G_m^p]_{t-}$*

$$\lambda^0(G_0^p - G^r) = \sum_{j=1}^{m} \lambda^j G_j^p \tag{9}$$

holds.

Proof: Let $P = [G_0^p \; G_1^p \; \dots \; G_m^p]$ an arbitrary (normalized) portfolio traded on the market. To build P, we need to find at any instant t a vector of weights h_t such that

$$\sum_{i=1}^{m+1} h_t^i X_t^i = P_t \qquad \text{and} \qquad \sum_{i=1}^{m+1} h_t^i = 1$$

or, equivalently,

$$\sum_{i=1}^{m+1} h_t^i (X_t^i - P_t) = 0 \qquad \text{and} \qquad \sum_{i=1}^{m+1} h_t^i = 1$$

which can also be written as $(G_{t-} - P_t\mathbf{I})h_t = 0$ and $\sum_{i=1}^{m+1} h_t^i = 1$. This system of linear equations must admit a non-zero solution because P is traded on the market. Therefore, its coefficients matrix has to be singular. Under the covering assumption, a necessary and sufficient condition for this to happen is that the first row is a linear combination of the other rows; that is, for any $t > 0$ there exists a non-null vector $\lambda_t = [\lambda_t^0 \; \lambda_t^1 \; \dots \; \lambda_t^m]$ such that

$$\lambda^0 (G_0^i - G_0^p) = \sum_{j=1}^{m} \lambda^j (G_j^i - G_j^p) \qquad i = 1, \dots, m+1 \qquad (10)$$

holds. In particular, substituting for P the riskless portfolio R we obtain

$$\lambda^0 (G_0^i - G^r) = \sum_{j=1}^{m} \lambda^j G_j^i \qquad i = 1, \dots, m+1 \qquad (11)$$

and the result follows subtracting (10) by (11) for any $i = 1, \dots, m+1$. To complete the proof, just remark that, for any $t > 0$, λ depends continuously on the adapted matrix $(G_{t-} - P_t\mathbf{I})h_t = 0$ and therefore all its components must be adapted as well. □

It is not difficult to check that the proofs of Propositions 1 and 2 extend immediately to the case of a generic semimartingale Z^0. This case may arise when in the attempt to reduce the number of state variables to some $m + 1 \leq n$, one is forced to coalesce time with other semimartingales. If we continue to call riskless all the assets which have zero diffusion coefficients, therefore, it follows that the linear equation (9) still holds. However, in this case the definition of riskless is given with respect to an arbitrary "reference" process. Assuming for instance that the components of $\mathbf{Z}$ are independent and that Z^0 represents the systematic risk in the market, this allows one to reinterpret (9) as an extension of the C.A.P.M. model.

3.2 Derivative securities in the extended model

The relationship between a security and one of its derivative securities is in general not linear. Whereas in the traditional model Ito's formula allows one to preserve a linear structure, in our more general formulation this is not possible anymore. However, a partial result can be still given under some further assumptions.

Suppose that a portfolio $X = [\mu\ \sigma^1\ \ldots\ \sigma^m]$ follows a Lévy process. If $f : \mathbf{R}^2 \to \mathbf{R}^+$ is a function of class C^2, let $Y_t = f(X_t, t)$ be a derivative security. By Theorem 5.33 in Protter [3] and Ito's formula for semimartingales (see Theorem 2.33 in Protter [3]), we obtain that

$$dY_t = \left(\frac{\partial f}{\partial t} + \mu_{t-}\frac{\partial f}{\partial x} + \frac{\alpha}{2}\frac{\partial^2 f}{\partial x^2}\right)(X_{t-}, t)\, dt +$$

$$+ \sum_{0<s\leq t} \left\{ f(X_s) - f(X_{s-}) - \frac{\partial f}{\partial x}(X_{s-})\Delta X_s \right\}$$

where $\alpha = \mathrm{E}\{[X, X]^c_1\}$. Since $Y \neq 0$ a.s., a suitable relabelling of its coefficients gives us the rates of return dynamics

$$\frac{dY_t}{Y_t} = q^0 dt + \sum_{j=1}^{m} q^j dZ^j_t + Q_t$$

where Q_t is the process defined by

$$Q_t = \sum_{0<s\leq t} \left\{ f(X_s) - f(X_{s-}) - \frac{\partial f}{\partial x}(X_{s-})\Delta X_s \right\}$$

Following Merton [1], we can further suppose that Q_t is the unsystematic risk intrinsic to Y while the rest represents the systematic risk. It is immediately seen that the systematic risk of the derivative security Y can be replicated by some portfolio and therefore can be "diversified away." This leads to some pricing relationships that it might be worth to explore in future research.

4 Conclusions

The main purpose of this paper is to point out that the linear structure of the standard model for asset pricing can be painlessly extended to more general assumptions on the coefficients of the stochastic differential equations describing price evolution. This is due to the formal simplicity of the model that makes it quite robust to changes in the assumptions. Briefly, the conclusion we would like to draw from this is that the analytic simplicity of a model that relies on heavy linearity assumptions is largely compensated by the richness of assumptions that it can carry.

So far, the restrictions that we have identified are two: (i) when writing the system of stochastic differential equations that defines the rates of return dynamics, one must guarantee the existence of a solution; (ii) an operator like Ito's formula is necessary in order to make it possible to include in the model the treatment of derivative securities. These restrictions are satisfied by the generalization that we consider here, but this does not exclude that further extensions might be proved possible.

References

[1] Merton, R.C. (1976): "Option pricing when underlying stock returns are discontinuous," *Journal of Financial Economics* **3**, 125–144.

[2] Merton, R.C. (1990): "Capital market theory and the pricing of financial securities," Working paper n. 90–024, Harvard Business School (forthcoming in B. Friedman and F. Hahn (eds.), *Handbook of monetary economics*, North-Holland, Amsterdam).

[3] Protter, P. (1990): *Stochastic integration and differential equations*, Springer-Verlag, Berlin.

A Definitions and results from stochastic calculus

In the discussion above, we have made extensive use of some definitions and results from the theory of stochastic calculus. To disecumber our discussion from these technicalities, we have confined those which are less known in this section. For a more complete treatment see for instance Protter [3], whose notation is followed here. Let $(\Omega, \mathcal{F}, P, \{\mathcal{F}_t\})$ be a filtered complete probability space satisfying the usual conditions (see [3]). Given a stochastic process X on $(\Omega, \mathcal{F}, P)$ we write X_t instead of $X(t,\omega)$ and X_{t-} for $\lim_{s\uparrow t} X(s,\omega)$. Moreover, we define $\Delta X_t = X_t - X_{t-}$ to be the jump at t. Finally, we set $X_{0-} = 0$ by convention; remark however that we do not require $X_0 = 0$.

A stochastic process X is *adapted* if X_t is $\mathcal{F}_t$-measurable for all $t \geq 0$ and it is *càdlàg* if it has a.s. right continuous sample paths with left limits. An adapted process is said a *Lévy process* if it has stationary independent increments and it is continuous in probability. Examples of Lévy processes include Brownian motions and Poisson processes. Denote by $\mathbf{D}$ the space of adapted processes with *càdlàg* paths. A process $M \in \mathbf{D}$ is a *local martingale* if there exists a sequence of increasing stopping times $\{T_n\}$ such that $\lim_{n\to+\infty} T_n = +\infty$ a.s. and $X_{t\wedge T_n} 1_{\{T_n>0\}}$ is a uniformly integrable martingale for each n. A process $V \in \mathbf{D}$ is a *finite variation process* if almost all of its paths are of finite variation on each compact interval of $\mathbf{R}^+$. A process $X \in \mathbf{D}$ is a *semimartingale* if it can be written $X = M + V$, where M is a local martingale with bounded jumps and V is a finite variation process. Examples of semimartingales include Lévy processes, square integrable martingales with càdlàg paths, and finite variation processes.

Given a semimartingale X and an adapted left continuous process H with right limits, it is possible to consistently define another stochastic process $J_X(H) = \int H_s dX_s$ which is called the *stochastic integral* of H with respect to the integrator X. When evaluated at t, we denote such process by

$$\left[\int H_s dX_s\right]_t = \int_0^t H_s dX_s$$

Whenever 0 is to be excluded from the integral, we use the notation

$$\int_{0+}^t H_s dX_s$$

The stochastic integral process preserves most of the crucial properties of the standard Lebesgue integral. Skipping the details of its construction (for which see [3]), we will only say that given two semimartingales X and Y the integral of Y_- with respect to X always exists and it is also a semimartingale.

Given two semimartingales X and Y, we define the *quadratic covariation* of X, Y as the stochastic process given by

$$[X, Y] = XY - \int X_- dY - \int Y_- dX$$

and denote by $[X, Y]^c$ its path by path continuous part. Then, we say that a semimartingale X is *quadratic pure jump* if $[X, X]^c = 0$. A simple sufficient condition for a semimartingale X to be quadratic pure jump is that X has paths of finite variation on compacts. Thus, for instance, any Poisson process is quadratic pure jump.

There are several results linking semimartingales with the theory of stochastic differential equations. We recall a very general theorem proved for instance in Protter [3]. Let $\mathbf{D}^n$ be the space of processes $\mathbf{X} = (X^1 \ \dots \ X^n)$ such that $X^i \in \mathbf{D}$, for all $i = 1, \dots, n$.

An operator $G : \mathbf{D}^n \rightarrow \mathbf{D}$ is said to be *functional Lipschitz* if it satisfies the following two conditions for any $\mathbf{X}, \mathbf{Y} \in \mathbf{D}^n$: (i) for any stopping time T, $\mathbf{X}_{T-} = \mathbf{Y}_{T-}$ implies $G(\mathbf{X})_{T-} = G(\mathbf{Y})_{T-}$; (ii) there exists an increasing finite process K such that

$$|G(\mathbf{X})_t - G(\mathbf{Y})_t| \leq K_t \sup_{0 \leq s \leq t} ||\mathbf{X} - \mathbf{Y}||_s \quad \text{a.s.} \qquad \forall t \geq 0$$

A functional Lipschitz operator G is typically (although not necessarily) of the form $G(\mathbf{X}) = g(t, \omega; \mathbf{X}_s, s \leq t)$. Remark that, although for any $t > 0$ its image $G(\mathbf{X})_t$ is in general a random variable, the operator $G : \mathbf{D}^n \rightarrow \mathbf{D}$ is not random itself unless it explicitly depends on ω.

Theorem 3 *Let $\mathbf{Z}_t = [Z_t^0 \ Z_t^1 \ \dots \ Z_t^m]$ be a vector of semimartingales such that $\mathbf{Z}_0 = 0$. Assume that the operators G_j^i are functional Lipschitz for any $i = 1, \dots, n; j = 0, 1, \dots, m$. Then the system of equations*

$$X_t^i = \sum_{j=0}^{m} \int_0^t G_j^i(\mathbf{X})_{s-} dZ_s^j \qquad i = 1, \dots, n \tag{12}$$

has a unique solution in $\mathbf{D}^n$. Moreover, $\mathbf{X}$ is also a vector of semimartingales.

Equation (12) is customarily written in the form

$$dX_t^i = \sum_{j=0}^{m} G_j^i(\mathbf{X})_{t-} dZ_t^j \qquad i = 1, \ldots, n \tag{13}$$

Other results of relevance are the following ones.

Theorem 4 (Ito's formula) *Let $X = [X^1 \ \ldots \ X^n]$ be a vector of semimartingales and let $f : \mathbf{R}^n \to \mathbf{R}$ be a function of class C^2. Then $f(X)$ is a semimartingale and the formula*

$$\begin{aligned} f(X_t) - f(X_0) &= \sum_{i=1}^{n} \int_{0+}^{t} \frac{\partial f}{\partial x_i}(X_{s-}) dX_s^i \\ &+ \frac{1}{2} \sum_{1 \le i,j \le n} \int_{0+}^{t} \frac{\partial^2 f}{\partial x_i \partial x_j}(X_{s-}) d[X^i, X^j]_s^c \\ &+ \sum_{0<s\le t} \left\{ f(X_s) - f(X_{s-}) - \sum_{i=1}^{n} \frac{\partial f}{\partial x_i}(X_{s-}) \Delta X_s^i \right\} \end{aligned}$$

holds.

Theorem 5 *Let $\mathbf{Z} = (Z^0 \ Z^1 \ \ldots \ Z^m)$ be a vector of independent Lévy processes such that $\mathbf{Z}_0 = 0$. Then $[Z^i, Z^j]^c = 0$ if $i \neq j$ and $[Z^i, Z^i]^c = \alpha t$ where $\alpha = E\{[Z^i, Z^i]_1^c\}$.*

STOCHASTIC BEHAVIOUR OF EUROPEAN STOCK MARKETS INDICES

Albert Corhay
University of Liège and University of Limburg
and
A. Tourani Rad
University of Limburg

1. Introduction

This paper is concerned with modelling return generating processes in several European stock markets. Distributional properties of daily stock returns play a crucial role in valuation of contingent claims and mean-variance asset pricing models, as well as in their empirical tests. A common assumption underlying a considerable body of finance literature is that the logarithm of stock price relatives are independent and identically distributed according to a normal distribution with constant variance, while little attention is paid to the the empirical fit of the postulated process. For instance, the mean-variance asset pricing models of Sharpe (1964) and the option pricing model of Black and Scholes (1973) are based on the assumption of normally distributed returns. Moreover, the normality assumption and the parameter stability are necessary for most of statistical methods usually applied in empirical studies.

As early as 1963, Mandelbrot observed that returns series tend not to be independent over time, but characterised by succession of stable and volatile periods, that is, "large changes tend to be followed by large changes - of either sign - and small changes tend to be followed by small changes". He also observed that the distributions of returns are leptokurtic and proposed the family of the stable Paretian distributions as an alternative to the normal distribution. Such Paretian distributions with characteristic exponent of less than two indeed exhibit heavy tails and conform better to the distributions of returns series. Fama (1965) contributed further evidence supporting Mandelbrot's hypothesis.

While the approach of these studies is based on the empirical fit of observed stock return distributions, an alternative approach relies on describing the process that could generate distributions of returns having fatter tails than normal distributions. For instance, Paretz (1972), Blattberg and Gonedes (1974) showed that the scaled-t distribution, which can be derived as a continuous variance mixture of normal distributions, fits better daily stock returns than infinite variance stable Paretian distributions. Other models using different mixtures of normal to generate distributions that would account for the higher magnitude of kurtosis, are, among others, the Poisson mixtures of Press (1967) and the discrete mixtures of Kon (1984). Furthermore, Clark (1973), Merton (1982) and Tauchen and Pitts (1983) put forward models where the distribution of variance is a function of the arrival of the information rate, the trading activity and the trading volume. Such models are, however, too complex to be used in empirical applications.

There is yet no unanimity regarding the best stochastic return generating model. One of the most recent proposed class of return generating process in the literature that can capture the empirical characteristics of stock return series, i.e. changing variance and high level of kurtosis, is the class of autoregressive conditional heteroskedastic processes introduced by Engle (1982) and its generalized version by Bollerslev (1986). Empirical studies showed indeed that such processes are successful in modelling various time series. See, for example, French, Schwert and Stambaugh (1987), Baillie and Bollerslev (1989), Hsieh (1989) and Baillie and De Gennaro (1990). Interested readers can consult Taylor (1990) who provides many references of applications of this class of models in finance.

As far as stock markets are concerned, this class of models has been mainly applied to American stock markets with the exception of the Amsterdam (Corhay and Tourani Rad, 1990) and the London (Taylor and Poon, 1992) stock exchanges. In this paper we apply these models to stock price indices of several European countries. To that end, we have selected the following five countries: France, Germany, Italy, the Netherlands and the United Kingdom. The study of stock price behaviour in these markets is interesting in that it can provide further evidence in favour of or against the use of this type of models for describing stock price behaviour in smaller and thinner markets.

The rest of this paper is organised as follows. Section two presents the data and descriptive statistics of all the five countries. Section three determines which univariate autoregressive moving average model fits the data best for the countries of which returns series are serially dependent. In section four, the class of autoregressive conditional heteroskedastic models is presented and tests for the presence of heteroskedasticity in the returns series are carried out. The next section is then devoted to the estimation of the best model for each country. In the final section, comparisons between countries and implications are drawn.

2. Data and descriptive statistics

The indices of five European stock markets were collected from DATASTREAM for the period 1/1/1980 to 30/9/1990. They are indices for France (CAC General), Germany (Commerzbank), Italy (Milan Banca), the Netherlands (general CBS) and the U.K. (FT All-Shares). The daily returns of these market indices are continuously compounded returns. They are calculated as the difference in natural logarithm of the index value for two consecutive days, $R_t=\log(P_t)-\log(P_{t-1})$.

We first carry out a detailed analysis of the distributional and time-series properties of the stock market indices of the five countries. Descriptive statistics for each country

Table 1 — Sample Statistics on Daily Returns Series*

Statistics	France	Germany	Italy	Netherl.	U.K.
Mean ($x10^3$)	.4699	.2933	.6819	.6047	.5109
t(mean=0)	2.3998	1.3757	2.5259	2.9956	2.9908
Variance ($x10^3$)	.1074	.1274	.2043	.1142	.0817
Skewness	-1.5118	-1.1168	-.9916	-.5427	-1.6873
Kurtosis	16.941	15.035	11.738	13.4161	9.662
Range	0.1979	0.2117	0.2315	0.2183	0.1778
Median ($x10^3$)	0.0000	0.1105	0.0985	0.0000	0.8475
IQR (Q3-Q1)	0.0093	0.0111	0.0119	0.0109	0.0103
D-statistic	0.0971	0.0749	0.0999	0.0678	0.0567
Log-Likelihood	11406.	11167.	10506.	11321.	11789.

* Values of the tests statistically significant at the one per cent level are underlined.

are presented in table 1. They include the following distributional parameters: mean, variance, skewness, kurtosis, range, median and inter-quartile range (IQR). The value of the maximized likelihood function when a normal distribution is imposed on the data is also reported. It can be observed that there are differences across the countries regarding the mean and variance of the returns series. All means are statistically significant, except for Germany. Italy has the highest mean and variance of returns. All distributions are negatively highly skewed, indicating that they are non-symmetric. Furthermore, they all exhibit high level of kurtosis meaning distributions are more peaked and have fatter tails than normal distributions. The presence of negative skewness can be due to the inclusion of the crash of

October 1987 in the sample period. Corhay and Tourani Rad (1990) show that the skewness of the distribution of the Dutch index is negative but not statistically significant for the period before the 1987 crash. A direct test of normality has been carried out. Under the null hypothesis of identically, independently normal distribution of returns, the coefficients of skewness and excess kurtosis are both zero. Their sample estimates have standard deviations of $\sqrt{6/n}$ and $\sqrt{24/n}$, respectively, where n is the number of observations in the series. This test always rejects the null hypothesis at a very high level of significance. Moreover, the Kolmogorov-Smirnov D-Statistic for the null hypothesis of normality has been calculated, and it also rejects the normality assumption at a significant level of one per cent in all cases. The results confirm the well known fact that daily stock returns are not normally distributed, but are leptokurtic and skewed, whatever the country concerned. It also appears that the size of non-normality in stock returns of European markets is much more pronounced than that observed by Akgiray (1989) in the American market.

In order to test the hypothesis whether returns are strict white noise, i.e. random walk, the Box-Pierce test statistics up to lag 25 is calculated and presented in the table 2. This is a joint test that the first k autocorrelation coefficients are zero. Under the null hypothesis, that the sample autocorrelations are not asymptotically correlated, the Box-Pierce statistic, $Q=n\sum_{i=1}^{k}\rho(i)^2$, has chi-square distribution with k degrees of freedom, where $\rho(i)$ is the i-th autocorrelation. The values of Q are all significant at the

Table 2 — Sample Autocorrelations of Daily Returns Series*

	France	Germany	Italy	Netherl.	U.K.
ρ_1	.1461	.0284	.1367	-.0308	.1367
	(.0292)	(.0440)	(.0351)	(.0510)	(.0651)
ρ_2	.0455	-.0545	-.0378	.0018	.0477
	(.0399)	(.0353)	(.0325)	(.0532)	(.0481)
ρ_3	.0273	.0169	.0447	.0003	.0261
	(.0353)	(.0329)	(.0372)	(.0438)	(.0394)
ρ_4	.0218	.0217	.0601	.0114	.0535
	(.0307)	(.0294)	(.0337)	(.0367)	(.0479)
ρ_5	.0177	.0207	.0062	.0507	.0153
	(.0285)	(.0298)	(.0300)	(.0422)	(.0385)
ρ_{10}	.0661	.0308	.0682	.0207	.0541
	(.0323)	(.0332)	(.0283)	(.0339)	(.0292)
ρ_{15}	-.0035	-.0131	.0283	.0116	.0294
	(.0292)	(.0297)	(.0259)	(.0365)	(.0255)
ρ_{20}	.0302	-.0027	.0413	.0011	.0099
	(.0277)	(.0271)	(.0267)	(.0218)	(.0269)
ρ_{25}	-.0249	-.0172	.0005	-.0319	-.0305
	(.0268)	(.0199)	(.0258)	(.0226)	(.0209)
Q(25)	154.23	56.03	139.58	46.69	111.13
Q*(25)	65.66	22.52	52.64	17.32	26.30

* Values of the tests statistically significant at the one per cent level are underlined. Numbers in parentheses are heteroskedasticity-consistent standard errors.

one per cent level, which means that the null hypothesis of strict white noise is rejected, reflecting a rather long range of dependency in the returns series. However, it can be questioned whether this test accounts for the full probability distribution of the returns series since heteroskedasticity can lead to the underestimation of the standard error, $\sqrt{1/n}$, of each sample, and therefore to the overestimation of the t- and χ^2-statistics. Diebold (1987) provided a heteroskedasticity-consistent estimate of the standard error for the i-th sample autocorrelation coefficient:

$$S(i) = \sqrt{\frac{1}{n}\left(1 + \frac{\gamma_R{}^2(i)}{\sigma^4}\right)} \tag{1}$$

where $\gamma_R{}^2(i)$ is the i-th sample autocovariance of the square data and σ is the sample standard deviation of the data. These adjusted standard errors are presented in the table 2 under their respective autocorrelation coefficient. It can be seen that only few autocorrelation coefficients are statistically different from zero. Using these adjusted standard errors, Diebold proposed an adjusted Box-Pierce statistic:

$$Q^* = \sum_{i=1}^{k}\left(\rho(i)/(S(i))^2\right) \tag{2}$$

which is asymptotically chi-square distributed with k degrees of freedom, under the null hypothesis of no serial correlation in the data. The values of Q^* which are presented in table 2 are much lower than the non adjusted ones. They are significant at one per cent level for France and Italy only. So, even after adjusting for heteroskedasticity, there remains some significant autocorrelations in the series of returns for these two countries.

Looking at the autocorrelation coefficients, we can observe that the first order coefficients are 0.1461 for France, 0.0284 for Germany, 0.1367 for Italy, -0.0308 for the Netherlands and 0.1367 for the UK. These are significant at one per cent level for France and Italy, and at five percent for the UK, indicating that the daily index returns for these countries are first order serially correlated. This is in accordance with empirical findings for other stock markets. Stock indices usually show a rather large first-order autocorrelation, even if autocorrelation coefficients of individual stocks returns are very low. The presence of autocorrelation in the index returns is due to the existence of intertemporal cross covariance between stock returns which is caused by some friction in the trading process (Cohen, Hawawini, Maier, Schwartz and Whitcomb (1980)). The rather low and insignificant coefficients of the first order serial correlation in the German and Dutch indices might be explained by the important weight of a few large, frequently and highly traded firms, of which returns are not autocorrelated, in the calculation of the indices.

A comparison between the values of Q and Q^* suggests that the rejection of serial independence using Q, which is based on the standard testing procedure, is due to the presence of heteroskedasticity in the returns series. The presence of significant values of Q^* in the French and Italian returns indices indicates, however, that these returns series are not white noise processes. Furthermore, the fact that the first lag autocorrelation is significant for these two countries at the one per cent level and for the UK at the five per cent level implies the rejection of white noise, i.e. uncorrelated process. Therefore, we have to eliminate the serial correlation in these three series before searching for appropriate models that could account for heteroskedasticity in the returns. One way to do this is to apply Autoregressive Moving Average (ARMA) models.

3. ARMA models

The class of univariate ARMA models might adequately represent the behaviour of the stock returns. Therefore, several ARMA models were applied to the returns of the three countries which exhibit rather significant serial dependence, namely, France, Italy and the UK. We found that an AR(1) fits all three returns series best.

$$R_t = \phi_0 + \phi_1 R_{t-1} + \varepsilon_t \qquad (3)$$

The estimates of the above regression model for each country are presented in table 3. In order to observe whether the residuals ε_t obtained from equation (3) are uncorrelated, we applied the same tests for normality and serial correlation as for the returns series. As before, the values of the autocorrelation coefficients and their respective standard errors adjusted for heteroskedasticity are presented in table 4. The first order autocorrelation coefficient for all three countries is not significantly

Table 3 — The Autoregressive Model*

	France	Italy	U.K.
	Estimates of the model $R_t = \phi_0 + \phi_1 R_{t-1} + \varepsilon_t$		
ϕ_0	.0004	.0006	.0004
$t(\phi_0)$	2.0704	2.1861	2.6220
ϕ_1	.1461	.1367	.1367
$t(\phi_1)$	7.8140	7.3012	7.3075
F-statistic	61.0810	53.3160	53.4100
R^2	0.0213	.0187	.0187
Fuller's test	2743.18	2750.64	2750.59

* Values of the tests statistically significant at the one per cent level are underlined.

Table 4 — Sample Statistics on Daily Residuals Series*

	France	Italy	U.K.
Mean (x10^3)	.0000	.0000	.0000
t(mean=0)	.0000	.0000	.0000
Variance (x10^3)	.1052	.2005	.0802
Skewness	-1.4215	-.8295	-1.3075
Kurtosis	17.3579	12.1476	16.8439
Range	0.2005	0.2361	0.1813
Median (x10^3)	-0.0035	-0.3102	0.2390
IQR (Q3-Q1)	0.0089	0.0116	0.0102
D-statistic	0.0969	0.0997	0.0480

* Values of the tests statistically significant at the one per cent level are underlined.

different from zero. Furthermore, the results indicate that the AR(1) transformation of the returns provides an uncorrelated series of residuals. One can indeed observe that while the standard Box-Pierce statistics rejects the null hypothesis of no serial correlation at the one per cent level of significance for France and Italy, and at the five per cent level for the UK, the adjusted one does not reject the null hypothesis at the one percent level for all three countries.

The estimate of ϕ_1 is statistically significant at the one percent level and the Dickey-Fuller test for unit roots indicates that ϕ_1 is significantly less than one. The three series of returns appear to follow a stationary random walk. As far as the assumption of normality of the residuals is concerned, it can be rejected by the direct test of normality as well as by the Kolmogorov-Smirnov D-statistic at one percent significance level. The residual series appear to be leptokurtic and skewed. Moreover, again a comparison between values of Q and Q^* in table 5 indicates that the three residuals series still exhibit heteroskedasticity.

The presence of heteroskedasticity in stock prices and in the market model has been documented by, for example, Morgan (1976) and Giaccoto and Ali (1982). But while they focused on unconditional heteroskedasticity, in this paper we use Engle's Autoregressive Conditional Heteroskedastic (ARCH) model which focuses on conditional volatility movements. It is interesting to note that, according to Diebold et al. (1988), the presence of ARCH effect appears to be generally independent of unconditional heteroskedasticity. Excess kurtosis

Table 5 — Sample Autocorrelations of Daily Residuals Series*

	France	Italy	U.K.
$\rho 1$	-.0036	.0075	-.0045
	(.0323)	(.0393)	(.0660)
$\rho 2$	.0216	-.0646	.0275
	(.0419)	(.0321)	(.0537)
$\rho 3$	.0185	.0431	.0131
	(.0336)	(.0384)	(.0431)
$\rho 4$	.0208	.0554	.0495
	(.0300)	(.0332)	(.0444)
$\rho 5$	-.0227	.0049	.0056
	(.0301)	(.0301)	(.0394)
$\rho 10$	.0514	.0642	.0457
	(.0321)	(.0281)	(.0305)
$\rho 15$	-.0047	.0213	.0344
	(.0291)	(.0261)	(.0259)
$\rho 20$	.0280	.0368	.0084
	(.0272)	(.0267)	(.0263)
$\rho 25$	.0205	.0010	-.0271
	(.0267)	(.0252)	(.0208)
Q(25)	<u>76.32</u>	<u>92.09</u>	43.95
Q*(25)	34.54	38.34	17.67

*statistical tests significant at the one per cent level are underlined. Numbers in parentheses are heteroskedasticity-consistent standard errors.

observed in both returns and residuals series can be related to conditional heteroskedasticity, that is, its presence can be due to a time varying pattern of the volatility. ARCH models and its extensions have been successfully applied, for instance, in foreign exchange markets by Baillie and Bollerslev (1989) and Hsieh (1989), and in stock markets by Akgiray (1989) and Baillie and De Gennaro (1990).

4. Conditional Heteroskedastic Models

a) ARCH and GARCH Models

The ARCH process imposes an autoregressive structure on the conditional variance which permits volatility shocks to persist over time. It can therefore allow for volatility clustering, that is, large changes are followed by large changes, and small by small, which has long been recognized as an important feature of stock returns behaviour. In this process, the conditional error distribution is normal, with a conditional variance that is a linear function of past squared innovations. The model, denoted by ARCH(p), is the following:

$$\varepsilon_t | \psi_{t-1} \sim N(0, h_t)$$

$$h_t = \alpha_0 + \sum_{i=1}^{p} \alpha_i \varepsilon_{t-i}^2 \qquad (4)$$

with $p>0$; $\alpha_i>0$, $i=0,\ldots,p$,

and where ψ_t is the information set of all information through time t, and the ε_t are obtained from a linear regression model.

An important extension of the ARCH model is the Generalized Autoregressive Conditional Heteroskedasticity (GARCH) process of Bollerslev (1986), denoted by GARCH(p,q). In this model, the linear function of the conditional variance includes lagged conditional variances as well. The equation (4) in the case of a GARCH model becomes:

$$h_t = \alpha_0 + \sum_{i=1}^{p} \alpha_i \varepsilon_{t-i}^2 + \sum_{i=1}^{q} \beta_j h_{t-j} \tag{5}$$

where also $q \geq 0$ and $\beta_j \geq 0$, $j=1,\ldots,q$. The GARCH(p,q) model reduces to an ARCH(p) for q=0.

Before estimating (G)ARCH models, it is useful to test for the presence of ARCH properties on the returns series. This is the object of the next subsection.

b) Testing for ARCH presence

In an ARCH process, the variance of a time series depends on past squared residuals of the process. Therefore, the appropriateness of an ARCH model can be tested by means of a LM test, i.e. by regressing the squared residuals against a constant and lagged squared residuals (Engle, 1982).

$$\varepsilon_t^2 = \gamma_0 + \sum_{i=1}^{n} \beta_i \varepsilon_{t-i}^2 \tag{6}$$

Under the null hypothesis of no ARCH process, the coefficient of determination R^2 can be used to obtain the test statistic TR^2 which is distributed as a chi-square with i degrees of freedom. This LM test has been applied to our series up to lag 10 for all the five returns series. The values we obtained for the TR^2 are reported in table 6. They are all statistically significant at the one per cent level, which strongly indicates the presence of an ARCH process in the series.

Table 6 — LM test statistic*

	France	Germany	Italy	Netherl.	U.K.
ARCH(1)	164.2	356.3	330.8	643.0	1089.5
ARCH(2)	264.7	370.6	347.8	859.6	1090.7
ARCH(3)	280.9	381.5	431.0	859.8	1091.1
ARCH(5)	285.4	389.1	442.7	922.1	1141.1
ARCH(10)	311.1	423.8	492.5	942.3	1160.2

* All LM test statistics for ARCH(p) are significant at the one per cent level.

c) Estimating (G)ARCH models

The parameters of a (G)ARCH model are obtained through a maximum likelihood estimation. Given the return series and initial values of ε_l and h_l, for $l=0,\ldots,r$ and with $r=\max(p,q)$, the log-likelihood function we have to maximise for a normal distribution is the following:

$$L(\phi \mid p,q) = -\frac{1}{2}T\ln(2\pi) + \sum_{t=r}^{T}\ln\left(\frac{1}{\sqrt{h_t}}\right)\exp\left(\frac{-\varepsilon_t^2}{2h_t}\right) \quad (7)$$

where T is the number of observations, h_t, the conditional variance, is defined by equations (4) and (5) for the ARCH and GARCH models respectively, ε_t^2 are the residuals obtained from the appropriate linear regression model according to the country in consideration.

As the values of p and q have to be prespecified in the model, we tested several combinations of p and q. The values of the maximised likelihood functions for all pairs of p and q are presented in table 7. We also calculated the generalized likelihood ratio $LR=-2\{L(\phi_n)-L(\phi_a)\}$ of the maximised likelihood functions under the null hypothesis, i.e., the normal distribution, and the various alternate hypothesis. Under the null hypothesis LR is chi-square distributed with degrees of freedom equal to the difference in the number of parameters under the two hypotheses. The third column of table 7 gives the values of the LR test for each model. It can be observed that the value of the LR test for all (G)ARCH models is statistically significant at the one percent level, which means that all of these models fit the data more likely than does the normal distribution. In order to distinguish between an improvement in the likelihood function due to a better fit and an improvement due to an increase in the number of parameters, we also calculated Schwarz's order selection criterion, $SIC=-2L(\phi)+(\ln T)K$, where K is the number of parameters in the model. According to this criterion, the model with the lowest SIC value fits the data best. The SIC values are reported in the fifth column of table 7. The

Table 7 — Maximum log likelihoods for (G)ARCH models

Model	p,q	Log likelihood	LR test	Schwarz criterion
		France		
Normal	-	11406.50		
ARCH	(1,0)	11560.95	308.90	-23113.96
ARCH	(2,0)	11664.35	515.70	-23312.82
ARCH	(3,0)	11677.31	541.62	-23330.80
		Germany		
Normal	-	11167.36		
ARCH	(1,0)	11335.34	335.96	-22662.74
ARCH	(2,0)	11396.47	458.22	-22777.06
ARCH	(3,0)	11490.67	646.62	-22957.52
GARCH	(1,1)	11576.18	817.64	-23136.48
GARCH	(2,1)	11578.72	822.72	-23133.62
GARCH	(1,2)	11569.26	803.80	-23114.70
		Italy		
Normal	-	10506.12		
ARCH	(1,0)	10653.91	295.58	-21299.88
ARCH	(2,0)	10757.64	503.04	-21499.40
ARCH	(3,0)	10886.73	761.22	-21749.64
GARCH	(1,1)	10992.68	973.12	-21969.48
GARCH	(2,1)	...		
GARCH	(1,2)	...		
GARCH	(2,2)	10998.15	984.06	-21964.55
		The Netherlands		
Normal	-	11321.07		
ARCH	(1,0)	11483.11	324.08	-22958.28
ARCH	(2,0)	11582.53	522.92	-23149.18
ARCH	(3,0)	11597.34	552.54	-23170.86
GARCH	(1,1)	11657.18	672.22	-23298.48
GARCH	(2,1)	11650.63	659.12	-23277.44
GARCH	(1,2)	11650.68	659.22	-23277.54
		The UK		
Normal	-	11789.03		
ARCH	(1,0)	11991.12	404.18	-23974.30
ARCH	(2,0)	12046.90	515.74	-24077.92
ARCH	(3,0)	12062.77	547.48	-24101.72
GARCH	(1,1)	12097.46	616.86	-24179.04
GARCH	(2,1)	...		
GARCH	(1,2)	12091.50	604.94	-24159.18
GARCH	(2,2)	...		

... indicates where the optimization routine failed.

GARCH(1,1) model has the lowest SIC values for all countries except France. For the latter the ARCH(3) supersedes the other models.

The sum of $\sum_{i=1}^{p}\alpha_i+\sum_{j=1}^{q}\beta_j$ in the conditional variance equations measures the persistence of the volatility. Engle and Bollerslev (1986) have shown that if this sum is equal to one, the GARCH process becomes an integrated GARCH or IGARCH process. Such integrated model implies the persistence of a forecast of the conditional variance over all future horizons and also an infinite variance of the unconditional distribution of ε_t. We calculated the sum of the parameters $\sum_{i=1}^{p}\alpha_i+\sum_{j=1}^{q}\beta_j$ for the appropriate GARCH models. They are respectively 0.9923, 1.0005, 0.9761, 0.9520 and 0.4329 for France, Germany, Italy, the Netherlands and the UK. It can be noticed that it is less than unity for four countries, though rather close to one, which indicates a long persistence of shocks in volatility. This means that this model is second order stationary and that the second moment exists for these four countries. The unconditional variances of residuals, shown in table 8, are respectively $\sigma_\varepsilon^2=\alpha_0/(1-\alpha_1-\beta_1)$ for Italy, the Netherlands and the UK and $\sigma_\varepsilon^2=\alpha_0/(1-\alpha_1-\alpha_2-\alpha_3)$ for France, and, for returns, it is $\sigma_R^2=\sigma_\varepsilon^2/(1-\phi_1^2)$.

As for Germany, the sum $\alpha_1+\beta_1$ is greater than unity, indicating that the series is not stationary and that an integrated model is more appropriate, i.e. the conditional variance follows an integrated process. The GARCH(1,1) model has therefore been reestimated with the restriction

Table 8 — Model Estimates*

	France	Germany	Italy	Netherl.	U.K.
ϕ_0 (thousands)	.6881	.6246	.8061	.9255	.6775
$t(\phi_0)$	4.1215	4.0899	3.8546	5.6614	4.6100
ϕ_1	.2031	–	.1909	–	.1519
$t(\phi_1)$	9.5706	–	7.7043	–	7.5064
α_0 (thousands)	.0581	.0021	.0064	.0053	.0053
$t(\alpha_0)$	24.7654	3.7088	6.2055	4.9619	5.1517
α_1	.1739	.1406	.1394	.1113	.1131
$t(\alpha_1)$	6.6687	8.5353	9.0820	7.6555	7.5200
α_2	.1612	–	–	–	–
$t(\alpha_2)$	6.4882	–	–	–	–
α_3	.0978	–	–	–	–
$t(\alpha_3)$	4.3288	–	–	–	–
β_1	–	.8594	.8367	.8407	.8153
$t(\beta_1)$	–	55.5779	52.0732	40.7251	35.6342
$\Sigma\alpha_i+\Sigma\beta_j$	.4329	1.0000	.9761	.9520	.9284
σ^2_ε ($\times 10^3$)	.1025	–	.2678	–	.0740
σ^2_R ($\times 10^3$)	.1069	–	.2779	.1104	.0758

* t statistics significant at the one percent level are underlined.

that $\alpha_1+\beta_1=1$. Table 8 contains the results of fitting GARCH(1,1) process to the returns series of Italy, the Netherlands and the UK, ARCH(3) to that of France, and finally IGARCH(1,1) for Germany. All estimated coefficients, except that of ϕ_0 and α_0 for Germany, are statistically significant at the one percent level. Interestingly, the estimates of α_0 are much smaller than the sample variances of returns or residuals reported in tables 1 and 4, indicating that conditional variances are changing over time.

5. Conclusions

This paper provides empirical support that the class of autoregressive conditional heteroskedasticity models is generally consistent with the stochastic behaviour of daily stock returns in five European countries. The results show that stock market indices exhibit a significant level of non linear dependence which cannot be accounted for by the random walk model. Descriptive statistics and normality tests reveal that the distribution of returns is not normal, whatever the country concerned, and that three out the five country indices exhibit significant first order autocorrelation. It has further been shown that the residuals obtained after applying an AR(1) model, which accounts for the presence of autocorrelation in the returns, exhibit non linear dependence and non normality. Then we observed the presence of ARCH in the returns series and tested various models belonging to the class of autoregressive conditional heteroskedasticity models. Our results reveal that this class of models supersedes the random walk model. And among the different models the GARCH(1,1) fits the data best for Italy, the Netherlands and the UK, the ARCH(3) for France and IGARCH(1,1) for Germany.

6. References

Akgiray, V. (1989), 'Conditional Heteroskedasticity in Time Series of Stock Returns: Evidence and Forecasts', *Journal of Business* 62, pp. 55-80.

Baillie, R.T. and T. Bollerslev (1989), 'The Message in Daily Exchange Rates: A Conditional-Variance Tale', *Journal of Business & Economic Statistics* 7, pp. 297-305.

Baillie, R.T. and R.P. De Gennaro (1990), 'Stock Returns and Volatility', *Journal of Financial and Quantitative Analysis* 25, pp. 203-214.

Black, F. and Scholes M. (1973), 'The Pricing of Options and Corporate Liabilities', *Journal of Political Economy* 81, pp. 637-654.

Blattberg, R.C. and N.J. Gonedes (1974), 'A Comparison of the Stable and Student Distribution of Statistical Models for Stock Prices', *Journal of Business* 47, pp. 244-280.

Bollerslev, T. (1986), 'Generalized Autoregressive Conditional Heteroskedasticity', *Journal of Econometrics* 31, pp. 307-327.

Cohen, K.J., Hawawini, G.A., Maier, S.F., Schwartz, R.A. and D.K. Whitcomb (1980), 'Implications of Microstructure Theory for Empirical Research on Stock Price Behavior', *Journal of Finance* 35, pp. 249-257.

Corhay A. and A. Tourani Rad (1990), 'Conditional Heteroskedasticity in Stock Returns: Evidence from the Amsterdam Stock Exchange', Research Memorandum 90-046, University of Limburg.

Diebold, F.X. (1987), 'Testing for Serial Correlation in the Presence of ARCH', Proceedings from the American Statistic Association, Business and Economic Statistics Section, pp. 323-328.

Diebold, F.X., Im, J. and C.J. Lee (1988), 'Conditional Heteroscedasticity in the Market', Finance and Economics Discussion Series, 42, Division of Research and Statistics, Federal Reserve Board, Washington D.C.

Engle, R. (1982), 'Autoregressive Conditional Heteroscedasticity with Estimates of the Variance of UK inflation', *Econometrica* 50, pp. 987-1008.

Fama, E.F. (1963), 'Mandelbrot and the Stable Paretian Hypothesis', *Journal of Business* 36, pp. 420-429.

Fama, E.F. (1965), 'The Behavior of Stock Market Prices', *Journal of Business* 38, pp. 34-105.

French, K.R. , Schwert, G.W. and R.F. Stambaugh (1987), 'Expected Stock Returns and Volatility', *Journal of Financial Economics* 19, pp. 3-29.

Giaccoto, C. and M.M. Ali (1982), 'Optimal Distribution Free Tests and Further Evidence of Heteroskedasticity in the Market Model', *Journal of Finance* 37, pp. 1247-1257.

Hinich, M. and D. Patterson (1985), 'Evidence of Nonlinearity in Daily Stock Returns', *Journal of Business & Economics Statistics* 3, pp. 69-77.

Hsieh, D.A. (1989), 'Modelling Heteroscedasticity in Daily Foreign-Exchange Rates', *Journal of Business & Economic Statistics* 7, pp. 307-317.

Kon, S. (1984), 'Models of Stock Returns: A Comparison', *Journal of Finance* 39, pp. 147-165.

Mandelbrot, B. (1963), 'The Variation of Certain Speculative Prices', *Journal of Business* 36, pp. 394-419.

Merton, R. (1982), 'On the Mathematics and Economics Assumptions of Continuous-Time Models', in *Financial Economics*, W. Sharpe and C. Cootner, eds., (Englewood Cliffs, N.J. Prentice-Hall, 1982).

Morgan, I. (1976), 'Stock Prices and Heteroscedasticity', *Journal of Business* 49, pp. 496-508.

Paretz, P.D. (1972), 'The Distribution of Share Price Changes', *Journal of Business* 45, pp. 49-55.

Perry, P. (1982), 'The Time-Variance Relationship of Security Returns: Implications for the Return-Generating Stochastic Process', *Journal of Finance* 37, pp. 857-870.

Press, S.J. (1967), 'A Compound Events Model for Security Prices', *Journal of Business* 40, pp. 317-335.

Poon S.H. and S. Taylor (1992), 'Stock Returns and volatility: An Empirical Study of the UK Stock Market', *Journal of Banking and Finance* 16, pp. 37-61.

Schwarz, G. (1978), 'Estimating the Dimension of a Model', *The Annals of Statistics* 6, pp. 461-464.

Sharpe, W. F. (1964), 'Capital Asset Prices: A Theory of Market Equilibrium under Conditions of Risk', *Journal of Finance*, 19, pp. 425-442.

Tauchen, G.E. and M. Pitts (1983), 'The Price Variability-Volume Relationship on Speculative Markets', *Econometrica* 51, pp. 485-505.

Taylor, S. (1990), 'Modelling a Stochastic Volatility', working paper, Department of Accounting and Finance, Lancaster University, UK.

MEASURING FIRM/MARKET INFORMATION ASYMMETRY:
The Model of Myers and Majluf or the Importance of the Asset Structure of the Firm

NATHALIE DIERKENS
E S C P, 79 Avenue de la République 75543 Paris Cedex 11 – France

This paper is based in part on the author's PhD dissertation at the Massachussets Institute of Technology. She would like to thank Stewart Myers, her chairman, and the other members of her committee, Paul Asquith and Patricia O'Brien, for their help. She thanks Richard Ruback and Robyn McLaughlin for the use of their programs Superday and variations. All remaining errors are hers. She has also received helpful comments from the participants of the AFFI Conference held in Paris in December 1989, the ESF-CEPR workshop in Gerzenzee in July 1990, the European Finance Association in Athens in September 1990, and the referees for the EURO Financial Modelling Studies, Curaçao and London, 1991.

This paper was written while the author was at INSEAD, Boulevard de Constance 77305 Fontainebleau Cedex, France.

ABSTRACT

This paper shows that measures of information asymmetry ought to be event-specific and model-specific in order to design correct tests of alternative models of information asymmetry. It shows that the traditional measures: volatilities, or residual volatilities, are not necessarily correct. The paper presents a correct measure of information asymmetry for the analysis of the equity issue process in the context of Myers and Majluf's model. This measure is a function of the asset structure of the firm, and captures the volatility of the assets in place only. Some empirical evidence suggests that the distinction can matter empirically.

I. INTRODUCTION

In recent years, the differences in information among several groups have received increased attention in the finance literature. Corporate finance discusses the asymmetry in information between the managers of the firm and the market. For example, Ross (1977) and Miller and Rock (1985) point out the influence of information asymmetry on the financial policy of the firm, and Myers and Majluf (1984) model the importance of information asymmetry for the equity issue process. Many models have expanded on these early papers.[1] In order to test empirically the predictions of the various models, a measure of information asymmetry is needed. Previous studies (e.g. Masulis and Korwar (1986), Bhagat, Marr and Thompson (1985), Dierkens (1991)) have used the volatility of the stock or the residual volatility for their empirical tests of models of information asymmetry without

[1] Since then many more complex models have been suggested. For example, the models of Krasker(1985), John and Williams (1985), Bradford (1987), Ambarish, John and Williams(1987), Narayanan (1988), Korajcyk, Lucas and McDonald (1990) extend Myers and Majluf's framework in several directions.

formal justifications of these measures.

This paper shows that the traditional measures are not always correct and may be misleading in some empirical tests. It chooses to focus on one specific model, the Myers and Majluf model. This model is very well known in the literature and often referred to explicitely in the type of empirical tests this paper discusses.[2] Furthermore, the Myers and Majluf model is based on the asset structure of the firm, which gives an interesting base for the discussion of the characteristics of the information asymmetry of the firm.

Section II defines the required characteristics for correct measures of information asymmetry. Section III checks whether several variables are or are not correct measures of information asymmetry in the context of Myers and Majluf's model. It shows that the volatility or the residual volatility of the firm is not correct. It suggests an alternative measure of information asymmetry, the volatility of the assets in place of the firm. Section IV discusses the relevance of the theoretical caveats for empirical work. It emphasizes especially the required conditions for the traditional measures to be good empirical proxies and presents some empirical results consistent with the analysis. Section V concludes the paper by giving general implications of this model-specific discussion. It also mentions some directions for future research.

II. REQUIRED CHARACTERISTICS FOR A MEASURE OF INFORMATION ASYMMETRY

The behavior of a firm in a world of information asymmetry can differ from the behavior of an otherwise identical firm in a world of symmetric information: the firm can have a different value, follow a

[2]See for example Masulis and Korwar (1986, p. 114) or Bhagat, Marr and Thompson (1985). Masulis and Korwar find non-significant results, Bhagat, Marr and Thompson and Dierkens find significant results (with the correct signs). Masulis and Korwar and Dierkens mention the problem in the case of Myers and Majluf's model but do not develop the source nor the implications of the problem. Bhagat, Marr and Thompson study information asymmetry through the concept of the risk to the underwriters.

different stochastic process and make different investment, financing and reporting decisions. Similarly, if all firms are not subject to the same level of information asymmetry, the behavior of a given firm can be a function of its level of information asymmetry. It would be useful to find one or several variable(s) summarizing the degree of information asymmetry faced by a given firm at a given point in time to predict the magnitude of the effects created by its level of information asymmetry. Possibly, some variable could capture the concept of information asymmetry satisfactorily for some applications, but not for some others. There could be information asymmetry about more than one aspect (e.g. per type of asset) of the firm, and different asymmetries could have different effects. In this sense one needs to specify the intended uses of the chosen measures.

This paper suggests a correct measure of information asymmetry for the empirical analysis of the equity issue process from the perspective of Myers and Majluf's model. The information asymmetry is noted IAE, with E expliciting the special case of equity issue taken into consideration. More specifically, the measures of information asymmetry are to be related to two *observable* events in the equity issue process: 1) the market-adjusted abnormal return of the firm observed at the equity issue announcement and 2) the magnitude of the information released by the announcement. These two events are traditional in the financial economics literature and have been the topics of numerous studies, for equity issues, but also for dividends, repurchases or any corporate restructurations.[3] Everything else constant, the existence and magnitude of these two events are considered to be driven by the existence and magnitude of information asymmetry. When the decision to issue equity reflects some of the managers-specific information as in the Myers and Majluf's model, a correct measure of information asymmetry should be monotonically negatively related to the magnitude of the abnormal return at the equity issue announcement. It should also, all other things equal, be decreased by the transfer to the market of some of the managers-specific information created at the equity issue announcement. Any measure always having these two

[3]The studies analyze the abnormal return at the announcements, the changes in abnormal returns of future announcements, the relationship to ex post changes in earnings (see for example Healy and Palepu (1988)).

characteristics qualifies as a correct measure. Later sections of the paper discuss examples and counter examples of correct measures for *IAE*.

III. MEASURES OF INFORMATION ASYMMETRY IN MYERS AND MAJLUF'S MODEL

Myers and Majluf show that the existence of information asymmetry between the managers of the firm and the market can create an economic loss in the value of the firm. Their model can also be used to study several *observable* (then empirically testable) differences between the behavior of the firm in a world of information asymmetry and the behavior of the firm in a world of perfect information symmetry. It can be used to predict the magnitudes of the proportional drop in price observed at the equity issue announcement and of the change in uncertainty in the assets of the firm before and after the announcement. This section shows by simulated examples how the structure of the assets of the firm fundamentally influences the process of issuing equity under asymmetric information and how as a consequence the structure of the assets of the firm determines the correct measures for *IAE*. The Myers and Majluf issue and invest model separates the total assets of the firm (V) into two groups: the assets in place of the firm (A), not influenced by the decision to issue and invest, and the growth opportunity (B), only available to the firm if the firm issues an amount I. The simulations show that the volatility of the assets in place is a correct measure of *IAE* but that the total volatility of the firm is not. First, some intuition is provided by highlighting the different roles of the assets in place and of the growth opportunity in the equity issue process. Then the simulated results are discussed.

A) An intuitive measure of *IAE*

In Myers and Majluf's model, the managers use their superior information about the assets of the firm to maximize the value of the firm to the old stockholders. Managers know a and b, the realized values of A and B respectively, when they decide to issue, but the market only knows the bivariate distribution of A and B at that time. When new shares are issued, a part of the issue (and thus a part of A and B) goes to new shareholders. New shareholders are afraid that the managers issue equity not only because they need to finance the new project B, but because they want to enrich the old shareholders at the expense of the new shareholders by selling overpriced securities before the bad news about A leaks out. As a result of this, the new shareholders will rationally protect themselves by discounting all new issues. All other things equal, the more a is worth, the less likely the firm is to issue, since the old shareholders can keep a to themselves instead of sharing it with the new shareholders. On the other hand, the more b is worth, the more likely the firm is to issue, since the old shareholders can share b instead of losing it.[4] When a firm announces a new issue, the market knows that this decision is created by a mixture of "unfavorable" news for a and "favorable" news for b. All other things equal, the market will impose a higher discount on the shares of the firm when the bad news concerning a is likely to be greater. This happens when the distribution for A is less centralized, i.e. when the volatility of A is higher. In the extreme case where A is constant, i.e. when its standard deviation is zero, no bad news about A could be hidden and the market will impose *no* discount on the shares of the firm. In this case, the firm will always issue, and both the ex-ante loss in the value of the firm and the drop in the value at the equity issue announcement are zero. The issue announcement brings no information in this case. No similar result, however, holds for the volatility of B: there can still exist an ex-ante loss in value and a drop in price at the announcement of the equity issue even if B is known (see Myers and Majluf (1984), p. 201 for a proof of this for the loss). This shows that A and B, and their respective volatilities, play different roles in the issue and invest decision. Therefore, intuitively, the volatility of A and the volatility of B should not be aggregated into the total volatility of the firm when measuring the IAE.

B) Simulated Results

No closed-form solution exists for the equilibrium prices and variances

[4]This can easily be seen in the figure 1, page 199, of Myers and Majluf's article.

in the Myers and Majluf model for commonly assumed distributions in finance, so the distributional characteristics are simulated for the case where the assets of the firm have initially a bivariate lognormal distribution in a world of symmetric information (indicated by the superscript ^{s}). The algorithm is an extension of the algorithm suggested by Myers and Majluf. The inputs to each simulation are $\overline{A}^s$, σ_A^s, $\overline{B}^s$, σ_B^s, ρ^s, and I, i.e. the mean and standard deviation of the assets in place, the mean and standard deviation of the growth opportunity, the correlation between A and B and the required amount of new equity. The algorithm computes the issue/non issue regions, the new distributional characteristics of A, B and V under asymmetric information, before and after the issue decision, and the proportional drop at the equity issue announcement. The simulations have been performed over a wide set of parameter values. The parameter set has been chosen in order to include all realistic cases.[5]

[Insert Table 1 here]

Over the whole parameter space, all other things equal, an increase in the uncertainty of the assets in place implies an increase in the proportional drop at the equity issue announcement and a decrease in the probability of the issue. Table 1 represents the proportional drop versus the volatility of the assets in place for several series. It can be seen that the drop at the issue announcement is negligible for low values of $\sigma_A/\overline{A}$ (e.g. $\sigma_A/\overline{A} = .10$). As $\sigma_A/\overline{A}$ increases, the drop increases. In the simulations, *no* other volatility is unambiguously related to the size of the proportional drop at the equity issue announcement. The article emphasizes the fact that the total volatility of the market value of the firm does not qualify, i.e., does not necessarily increase

[5] Here are the elements of the parameter set: The assets in place are used as a reference point; they always have a mean $\overline{A} = 100$.The amount of new equity needed to finance the new project, I, varies between 1 and 100 (i.e. between 1 percent and 100 percent of the mean value of the assets in place), in increments of approximately 10. The expected value of the growth opportunity, $\overline{B}^s$, varies between .01 and 50 (i.e. between 1 percent and 50 percent of I or between .01 percent to 50 percent of A), in increments of 5. $\sigma_A/\overline{A}$ varies between 5 percent and 50 percent, in increments of 10 percent. $\sigma_B^s/\overline{B}^s$ is chosen so that, once the project has been implemented (i.e. once I has been invested), it varies between .25 and 4 times $\sigma_A/\overline{A}$. The correlation between A and B varies between 0 and .9, in increments of .1.

the drop, because this measure is readily available from trading data, and is used in several papers.[6] Table 2 gives two examples where an increase in the total uncertainty of the market value of the firm (measured by the volatility) implies a decrease in the proportional drop at the equity issue (.22 < .29 but .04 > .01 and .32 < .36 but .02 > .01). This typically happens when $\overline{B}/\overline{A}$ is high.[7] [8]

[Insert Table 2 here]

Over the whole parameter space, the volatility of the assets in place conditional on the firm deciding to issue is lower than the volatility of the assets in place before the decision. Table 3 gives several representative examples. On the other hand, the volatility of the market value of the firm does not necessarily decrease after the announcement. Intuitively this happens because the growth opportunity is undertaken once the firm issues equity; the standard deviation of the growth opportunity can be fairly high and can increase the total uncertainty of the firm. Table 4 provides two examples where the announcement of the decision to issue *increases* the uncertainty of the market value of the firm (.25 > .24, .31 > .29).[9] [10] [11]

[Insert Table 3 and Table 4 here]

---

[6]We also replicate Myers and Majluf results that σ_A is the only volatility systematically (positively) related to the loss in the value of the firm created by the existence of information asymmetry (and not $\sigma_V/\overline{V}$ or $\sigma_B/\overline{B}$).

[7]The same results obtain for $\sigma_A, \sigma_A^2/\overline{A}$, or any positive function of these variables.

[8]Similarly, no systematic behavior can be observed for σ_B or $\sigma_B/\overline{B}$, σ_V, or $\sigma_V/\overline{V}$.

[9]Same comments as in footnotes 7 and 8.

[10]The results shown in this section are distribution specific. Some more extreme examples and counter examples exist when A and B follow binomial distributions (see Dierkens (1988)).

[11]The presentation in this section is made for an unlevered firm. The results are easily extended to the case of a firm with riskless debt.

IV. IMPLICATIONS FOR EMPIRICAL ANALYSES

A) Required characteristics of proxies for *IAE*

There is only manager-specific uncertainty in Myers and Majluf's model.[12] The empirical tests, however, will be run with data for which there exists also another type of uncertainty, the uncertainty shared by the managers of the firm and the market, for example related to the general economy, to exchange rates, or to specific industries. The empiricist is confronted to a double requirement for its proxies of *IAE*: they should only concern the assets in place and they should not incorporate any of the uncertainty shared by the managers of the firm and the market. This paper focuses on the former problem. The latter concern is addressed by using only residual volatility.

B) Importance of the distinction between assets in place and total assets

Section III has shown that the volatility for the total assets of the firm is not theoretically correct for the analysis of the equity issue process, in the context of the Myers and Majluf model. However, the approximation may be more acceptable in some cases than in others. One would then expect empirical results to be more valid in these cases. The Myers and Majluf model makes a distinction between the assets in place and the growth opportunity. That distinction has proved to be important for the measure of *IAE*. The growth opportunity represents a project with a positive net present value that is completely lost if the firm does not issue equity at this point in time. The magnitude and the nature of the project can vary widely.[13] When

[12] So, in their model, the concepts of information asymmetry, volatility and uncertainty are equivalent.

[13] B can be a strategic investment, the usual meaning of the term growth opportunity, for example an investment in the development of a new technology, but it can also represent a favorable change in the debt/equity ratio of the firm, or the implementation of some improvements to the existing machines of the firm. If the firm can issue and invest later if it decides not to issue now, b represents the loss of value asociated with delaying the project. If the firm can finance the project with sources other than an equity issue, b is the additional cost of that financial source over the equity issue. The "assets in place" include all the assets of the firm that

B is defined as the value lost if the firm does not issue new equity *now*, B can be fairly small in many cases. Then the value of the firm is approximately equal to the value of the assets in place, and the volatility of the firm can be approximately equal to the volatility of the assets in place.

More formally:

$$\left(\frac{\sigma_V}{\overline{V}}\right)^2 = \left(\frac{\sigma_A}{\overline{A}}\right)^2 \left(\frac{\overline{A}}{\overline{V}}\right)^2 + 2\rho \frac{\sigma_A}{\overline{A}} \frac{\sigma_B}{\overline{B}} \frac{\overline{A}}{\overline{V}} \frac{\overline{B}}{\overline{V}} + \left(\frac{\sigma_B}{\overline{B}}\right)^2 \left(\frac{\overline{B}}{\overline{V}}\right)^2 \tag{1}$$

or

$$\left(\frac{\sigma_V}{\overline{V}}\right)^2 - \left(\frac{\sigma_A}{\overline{A}}\right)^2 = 2\rho \frac{\sigma_A}{\overline{A}} \frac{\sigma_B}{\overline{B}} \frac{\overline{A}}{\overline{V}} \frac{\overline{B}}{\overline{V}} + \left(\frac{\sigma_B}{\overline{B}}\right)^2 \left(\frac{\overline{B}^2}{\overline{V}}\right) - \left(\frac{\sigma_A}{\overline{A}}\right)^2 \left(\frac{2\overline{AB} + \overline{B}^2}{\overline{V}^2}\right) \tag{2}$$

which shows that $\sigma_V/\overline{V}$ is a perfect measure for $\sigma_A/\overline{A}$ when $\rho = 1$ and $\sigma_B/\overline{B} = \sigma_A/\overline{A}$. Other combinations of the parameters can also justify the equivalence between $\sigma_V/\overline{V}$ and $\sigma_A/\overline{A}$, as for example a low ratio $\overline{B}/\overline{V}$. All other things equal, equation (2) goes to zero when $\overline{B}/\overline{V}$ goes to zero. The case of ρ equal to one and $\sigma_A/\overline{V}$ equal to $\sigma_B/\overline{B}$ would be hard to find and hard to prove.[14] The case of $\overline{B}/\overline{V}$ small can at least be checked, even if only with a small level of precision. So in the case of $\overline{B}/\overline{V}$ small, the empiricist might prefer proxies that are easy to estimate over short periods of time and easy to estimate with precision (and that handle well the separation between total uncertainty of the firm and information asymmetry), over proxies that focus on the separation between assets in place and growth opportunities but are much harder to estimate. This justifies the use of "traditional" proxies of information asymmetry used or suggested in the literature like the residual volatility of the stock, the intensity of

that are *not* influenced by the decision to issue, possibly including some expansion plans that can be financed immediately by internal resources or are planned for later periods.

[14]Exceptions could be cases of pure expansion of the firm.

trading, the magnitude of the bid-ask spread, the intensity of insiders trading, the dispersion of analysts forecasts or the (lack of) intensity of public announcements.

The relevance of the distinction between the total information asymmetry and the information asymmetry for the assets in place only can be tested empirically. Two types of tests are possible. The first type of test consists in finding proxies for IAE that respect the distinction between the assets in place and the growth opportunity and in comparing the results obtained with more traditional proxies. Unfortunately, such proxies are very hard to find.[15] The second type of test uses traditional proxies and compares their behavior in several subsamples: if Myers and Majluf's model is true and if the ratio $\overline{B}/\overline{V}$ can be adequately measured, the proxies should capture the consequences of the existence of information asymmetry much better when $\overline{B}/\overline{V}$ is low than when it is high. The results of such a test are provided below.

C) Some empirical evidence

This section tests whether, all other things equal, an increase in IAE increases the drop observed at the equity issue announcement for two "traditional" measures of information asymmetry, σ_ϵ^2 and $DNBAN$. σ_ϵ^2 is the variance of the stock return.[16] It recognizes that the information asymmetry is a subset of the total uncertainty of the firm, from which it deducts all the market uncertainty, obviously shared by the managers of the firm and by the market. $DNBAN$ is a dummy variable describing the informational environment of the firm by the number of announcements of the firm. It is set equal to one (zero) when the firm has on average relatively few (many) announcements made to the market. It captures the idea that, all other things equal, the information asymmetry is high (low) when there exists few (many) announcements made about a firm. Both measures have no reason to be related to the assets in place of the firm only, so they will per-

[15] Dierkens (1988) discusses some of the problems. She suggests a proxy, more specifically related to the assets in place of the firm, the average surprise at earnings announcements. The empirical results, however, are not better for this proxy, probably because it was estimated over too long a time period (five years).

[16] Unlevering the variance does not change the results. See also footnote 11.

form better in the low $\overline{B}/\overline{V}$ subsample if Myers and Majluf's model holds and if the distinction between assets in place and total assets matters. Table 5 presents the results of the cross-sectional regression of the market-adjusted two-day abnormal return at the equity issue announcement by *IAE*, the relative size of the equity issue (*RSIZE*) and two control variables, the relative importance of the growth opportunity (*RMEBE*), for the subsamples for high and low *RMEBE* for a total sample of 197 industrial firms. The relative importance of the growth opportunity for a firm is approximated by the ratio of the market value of the equity of the firm to the book value of the equity of the firm, in the spirit of Tobin's Q-ratio. [17] [18]

[Insert Table 5 here]

Table 5 shows that in the case of a low *RMEBE*, i.e. in the case where the empirical proxies come closest to the theoretically correct measure of *IAE*, the cross-sectional variations in *IAE* explain very well the cross-sectional variations in the reaction at the equity issue announcement. *IAE* is the best explanatory variable and the t-statistics for two mesures of *IAE*, σ_ϵ , and *DNBAN* are negative and significant respectively at the 1% and the 5% level in one-tailed tests. The constant is even not significant, which is an unusual result for this type of study. On the other hand, only the constant is significant for the subsample of firms with high *RMEBE* and the proxies for *IAE* explain absolutely nothing in this case. Also, the abnormal return at the equity issue announcement is significantly higher (i.e. the drop

[17]The simulations of Myers and Majluf's model have shown that *RSIZE* and *RMEBE* should decrease (increase) *AREI*.

[18]The sample of 197 equity issue announcements has been constructed in a traditional way, e.g. with no joint announcement of mergers, earnings, dividends, or other financial changes on the days of the equity issue announcements. It only considers industrial firms and has a standard time and industry clustering. The total sample reaction at the equity issue announcement(average market-adjusted two-day abnormal return of −2.4,
80 % negative) is fully consistent with the existing literature (see Bhagat, Marr and Thompson (1985), Asquith and Mullins(1986), Masulis and Korwar (1986), Mikkelson and Partch (1986)). Even the non-significance of the relative size of the issue has been noted before.

is lower), at the 5% level, for firm with high *RMEBE*.[19] Overall, the results show that the distinction between information asymmetry for the assets in place only and for the total value of the firm matters in some cases.[20] [21] The evidence is especially compelling when one considers how hard it is to capture empirically the concept of growth opportunity and the ratio $\overline{B}/\overline{V}$.

V. CONCLUSION

This paper offers a correct measure of information asymmetry for the study of the equity issue process in the context of the Myers and Majluf model. It shows by simulations that a correct measure of information asymmetry is a function of the volatility of the assets in place of the firm only. Its dependence on the assets structure of the firm reflects the importance of the asset structure throughout Myers and Majluf's model.[22] The simulations also show that an "obvious" candidate, the volatility (or the residual volatility) of the firm does not qualify as an unambiguously correct measure of information asymmetry in this context. Furthermore, both theoretical and empirical evidence show that the distinction matters. The results of this paper should be used to understand better the limitations of traditional proxies and use them better. In this case, the tests can be improved either by finding more correct proxies for *IAE*, i.e. more directly re-

[19] This result is also consistent with the model of Ambarish, John, and Williams (1987).

[20] The effect is not observable continuously: I have not found a continuously decreasing *t*-statistics for decreasing levels of *RMEBE* by separating the subsample in 5 or 10 subsamples.

[21] σ_ϵ^2 is significantly decreased by the equity issue announcement, however, at the same level (i.e. with no significant difference at usual level of significance) for high *RMEBE* and for low *RMEBE* firms.

[22] The importance of the asset structure is even more extreme in some other models, such has Ambarish, John and Williams (1987), where the equity issue announcement implies negative abnormal return when the manager-specific information concerns primarily the assets in place but positive when the manager-specific information concerns primarily the opportunities to invest, whereas the equity issue announcement is always negative in Myers and Majluf's model. Such models will of course also have strong implications for the correct measures of information asymmetry.

lated to the assets in place of the firm only, or by limiting the use of more the traditional proxies to the cases where the approximation is the most valid, i.e. when $\overline{B}/\overline{V}$ is low. Further tests could try to approximate the growth opportunity with more precision. For example Williamson (1981) or Long and Malitz(1983) discuss the problem and suggest some alternative estimations of $\overline{B}/\overline{V}$. Also, Lindenberg and Ross (1981) and Lang, Stulz and Walkling (1989) define alternative measures of Tobin's Q that could be used in this context.

The paper discusses a very precise problem: it specifies the event (equity issue announcement), the model (Myers and Majluf's model) and even the tests (cross-sectional variation in the reaction at equity issue and pre-post comparisons of the level of information asymmetry). However this result indicates that in general measures of information asymmetry ought to be event-specific and model-specific in order to design correct tests of alternative models of information asymmetry. Now, with the expansion of theoretical and empirical work, the case for the relevance of information asymmetry in general, especially for the equity issue process, need not be defended any more, but we need to know which modelling approach is the most productive in specific cases.[23] Up to now the difference among different models based on information asymmetry was done through other implications of the models not by a specific measure of the information asymmetry relevant in that model.[24] The kind of information asymmetry needed for empirical tests should be defined in each case, and then tests of this specific asymmetry can be devised. The time has come to design more precise tests to differentiate among alternative modelling approach. This paper shows a direction for future tests.

---

[23]Although several (non mutually exclusive) explanations have been provided for the average negative stock price reaction at the equity issue announcement, theories of information asymmetry seem the most consistent with the evidence (see Smith (1986) for a general overview).

[24]For example Myers and Majluf's model implies a lower drop in stock price at the issue announcement of securities of lower risks, contrary to Miller and Rock model. There is a general tendency for this to be observed (Compare the reaction at the issue announcement of equity, preferred stocks (Linn and Pinegar (1988)), convertible debt (Mikkelson and Partch,(1986)). Also Bruner (1988) shows that mergers happen in order to prevent the potential loss in the value of the firm for projects-rich but cash-poor firms as predicted by Myers and Majluf's model.

REFERENCES

Ambarish, Ramasastry, Kose John, and Joseph Williams. "Efficient Signalling with Dividends and Investments." *Journal of Finance*, Vol. 42, No. 2, (June 1987), 321-373.

Asquith, Paul and David Mullins. "Equity Issues and Offering Dilution." *Journal of Financial Economics*, Vol. 15, No. 1/2, (January/ February 1986), 61-90.

Bhagat, Sanjay, Wayne Marr, and Rodney Thompson. "The Rule 415 Experiment: Equity Markets.", *Journal of Finance*, Vol. 40, No. 5, (December 1985), 1385-1401.

Bruner, Robert. "The Use of Excess Cash and Debt Capacity as a Motive for Merger." *Journal of Financial and Quantitative Analysis*, Vol. 23, No. 2, (June 1988).

Dann, Larry Y., Ronald W. Masulis and David Mayers. "Repurchase Tender Offers and Earnings Information." *Journal of Accounting and Economics*, Vol. 14, (1991), 217-251.

Dierkens, Nathalie. "Information Asymmetry and Equity Issues." Unpublished Ph.D. Dissertation, Sloan School of Management, M.I.T., (March 1988).

Dierkens, Nathalie. "Information Asymmetry and Equity Issues." *Journal of Financial and Quantitative Analysis*, Vol. 26, No. 2, (June 1991), 181-199.

Healy, Paul, and Krishna Palepu. "Earnings Information Conveyed by Dividend Initiations and Omissions." *Journal of Financial Economics*, Vol. 21, No. 2, (September 1988), 149-175.

Hertzel, Michael and Prem C. Jain. "Earnings and Risk Changes around Stock Repurchase Tender Offers." *Journal of Accounting and Economics*, Vol. 14, (1991), 253-274.

John, Kox and Joseph Williams. "Dividends, dilution and Taxes: A Signalling Equilibrium." *Journal of Finance*, Vol. 40, No. 4, (September 1985), 1053-1070.

Korajczyk, Robert, Deborah Lucas, and Robert McDonald. "The Effect of Information Releases on the Pricing and Timing of Equity Issues: Theory and Evidence." in *Asymmetric Information, Corporate Finance and Investment*, NBER, Edited by R. Glenn Hubbard, the University of Chicago Press, (1990).

Krasker, William. "Stock Price Movements in Response to Stock Issues and Aymmetric Information." *Journal of Finance*, Vol. 41, No. 1, (March 1986), 93-105.

Lang, J. H., R. S. Stulz and R. A. Walkling. "Managerial Performance, Tobin's Q and the Gains from Sucessful Tender Offers." *Journal of Financial Econmics*, Vol. 24, No. 1, (September 1989), 137-154.

Lindenberg, E. and S. Ross. "Tobin's Q Ratio and Industrial Organization." *Journal of Business*, Vol. 54, No. 1, (1981), 1-32.

Linn, Scott and Michael Pinegar. "The Effects of Issuing Preferred Stock on Common and Preferred Stockholder Wealth." *The Journal of Financial Economics*, Vol. 22, No. 1, (October 1988), 155-184.

Long, Michael and Ileen Malitz. "Investment Patterns and Financial Leverage." NBER working paper, #1145, (June 1983).

Masulis, Ronald and Ashok Korwar. "Seasoned Equity Offerings: An Empirical Investigation." *Journal of Financial Economics*, Vol. 15, No. 1/2, (January/February 1986), 91-118.

Mikkelson, Wayne and Megan Partch. "Valuation Effects of Security Offerings and the Issuance Process.", *Journal of Financial Economics*, Vol. 15, No. 1/2, (January/February 1986), 31-60.

Miller, Merton and Kevin Rock. "Dividend Policy Under Asymmetric Information.", *Journal of Finance*, Vol. 40, No. 4, (September 1985), 1031-1050.

Myers, Stewart and Nicolas Majluf. "Corporate Financing and Investment Decision When Firms Have Information Investors Do Not Have." *Journal of Financial Economics*, Vol. 13, No. 2, (July 1984), 187-221.

Narayanan, M. "Debt versus Equity and Asymmetric Information." *Journal of Financial and Quantitative Analysis*, Vol. 23, No. 1, (March 1988), 39-51.

Ross, Stephen. "The Determination of Financial Structure: The Incentive Signalling Approach." *Bell Journal of Economics*, Vol. 8, No. 1, (Spring 1977), 23-40.

Smith, Clifford. "Investment Banking and the Capital Acquisition Process." *Journal of Financial Economics*, Vol. 15, No. 1/2, (January/ February 1986), 3-29.

Williamson, Stewart. "The Moral Hazard Theory of Corporate Financial Structure : Empirical Tests." Unpublished PhD Dissertation, Sloan School of Management, M.I.T., (1981).

Table 1
The uncertainty of the assets in place
increases the drop

Simulated series showing that, all other things equal, an increase in the uncertainty of the assets in place, monotonically increases the proportional drop observed at the announcement of the new equity issue and monotonically decreases the probability of issue.

	$\overline{B}^s = 10,\ I = 50$	$\overline{B}^s = 20,\ I = 50$	$\overline{B}^s = 10,\ I = 75$
$\sigma_A/\overline{A}$	*DROP*(%) (*PROB*(%))	*DROP*(%) (*PROB*(%))	*DROP*(%) (*PROB*(%))
.10	0 (99)	0 (99)	0 (99)
.20	3 (85)	0 (99)	4 (81)
.30	7 (71)	0 (97)	13 (59)
.40	14 (62)	4 (91)	24 (45)
.50	23 (54)	10 (85)	35 (36)
.60	30 (49)	16 (79)	43 (31)
1.00	52 (39)	35 (66)	62 (28)

DROP is proportional drop in the value of the firm, V, at the equity issue announcement.
PROB is the probability of the firm deciding to issue and invest.
σ_A is the standard deviation of the assets in place.
I is the amount of new equity required to finance the new project.
$\overline{B}^S$ is the mean of the growth opportunity under symmetric information.

The assets in place, A^s , and the growth opportunity, B^s , follow a bivariate lognormal distribution under symmetric information.
The mean of the assets in place is 100.
The standard deviation of the growth opportunity under symmetric information is 1.5.
The correlation between the assets in place and the growth opportunity under symmetric information is 0.

Table 2
The total uncertainty may decrease the drop

Two simulated lognormal examples where an increase in the uncertainty of the firm implies a decrease in the proportional drop at the equity issue announcement.

	$\overline{B}^S$	$\sigma_A^S/\overline{A}^S$	$\sigma_B^S/\overline{B}^S$	ρ^S	$\sigma_V/\overline{V}$	*DROP*
Example 1	10	.20	4.4	0	.29	1%
	10	.25	1.0	0	.22	4%
Example 2	25	.30	.9	.5	.36	0%
	25	.40	.2	.5	.32	2%

For X in (A, B, V),
$\sigma_X^S/\overline{X}^S$ is the coefficient of variation (volatility) of X under symmetric information.
σ_X/X is the coefficient of variation (volatility) of X under asymmetric information.

$\sigma_V/\overline{V}$ is endogeneous.

V is the value of the firm under asymmetric information.
The assets in place, A, and the growth opportunity, B, follow a bivariate lognormal distribution under symmetric information.
The mean of the assets in place is 100.
The amount of new equity required to finance the new project is 50.
$\overline{B}^S$ is the mean of the growth opportunity under symmetric information.
ρ^S is the correlation between the values of the assets in place and the equity issue announcement.

Table 3
Equity issue announcements decrease the uncertainty of the assets in place

	$\overline{B}^S$	$\sigma_B^S/\overline{B}^S$	I	$\sigma_A/\overline{A}$	$\sigma_A/\overline{A} \mid I$
Example 1	10	1.2	50	.20	.16
Example 2	4	3	20	.50	.16
Example 3	.2	5	20	.05	.03
Example 4	.1	2	1	.20	.14
Example 5	20	.5	90	.20	.18

For X in (A, B),
σ_X^S is the standard deviation of X under symmetric information.
$\sigma_X/\overline{X} \mid I$ is the coefficient of variation (or volatility) of X conditional on the firm deciding to issue equity, under asymmetric information.
$\sigma/\overline{X} \mid I$ is endogeneous.

The assets in place, A, and the growth opportunity, B, follow a bivariate lognormal distribution under symmetric information.
The mean of the assets in place is 100.
The correlation between the values of the assets in place and the growth opportunity under symmetric information is 0.
$\overline{B}^S$ is the mean of the growth opportunity under symmetric information.
I is the amount of new equity needed to finance the new investment.

Table 4
Equity issue announcements may increase the total uncertainty

Two simulated examples where the volatility of the firm conditional on the firm deciding to issue and invest is higher than the volatility of the firm before the announcement of the issue.

	I	$\sigma_B^S/\overline{B}^S$	$\sigma_A/\overline{A}$	$\sigma_V/\overline{V}$	$\sigma_V/\overline{V} \mid I$	$\sigma_A/\overline{A} \mid I$
Example 1	90	2.0	.20	.29	.31	.15
Example 2	50	4.4	.20	.29	.31	.16

For X in (A, B, V),
$\sigma_X/\overline{X}^S$ in the coefficient of variation (volatility) of X under symmetric information.
σ_X/X is the coefficient of variation (volatility) of X under asymmetric information.
$\sigma_X/\overline{X} \mid I$ is the coefficient of variation (volatility) of X conditional on the firm deciding to issue equity, under asymmetric information.

σ_V, and $\sigma_V/\overline{V} \mid I$ are endogeneous variables, but σ_A is equivalent to σ_A^2

The assets in place, A, and the growth opportunity, B, follow a bivariate lognormal distribution under symmetric information.
The mean of the assets in place is 100.
The mean of the growth opportunity under symmetric information is 10.
The correlation between the assets in place and the growth opportunity under symmetric information is 0.
V is the value of the firm under asymmetric information.
I is the amount of new equity required to finance the new project.

Table 5
Impact of information asymmetry on the drop

OLS estimates of the coefficients from the cross-sectional regressions:

$$AREI_i = a_0 + a_1\ IAE_i + a_2\ RSIZE_i + a_3\ RMEBE_i + \epsilon_i$$

for 197 primary seasoned equity issues offered between 1980 and 1983, divided in 2 subsamples of high and low *RMEBE* (1) (2), with low (high) *RMEBE* proxying for better (worse) approximation of *IAE* by σ_ϵ^2.
(*t*-statistics are given in parentheses)

For Low *RMEBE*

Measures of *IAE*	CONSTANT	*IAE*	*RSIZE*	*RMEBE*	$\overline{R}^2$
σ_ϵ^2:	-.008	-16.350	.029	.010	6.2%
	(.58)	(−2.85)**	(.78)	(1.22)	
DNBAN	-.013	-.010	.033	.011	3%
	(.96)	(−2.17)*	(.84)	(1.92)	

For High *RMEBE*

Measures of *IAE*	CONSTANT	*IAE*	*RSIZE*	*RMEBE*	$\overline{R}^2$
σ_ϵ^2	-.032	5.780	.007	.002	≤ 0
	(−3.55)**	(0.54)	(.19)	(1.50)	
DNBAN:	-.027	-.005	.023	.002	≤ 0
	(−3.31)**	(-.62)	(.60)	(1.47)	

(1) The subsample of low (high) *RMEBE* has 99 (98) observations.

(2) The average *AREI* is -.027 (-.020) for the subsample of firms with low (high) *RMEBE*, with a *t*-statistics on the difference of the means of −2.17.

$\overline{R}^2$ is adjusted for the number of degrees of freedom.
** and * indicate that the *t*-statistic is significant at the 1- and 5-percent levels.

AREI is the market-adjusted two-day abnormal return at the equity issue annoucement.

IAE is the degree of information asymmetry.

σ_ϵ is the residual standard deviation of the daily stock returns estimated by the market model for the year preceding the equity issue announcement.

DNBAN is a dummy variable set equal to 1 when the firm has 16 or less announcements listed in the *WSJI* for the year of the equity issue announcement.

RSIZE is the number of shares to be issued based on the first announcement of the equity issue divided by the number of shares outstanding at the time of the annual earnings before the equity issue announcement.

RMEBE is the ratio of the market value of the equity divided by the book value of the equity at the last annual earnings announcement before the equity issue announcement.

THE CONSTRUCTION OF SMOOTHED FORWARD RATES

Richard Flavell and Nigel Meade
The Management School
Imperial College

1. Introduction

The concept that money due at some time in the future is worth less than money received today is fundamental to most financial analyses. Before such analyses may be performed, it is necessary to estimate a discount function δ such that

$$c_t * \delta_t = c_0 \quad \forall\, t \geq 0 \qquad (1)$$

where c_t is cash at time t and c_0 its value at time 0. Associated with the concept of a discount function is that of forward rates, ie. what rate of interest should be applied to c_t over a time period $(t'-t)$ to estimate the worth of the cash at time t'? The forward rate may be easily constructed from the discount function, namely

$$f_{t,t'} = (\delta_t/\delta_{t'}) - 1 \quad \forall\, t' \geq t \qquad (2)$$

Obviously the concepts of discounting and forward rates are not merely theoretical but of intense practical interest. So how are these functions estimated in practice? Most market practitioners use three different sources of interest rates from which they would imply the discount function, ie.

- cash market
- short interest rate futures markets
- interest rate swap market

The cash market, or interbank market whereby banks borrow and deposit money, is highly active upto a maturity of 1 year. The swaps market will typically have liquidity between 1 and 10 years maturity. The futures market depends very much upon the particular country, and can range in maturity from 4 years to 3 months if it exists at all. The reliance a practitioner will place upon each market depends crucially on his or her perception of their relative liquidities. For example, in US dollars:

- cash rates to maturity of first future
- futures out to 2-3 years
- swaps from 2-3 years out to 10 years

and the result would be termed a "blended" curve. In sterling, the <u>active</u> futures contracts would probably not extend beyond 1 year maturity; there is poor liquidity in the longer-dated futures. For simplicity, futures rates will not be included in the analysis below; as will be seen, this has no effect on the overall results and creates a clearer picture.

Typical data would be as shown in Table 1 below. Notice in particular that the swap data does not possess all annual maturities, and that the missing ones have to be estimated by some process[1].

	US dollars	Sterling
cash	ACT/360	ACT/365
6 month	5.5 %	10.1875%
12 month	5.935	10.1875
swap	ACT/360 annual	ACT/365 semiannual
2 year	6.49	9.99
3 year	6.96	10.00
4 year	7.31	10.00
5 year	7.535	10.01
7 year	7.99	10.04
10 year	8.115	10.05

Table 1: Market data for 20 September 1991

The (zero coupon) discount function is calculated from the formula:

$$\delta_t = (1 + i_t * d_t)^{-1} \quad \text{for cash rates} \qquad (3a)$$

$$\delta_t = \frac{100 - Q_t * s_t}{100 + s_t * \Delta_t} \quad \text{for } t \geq 2 \text{ years} \qquad (3b)$$

[1] For those readers unfamiliar with the swaps market, a brief explanation is provided in Appendix 1.

where: i_t is the cash rate of maturity d_t years
s_t is the swap rate of maturity d_t years
$\Delta_t = d_t - d_{t'}$
$d_{t'}$ is the maturity of the previous par swap

$$\text{and} \quad Q_t = \sum_{k \le t'} \delta_k * \Delta_k$$

Details of the derivation of this formula are given in Appendix 1.

As a result we can derive the functions shown in Figures 1 and 2. Notice that in both currencies the underlying par swap data and the discount function are both relatively smooth, but the implied one-year forward rates are not. This lack of smoothness is not acceptable in practice as interest rates should not portray such implicit discontinuities. There are two likely causes to this problem:

a. inefficiencies in the markets may cause market-quoted rates to be out of alignment;
b. it is necessary to estimate non-market-quoted rates before the forward rates may be calculated

The purpose of this paper is to examine the minimal adjustments that would be required to the underlying data in order for the forward rates to exhibit a more acceptable behaviour. The next section discusses a linear programming formulation that will be used to test various smoothing formulations.

2. The construction of a LP formulation

As a first step, it is necessary to relate the forward rates directly to the underlying par data. This may be done by combining equ's (2) and (3), to generate an highly non-linear closed form analytic relationship. Unfortunately any attempt to linearize the relationship directly would result in substantial errors. From experimentation, we find that the <u>changes</u> in the underlying data to produce a relatively smooth curve are quite small, say no more than 20 basis points maximum. This suggests that if the original forward curve is used as a starting point, then linearization around it is likely to be reasonably accurate for the purposes of this work.

Define $\sigma_k = s^N_k - s_k$ to be the (unknown) change in the kth par swap rate. There is no precise definition of what constitutes "smoothness" but conceptually define S{f} to be the smoothness of a series f such that S{f} = 0 implies perfect smoothness. Thus we need to determine the set of σ_k such that

$$\mathcal{S}\{f^N_{t,t'} \mid \sigma_k,\ k \in \text{set of par swaps}\} = 0$$

As a first order approximation we get from Taylor's theorem

$$\mathcal{S}\{f^N_{t,t'}\} = \mathcal{S}\{f_{t,t'}\} + \Sigma \frac{\partial \mathcal{S}}{\partial s_k} * \sigma_k \qquad (4)$$

The remainder of the model is:

$$\left.\begin{array}{ll} \text{Minimise} & \Sigma\,(u_k + v_k) \\ \text{subject to:} & \\ & \sigma_k - u_k + v_k = 0 \quad \forall\, k \\ & u_k,\ v_k \geq 0 \end{array}\right\} \qquad (5)$$

In the rest of the paper we explore different definitions of S{.}, both local and global, and the resulting impact on the smoothness of the forward rates.

3. Local smoothing constraints

One of the localized conditions that makes the curve of forwards rates unacceptable is the frequent and significant changes in direction. Thus constraints on the change of gradient would impose a degree of smoothness. For example, if we define the gradient as:

$$g_{t,t-1'} = (f_{t,t'} - f_{t',t-1'})/\Delta_t \qquad (6)$$

then

$$\theta^u \geq g^N_{t,t-1'} - g^N_{t+1,t'} \geq \theta^1 \qquad (7)$$

would act as constraints. Using (4) above, ie.

$$f^{N}_{t,t'} = f_{t,t'} + \Sigma \frac{\partial f}{\partial s_k} * \sigma_k$$

we can substitute into (6) and (7) to generate a set of linear constraints.

The results below were all obtained by setting $\theta^u = -\theta^l = \theta$ Figures 3a-d show the progressive impact of reducing θ on the shape of the dollar forward curve. Only the interpolated swap rates are permitted to change, ie. those rates quoted in the market-place are fixed, which implies that there would be no effect before year 5. The forward curve becomes increasing smooth, in terms of both the number of turning points and also the rate of change of gradient. The adjustments to the interpolated rates (in terms of basis points) are shown below:

θ	1.0	0.8	0.7	0.61
6 year	4.0	3.6	2.7	1.5
8 year	0.6	3.3	6.0	9.5
9 year	0	0.9	3.5	9.2

The problem becomes infeasible for values of θ below 0.61 If however we now permit some of the quoted rates also to vary, perhaps implying that there are slight misalignments in the market, the value of θ may be reduced still further. Figure 4a shows the result of adjusting the 7 year swap rate, and Fig 4b the effect of permitting 5 year rates and above to move. Adjustments to the rates (in basis points) are:

θ	0.45	0.40
5 year	-	0.5
6 year	2.9	2.8
7 year	-8.0	-8.5
8 year	1.3	1.1
9 year	0	0
10 year	-	0

These curves are considerably smoother than before, in terms of change of gradient. But they still display perceived undesirable characteristics in terms of the number of changes of gradient sign.

If the same model is applied to the sterling data, we find similar results, as shown in Figures 5a and 5b. The limiting value of θ is much smaller (the problem goes infeasible for θ≤0.05) probably because the underlying rates are very much flatter and also because there are 12 estimated rates as opposed to only 3 in dollars. The adjustments that have to be made are:

θ	0.1	0.05
1½ year	0.4	0.60
2½ year	0	0.20
3½ year	0.02	-0.04
4½ year	0	-0.2
5½ year	0	0
6 year	0.04	0.2
6½ year	0.10	0.1
7½ year	0.07	0.06
8 year	0	0.06
8½ year	0	0
9 year	0	0
9½ year	0	0
Total absolute	0.65	1.46

For $\theta = 0.05$ these changes average out at just over 0.1 of a basis point, a negligible amount for most purposes, and yet it is evident from Figure 5b that the change in the forward curve is quite significant, amounting to some 20bp in the 7 year forward!

4. Global smoothing constraints

Whilst the imposition of constraints on local properties such as the first differential considerably improved the perceived shape of the forwards curve, we can see from Figure 5b that there are probably still too many turning points for the curve to be acceptable. To attempt to overcome this, a more global definition of smoothness was used by trying to fit the forward rates to a specified smooth polynomial in time. The objective of the model was then to estimate the minimal changes required to the underlying rates so that the resulting forwards lay as close as possible to a polynomial. This is formulated as:

$$f^{N}_{t,t'} - P(t \mid \boldsymbol{\alpha}) + a_t - b_t = 0 \quad \forall\, t \qquad (8)$$
$$a_t\ ,\ b_t \geq 0$$

where $\boldsymbol{\alpha}$ is the set of unknown polynomial parameters. This model was applied in two different ways. First, the polynomial was estimated from the original forward rates using linear regression and then a LP model was constructed to estimate the minimal adjustments required to the underlying interpolated swap rates so that the resulting forwards lay on the polynomial. The second approach, as discussed in the next section, was to estimate the polynomial and the minimal adjustments simultaneously in a single model.

Fig. 6a shows the original sterling forward rates together with the regressed cubic polynomial produced by giving equal weights to all rates. A LP is then constructed to calculate the minimal changes required to the rates so that the smoothed forwards lie close to the cubic, ie.

$$\text{Minimise} \quad \Sigma_k \, (u_k + v_k) + W * \Sigma_t \, (a_t + b_t)$$

subject to:

$$- \Sigma \frac{\partial f}{\partial s_k} * \sigma_k + a_t - b_t = P(t \mid \alpha) - f_{t,t'} \quad \forall\, t$$

$$\sigma_k - u_k + v_k = 0 \quad \forall\, k$$

$$u_k, \; v_k \geq 0$$

$$a_t, \; b_t \geq 0$$

The result of permitting all rates to be adjusted is shown in Fig. 6b. Whilst this produces a good fit (as one would expect) however the movements required in the rates (particularly thosed quoted in the marketplace) are far too large for practical purposes, as may be seen in Table 1 below. On the other hand, if movements in the market-quoted rates are very heavily penalised, then the fit is still extremely good except for two forward rates; see Fig. 6c. Compromises are feasible, as we shall see in the next section.

When constructing the regression model, it is possible to weight the forward rates differently depending whether they were calculated directly from swap rates in the marketplace or used some interpolated rates. The thinking here is that if a forward rate is determined solely from market-based swap rates, then perhaps it should be given more emphasis than one based upon (estimated) interpolated rates. Some limited experimentation was done with different weighting schemes. For example, the polynomial in Fig. 6a was produced by a regression that treated all forward rates the same. Alternatively Fig. 6d was calculated by performing the same regression, but introducing a vector of weights as follows:

+ each market rate was given a weight of 1
+ each interpolated market rate was given a weight equal to the product of the weights of the two extremes
+ these weights were then allocated to the discount factors
+ each forward rate was allocated a weight equal to the product of the weights of the two appropriate discount factors

		Figure 6b	Figure 6c
1	year	7.0	0
1½	year	-1.5	3.0
2	year	-1.7	0
2½	year	-0.2	-0.2
3	year	-1.6	-0.3
3½	year	0	-0.6
4	year	0.1	0.1
4½	year	0	0
5	year	0.7	0.6
5½	year	0	0
6	year	0.2	0.1
6½	year	0	0
7	year	-0.3	-0.3
7½	year	0	0
8	year	0.1	0.1
8½	year	0	0
9	year	0.1	0.1
9½	year	0	0
10	year	0	0

Table 1: Changes in rates (in bp)

5. Simultaneous estimation of a smooth forward curve

A major drawback of the previous method is that the polynomial is estimated from the <u>old</u> forwards, which of course are to be changed! Hence it would appear to be more sensible to estimate the polynomial and rate changes simultaneously. Substituting from equs (4) and (8), we get as an overall model, again using a cubic polynomial:

$$\text{Minimise} \quad \Sigma_k \, (u_k + v_k) + W * \Sigma_t \, (a_t + b_t)$$

subject to:

$$- \Sigma \frac{\partial f}{\partial s_k} * \sigma_k + \alpha_1 + \alpha_2 * t + \alpha_3 * t^2 + \alpha_4 * t^3 + a_t - b_t = -f_{t,t'} \quad \forall \, t$$

$$\sigma_k - u_k + v_k = 0 \quad \forall \, k$$

$$u_k, \quad v_k \geq 0 \qquad a_t \, , \, b_t \geq 0$$

where W relatively weights the two minimisations; a value of 10 was used throughout.

Figure 7a shows the sterling rates without any restrictions on the rates that could be changed. The curve is smooth and acceptable. Notice however that, from Table 2, the changes required in the rates are all very small with the exception of the 1 year rate. This is obviously unacceptable at 9bp. If we do not permit market rates to change at all, we find the curve shown in 7b is smooth but not as acceptable. Possibly a compromise is more satisfactory; Figure 7c shows the result when market rates are permitted to change by a maximum of only 1bp. Such a curve is quite acceptable except possibly at the long end, which curves away rapidly. By introducing a local constraint on the gradient only at the long end, ie. restricting change in the forwards over a year to less than 1 bp, then we ended up with Figure 7d. This shows a smooth flat forward curve, whilst adjusting the rates by less that 1.1bp. The curve is not good at the very short end, but this displays the inefficiency between the cash and swap markets.

	Figure 7a	Figure 7b	Figure 7c	Figure 7d
½ year	0	0	0	1.1
1 year	9.3	0	1.0	1.1
1½ year	-1.3	1.4	0.1	0
2 year	0	0	-1.0	-1.1
2½ year	-0.2	0.7	0.1	0.1
3 year	-0.9	0	-0.2	-0.3
3½ year	0	-0.2	0.1	0
4 year	0	0	1.0	1.1
4½ year	0	-0.1	0	0
5 year	0.1	0	0.9	1.1
5½ year	0	0	0	0
6 year	0.1	0	0.1	0.1
6½ year	0	0	0	0
7 year	-1.1	0	-1.0	-0.8
7½ year	0	0.1	0	0
8 year	0.1	0.8	-0.1	0.1
8½ year	0	0.1	0	0
9 year	0.1	1.0	-0.2	0
9½ year	0	0.2	0	0
10 year	0	0	0	-1.1

Table 2: Changes in sterling rates (in bp)

6. Conclusions

This paper started from the premise that yield curves, whether of spot or forward rates, should be relatively smooth. It demonstrated that the implied forward rates from market-quoted spot rates are not smooth, but also showed that by making small changes, a smooth forward curve could be estimated. The final point to examine is the changes in the spot rates and the discount factors as a result of these small changes. Figure 7e shows that whilst the spot rates are adjusted by a maximum of 1.1bp (see Table 2), the discount factors are virtually identical!

This paper has demonstrated a mechanism by which small (ie. market acceptable) changes may be made to rates so that:

discount factors are negligibly affected
forward rates are considerably smoothed

Such an approach may be generally applied to any set of market rates.

7. Reference

1. Flavell R, Interest Rate Swaps Workbook, published by Euromoney, 1991

Appendix 1: A brief introduction to interest rate swaps [1]

A swap is an agreement freely entered into between two counterparties to exchange two streams of cash flows of perceived equal value. Equal value is invariably interpreted as being of equal present value. The agreement must obviously contain a definition of the two streams, and the two commonest definitions are:

a. regular fixed payments quoted as an interest rate on some notional principal
b. regular variable payments quoted as based on a floating interest rate again applied to some notional principal

For example, using the data in Table 1 above, a 3 year US dollar swap would involve, say, 3 annual payments of 6.96% in arrears on a notional principal. The calculation is slightly more complex in practice, ie.

notional principal * 6.96% * (actual days in year/360)

In return for these payments, the party would receive regular floating rate payments, ie. 6 semiannual payments in arrears of

notional * 6 month Libor * (actual days in last 6 months/360) principal

Alternatively it may be 12 quarterly payments based upon 3 month Libor. The important point to note is that, for what is termed a generic swap, the frequency of the floating interest rate matches the frequency of payment.

The calculations for sterling swaps are similar but not identical, for example a 3 year sterling swap would involve 6 semiannual payments of:

notional * 10.00% * (actual days in last 6 months/365)
principal

against 6 floating receipts of:

notional * 6 month Libor * (actual days in last 6 months/365)
principal

The derivation of the discount function occurs in a number of steps.

a. Estimate the complete set of par swap rates[2]. This is quite straightforward for US dollars; as these swaps have annual fixed payments, then simply estimate the 6, 8 and 9 year swap

[2]The complete set of par swaps is all swaps with the fixed side increasing in maturity at the same rate as the frequency of payment.

rates by some form of interpolation such as linear or exponential.

As sterling swaps have <u>semiannual</u> fixed payments, The process is more complicated. It is necessary to estimate not only the 6, 8 and 9 year rates but also swap rates for semiannual maturities such as 1½, 2½, ..., 9½ years. There is a particular complication in the early maturities because the 1 year swap rate is not quoted, and hence the 1½ year rate cannot be interpolated. This point will be covered later.

b. Calculate the discount function up to 1 year from the cash rates, ie. for dollars

$\delta(\frac{1}{2})$ = (1+0.055 * [20 March - 20 Sept]/360)$^{-1}$ = 0.9729
$\delta(1)$ = (1+0.05935 * [20 Sept 92 - 20 Sept]/360)$^{-1}$ = 0.9431

and for sterling

$\delta(\frac{1}{2})$ = (1+0.101875 * [20 March - 20 Sept]/365)$^{-1}$ = 0.9517
$\delta(1)$ = (1+0.101875 * [20 Sept 92 - 20 Sept]/365)$^{-1}$ = 0.9073

etc.

c. Calculate the discount function for beyond 1

year from the swap rates. First for dollars; the fixed cash flows for the 2 year swap are, on a notional principal of $100m :

year	day count	cash flow
0	0	
1	1.0167	6.49% * 1.1067 * 100m = 6.598m
2	1.0000	6.49% * 1.0000 * 100m = 6.490m

It may be shown that, if the notional principal is included in the cash flows in the following fashion, then the (present) value of the entire fixed cash flows is equal to zero[3], ie.

year	cash flow	discount function	discounted cash flow
0	-100 m	$\delta_0 = 1$	-100
1	6.598m	$\delta_1 = 0.9729$	6.4192
2	100 + 6.490m	δ_2	$106.4900*\delta_2$
		Total present value =	0

Solving this equation gives $\delta_2 = 0.8788$ Obviously this procedure may be continued recursively to generate δ_3, δ_4, etc.

If the procedure were described algebraically, then we would arrive at equ. (3) in the main text above. For example, the discounted cash

---

[3] See [1] for a full explanation.

flows above total

$$-100 + \Delta_1 * s_2 * \delta_1 + (100 + \Delta_2 * s_2) * \delta_2 = 0$$

ie.

$$\delta_2 = \frac{100 - \Delta_1 * s_2 * \delta_1}{100 + \Delta_2 * s_2}$$

For sterling, it is first necessary to estimate s_1 using the above result, ie.

$$-100 + \Delta_{\frac{1}{2}} * s_1 * \delta_{\frac{1}{2}} + (100 + \Delta_1 * s_1) * \delta_1 = 0$$

which gives: $s_1 = \dfrac{100 * (1 - \delta_1)}{\Delta_{\frac{1}{2}} * \delta_{\frac{1}{2}} + \Delta_1 * \delta_1}$

ie. $s_1 = 9.9458\%$ Then the above procedure may be repeated recursively for $\delta_{1\frac{1}{2}}$, δ_2, etc.

An Index of De-stability for Controlling Shareholders

Gianfranco Gambarelli
Dept. of Mathematics, Statistics, Informatics and Applications
University of Bergamo, Italy.

This paper presents an index of de-stability for firms' control groups, based on a game-theoretical approach.

1. Introduction

The considerable economic interests regarding the climbing to shares' control have led to the research of appropriate descriptions of such phenomena. The aim of the research is to optimize defensive strategies for the control group and hostile ones for the raiders. The benefits coming from controlling a firm can be of various types: from better management capable of raising the company's share price (thus, directly benefiting the investors) to the changing of company goals in order to optimize also the indirect interests of the "raider" (for example, the use of other associated firms' services, special salaries and benefits granted to trustworthy persons, the use of inside information, etc.). Certainly, the concrete application of such deviations depends on local legislation. However, the large amount of capital invested in the takeover transactions leads us to believe that the interests involved in the game are of considerable importance (see f.i.[15]). It is a well known fact that is not necessary to possess the absolute majority of the shares in order to control a firm. Coalitions with other shareholders may provide a relative majority which is able to defeat possible competitors, leaving most of the shares in the hands of small shareholders who are unable to form a coalition. The first problem lies in determining a reasonable expectancy of the control quota which can be achieved after having purchased a certain number of shares. Many indices of power have been proposed in order to give such an expectation (see [6]). Among these, the Shapley-Shubik index [17] seems to be the most appropiate one in shareholding context, owing to its axiomatic assumptions and the bargaining model on which it is based. For example, a strict connection between such an index and the increase in share prices on the Swedish market, in the presence of speculation phenomena, has been found in [16]. As known, the Shapley-Shubik index assigns to each of n shareholders the expected control quota

$$\Sigma\ [(s - 1)\ !\ (n - s)\ !]\ /\ n\ !$$

where the sum is extended over all the coalitions of s members for which the shareholder is "crucial", i.e. over the coalitions that would be major with his contribution and minor without it (remember that 0!=1 and n!=1x2x...xn).

It is necessary, however, to introduce some corrections to such an index should some shareholder groups have a major propensity to ally among themselves rather than with others (due to kinsmanship, friendship, common interests in other activities and so on). In such a case, G. Owen suggested modifying the Shapley-Shubik index by assigning to each coalition calculated in the summation a probability of its actual performance (see [12]). More recent works have enabled us to better quantify critical stocks, corresponding increases in power, the most competitive partner in purchase-sale for each investor and computational methods, with some applications to portfolio selection and management (see [3], [1], [10], [5 and 11], [2] and [4] respectively). Such results, on one hand, are encouraging because of the model's conformity with the real phenomenon. On the other hand, they require further investigations concerning forecasts of an increase in market price in relation to the climbing, the propensity of some shareholders to form coalitions among themselves rather than with others, as well as the indirect control that may be exercised over a co-owned company. These problems are connected with the individualization of a de-stability index for each company. The aim of this paper is to build such an index.

The most important information involved in this model is shown in section 2. Section 3 presents the problem of computing the indirect control of an investor who owns shares of firms which control other firms. A "dissatisfaction index" for shareholders is pointed out in section 4. Variations of this index, due to propensities and aversions among the investors, are studied in section 5. Finally, a global index of de-stability is introduced in section 6.

2. De-stability

For the purpose of the concrete application of the above results, it is necessary to proceed to a global quantification of a firm's de-stability. It should be done in a way which, on one hand, would allow the present majority shareholders to realize how secure their position is, and on the other hand, would enable the investors interested in takeover operations to obtain information about the most attractive companies for climbing.

The principal components necessary to identify such an index are: the quantity of shares possessed by the raider, the vicinity to the threshold of 50 per cent of the present control shareholding, the quantity still available on the market, the internal cohesion and the economic power of the control group. These components contribute to the forecast of an increase in prices that may take place during climbing. In turn, this forecast should be compared with the forecast of the control position, taking into consideration the investor's available capital. It should be noted that on a perfect market with complete information, the increase in prices is followed by a growth in power, while the presence of numerous minority shareholders makes the two functions different: in such just a difference lies the gain of the raider. It is also possible to control a company through the shares of another one which is its co-partner. Our investigation will start with this problem.

3. Indirect control

Let us consider n companies, m chief shareholders that belong to at least one of these firms and many small shareowners supposedly unable to participate in control coalitions. Let A be the n x m matrix of the co-participating companies of which the generic element a_{ik} indicates the percentage of shares from k-th company possessed by i-th one (i=1,..,n); let A* be the m x n matrix of co-participating investors, with generic element a^*_{ik}, and define $\underline{o}$ = =(o_i,...,o_n) the vector of the minor co-participants in various companies. Thus, for all the i and the k from 1 to n, we have the following percentage conditions:

$$\sum_{i=1}^{n} a_{ik} + \sum_{i=1}^{m} a^*_{ik} + o_k = 1$$

$$a_{ik} \geq 0, \quad a^*_{ik} \geq 0, \quad o_k \geq 0$$

The impossibility of self-control ($a_{ii} = 0$) can be obtained by putting to zero and normalizing.

Let S be the m x n matrix, of which the columns s_k are the Shapley-Shubik indices related to the corresponding columns of A; let us define the analogous m x n matrix S^* with reference to A^*. So, for all the i,k:

$$s_{ik} \geq 0, \qquad s^*_{ik} \geq 0$$

$$\sum_{i=1}^{n} s_{ik} + \sum_{i=1}^{m} s^*_{ik} = 1$$

It should be noted that, by hypothesis, the control power of minor co-participants is null.

Let i be a generic shareholder of k. The element s^*_{ik} represents only a part of the controlling capacity of i over k. In fact, if i possesses also the shares of h (with the corresponding control s^*_{ih}) and if the company h co-participates in k (with the corresponding control s_{hi}), then i controls k not only directly (with the power s^*_{ik}), but also indirectly (with the power s^*_{ih}).

More generally, if a chain of two or more companies exists j_i, ..., j_k each of which co-participates in the following one, the global control s_{ik} of the company j_i over j_k is difficult to evaluate. This problem has been solved in [9] (using the multilinear extensions introduced in [13]), for all cases where indirect controls are not in loop, that is when no participations of a firm into itself exist, through shares of other firms. Such a situation is in line with some European laws (for Italy see n. 281 of 4/6/1985). For a global European law, we have to wait until 1993.

4. The Dissatisfaction index

Let C be the m x n matrix of which the generic element c^*_{ik} represents the global control of the shareholder i in the company k.

Each column c_k of C explains the actual distribution of control power exercised over the k-th company by the investors, with $c_{ik} > 0$ and

$$\sum_{i=1}^{m} c_{ik} = 1 \text{ for all } i, k.$$

Let V be the m x n matrix with the generic element v_{ik}, which represents the actual percentage of power (the controlled members of the board of directors, etc.) exercised by the i-th shareholder over the k-th firm. The difference matrix D = C-V explains the shareholders' dissatisfaction with the present situation. It also gives an important indication about the de-stability: the columns d_k close to zero represent the stable situations, while those far from zero reflect dissatisfaction (on behalf of the shareholders with the positive values d_{ik}) with the present distribution of power.

An index of dissatisfaction w_k for the k-th company can, therefore, be the sum of positive elements of the column d_k. Such a sum can be computed using the absolute values d_k as follows:

$$u_k = 1/2 \sum_{j=1}^{m} (d_{jk} + \left| d_{jk} \right|)$$

Then, each element of the sum vanishes if d_{jk} is not positive.

5. Propensity and aversion

It is necessary to take into consideration the propensity of some shareholders to form coalitions among themselves for reason of kinsmanship, friendship or common interests of various kinds. Such propensity requires Owen's modification quoted above of the Shapley-Shubik index. The question is: how to individualize such propensity if it is not known on the exchange market? A possible method would consist in searching the matrix V for the groups of shareholders which often appear together in control committees. Then, we go to the matrix D and check the level of dissatisfaction that these shareholders are ready to face to remain in the coalition. Having obtained this information, the next step is to recreate the matrix S* weighting the Shapley-Shubik indices in the way suggested by Owen in [12] or, if more detailed information is available, using [7]. The new S* should, thus, generate a matrix D closer to zero, more reliable in terms of actual de-stability caused by dissatisfaction.

6. A global index of de-stability

A global index of a firm as de-stability depends on various components: the dissatisfaction index u above presented, the current allotment of the shares (among control group and raider), and the fall of the share quotation. This fall f (of the current quotation q_{cur} in respect to a reference quotation q_{old}) can be measured by the value

$$f = \max (0, (q_{old} - q_{cur})/ q_{old}).$$

This value is limited from 0 and 1; it is worth 0 for a rise or null variation, and it linearly tends towards the maximum value 1 (which corresponds to the maximum danger of de-stability), when the current quotation q_{cur} vanishes.

The allotment of shares between control group and raider contributes in three different ways. Let r and c be, for the company being considered, the percentages of shares possessed by the raider and the control group. Each one of the three above components can be expressed by an index varying from 0 (= minimal de-stability) to 1 (= maximal de-stability). The indices are:

$p = r/c$ the relationship between the raider's power and the controllers' power;

$m = 1-r-c$ the availability of shares on the market;

$v = 1-2c$ the vicinity of the absolute majority quota among the controlling shareholders.

The global index i has to group all the above indices, so that a great value of i requires the concurrence of great values of all these indicators, nothing excluded. Then, a muliplicative conjunction is opportune, weighting, if necessary, some components with suitable exponents. The proposed global index i is then:

$$i = u^{a1} . f^{a2} . p^{a3} . m^{a4} . v^{a5}$$

where $a_1,...,a_5$ are positive exogenous parameters, which can be worth 1, in a first approximation, but can be better estimated using statistical methods on historical series of past takeovers.

Notice that the resulting index i is still limited from 0 and 1, and it is worth 0 for minimal, 1 for maximal de-stability.

This global index has to be used together with other very important information: the political and economic power (and consequently the reacting capacity) of the control group. This information is qualitatively well-known by the market operators, but reliable quantification is very difficult in practice: a new open problem starts here.

7. Acknowledgments

This paper has been sponsored by Committee 10 of the National Council of Research. It is based on a previous work presented at the XII AMASES meeting in cooperation with Leopoldo Roviello, and from many discussions held with Guillermo Owen, during his visits to Bergamo and Brescia, sponsored by GNAFA of C.N.R.

REFERENCES

[1] Arcaini G., Gambarelli G. (1986) "Algorithm for Automatic Computation of the Power Variations in Share Tradings" Calcolo, 23, 1, 1986, 13-19.

[2] Gambarelli G. (1982) "Portfolio Selection and Firms' Control" Finance, 3, 1, 1982, 69-83 or VIII Annual Meeting of the European Finance Association (Sheveningen, the Netherlands, 10-12/9/1981).

[3] ------------- (1983) "Common Behaviour of Power Indices" International Journal of Game Theory, 12, 4, 237-244.

[4] ------------- (1987) "Portfolio Management for Firms' Control" Allied Sciences Association Meeting, Dallas, Texas or Euro Working Group on Financial Modelling, Paderborn, Germany.

[5] ------------- (1990) "A New Approach for Evaluating the Shapley Value" Optimization 21, 3, 445-452 or 11-th Triennal Conference on Operations Research (IFORS), Buenos Aires.

[6] ------------- (1991) "Political and Financial Applications of the Power Indices" Decision Processes in Economics (G. Ricci ed.), Springer-Verlag, pres. at XII IFORS, Athens.

[7] ------------- (1991) "Survival Game: a Dynamic Approach for

Controlling Coalition" I APORS Meeting, Seoul, Corea.

[8] Gambarelli G., Holubiec J. and Kacprzyk J. (1988) "Modeling and Optimization of International Economic Cooperation via Fuzzy Mathematical Programming and Cooperative Games" Control and Cybernetics, 17, 4, 325-335.

[9] Gambarelli G., Owen G. (1992) "Indirect Sharing Control" (forthcoming).

[10] Gambarelli G., Szegö P.G. (1982) "Discontinuous Solutions in n-Person Games" New Quantitative Techniques for Economic Analysis, ed. Academic Press, New York, 1982, 229-244.

[11] Mann I., Shapley L.S. (1962) "Value of Large Games, VI: Evaluating the Electoral College Exactly" Rand Corporation, RM 3158, Santa Monica, California.

[12] Owen G. (1977) "Value of Large Games with a Priori Unions" Lect. Notes in Econ. and Mathem. Systems, 141, 76-88.

[13] ----------- (1972) "Multilinear Extensions of Games" Management Science, 18, 64-79.

[14] ----------- (1982) Game Theory (II ed.), Academic Press, New York.

[15] Ragazzi G. (1981) "On the Relation between Owner- ship Dispersion and the Firm's Market Value" Journal of Banking & Finance, 5, 2, 261-276.

[16] Rydqvist K. (1986) "The Pricing of Shares with Different Voting Power and the Theory of Oceanic Games" School of Economics, the Economic Research Institute, Stockolm.

[17] Shapley L.S., Shubik M. (1954) "A Method for Evaluating the Distributions of Power in a Committee System" American Political Science Review, 48, 787-792.

ON IMITATION

M. L. Gota and L. Peccati
Istituto di Matematica Finanziaria dell'Università di Torino
Facoltà di Economia e Commercio
Piazza Arbarello, 8 — I-10122 Torino (Italy)

1 Introduction

The main focus of this paper is on the construction of a micro-model of stock-market speculator consistent with the assumptions on imitative behaviour used in FERRARI–LUCIANO–PECCATI (1990)[1]. Our work is partially related to GROSSMAN - STIGLITZ (1980).

Our idea is precisely to study the case of an agent, the *follower*, who partially models his decisions by observing the behaviour of another one, the *leader*.

The variable we are interested in is the amount of a transaction an agent wishes to make on a given stock-market[2].

While building this approach some relations have been naïvely assumed. The underlying philosophy assumed that a typical agent proposes transactions whose amount is a linear combination of:

- what should arise from a simple comparison between fundamental value of a stock and current market price with
- what is plainly suggested by imitation of proposals made by other (possibly) better informed agents.

Although this assumption may appear to be natural, this model cannot find an immediate foundation in the existing economic literature, mainly owing to the traditionally assumed individualistic behaviour of agents in a financial market.

[1]These hypotheses were first introduced in FERRARI–PECCATI (1989) and ulteriorly exploited in CORNAGLIA(1990) and (1991), LUCIANO (1989) and (1990), and in CENCI–CERQUETTI (1991).

[2]Our model does not consider clearing problems for our market because it is focussed only on transactions proposals. One cannot deny that these proposals do influence the market behaviour. This is precisely what is shaped in the literature concerning our approach.

The main aim of this paper is to fill this lack of foundations for the approach showing that it is not difficult to frame the imitative approach in a (slightly) modified version of paradigms currently accepted in the economic literature.

Although our main objective is to model imitation, we are forced to devote some attention to the individual behaviour of the *leader*. Once available a model for the leader behaviour, we will be able to get a model for the *follower* behaviour.

We begin with the case of only one stock that can be traded. In section 2 we shall analyse the behaviour of the leader, while in section 3 we shall deal with the more difficult problem of the follower. In sections 4 and 5 we shall explore the case of more than one stock. Section 6 collects some final remarks.

2 The behaviour of the leader

Let us consider a given stock, whose present market price is p. Let us denote by $\mathbf{X}$ its "true" value. This is a random variable (r.v.). About its distribution leader and follower have possibly different opinions. Let L be the distribution function of $\mathbf{X}$, let also m_L, v_L be, respectively, its mean and variance. To fix our ideas suppose now that $p < \mathbf{E}(\mathbf{X})$. It is obvious that buying this stock gives a (random) profit with positive expectation. The question we wish to investigate is quite natural: "How much to buy?"[3]. An easy answer can be obtained in the framework of the expected utility theory. If A denotes the amount that is bought, the expected utility principle suggests that a rational leader, with utility function u, should choose the amount A^*, which maximizes:

$$U(A) \stackrel{d}{=} \mathbf{E}\left[u[A(\mathbf{X}-p)]\right] \tag{1}$$

It is reasonable to assume that there exists an upper bound for the purchased amount A, say $A \leq A^{\#}$. We assume that $U(A^{\#})$ exists. It is easy to check that under this hypothesis $U(A)$ exists $\forall A \in [0, A^{\#}]$.

2.1 The exact optimal amount purchased

Under suitable hypotheses about u, we study immediately some useful properties of U

[3]A problem with some analogy with this one has been studied in ARROW (undated), as reported in a footnote of PRATT (1964).

Theorem 1 *If u is increasing and strictly concave then U is continuous on $[0, A^{\#}]$ and strictly concave.*

Although the concavity of U may seem obvious, its continuity properties on a *closed* interval deserve a proof. The theorem is proved in Appendix A.

The continuity and strict concavity of U on $[0, A^{\#}]$ guarantee existence and uniqueness of an optimal value A^* on the interval.

An interesting question to be investigated concerns conditions implying that the optimal purchase is positive. Intuitively this should be guaranteed when:

- the randomness of the security is mainly on the favourable side, *i.e.*, when the probability distribution of $\mathbf{X}$ has a heavy right tail and
- when the agent is not too much risk averse.

We can prove that under suitable hypotheses, which simply precise the intuition above, the optimal purchase is positive.

A possible index to appreciate the randomness of the result of an investment in a given stock with random value $\mathbf{X}$ and market price p is $\mathbf{E}(|\mathbf{X}-p|)$, the first absolute moment of $\mathbf{X}$ from the pole p. This quantity may be expressed as the sum of two addenda being the absolute values of possible losses and gains stemming from the investment:

$$\mathbf{E}(|\mathbf{X}-p|) = \int_0^p (p-x)\mathrm{d}L(x) + \int_p^{+\infty} (x-p)\mathrm{d}L(x) \qquad (2)$$

A naïve way to describe how this quantity is divided in "favourable" and "unfavourable" randomness is, of course, given by the quotient:

$$Q(p,\mathbf{X}) \stackrel{d}{=} \frac{\int_p^{+\infty}(x-p)\mathrm{d}L(x)}{\int_0^p (p-x)\mathrm{d}L(x)}$$

The higher the quotient $Q(p,\mathbf{X})$ is, the more favourable the investment appears. We could call it "favourableness quotient".

Again naïvely it is possible to describe the attitude of an expected utility maximizer through the quotient between the one sided derivatives of the utility function u at 0:

$$q_u(0) \stackrel{d}{=} \frac{u'_-(0)}{u'_+(0)}$$

The higher the quotient $q_u(0)$ is, the higher the fear of (small) losses in comparison with the appreciation of possible (small) gains. We could call it "fear quotient".

The theorem we are giving next simply states that $A^* > 0$ if the favourableness quotient of the business is grater than the fear quotient of the agent:

Theorem 2 *If:*

$$Q(p, \mathbf{X}) > q_u(0) \tag{3}$$

then $A^* > 0$.

The proof is given in Appendix B.

Remark

If u is differentiable at 0 then $q_u(0) = u'_-(0)/u'_+(0) = 1$ and the condition of the preceding theorem reduces to $m_L > p$, which is true by assumption (see the beginning of this section).

An interesting question concerns, of course, the type of dependence of A^* (when internal) on the expected value m_L of $\mathbf{X}$.

The following theorem gives us a sufficient condition on this point.

Theorem 3 *If:*

- *u is twice differentiable,*
- $\mathbf{E}\left[(\mathbf{X} - p)u'(\mathbf{X} - p)\right]$ *and,*
- $\mathbf{E}\left[(\mathbf{X} - p)u''(\mathbf{X} - p)\right]$ *exist,*

then an internal A^* increases with m_L if the average relative risk aversion of u weighted by the product of u' and probability is less than 1.

For the proof see Appendix C.

Remarks

1. Owing to frequent assumptions in the financial literature a special case deserves interest. It is the one of constant (absolute) risk-aversion utility[4]:

$$u(x) = -\exp(-\lambda x) \tag{4}$$

[4]We have explored also the case of decreasing risk-aversion utility function $u(x) \stackrel{d}{=} x^c/c$. Unluckily in this case the problem becomes trivial.

In this special case Theorem 3 provides the following monotonicity sufficient condition:

$$\frac{g'(-\lambda A^*)}{g(-\lambda A^*)} - p < \frac{1}{\lambda A^*} \tag{5}$$

that is certainly satisfied owing to the fact that the first order condition on U, defining internal values for A^*, is:

$$\frac{g'(-\lambda A^*)}{g(-\lambda A^*)} - p = 0 \tag{6}$$

It is interesting to get the same result independently of Theorem 3, because some steps of this alternative proof are new and interesting in themselves. In the Appendix D some relevant implications of these results for probability and portfolio selection are collected.

To prove that, in the case of constant absolute risk aversion, A^* increases with m_L we need the following result:

Theorem 4 *Every moment generating function (m.g.f.) is log-convex.*

Proof – It suffices to remark that e^{tx} is log-convex as a function of t for each given x. A m.g.f. is a mixture of functions e^{tx} w.r.t. x. A theorem proved in ARTIN (1931), as reported in MARSHALL–OLKIN (1979), p. 452, states that log-convexity is preserved under mixture[5]. The thesis follows.•

At this point the increasing monotonicity of A^* as a function of m_L is at hand:

Theorem 5 *If $A^* < A^\#$ then the optimal quantity under exponential utility A^* increases with m_L.*

Proof – In this case:

$$U(A) = -\mathbf{E}\left[e^{-\lambda A(\mathbf{X}-p)}\right] = -\mathbf{E}\left[e^{-\lambda A(\mathbf{Y}+m_L-p)}\right] \tag{7}$$

where $\mathbf{Y} = \mathbf{X} - m_L$. Let also g be the m.g.f. of $\mathbf{Y}$ so that we can write:

$$U(A) = -e^{\lambda A(p-m_L)} g(-\lambda A) \tag{8}$$

[5] The fact that log-convexity is preserved under addition (and hence under mixture) has been proved by different techniques in MONTRUCCHIO–PECCATI (1990).

Suppose that $A^* < A^\#$. The correspondent first order condition for U is equivalent to:

$$\frac{g'(-\lambda A^*)}{g(-\lambda A^*)} = p - m_L \tag{9}$$

The optimal value A^* increases with m_L iff the l.-h.s. of the equation decreases when A^* increases. This happens iff g'/g is increasing or iff g is log-convex. Thanks to Theorem 4 this is true and the proof is complete.•

2. Let $\gamma \stackrel{d}{=} g'/g$. Owing to the fact that g is log-convex, γ is invertible and A^* admits the following representation:

$$A^* = -\gamma^{-1}(p - m_L)/\lambda \tag{10}$$

It is interesting to note that the optimal amount increases with the expected profit $m_L - p$ and decreases when the risk aversion increases.

3. Consider the case of normal **Y**, or $\ln g(t) = v_L t^2/2$. In this case $\gamma(t) = v_L t$. The preceding representation becomes simply:

$$A^* = \frac{m_L - p}{\lambda v_L} \tag{11}$$

In this special case we see that A^* decreases when the uncertainty in the opinions, conveyed by v_L, increases.

Further, this expression of A^* is very similar to standard solutions for portfolio selection problems in the CAPM framework.

2.2 An approximation of the optimal amount

Let us consider the first order Taylor approximation for γ:

$$\gamma(t) \approx \gamma(0) + t\gamma'(0) = t\,\frac{g(0)g''(0) - g'^2(0)}{g^2(0)} \tag{12}$$

Owing to the fact that:

$$g(0) = 1;\ g'(0) = 0;\ g''(0) = v_L \tag{13}$$

we can approximate the optimal value by solving the equation:

$$p - \left[m_L + (-\lambda \hat{A})v_L\right] = 0 \tag{14}$$

that gives:

$$\hat{A} = \frac{m_L - p}{\lambda v_L} \tag{15}$$

Remark – In the *normal* case $A^* = \hat{A}$ and $\hat{A}$ is exact.

3 The behaviour of the follower

Two models seem interesting. The *first* one has correct foundations but appears to be very complex and it is not easy to deduce from it general relevant information about the behavioural links.

The *second* one is very simple and allows us to find a useful relationship between the actions of leader and follower.

A somewhat intermediate approach is presented il Appendix E. Under the hypothesis of normality of the r.v. involved the same results as in the simple model are obtained.

3.1 Complex model

Let F be the d.f. of the stock value following the own opinions of the follower and L the analogous d.f. from the viewpoint of the leader. We assume now that when the follower chooses his course of action he uses instead of F a mixture H of two d.f., F, and L, the d.f. that describes the leader opinion.

We have then:

$$H(x) = \eta F(x) + \overline{\eta} L(x) \tag{16}$$

where η can be seen as the degree of self-confidence of the follower and $\overline{\eta} \stackrel{d}{=} 1 - \eta$ is the degree of confidence he attaches to the opinion of the leader.

The quantity B^* maximizing the expected utility for the follower is the solution of the following problem:

$$\max_{B} \quad \mathbf{E}^{(H)}\{v[B(\mathbf{X} - p)]\}$$

where v is the vN-M utility function for the follower and the symbolic "exponent" attributed to the expectation operator indicates the d.f. used to compute the expected value. The function to be maximized $Q(B) = \mathbf{E}^{(H)}\{v[B(\mathbf{X} - p)]\}$ can be analogously rewritten as follows:

$$Q(B) = \eta \mathbf{E}^{(F)}\{v[B(\mathbf{X} - p)]\} + \overline{\eta} \mathbf{E}^{(L)}\{v[B(\mathbf{X} - p)]\} \tag{17}$$

Let us simplify the notation. Let $k(B) = \mathbf{E}^{(F)}\{v[B(\mathbf{X} - p)]\}$ and $h(B, m_L) = \mathbf{E}^{(L)}\{v[B(\mathbf{X} - p)]\}$. We get:

$$Q(B) = \eta k(B) + \overline{\eta} h(B, m_L) \tag{18}$$

Reasonable assumptions about k, h are concavity and increasing maximum point for h (w.r.t. B) when m_L increases. If we further require the comfort of differentiability some conclusions can be drawn.

To fix ideas, assume for a while that $p < m_F < m_L$. Both the agents think of underpricing of the stock, but the leader has a stronger opinion about this.

In the extreme case $\eta = 1$ the follower would choose B' such that $k'(B') = 0$, in the opposite extreme case ($\eta = 0$) he would choose $B'' > B'$ ($h_1'(B'', m_L) = 0$). Obviously $\forall \eta \in (0,1)$, Ψ is concave too and maximum at[6] $B^* \in (B', B'')$. The problem consists in finding conditions such that B^* increases with m_L. From the relation:

$$\eta k'(B) + \overline{\eta} h_{12}'(B, m_L) = 0 \tag{19}$$

one can try to understand how B depends on m_L. Using the implicit function theorem one finds:

$$\frac{\mathrm{d}B}{\mathrm{d}m_L} = -\frac{h_{12}''(B, m_L)}{g''(B)} \tag{20}$$

The sign of this derivative is the same of the numerator $h_{12}''(B, m_L)$.

In general nothing can be said, but some interesting conditions can be found in the usual exponential specification. In this special case we have:

$$h(B, m_L) = -\exp[-\phi B(m_L - p)]g(-\phi B) \tag{21}$$

where, as before, we denote by g the m.g.f. of the r.v. $\mathbf{Y} = \mathbf{X} - m_L$.

Tedious computations bring to the following expression:

$$h_{12}''(B, m_L) = \phi e^{-\phi B(m_L - p)} g(-\phi B)\left[1 - \phi B\left(m_L - p + \frac{g'(-\phi B)}{g(-\phi B)}\right)\right] \tag{22}$$

whose sign is the same of:

$$1 - \phi B\left[m_L - p + \frac{g'(-\phi B)}{g(-\phi B)}\right] = 1 - \phi B[m_L - p + \gamma(-\phi B)] \tag{23}$$

where, again, γ is the logarithmic derivative of g. As above we can count on the fact that g is log-convex. This implies that if $m_L - p < 0$ then $h_{12}''(B, m_L) > 0$ and there is concordance between opinion shift

[6] Remember that $Q'(B') = \eta k'(B') + \overline{\eta} h_1'(B', m_L) > 0$, and, analogously, $Q(B'') < 0$.

of the leader and behaviour of the follower. On the other hand, when $m_L - p > 0$ it is necessary that $\gamma(-\phi B)$ is "sufficiently negative". Owing to the fact that $\lim_{\phi \to +\infty} \gamma(-\phi B) = y_0$ where y_0 is the GLB of the support of $\mathbf{Y}$, for sufficiently risk-averse follower the same can be asserted.

Remark – Consider the special case of normal distributions and exponential utility of the follower. In this case the expression determining the sign of $h''_{12}(B, m_L)$ becomes

$$1 + B\phi(B\phi v_L - m_L + p) \tag{24}$$

There is concordance

- if $p \geq m_L$ or
- in the case $p < m_L$, under obvious conditions about B and the parameters.

Anyway this framework does not appear very appealing. This fact increases the interest of the next subsection where we present a much more simple model.

3.2 Naïve model

We assume that the follower has a psychology of the same type as the leader in the model of sec. 2, *i.e.*, that he is a vN-M decision maker with utility function $v(x) = -\exp(-\phi x)$. From these assumptions, as seen above, a linear decision rule stems (at least approximately in the non-normal case). We assume that the expected value of the stock in the opinion of the follower is a mixture of his personal opinion m_F and of the corresponding leader opinion m_L:

$$m = (1 - z)m_F + zm_L \tag{25}$$

where z is the "credibility" of the leader.

Would he know m_L, his decision should be (at least approximately):

$$\hat{B} = [(1 - z)m_F + zm_L - p]/(\phi v_F) \tag{26}$$

where v_F is the variance of the probability distribution he attributes to the true value of the stock.

However it is unsuitable to assume that the follower knows m_L, but a good idea is to assume that he can observe at least the decisions of the leader, namely $\hat{A} = (m_L - p)/(\lambda v_L)$. Substitute in (26) the expression for m_L that can be deduced by solving the last equation:

$$\hat{B} = (m-p)/(\phi v_F) = [(1-z)m_F + z(p+\lambda v_L \hat{A}) - p]/(\phi v_F) \quad (27)$$

Trivial computations bring to:

$$\hat{B} = \frac{(1-z)}{\phi v_F}(m_F - p) + \frac{z\lambda v_L}{\phi v_F}\hat{A} \quad (28)$$

With the positions $(1-z)/(\phi v_F) = b$ and $z\lambda v_L/(\phi v_F) = b'$ we get:

$$\hat{B} = b(m_F - p) + b'\hat{A} \quad (29)$$

that is precisely the relation assumed in FERRARI–PECCATI (1989).

Remark – To get such relation we have to assume also that the follower knows v_L (although he doesn't know m_L). This can be assumed at least in the significant case where the information asymmetry affects *only* the mean value of $\mathbf{X}$, making its volatility in some sense *public*. The value of λ too should be known to the follower. After a sufficiently long observation period this can be safely assumed.

4 Many stocks: the leader behaviour

We consider n stocks, the vector $\mathbf{p} \in \mathbf{R}^n$ collects their market prices. We continue to use the symbol $\mathbf{X}$, with the new meaning of random n-vector collecting the true values of the stocks. We shall denote by $\mathbf{m}$ the n-vector expectation of $\mathbf{X}$. We shall denote by $g(\mathbf{t})$ the m.g.f. of $\mathbf{X}$ at $\mathbf{t}$. We use the symbol $\gamma(\mathbf{t})$ to denote the gradient of the logarithm of the m.g.f. g of $\mathbf{Y} = \mathbf{X} - \mathbf{m}$. $\gamma(\mathbf{t})$ is a n-vector. The symbol $\mathbf{A}$ denotes the vector of the purchased amounts of the n stocks under the assumption that $\mathbf{m}>\mathbf{p}$. In a way quite similar to that of sec. 2 we can transform the maximization problem:

$$\max_{\mathbf{A}} \ \mathbf{E}\left[-e^{(-\lambda\langle \mathbf{A}, (\mathbf{X}-\mathbf{p})\rangle)}\right]$$

into the following:

$$\min_{\mathbf{A}} \ \exp(\lambda\langle \mathbf{A}, \mathbf{p}\rangle) g(-\lambda \mathbf{A})$$

Let $G : \mathbf{R}^n \to \mathbf{R}$ be the objective function of the minimization problem. It is easy to check that its gradient at $\mathbf{0}$ is $-\lambda(\mathbf{p}-\mathbf{m}) < \mathbf{0}$, so that the optimal policy consists in buying a positive amount of each stock.

The first order conditions that characterize an internal optimal purchase vector $\mathbf{A}^*$ can be written as:

$$\mathbf{p} - \mathbf{m} - \gamma^T(-\lambda\mathbf{A}^*) = 0 \tag{30}$$

If $\mathbf{X}$ possesses second order moments and the $(n \times n)$-matrix γ' is non-singular at $-\lambda\mathbf{A}^*$ at least locally the optimal quotae are functions of $\mathbf{m}$ owing to the implicit function theorem.

The quotae are increasing functions of the corresponding mean values if the diagonal elements of γ'^{-1} are positive. Sufficient conditions to get this result can be found in the standard theory of dominant diagonal matrices. See *e.g.* TAKAYAMA (1974), p. 380. Their financial meaning becomes quite obvious if we consider the special case of stochastically independent stocks values. Under this assumption, γ' is diagonal and all boils down to apply to each stock separately the results of sec. 2. The general case is different from this special one because of the connections among the values of the different stocks implicit in the joint probability distribution of $\mathbf{X}$. Well: the desired monotonicity holds when these connections are sufficiently weak.

It is illuminating to write down the calculations in the normal case.

Assume that $\mathbf{X} \sim N(\mathbf{m}, \mathbf{V})$, where $\mathbf{V}$ is the variances-covariances matrices of the components of $\mathbf{X}$. In this case the log of the m.g.f. of $\mathbf{X}$ is $\ln g(\mathbf{t}) = \frac{1}{2}\,\mathbf{t}^T\mathbf{V}\mathbf{t}$.

The optimal vector $\mathbf{A}^*$ is then provided by:

$$\mathbf{A}^* = (1/\lambda)\mathbf{V}^{-1}(\mathbf{m}-\mathbf{p}) \tag{31}$$

that obviously generalizes the last formula of subsection 2.1.

5 Many stocks: the follower behaviour

Owing to the complications we have described in the complex model, already in the scalar case, we confine ourselves to the naïve scheme in presence of n stocks.

The construction of the model follows strictly the route we have chosen in subsection 3.1, so that we shall rapidly sketch the main points.

We shall denote by $\mathbf{m}_L, \mathbf{m}_F$ the stocks expected values vectors in the opinion, respectively, of the leader and of the follower. Analogously we shall indicate with $\mathbf{V}_L$ and $\mathbf{V}_F$ the two variances-covariances matrices. Under exponential utility for the follower with constant risk-aversion ϕ, the optimal (approximate) purchased amounts vector $\hat{\mathbf{B}} \in \mathbf{R}^n_+$ is given by:

$$\hat{\mathbf{B}} = (\phi \mathbf{V}_F)^{-1} \left[(\mathbf{I} - \mathbf{Z})\mathbf{m}_F + \mathbf{Z} \left(\mathbf{p} + \lambda \mathbf{V}_L \hat{\mathbf{A}} \right) - \mathbf{p} \right] \tag{32}$$

where $\mathbf{I}$ is the n-th order identity matrix and $\mathbf{Z}$ a diagonal matrix collecting the "credibilities" of the leader with reference to each of the n stocks.

A simple rearrangement brings to:

$$\hat{\mathbf{B}} = \mathbf{b}(\mathbf{m}_F - \mathbf{p}) + \mathbf{b}'\hat{\mathbf{A}} \tag{33}$$

where:

$$\mathbf{b} = \frac{1}{\phi} \mathbf{V}_F^{-1}(\mathbf{I} - \mathbf{Z}) \quad \mathbf{b}' = \frac{\lambda}{\phi} \mathbf{V}_F^{-1} \mathbf{Z} \mathbf{V}_L \tag{34}$$

that clearly generalizes both our results in the scalar case and the assumptions made in the articles cited in sec. 1.

6 Conclusions and further research

In this paper we have tried to show what kind of rationality can generate the imitative behaviour assumed in FERRARI – PECCATI (1989). Looking for this explanation we have found interesting and general propositions about the behaviour of the leader who in our scheme is unaffected by imitation. Some of these propositions in the special case of constant risk aversion are proved very simply owing to the remark about the log-convexity of every m.g.f. (Theorem 4).

Acknowledgements

We are indebted with Luigi Montrucchio for some suggestions about an earlier version of this paper that have brought us to improve and generalize some results. Richard Flavell and an anonymous referee gave us precious hints to improve significantly the readability of this paper. We acknowledge a further debt towards Michael Brennan, who provided us with precious references and inspired, during a visit in Turin, the content of Appendix E.

REFERENCES

K.J. ARROW (undated): 'Liquidity Preference', Lecture VI in *Lecture Notes for Economics 285, The Economics of Uncertainty*, pp. 33-53, Stanford University.

E. ARTIN (1931): *Einführung in die Theorie der Gammafunktion*, Hamburger Mathematische Einzelschriften, Heft 2, transl. by M. BUTLER (1964): *The Gamma function*, Holt Rinehart Winston, New York.

M. CENCI – A.M. CERQUETTI (1991): 'Modelli evolutivi per un mercato azionario con valori fondamentali variabili nel tempo e asimmetria di informazioni', *Atti del Quindicesimo Convegno AMASES*, Grado (I), 26-29 sett.

A. CORNAGLIA (1991): 'A Non-linear Model of Stock-Market Behaviour and Imitation', *Quaderni dell'Istituto di Matematica Finanziaria dell'Università di Torino.*

A. CORNAGLIA (1990): 'A nonlinear model of stock market with institutionally different agents and imitation', 8th Meeting of the EURO Working Group on Financial Modelling, Gieten.

L. FERRARI – L. PECCATI (1989): 'Stock Market Behaviour and Imitation: a Simple Model', 6th Meeting of the EURO Working Group on Financial Modelling, Liège. *Quaderni dell'Istituto di Matematica Finanziaria dell'Università di Torino*, 1991.

L. FERRARI – E. LUCIANO – L. PECCATI (1990): 'Institutionally Different Agents in an Imitative Stock-Market with Asymmetric Information', 8th Meeting of the EURO Working Group on Financial Modelling, Gieten.

S.J. GROSSMAN – J.E. STIGLITZ (1980): 'On the impossibility of informationally efficient markets', *American Economic Review*, **70**, pp. 393-408.

E. LUCIANO (1989): 'Equilibrium in a Financial Market with Asymmetric Information', 6th Meeting of the EURO Working Group on Financial Modelling, Lièges. *Quaderni dell'Istituto di Matematica Finanziaria dell'Università di Torino*, 1991.

E. LUCIANO (1990): 'Market Making with Irrationalities: the Case of a Specialist Financial Market with Heterogeneous Traders', 8th Meeting of the EURO Working Group on Financial Modelling, Gieten.

A.W. MARSHALL – I. OLKIN (1979): *Inequalities: Theory of Majorization and Its Applications*, Academic Press, New York.

L. MONTRUCCHIO – L. PECCATI (1990): 'Log-convexity and Global Portfolio Immunization', in A. CAMBINI – E. CASTAGNOLI – L. MARTEIN – P. MAZZOLENI – S. SCHAIBLE: *Generalized Convexity and Fractional Programming with Economic Applications.* Lecture Notes in Economics and Mathematical Systems, n. 345, pp. 276-286.

J.W. PRATT (1964): 'Risk aversion in the small and in the large', *Econometrica*, 32, pp. 122-136, reprinted in P. DIAMOND–M. ROTHSCHILD(eds.) (1989): *Uncertainty in Economics. Readings and Exercises*, Academic Press, New York.

A. TAKAYAMA (1974): *Mathematical Economics*, 1st Ed.. The Dryden Press, Hinsdale, Ill.

Appendix A

Proof of Theorem 1 – We divide the proof in three points.

1. Concavity - Let $\theta \in (0,1)$ and $\overline{\theta} \overset{d}{=} 1-\theta$. We have:

$$U(\theta A+\overline{\theta}A') = \int_{\mathbf{R}^+} u[(\theta A+\overline{\theta}A')(x-p)]\mathrm{d}L(x) >$$
$$> \int_{\mathbf{R}^+} \theta u[A(x-p)]\mathrm{d}L(x) + \int_{\mathbf{R}^+} \overline{\theta} u[A'(x-p)]\mathrm{d}L(x) =$$
$$= \theta U(A) + \overline{\theta} U(A') \quad \forall A, A' \in [0, A^{\#}]$$

This implies that U is strictly concave on $[0, A^{\#}]$ and hence continuous on the open interval $(0, A^{\#-})$. It is easy to prove that U is continuous also at 0^+ and at $A^{\#}$.

2. Right-continuity at 0. Recall that $A \geq 0$. We have:

$$u(-Ap) \leq u[A(\mathbf{X}-p)] \leq u(0) + \mu A(\mathbf{X}-p) \tag{35}$$

where[7] $\mu \in -\partial u(0)$.

[7] We denote by $\partial u(x^*)$ the subdifferential of the function u at x^*, *i.e.*, the set of numbers $\{\mu \mid u(x) \geq u(x^*) + \mu(x-x^*)\}$.

By taking expectations:

$$u(-Ap) \leq U(A) \leq u(0) + \mu A(m_L - p) \tag{36}$$

If $A \to 0^+$ both the quantities bounding $U(A)$ converge to $u(0)$ and we get therefore $U(A) \to u(0) = U(0)$.

3. Left-continuity at $A^{\#}$. It is easy to check that:

$$0 \leq |u[A(x-p)] - u(0)| \leq \left|u[A^{\#}(x-p)] - u(0)\right| \tag{37}$$

Lebesgue's dominated convergence theorem implies then that:

$$U(A) \to U(A^{\#}) \quad \text{when } A \to A^{\#-} \tag{38}$$

The proof is complete.•

Appendix B

Proof of Theorem 2 – The thesis will follow from conditions implying the positivity of the right-hand derivative of U at 0. Its expression, $U'_+(0)$, can be given in terms of left-hand and right-hand derivatives of u at 0, resp. $u'_-(0), u'_+(0)$, which exist owing to the concavity of u.

Let $r(A,x) \stackrel{d}{=} \{u[A(x-p)] - u(0)\}/[A(x-p)]$. We can write:

$$\frac{U(A) - U(0)}{A} = \int_0^p r(A,x)(x-p)\mathrm{d}L(x) + \int_p^{+\infty} r(A,x)(x-p)\mathrm{d}L(x) \tag{39}$$

It follows from the dominated convergence theorem that the two addenda in the right-hand side converge if $A \to 0^+$. We get then:

$$U'_+(0) = u'_-(0)\int_0^p (x-p)\mathrm{d}L(x) + u'_+(0)\int_p^{+\infty}(x-p)\mathrm{d}L(x) \tag{40}$$

Trivial computations allow us to prove the thesis.•

Appendix C

Proof of Theorem 3 – Start from the first order condition:

$$\mathbf{E}\left[(m_L + \mathbf{Y} - p)u'[A^*(m_L + \mathbf{Y} - p)]\right] = 0 \tag{41}$$

that is of the type $\Phi(m_L, A^*) = 0$. Obviously $\partial\Phi/\partial A^* < 0$, so that by the implicit function derivative formula we must require $\partial\Phi/\partial m_L > 0$ or:

$$\mathbf{E}\left[u'[A^*(m_L + \mathbf{Y} - p)]\right] + \mathbf{E}\left[A^*(m_L + \mathbf{Y} - p)u''[A^*(m_L + \mathbf{Y} - p)]\right] > 0 \tag{42}$$

The last equation can be rewritten as:

$$\frac{\int_0^{+\infty} \rho[A(x-p)]u'[A(x-p)]\mathrm{d}L(x)}{\int_0^{+\infty} u'[A(x-p)]\mathrm{d}L(x)} < 1 \tag{43}$$

where $\rho(x) \stackrel{d}{=} -xu''(x)/u'(x)$ is the relative risk-aversion of u.•

Appendix D

Some interesting consequences of Theorem 4 are listed below.

1. The log of the m.g.f. is the cumulants generating function. Theorem 4 can be restated: *Every cumulants generating function is convex.*

2. The proposition holds for random vectors too. It is an immediate consequence of the proof of Artin theorem cited above. The theorem is stated with reference to one-dimensional mixtures, but the argument holds also in the n-dimensional case.

3. The implications of this simple proposition appear to be interesting. Consider the recurrent problem consisting in maximizing w.r.t. $\mathbf{a} \in \mathbf{R}^n$ the certainty equivalent under exponential utility of the random amount $\langle \mathbf{a}, \mathbf{X} \rangle$, where $\mathbf{X}$ is a random vector in $\mathbf{R}^n$ and $\langle .,. \rangle$ denotes the vector dot product. We have

$$\mathbf{E}\left[-e^{-\lambda\langle \mathbf{a}, \mathbf{X}\rangle}\right] = -g(-\lambda \mathbf{a}) \tag{44}$$

where g is the m.g.f. of the random vector $\mathbf{X}$, so that the certainty equivalent, solution of:

$$-\,e^{-\lambda c} = -g(-\lambda \mathbf{a}) \tag{45}$$

which entails:

$$c = -\,\frac{1}{\lambda}\,g(-\lambda \mathbf{a}) \tag{46}$$

The proposition implies that c is a concave function of $\mathbf{a}$ and this is obviously advantageous under a lot of aspects.

Appendix E

In this appendix, following a suggestion by M.J. Brennan, we show how it is possible to arrive to our simple relations about imitation through a different set of hypotheses.

Suppose that at a given moment the leader and the follower share the same opinion about the value of a stock and that this opinion can be summarized by a Normal distribution: $\mathbf{X} \sim N(m_x, \sigma_x^2)$. The leader receives a signal $e \sim N(m_e, \sigma_e^2)$ having known variance. His posterior opinion is $\mathbf{W} = \mathbf{X} + e$, with $\mathbf{W} \sim N(m_x + m_e, \sigma_x^2 + \sigma_e^2)$. The expected value:

$$\mathbf{E}\{u[A(\mathbf{W} - p)]\} \tag{47}$$

is internally maximized at:

$$A^* = \frac{m_x + m_e - p}{\lambda(\sigma_x^2 + \sigma_e^2)}$$

By observing A^* the follower infers about $\mathbf{W}$:

$$\mathbf{W}_f \sim N[\lambda A^*(\sigma_x^2 + \sigma_e^2) + p, \sigma_x^2 + \sigma_e^2] \tag{48}$$

The follower receives also a signal $f \sim N(m_f, \sigma_f^2)$.

His posterior opinion is then:

$$\mathbf{Z} = (1 - z)(\mathbf{X} + f) + z\mathbf{W} \tag{49}$$

where z is the leader credibility.

The expected value of $\mathbf{S}$ is:

$$m_z = (1 - z)(m_x + m_f) + z[\lambda A^*(\sigma_x^2 + \sigma_e^2) + p] \tag{50}$$

The sum $m_x + m_f$ is the mean value of $\mathbf{X} + f$, the posterior opinion of the follower, while the expression in [ ] is the posterior mean for the leader. By introducing m_z in the formula:

$$\hat{B} = \frac{m_z - p}{\phi v_z} \tag{51}$$

one obtains:

$$\hat{B} = \frac{1 - z}{\phi v_z}(m_x + m_f - p) + \frac{z\lambda(\sigma_x^2 + \sigma_e^2)}{\phi v_z} A^* \tag{52}$$

already obtained in our naïve model.

FINANCIAL FACTORS AND THE DUTCH STOCK MARKET:

SOME EMPIRICAL RESULTS *)

Winfried G. Hallerbach
Dept of Finance, Erasmus University Rotterdam
POB 1738, NL-3000 DR ROTTERDAM, The Netherlands

1. INTRODUCTION AND SUMMARY

A financial security represents a prospect to future receipts. The expected value of these receipts will be surrounded with risk. Hence, a financial security can be viewed as a claim on a specific but uncertain pattern of future cash flows, or equivalently as a particular distribution of risky future returns. Future cash flows (and thus the returns) to be received from a financial security will be influenced by economic events or 'factors'. In this view, when buying a security, an investor is actually buying an exposure to these factors. In a factor model, this exposure is measured in terms of response coefficients or sensitivities of the security's return for the factor movements. In giving economic content to factor models, one encounters the problems of how to identify and measure the factors (proxies) and how to measure the sensitivities.

*) I would like to thank Jaap Spronk for stimulating discussions and an anonymous referee for critical remarks. Of course, all remaining errors are mine.

In this paper, we investigate some aspects of factor models for the Dutch stock market and illustrate some practical applications. We do not strive to formulate 'the' factor model (which in our opinion is impossible) nor do we analyze the pricing aspects in an APT framework. Instead, we focus on factor models as risk models and present some empirical results. Some economic underpinnings for the econometric exercises are provided and discussed in Hallerbach [1990].

In section 2, we briefly discuss the concept of factor models. Section 3 is devoted to the relation between three Dutch stock market indices (general, locals & internationals) and three financial variables: the dollar/guilder exchange rate, the US long term interest rate and the low grade corporate bond yield. We discuss the construction of the factors and estimate the sensitivities for the indices over the period October 1986 to June 1991. The coefficients for all factors are significant at 5%, at least. These results are encouraging, as they clearly show a link between stock market returns and some economic key variables. We also pay attention to the stability and stationarity of the relationships with the factors. We find that sensitivities, estimated on the basis of 4-weekly return data, are not significantly different from the weekly sensitivities. Dividing the total sample period into sub-periods, we observe quite large changes in the sensitivities; however, only the changes in the dollar sensitivities are significant.

Section 4 is devoted to the estimation of factor sensitivities for individual stocks. We illustrate the effect of portfolio diversification on the significance of sensitivity estimates and present an example in which a factor-tilted index tracking portfolio is constructed. Observing the changes in portfolio weights when the portfolio sensitivities are adjusted, yields information about the marginal contribution of individual stocks to the portfolio sensitivities.

Section 5 adresses the question whether stock returns exhibit symmetrical responses to factor changes, i.e. whether an increase in a factor has approximately the same impact on stock returns as a decrease. Our results indicate that there exist asymmetric responses, especially for changes in the US interest rate. Stock returns show a severe response to interest rate increases, but only a modest (if significant at all) response to interest rate decreases. One explanation for this effect could be that stock returns show an immediate (over-) reaction to the bad news of interest rate increases, but a lagged ('prudent') reaction to the good news of interest rate decreases.

In section 6, finally, the sources of dollar sensitivity are analyzed. We find that the major part of the dollar impact on the Dutch stock market does not stem from comovements with the US stock market.

2. FACTORS AND SECURITY RETURNS

Future cash flows, to be received from a financial security, will be influenced by economic events or "factors". A common stock security e.g., represents a residual claim on part of the profits of a firm. These profits will depend on various forces or influences that the firm experiences from the dynamic economic environment in which it operates its capital assets and in which it generates its income. Hence, the return on the security reflects the factors' influences. (Stated accurately, the issue is more complex: the return on the security reflects the perception and the interpretation of these factors by the investors in the capital market.)

In this view, when buying a security, an investor is actually buying an exposure to these factors. This exposure can be measured in terms of response coefficients or sensitivities of the security's return for the factor movements. As the portfolio problem is prospective in nature, an investor is interested in *future* sensitivities. Moreover, since in a fairly efficient market the expected influences from factors on the returns are likely to be already incorporated in the market prices of the securities, he is interested in the sensitivities to the *unanticipated changes* in the factors. (This implicitely assumes that changes in expectations are driven by unforeseen changes.) The sensitivities to the factors provide a link between the general economic explanatory variables and the security returns.

In a general form, we can express the return generating process of a security as:

$$r_{i,t} = E(r_{i,t}) + \epsilon_{i,t} \tag{2.1}$$

where $r_{i,t}$ = the return of security i over the period t,

$\epsilon_{i,t}$ = zero-mean disturbance term.

E(.) is the operator for the expectation, performed at t-1. The general error process ϵ is the source of risk. A factor model now makes specific assumptions with respect to this error process. Compared with eq. (2.1), the error process is decomposed and related to changes in pervasive factors:

$$r_{i,t} = E(r_{i,t}) + b_{i1}U(f_{1,t}) + \ldots + b_{ik}U(f_{k,t}) + \xi_{i,t} \tag{2.2}$$

where b_{ij} denotes the sensitivity of security i for the unexpected movements $U(f_j)$ of the factors f_j. The idiosyncratic return component $\xi_{i,t}$ is often assumed to be un(cor-)related over the securities. The variability of this idiosyncratic return component is the source of idiosyncratic risk. In large, well diversified portfolios, the latter return components will compensate each other to a certain extent, so that this type of risk can be reduced. The unanticipated movements of the factors are also responsible for a discrepancy between the expected return and the realized return. These factors are the sources of factor risk. As the factor sensitivity coefficients determine the degree in which a factor movement is passed on to the security's return, these sensitivities are measures of risk. In a portfolio context, we expect the factor risk to constitute the major part of the total risk. However, the residual portfolio return component may be too large to be neglected.

By decomposition of the general error process in eq. (2.2), investment risk has become a multi-dimensional concept, in which the sensitivities are attributes of the securities. If, in addition, we would be able to relate the thusfar anonymous general factors to identifiable economic variables, then the transparancy of the risk concept is also enlarged. However, in giving economic content to factor models, one encounters the problems of how to measure the factors (proxies) and how to measure the sensitivities. Chen, Roll & Ross [1986] suggested four variables that are candidate sources of systematic risk: *(1)* unexpected changes in the growth rate of industrial production; *(2)* unexpected changes in the inflation rate; *(3)* unanticipated changes in the long term real interest rate or shape of the term structure, measured as the difference between the long term government bond return and the Treasury Bill rate; *(4)* unanticipated changes in risk premia, measured by the difference between low grade corporate bonds and long term government bonds. As their research is intended to be a test of Ross' [1976] Arbitrage Pricing Theory, they do not provide much information on the estimation results of the underlying factor model. Many other researchers have gratefully used the factor definitions, proposed by Chen, Roll & Ross [1986], as a starting point for their own analyses (for example Chan, Chen & Hsieh [1985] and Berry, Burmeister & McElroy [1988]).

In contrast with this statistical approach, Salomon Brothers have developed a Fundamental Factor Model (Estep et al. [1984]). It is argued that the means through which the factors affect the value of a firm (and hence, the return on its stock) is their influence on the growth rate of earnings. Five relevant factors are proposed. They include unanticipated changes in successively *(1)* the inflation rate; *(2)* the growth rate of the real Gross National Product; *(3)* the real interest rate; *(4)* the rate of change in real oil prices; and *(5)* the growth rate of real defense spendings. The sensitivities of stock returns for these factors are determined via revenue-cost models of the firms' profits. Apparently, Salomon Brothers has left this fundamental approach and replaced it with the statistical (regression) approach (Sorensen, Mezrich & Thum [1989]). In this model, seven factors appear: *(1)* economic growth (proxied by industrial production); *(2)* business cycle (return difference on long term investment grade corporate bonds and long term US Treasuries); *(3)* long term interest rate; *(4)* short term interest rate; *(5)* inflation shock; *(6)* US dollar exchange rate against a trade-weighted basket of 15 currencies; and *(7)* the S&P-Index, after accounting for the other six factors.

In applications of factor models, the prospective value of the model (stationarity) is important. By tuning the sensitivity coefficients, a specific risk profile of the investment portfolio can be chosen. For a discussion of several strategies that can be followed, we refer to Roll & Ross [1984], Burmeister, Berry & McElroy [1988] and

Hallerbach & Spronk [1991]. In the next sections, we'll touch upon some of these issues; however, many lines for future research are open yet.

3. STOCK MARKET INDICES AND FINANCIAL FACTORS

After discussing the data in section 3.1, we provide in section 3.2 estimation results of a limited factor model for Dutch stock market indices. In section 3.3 we investigate the stationarity and stability of the model.

3.1 The data

Unless stated otherwise, we use weekly price data from 29 October 1986 to 19 June 1991. We deleted the 4 observations for the month October 1987, which leaves a total of 238 return observations.

We use three stock market indices: the CBS-General Index (*CBS-G*) and the indices CBS-Locals (*CBS-L*) and CBS-Internationals (*CBS-I*). The general index is capitalization weighted and includes the total returns (with dividends reinvested) of all common stocks, listed on the Amsterdam Stock Exchange (real estate funds and investment funds excluded). The Locals and Internationals are sub-indices and comprise local and international firms, respectively. For these indices, we computed logarithmic returns.

For our factor model, we use only three factors. The first factor is the dollar/guilder ($/*f*) exchange rate, which is of interest because of international trade and its price effects. From October 1986, the dollar slides down from about *f*2,30 to below *f*1,80 at the 1987 crash. At mid

1989, the dollar almost reaches ƒ2,30 again, then falls to below ƒ1,65 at the beginning of 1991. As of the end of the Gulf War, the dollar recovers quickly and ends just over ƒ2,- in June 1991. In the factor model, we use the weekly changes in the logarithm of the $/ƒ-rate (*d$*).

The second factor is the yield to maturity on US Treasury Bonds with a remaining maturity of 10 years, which serves as a proxy for the US long term interest rate. The rate starts at about 7% in October 1986 and rises sharply to over 9.5% at the time of the 1987 crash. The rate roughly stays within the range of 8-9% and ends just over 8% in June 1991. We measure this factor *dUSL* by the change in the log of one plus the yield.

The last factor is the yield to maturity on low grade US corporate bonds. The low grade bond yield provides information about the premium investors demand for business risk or default risk. Following Chen, Roll & Ross [1986], we first tried the difference between the low grade bond yield and the government bond yield as a proxy for this default risk premium. To our surprise, the index returns showed no significant relations with this variable. For this reason, we chose the total of the low grade yield as a factor. Up to the middle of 1989, the low grade bond yield moved parallel to the US long term rate, at about 4% higher level. Until the middle of 1990 the difference between the two yields gradually increases. At the beginning of the Gulf War, the low grade bond yield rises sharply to over 19%. After the US invasion of Kuwait, the rate rapidly decreases to 15% in June 1991. The low grade yield is transformed the same way as the US long interest rate and denoted as *dDef*.

The high-yield bond data come from Bloomberg and are only available for Fridays; all other data are from Datastream.

Because of the relatively short sample period, we

focussed on financial rather than economic factors (like business cycle, economic growth). Because of the Dutch open economy, we've selected factors of an international nature. As we wanted to include the $/ƒ-rate in any case and as the low grade bond yields only were available for the US, we thought it consistent to choose the US interest rate instead of a Dutch rate. Detailed estimation results for Dutch as well as US interest rates are reported in Von Eije, Hallerbach & Versteeg [1991].

The time series of the three factors, transformed to logarithmic changes, can be considered as white noise and are therefore directly used in the factor model[1]. As the three factors are related to financial (exchange and bond) markets that can be considered as efficient, we could have expected this. As we use changes in logs for the indices as well as for the factors, we can interprete the sensitivities as elasticities of stock prices with respect to the factors.

As the low grade bond yields are only available on Fridays, it would be straightforward to compute weekly returns from Friday to Friday. However, it would not be wise to use the weeks' closing prices. Table 3.1 reports results from regressions of the CBS-General Index return on the changes in the dollar and the US long rate, based on Wednesday and Friday data, respectively. The sensitivities for dollar changes are virtually the same, but the sensitivities for interest rate changes show a remarkable difference. As the results from the Wednesday data are in line with

---

1) As the models did not exhibit first order residual autocorrelation, significant at at least 5%, we do not report Durbin-Watson statistics. As we are interested in factor models as risk models, we neither report the intercepts of the regression equations. Also, we only report unadjusted R^2, indicating the proportion explained variance. Finally, for the sake of completeness and fashion, we admit that we looked for traces of autoregressive conditional heteroskedasticity (ARCH). We couldn't find any.

estimations based on monthly returns, we decided to use Wednesday data for the index returns and the dollar and the US long interest rate. This implies a compromise for the low grade bond yield: we measure it on the Fridays that immediately follow the Wednesdays (2 day lead).

Table 3.1: Estimation results from regression of CBS-G on d$ and dUSL, 10/86 - 6/91, 10/87 omitted (t-statistics in parentheses).

	Friday data		Wednesday data	
d$	.44	(5.66)	.49	(6.93)
dUSL	-.75	(-.86)	-4.35	(-5.26)
R^2	.13		.24	

The changes in the dollar (d$) are uncorrelated with changes in the US interest rate (dUSL). The changes in the low grade bond yield dDef, however, show a correlation of .16 with dUSL (significant at 5%). This correlation can be traced to the first half of the sample period, where both factors move in lockstep. In fact, from 10/29/86 to 2/1/89 (115 observations) the correlation is .40, whereas in the rest of the period (2/8/89 - 6/12/91, 123 observations) the correlation is zero. To obtain orthogonal factors, we regressed dDef on dUSL in the first subperiod. The residual from that regression is taken as the corrected change in the low grade bond yield, dDef.

3.2 The sensitivities of the indices

Table 3.2 reports the estimated sensitivities of the indices for the 3 constructed factors. All coefficients are significant at 5%, at least. These results are encouraging, as they clearly show a link between stock market returns and some financial key variables.

Table 3.2: Estimation results from regression of CBS-G, -L and -I on d$, dUSL and dDef, 10/86 - 6/91, 10/87 omitted (|t|-statistics in parentheses).

	CBS-G		CBS-L		CBS-I	
d$	.47	(6.75)	.29	(3.43)	.60	(8.10)
dUSL	-4.36	(5.36)	-5.39	(5.49)	-3.46	(3.94)
dDef	-2.35	(3.17)	-3.17	(3.53)	-1.74	(2.17)
R^2	.27		.19		.28	

The elasticities with respect to the dollar are, as could be expected, all positive. As a change in the exchange rate implies a change in the terms of trade, the competitive position of firms is affected. It is then important how much dollar denominated income is generated and what part of the dollar changes can be passed through. The signs for the elasticities with respect to the interest rate and the low grade bond yield are negative and also according to intuition. A higher interest rate raises the opportunity cost for holding stocks (i.e. raises the discount rate for the future dividend stream) and consequently lowers stock prices. (As increasing interest rates also are a sign of increased economic activity, we have a second effect of interest rate changes on the projected earnings, but in general we do not expect this effect to compensate the discounting effect.) Finally, a higher business risk premium will increase the required return on stocks and lower their price.

From the table, we note a considerable difference between dollar sensitivities of the Locals (CBS-L) and Internationals (CBS-I). A highly significant dollar sensitivity for international firms cannot surprise us. That local firms also show a significant dollar sensitivity can have two reasons. First, the stock market as a whole reacts to some degree to dollar changes. As the Locals in turn 'go with the market', they will show some sensitivity to dollar changes. Second, that firms are labelled 'local' by some criterion, does not exclude the fact that many commodities and resources, directly or indirectly, are denominated in dollars. To the extent that these resources are inputs for local firms, these firms will import a dollar sensitivity. In section 6, we will further analyze the dollar sensitivity.

Considering the sensitivities to changes in the US long rate and the low grade bond yield, we see the opposite, although not so clear: Locals seem more sensitive than Internationals. We performed a test whether the sensitivities of CBS-L were significantly different from the sensitivities of CBS-I. It followed that the differences in dollar and interest rate sensitivities are significant at a 5% level (t=4.18 and 2.16 respectively), whereas the difference in sensitivities for dDef is not (t=1.75).

We can also reformulate the question and analyze the differences in sensitivity of the strict local and strict international part of the general stock market index. To obtain the returns of the strict local part of the market, we regres the returns on CBS-G on CBS-I; the residual is the part of the general market index return that cannot be explained by the return on the Internationals. Likewise, we ran a regression of CBS-G on CBS-L; this time, the residual represents the strict international return component of the general market index.

Table 3.3 reports the estimation results of the intermediate regressions (panel A) as well as of the factor models (panel B). By running the intermediate regressions, as indicated in panel A, we decompose the general stock market index in three parts: the strict local part (e_{Loc}), the strict international part (e_{Int}) and the part that comoves with returns of locals as well as internationals. From panel B of the table, we see that the strict local

Table 3.3: Estimation results for strict local and strict international stock market returns; 10/86 - 6/91, 10/87 omitted (t-statistics in parentheses).

A:

$$\text{CBS-G} = .00004 + \underset{(36.53)}{.852}\ \text{CBS-I} + e_{Loc} \qquad R^2 = .85$$

$$\text{CBS-G} = .00135 + \underset{(26.68)}{.755}\ \text{CBS-L} + e_{Int} \qquad R^2 = .75$$

B:

	e_{Loc}		e_{Int}	
d$	-.05	(-1.62)	*.25*	*(6.77)*
dUSL	*-1.41*	*(-4.00)*	-.29	(-.66)
dDef	*-.87*	*(-2.71)*	.04	(.10)
R^2	.10		.17	

development of the stock market (e_{Loc}) is significantly related to changes in the interest rate and the low grade bond yield. The strict international development of the stock market is only significantly related to changes in the dollar. To our surprise, it shows no significant link with the US interest rate nor the low grade bond yield.

3.3 Stability and stationarity

For the CBS-General Index, we finally investigated the stability and stationarity of the factor models. We have stability when the model is invariant under changes in the length of the observation interval, given the length of the sample period. For this, we recomputed the returns of CBS-G and the factors over 4-week periods and reran the regressions on the factors. Table 3.4 reports the estimation results.

As we would expect for non-autocorrelated series, the standard deviation of the 4-week returns is roughly $\sqrt{4}$ times the weekly standard deviation. Apart from the interest rate sensitivity, we observe that the sensitivities have changed

Table 3.4: Standard deviations and regression coefficients of CBS-G using weekly and 4-weekly returns, 10/86 - 6/91, 10/87 omitted (t-statistics in parentheses).

	weekly data (238 obs)			4-weekly data (59 obs)		
	σ	coefft		σ	coefft	
CBS-G	.0194			.0377		
d$	.0157	.47	(6.75)	.0315	.37	(2.97)
dUSL	.0013	-4.36	(-5.36)	.0029	-4.33	(-3.17)
dDef	.0015	-2.35	(-3.17)	.0038	-3.66	(-3.45)
R^2		.27			.42	

and that the R^2 has increased. Within the 3-factor model, however, the 4-weekly sensitivities are not significantly different from the weekly sensitivities at a level of less than 10%.

We have stationarity when the model is invariant under a change in the sample period. As a rough test for stationarity, we divided the total sample period into 2 sub-periods. Table 3.5 shows that the sensitivity for low grade bond yield changes is virtually the same in both periods; the sensitivities for changes in the dollar and the interest rate, however, are quite different. When we test the coefficients in the first and second sub-period against the sensitivities in the overall period, we find that only the dollar sensitivity is significantly different at a 5% level (with t=2.54 and t=-2.16 in the first resp. second sub-

Table 3.5: Regression coefficients of CBS-G over the two sub-periods, 10/87 omitted (t-stats in parentheses).

	10/29/86-2/1/89 (115 obs)		2/8/89-6/12/91 (123 obs)	
d$	.77	(6.51)	.29	(3.63)
dUSL	-2.94	(-2.34)	-4.93	(-4.73)
dDef	-2.62	(-1.15)	-2.55	(-3.57)
R^2	.34		.28	

period). Testing the coefficients in the two sub-periods against each other, we also find that only the dollar sensitivities are significantly different (with t=4.06).

Table 3.6 presents more detailed information about the development of the sensitivities over time. We ran regressions over 52-week windows that are shifted 4 weeks at a time. The table presents a summary of these estimation results; the non-overlapping windows starting at the beginning of the sample period are in italics. The F-values indicate that the regressions (as a whole) are significant at a level of at least 1%, except for windows 34 and 35 (3%), 36 (5%), 28 (6%), 29 - 32 (8%) and 33 (9%). The dollar is significant in practically any year. The results for the US interest rate show a mixed pattern: we see a significant (at 5%) effect starting at the end of 1989. As could be expected from the discussion of the course of the low grade

Table 3.6: Regression coefficients of CBS-G over 52-week windows, 10/87 omitted (|t|-statistics & F-value in parentheses).

wind./week	d$	dUSL	dDef	R^2 F
1/ 1- 52	*.88 (5.26)*	*-2.65 (1.62)*	*-3.48 (1.30)*	*.45 (12.88)*
4/ 13- 64	1.17 (5.46)	- .76 (.40)	-2.53 (.76)	.42 (11.61)
7/ 25- 76	1.26 (5.50)	- .22 (.11)	-1.97 (.61)	.41 (11.32)
10/ 37- 88	1.11 (5.19)	-2.97 (1.35)	-2.04 (.52)	.40 (10.88)
13/ 49-100	.90 (4.13)	-3.56 (1.46)	-1.69 (.34)	.29 (6.57)
14/ 53-104	*.81 (3.90)*	*-3.68 (1.62)*	*-2.51 (.53)*	*.29 (6.54)*
17/ 65-116	.54 (3.70)	-5.57 (3.32)	2.93 (.71)	.39 (10.44)
20/ 77-128	.43 (3.49)	-5.75 (4.20)	-3.12 (1.14)	.39 (10.41)
23/ 89-140	.31 (2.85)	-2.94 (2.32)	-3.30 (1.27)	.24 (5.16)
24/ 93-144	.30 (2.93)	-2.52 (2.07)	-2.84 (1.14)	.22 (4.64)
27/105-156	*.40 (3.48)*	*-1.55 (1.06)*	*- .68 (.36)*	*.23 (4.80)*
30/117-168	.32 (2.37)	-1.42 (.81)	.34 (.18)	.13 (2.37)
33/129-180	.29 (2.11)	-1.09 (.64)	1.57 (.82)	.12 (2.28)
34/133-184	.38 (2.68)	-1.94 (1.03)	1.29 (.70)	.16 (3.16)
37/145-196	.37 (2.04)	-5.91 (3.38)	-1.24 (.81)	.27 (5.77)
40/157-208	*.28 (1.48)*	*-5.85 (3.76)*	*-3.61 (3.11)*	*.39 (10.17)*
43/169-220	.31 (2.11)	-6.61 (4.62)	-3.07 (3.51)	.49 (15.35)
44/173-224	.27 (1.77)	-6.10 (3.90)	-3.26 (3.93)	.47 (14.34)
47/185-236	.37 (3.22)	-8.06 (5.05)	-3.27 (4.31)	.55 (19.37)

bond yield in section 3.1 and the results presented in Table 3.5, this variable is only significant at the end of the sample period (on a yearly basis from about mid-1989).

The R^2's start at a high level of 45%, gradually decreasing to just 12% in 1989 and then rising again to well over 45%. From Table 3.6, we infer that the explanatory power of the model in the first part of the sample period depends solely on the effect of dollar changes. In that period we observe an increasing $/ƒ-rate (we could however find no relation with the volatility of the dollar changes). The high explanatory power of the model in the last part of the sample period seems to depend on the effect of changes in the US interest rate and, above all, in the low grade bond yield. In this part of the sample period, the last variable shows a rapid increase, followed by a rapid decrease; this is accompanied by a relatively high volatility of the changes in the low grade bond yield. As noted in section 3.1 the low grade bond yield moves parallel with the US interest rate in the first part of the sample period, it therefore adds no explanatory power to the effect of the US rate.

4. ESTIMATING FACTOR SENSITIVITIES OF INDIVIDUAL STOCKS

When estimating factor sensitivities for individual stocks, we must consider the fact that these securities will be combined into a portfolio. This implies that to some extent a beneficial diversification effect will work (Samuelson [1967]). As a result, when applying optimization procedures to the portfolio composition process (for example, as illustrated by Hallerbach & Spronk [1986, 1991]), we are only interested in factor sensitivities in a portfolio context.

We want to illustrate the effects of diversification by means of some examples. For this, we used a data set consisting of 58 monthly return observations from August 1985 to July 1990 (dividend yield not included, October and November 1987 deleted). We use two factors: the changes in (the log of) the \$/ƒ-rate, d\$, and the changes in (the log of one plus) the yield of Dutch long term government bonds, dNLL.

We first look at the estimation of the factor sensitivities for one stock in isolation. Table 4.1 presents the factor elasticities for the Dutch firm Heineken (beverages). Neither the dollar nor the interest rate show a significant (5%) effect on its return. It would be uncorrect however, to conclude that its sensitivities to these factors would be zero. The residual variance of the regression is only so high, that insignificant coefficients result. If we are able to attribute part of the residual variance to some

Table 4.1: Regression results for Heineken, factors only and extended factor model, 8/85 - 7/90 (10-11/87 deleted) (t-statistics in parentheses).

	factors only		factors plus residual market factor	
d\$	.36	(1.34)	.36	(1.79)
dNLL	-8.77	(-1.77)	-8.77	(-2.36)
UCBS-G			1.41	(6.62)
R^2	.07		.49	

sources, then this significance will change. For this reason, we estimate the factor model for the CBS-G Index and consider the residual (unexplained) index return, UCBS-G, as a residual factor (in tests of the APT, this residual factor is proposed by McElroy & Burmeister [1988]). UCBS-G accounts for a mixture of omitted factors, as well as for market movements that are not related to 'fundamental' economic factors. By construction, the residual market factor is uncorrelated with the factors. This implies that the magnitude of a stock's factor sensitivities will not change when this factor is incorporated in the estimation. As Table 4.1 shows, however, the significance of the estimates will improve, yielding a more clear picture of the relevance of Heineken's sensitivities in a portfolio context.

When combining individual stocks into a portfolio, a comparable effect takes place. Because of diversification, the variance of the factor model's residuals will decrease. As this implies that the proportion of the variance that can be attributed to the factors will increase, the significance of the sensitivities for these factors will also increase. When combining stocks like Heineken into a portfolio, the resulting diversification process will have the same effect as the incorporation of the residual market factor in individual regressions.

As a second example of factor sensitivities in a portfolio context, we consider the case of index tracking. We assume that the CBS Index serves the role of an investor's reference portfolio. Using the 'full covariance' method for index tracking, as presented by Haugen [1990, pp.173ff] and Haugen & Baker [1990], we used 15 actively traded and large capitalization stocks to construct a tracking portfolio for CBS-G. The composition of the tracking portfolio is presented in Table 4.2 (note the large capitalization of Royal Dutch). The factor sensitivities of the stocks are presented on the right. The sensitivities of the index and the tracking portfolio are presented in the bottom of the table. The R^2 of their models clearly shows the diversification effect. Also the correlation (rho) between the index and the tracker is shown.

Next, we constructed a 'dollar tilted' index tracking portfolio, i.e. a portfolio that mimicks the CBS-G Index,

Table 4.2: The composition of the index tracking portfolio and the tilted tracking portfolio, together with the sensitivities of the individual stocks, 8/85 - 7/90 (10-11/87 deleted).

	portfolio composition			factor model		
	CBS-tracker	CBS$-tracker	revision portf.	dollar	interest rate	R^2
AEGN	6.78	5.33	-1.44	.59	-7.9	.13
AH	2.83	7.59	4.76	1.04	-5.6	.20
AKZO	6.50	7.30	0.80	.81	-6.0	.15
AMEV	6.18	3.50	-2.69	.36	-4.6	.03
GIST	3.99	3.66	-0.33	.84	-9.5	.12
HBG	2.30	4.18	1.88	1.01	-14.0	.25
HEIN	7.40	2.76	-4.64	.36	-8.8	.07
HOOG	0.38	1.29	0.90	1.22	-6.8	.11
INT-M	0.86	0	-0.86	.88	-10.3	.15
KLM	4.76	5.44	0.68	1.14	-16.2	.25
KNP	1.30	0.81	-0.49	.79	-15.1	.12
NIJV	2.80	3.32	0.53	.87	-9.9	.13
RD	42.52	42.12	-0.41	.63	-5.9	.20
UNIL	8.57	9.33	0.75	.80	-9.9	.23
VNU	2.83	3.37	0.54	.63	-5.1	.09
total:	100 %	100 %	0 %			
CBS				.60	-6.4	.31
CBS -tracking portfolio (rho = .985)				.68	-7.6	.34
CBS$-tracking portfolio (rho = .920)				.76	-8.6	.28

but has a higher sensitivity for dollar changes. The composition of this portfolio, CBS$, is also shown. Whereas the tracker already has a higher dollar sensitivity, the dollar tilted tracker shows an even higher sensitivity. As we expected, the increased sensitivity goes together with an increased tracking error. From the bottom of Table 4.2, we also note the unpleasant fact that the interest rate sensitivity has increased with the dollar sensitivity (we did not correct for this effect here).

Now, when we look at the changes in portfolio holdings that are necessary to convert the tracking portfolio into the tilted tracker (i.e. the revision portfolio), we obtain information about the marginal contribution of individual stocks to the tracking portfolio's sensitivity to dollar changes. This gives us an impression of the individual stocks' sensitivities in that particular portfolio context. We expect that the portfolio weights of stocks that possess a more (less) than average dollar sensitivity are increased (decreased). Indeed, the revision in portfolio weights for Ahold (AH) and Heineken (HEI) are nice examples of both cases. As, in this data set, there exists a slight tendency for high dollar sensitivities to go together with high interest rate sensitivities, we get the undesired effect of an increased interest rate sensitivity for the dollar tilted tracker. A correction for this effect would further increase the tracking error. However, by using the full covariance method, we explicitly take account of the diversification effect in constructing the portfolios.

5. THE SYMMETRY OF FACTOR RESPONSES

We return to our data set of weekly returns, as described in section 3.1. We ask ourselves whether stock returns exhibit symmetrical responses to factor changes, i.e. whether an increase in a factor has approximately the same impact on stock returns as a decrease. We therefore decomposed the time series of each factor change dF into two parts:

$$dF^{+} = \max [\ E(dF),\ dF\ ]$$
$$dF^{-} = \min [\ E(dF),\ dF\ ]$$

where E(.) stands for the average of the factor over the

total sample period. Next, we regressed the return on CBS-G on the 'positive' and 'negative' parts[2)] of the factor changes. The results are shown in Table 5.1. With the low grade bond yield as a possible exception, the positive and negative parts of the time series are quite evenly distributed over the sample period. Also, the standard deviations of the positive and negative factor components, are almost identical.

The sensitivities of CBS-G for the decomposed factors, however, indicate that there exist asymmetric responses to the factor components. The difference between the responses to the components of the dollar changes is insignificant and the response asymmetry with respect to the low grade bond yield is only significant at a level of 10%. The difference between the sensitivities for interest rate increases and decreases, however, is significant at a level of .1% (t=-3.58). This result implies that stock returns show a severe response to interest rate increases, but only a modest (if significant at all) response to interest rate

Table 5.1: Standard deviations and regression coefficients of CBS-G on decomposed factors, 238 weekly returns, 10/86-6/91, 10/87 omitted (t-stats in parentheses).

	$\sigma \cdot 100$	coefft		average	aggregated
$d\$^+$	.929	.39	(2.94)	.47	.47
$d\$^-$	.913	.55	(4.13)		
$dUSL^+$	.081	-6.81	(-4.64)	-4.19	-4.36
$dUSL^-$	.076	-1.56	(-1.00)		
$dDef^+$	.103	-3.21	(-2.99)	-2.21	-2.35
$dDef^-$	.083	-1.20	(-.88)		
R^2		.29			.27

2) As the average of the factor changes over the sample period is not equal to zero, we define the 'positive' and 'negative' part of a factor change with respect to its average. We repeated the analysis for the 'real' positive and negative changes (i.e. E(dF)=0), but this yielded virtual identical results.

decreases. We've checked this result for other data sets which cover different interest rate regimes (monthly data, over the period 1978-1990 and several sub-periods), but found the same effect (although sometimes to a lesser extent). This puzzles us. One hypothesis is that the effect is spurious. Another hypothesis is that stock returns show an immediate (over-) reaction to the bad news of interest rate increases, but a lagged (or 'prudent') reaction to the good news of interest rate decreases. So, investors might be overly sensitive to perceived risks and react overly dramatic to negative news. This asymmetric effect is consistent with overreactions, explored by De Bondt & Thaler [1985, p.799; 1987, p.575] in the context of the performance of winner and loser portfolios: the price correction for losers is much larger than for winners. This issue calls for more detailed research.

Finally, as a check, the table also reports the average of the sensitivities for the factor components, as well as the sensitivities for the total factor changes (duplicated from Table 3.2); for each factor, the two numbers are quite close.

6. DOLLAR SENSITIVITY REVISITED

In section 3.2, we touched upon the sources of dollar sensitivity. It is often argued, that the sensitivity of the Dutch stock market (and especially of the Locals) to changes in the $/ƒ-rate is induced by the comovement with the US stock markets. To shed some light on this issue, we followed a simple procedure. Using the S&P-500 Index as a representative for the US stock markets, we regressed first the CBS-G Index on the S&P Index (both indices without dividend yield). The residual of this regression is the strict non-US part of the Dutch index. We then regressed this residual variable on the changes in the dollar. A significant (slope) coefficient for this regression indicates that at least some part of the dollar impact on the Dutch stock market does not stem from comovements with the US stock market. For completeness, we also followed the complementary procedure: correcting CBS-G for dollar changes and then looking for a relation with S&P. Table 6.1 reports the results for the CBS-G, as well as for the sub-indices Locals and Internationals.

Table 6.1: Regression results for S&P-corrected indices on dollar changes and for dollar-corrected indices on S&P, 238 weekly returns, 10/86 - 6/91, 10/87 omitted (t-statistics in parentheses).

	d$		R^2	S&P		R^2
CBS-G | S&P	.39	(5.76)	.12			
CBS-G | $				.42	(9.35)	.27
CBS-L | S&P	.24	(3.12)	.04			
CBS-L | $				.41	(7.83)	.21
CBS-I | S&P	.51	(6.73)	.16			
CBS-I | $				.42	(8.26)	.22

Note: y|x denotes the residual of y from regression on x.

Comparing Table 6.1 with Table 3.2, we see that the correction for the comovement with the S&P Index slightly lowers the dollar sensitivities, but they remain highly significant. The right hand side of Table 6.1 yields no surprises. We conclude that most part of the dollar sensitivities is not induced by a comovement with the US stock market.

REFERENCES:

Berry, M.A., E. Burmeister & M.B. McElroy, 1988, Sorting Out Risks Using Known APT Factors, *Financial Analysts Journal* March/April, pp. 29-42

Chan, K.C., N.-F. Chen & D.A. Hsieh, 1985, An Exploratory Investigation of the Firm Size Effect, *Journal of Financial Economics* 14, pp. 451-71

Chen, N.-F., R. Roll & S.A. Ross, 1986, Economic Forces and the Stock Market, *Journal of Business* 59, pp. 383-403

De Bondt, W.F.M. & R.H. Thaler, 1985, Does the Stock Market Overreact?, *The Journal of Finance* 40/3, pp. 793-805

De Bondt, W.F.M. & R. Thaler, 1987, Further Evidence On Investor Overreaction and Stock Market Seasonality, *The Journal of Finance* 42/3, pp. 557-581

Estep, T., M. Clayman, C. Johnson & K. McMahon, 1984, *The Evolution of a* New Approach to Investment Risk, *Salomon Bros Inc., May*

Hallerbach, W.G., 1990, Present Value Models and Multi-factor Risk Analysis, paper presented at the VIIth Meeting of the EURO Working Group on Financial Modelling, Sirmione, Italy, April, 39 pp.

Hallerbach, W.G. & J. Spronk, 1986, An Interactive Multi-Factor Portfolio Model, Report 8610/F, Centre for Research in Business Economics, Erasmus University Rotterdam, 20 pp.

Hallerbach, W.G. & J. Spronk, 1991, A Multi-Attribute Approach to Portfolio Selection, *Proceedings of the IXth Meeting of the EURO Working Group on Financial Modelling*, Curaçao, Netherlands Antilles, April, 19 pp.

Haugen, R.A., 1990, *Modern Investment Theory*, Prentice Hall, Englewood Cliffs, N.J.

Haugen, R.A. & N.L. Baker, 1990, Dedicated Stock Portfolios, *The Journal of Portfolio Management* Summer, pp. 17-22

McElroy, M.B. & E. Burmeister, 1988, Arbitrage Pricing Theory as a Restricted Nonlinear Multivariate Regression Model, *Journal of Business & Economic Statistics* January, vol. 6/1, pp. 29-42

Roll, R. & S.A. Ross, 1984, The APT Approach to Strategic Portfolio Planing, *Financial Analysts Journal*, pp. 14-26

Ross, S.A., 1976, The Arbitrage Theory of Capital Asset Pricing, *Journal of Economic Theory*, pp. 341-360.

Samuelson, P.A., 1967, General Proof that Diversification Pays, *Journal of Financial and Quantitative Analysis*, March

Sorensen, E.H., J.J. Mezrich & C. Thum, 1989, The Salomon Brothers U.S. Stock Risk Attribute Model, Salomon Bros Research, 17 pp.

Von Eije, J.H., W.G. Hallerbach & H.C. Versteeg, 1991, Measuring Interest Rate Risk of Common Stocks, paper presented at the Dutch Financial Analysts Association's seminar 'Portfolio Management in a Changing World', Maastricht, The Netherlands, May 31, 25 pp. (in Dutch)

A Present Value Approach to the Portfolio Selection Problem

Klaus Hellwig, University of Ulm, Helmholtzstrasse 18, 7900 Ulm

1 Introduction

The traditional approach to the single-period portfolio problem is to assume that there is some given utility function such that an optimal portfolio can be found by maximizing expected utility (see, for example, [4]). However, the determination of such a utility function may cause substantial difficulties. This, in particular, holds for an investment company, which generally does not know the investors' preferences or is able to aggregate them.

This raises the question of an alternative approach. One possible approach to be followed here is to look for a decision that is consistent with the present value method. The meaning of this will become clear by the following example.

An investor has to choose between a risky and a risk free security A and B respectively. He estimates the return of A to be either zero or twenty one per cent with equal probability. The return of B is ten per cent.

The investor first examines whether he should choose B and reject A. Choosing B offers a 10% return in both states. Thus, using 10% as the appropriate discount rate in both states, the present value of this opportunity, PV_B, is zero. In order to justify the decision for B, PV_A, should at most be zero. But $PV_A = -1 + 0.5\frac{1}{1.1} + 0.5\frac{1.21}{1.1} > 0$. Therefore the investor concludes, that A should not be rejected after all.

If the investor on the other hand chooses A and rejects B, then the return in state 1 and 2 will be 0% and 21% respectively. Invoking a similar argument, to justify this decision, PV_B should at most be zero. But $PV_B = -1 + 0.5\frac{1.1}{1} + 0.5\frac{1.1}{1.21} > 0$. As a consequence, B should not be rejected.

It remains to examine, whether a combination of A and B is consistent with the present value method. Suppose the investor invests fifty per cent of his funds in A and fifty per cent in B. Then the return in state 1 is $0.5 \cdot 1 + 0.5 \cdot 1.1 - 1 = 5\%$ and the return in state 2 is $0.5 \cdot 1.21 + 0.5 \cdot 1.1 - 1 = 15.5\%$. As a consequence, the present values of A and B, using these discount factors, are zero. Therefore, the decision to choose this combination, is consistent with the present value method.

The described procedure can also be viewed as an axiomatic approach to the portfolio selection problem. First, the investor requires that the portfolio finally choosen should not permit arbitrage. Let x be the proportion of A in the portfolio. Then this portfolio does not permit arbitrage, if and only if state-prices w_1, w_2 exist, such that the following conditions are met

1. $PV_A = -1 + w_1 + 1.21w_2 \leq 0. \quad x > 0 \Rightarrow PV_A = 0.$

2. $PV_B = -1 + 1.1w_1 + 1.1w_2 \leq 0. \quad 1 - x > 0 \Rightarrow PV_B = 0.$

w_1 and w_2 can be decomposed into a probability and a discount factor, $w_1 = 0.5b_1, w_2 = 0.5b_2$, where $b_1 = (1+i_1)^{-1}, b_2 = (1+i_2)^{-1}$ and i_1, i_2 are the interest rates for state 1 and 2 respectively.

PV_A and PV_B can be interpreted as present values. With this interpretation conditons 1 and 2 state that the present values of A and B should at most be zero, and that an alternative with a negative present value should be rejected.

Because generally more than one portfolio exists, that does not permit arbitrage, at least one additional condition is needed. Such a condition can be found by noting that, if x is invested in A, then every unit invested in this portfolio has a return $r_1 = x + 1.1(1-x) - 1$ in state 1 and $r_2 = 1.21x + 1.1(1-x) - 1$ in state 2. r_1 and r_2 may thus be interpreted as opportunity costs associated with the given portfolio in states 1 and 2 respectively. Since one should discount with opportunity costs, as a second condition $r_1 = i_1$ and $r_2 = i_2$ is required, which, together with the no arbitrage condition, leads to a portfolio where fifty per cent are invested in A and fifty per cent in B.

In the following paragraph the example will be generalized. In paragraph three, the existence and uniqueness of a solution of the model will be proved. In addition it will be shown, that the solution is consistent with expected utility maximization with a log utility function. In the final paragraph, the case is analysed, where the return of the risky security is log normally distributed.

2 The model

Let A be risky and B a risk free security respectively.[1]

Assume the following notations:

$x: \;=$ proportion of the funds, that is invested in A.
$a_i: \;=$ 1 + the return of A in state i $(i = 0, \dots, n)$.
$b: \;=$ 1 + the return of B.
$b_i: \;=$ 1 + the portfolio return in state $i (i = 0, \dots, n)$.
$p_i: \;=$ probability of state $i (i = 0, \dots, n)$.

Let P_x be the portfolio where x is invested in A and $1 - x$ in B. The return of P_x is given by

$$b_i - 1 = a_i x + b(1 - x) \qquad (i = 0, \dots, n). \tag{1}$$

$b_i - 1$ is the opportunity cost in state i associated with P_x. Discounting with this opportunity cost leads to the present values of A and B,

$$PV_A^{(n)} := \sum_{i=0}^{n} p_i \frac{a_i}{b_i} - 1, \qquad PV_B^{(n)} := \sum_{i=0}^{n} p_i \frac{b}{b_i} - 1. \tag{2}$$

In order to reproduce P_x with the present value method, the following conditions have to be met.

[1] Alternatively, A and B can be risky and risk free portfolios.

$$PV_A^{(n)} \leq 0 \,.\, x > 0 \Rightarrow PV_A^{(n)} = 0. \tag{3}$$

$$PV_B^{(n)} \leq 0 \,.\, x < 1 \Rightarrow PV_B^{(n)} = 0. \tag{4}$$

Let (1), (3) and (4) be satisfied for P_x. Then P_x will be called return-oriented.

3 Existence and uniqueness of the return-oriented portfolio

Substituting (1) and (2) gives the present values of A and B as a function of x.

$$PV_A^{(n)}(x) = \sum_{i=0}^{n} p_i \frac{a_i}{a_i x + (1-x)b} - 1, \tag{5}$$

$$PV_B^{(n)}(x) = \sum_{i=0}^{n} p_i \frac{b}{a_i x + (1-x)b} - 1. \tag{6}$$

Assume $a_i > 0$ for $i = 0, \ldots, n$. Then $PV_A^{(n)}(x)$ and $PV_B^{(n)}(x)$ are defined for all $x \in [0.1]$. Since the second derivatives are positive, both $PV_A^{(n)}(x)$ and $PV_B^{(n)}(x)$ are strictly convex functions.

In order to prove the existence and uniqueness of the return-oriented portfolio, $PV_A^{(n)}(x)$ and $PV_B^{(n)}(x)$ will be analysed first.

Let $E_n := \sum_{i=0}^{n} p_i a_i$ be the expected return of A. Then

$$PV_A^{(n)}(0) = \frac{E_n}{b} - 1, \; PV_A^{(n)}(1) = 0, \tag{7}$$

$$PV_B^{(n)}(0) = 0, \; PV_B^{(n)}(1) = b \sum_{i=0}^{n} \frac{p_i}{a_i} - 1. \tag{8}$$

Multiplying (1) by p_i/b_i and summing up yields

$$xPV_A^{(n)}(x) + (1-x)PV_B^{(n)}(x) = 0, \qquad \text{for all } x \in [0.1]. \tag{9}$$

If $PV_A^{(n)}(0) > 0$, then according to (7), the expected return of A is greater than the return of B. Furthermore, because of the strict convexity of $PV_A^{(n)}(x)$, there exists at most one x_1 with $0 < x_1 < 1$ and $PV_A^{(n)}(x_1) = 0$. From (9), in such a case $PV_B^{(n)}(x_1) = 0$. Because of the strict convexity of $PV_A^{(n)}(x)$ and $PV_B^{(n)}(x)$

$$PV_A^{(n)}(x) > 0, PV_B^{(n)}(x) \leq 0 \text{ if } x < x_2,$$
$$PV_A^{(n)}(x) \leq 0, PV_B^{(n)}(x) > 0 \text{ if } x > x_2.$$

Thus, if an x_1 with $0 < x_1 < 1$ and $PV_A^{(n)}(x_1) = 0$ exists, $\bar{x} = x_1$ yields the uniquely determined return-oriented portfolio. If such an x_1 does not exist, then $\bar{x} = 1$ yields a return-oriented portfolio, which again is uniquely determined.

Now assume $PV_A^{(n)}(0) \leq 0$. Then $PV_A^{(n)}(x) < 0$ for all $x \in (0.1)$. The first derivative of $PV_B^{(n)}(x)$ at $x = 0$ is given by $1 - \frac{E_n}{b}$ and is therefore non-negative for $E_n \leq b$. Because $PV_B^{(n)}(x)$ is strictly convex, it follows that $PV_B^{(n)}(x) > 0$ for all $x \in (0.1]$. Thus, the only return-oriented portfolio is realised for $\bar{x} = 0$. Therefore, also in this case the choice of the return-oriented portfolio is compatible with risk-averse behaviour.

Summarizing the above considerations, the return-oriented portfolio is uniquely determined. Moreover, the return-oriented portfolio is a utility maximizing solution for the log utility function. That is, the return-oriented portfolio is an optimal solution of

$$\max_{0 \leq x \leq 1} \{ \sum_{i=0}^{n} p_i \log(a_i x + b(1-x)) \}.$$

This follows, since (3) and (4) can be identified with the Kuhn-Tucker conditions of this optimization problem.

In particular, the log function can be justified by the no arbitrage condition and the condition, that consumption should be discounted with opportunity costs.

4 The log-normal case

The solution of the model presented in section three depends upon the probability distribution of A. Therefore, in order to prove additional results, the solution has to be examined for particular distributions.

In practical applications, the binomial model has proved to be a suitable approach to describe the price behaviour of risky securities. The basic idea underlying this approach is to divide the planning period (e.g. one year) in n subperiods where in every subperiod independently only two price movements u ("up") and d ("down") with probability p and $1-p$ resp. occur.

If u, d and p are suitably defined, then it can be shown, that the binomial process for $n \to \infty$ converges to a continuous process, where the return is (dependent upon the definition of u, d and p) distributed log −normal or log −poisson [1].

If, for example u, d and p are defined by $p = 0.5$, $g = \exp(\mu/n + \sigma/\sqrt{n})$, $s = \exp(\mu/n - \sigma/\sqrt{n})$, then the limiting distribution of the return A is a log-normal distribution with mean μ and standard deviation σ [5], p. 188.[2]

Applying the same technique, that Feller used to prove the Limit theorem of De-Moivre and Laplace [2], pp. 182 and using the above given definitions of u, d and p, the limiting functions $PV_A(x) := \lim_{n\to\infty} PV_A^{(n)}(x), PV_B(x) := \lim_{n\to\infty} PV_B^{(n)}(x)$ can be found to be

$$PV_A(x) = \frac{1}{\sqrt{2\pi}} \int_{-\infty}^{+\infty} \frac{\exp(-y^2/2)}{x + (1-x)b\exp(-\mu - \sigma y)} dy - 1, \qquad (10)$$

[2]In this case $p_i = (0.5)^n(\binom{n}{i})$, $a_i = g^i s^{n-i} = \exp(2i\sigma/\sqrt{n})\exp(\mu - \sqrt{n}\sigma)$.

$$PV_B(x) = \frac{b}{\sqrt{2\pi}} \int_{-\infty}^{+\infty} \frac{\exp(-y^2/2)}{x\exp(\mu+\sigma y)+(1-x)b} dy - 1. \qquad (11)$$

$PV_A(x)$ and $PV_B(x)$ are strictly convex. Consequently, the existence and uniqueness of the return-oriented portfolio for the limiting case can be proved analogue to the finite case.

Evaluating $PV_A(x)$ at $x = 0$ yields the limiting value for the expected return $E := \lim_{n\to\infty} E_n$. One gets $E = \exp(\mu+\sigma^2/2)$. Thus the expected return of A does not only increase with μ, but also with the volatility σ.

However, this does not mean, that the proportion $\bar{x}$ of A in the return-oriented portfolio always increases with σ. Analysing the derivation of PV_A with respect to σ leads to the result, that $PV_A(x)$ increases, if $\bar{x} < b(e^\mu + b)^{-1}$, and decreases, if $\bar{x} > b(e^\mu - b)^{-1}$ (see theorem 1 in the appendix). As a consequence, $\bar{x}$ increases (decreases) with σ, if $\bar{x} < b(e^\mu + b)^{-1}(\bar{x} > b(e^\mu + b)^{-1})$. If $\bar{x} = 0.5$, then, as a special case, $\mu = \log b$.

Since $\bar{x}$ c.p. increases with μ, as a consequence, $\bar{x}$ is not greater (smaller) than 0.5, if $\mu < \log b(\mu > \log b)$.

5 Conclusion

The primary goal of the model presented above was to present a solution for the portfolio selection problem, that is not based on a specific utility function. However, it appeared, that the model is consistent with expected utility maximization with a log utility function. As a result, the log utility function can be established by two conditions, namely, that a portfolio should not permit arbitrage and that the opportunity costs associated with the demanded portfolio should be used for discounting. As done for the case of a log normally distributed return, the solution can be analysed under different distributional assumptions. The extension to the case with more than two securities is straightforward.

Appendix

Theorem 1: $PV_A(x)$ is increasing (decreasing) with respect to σ, if $x < x^* := b(e^\mu + b)^{-1}$ $(x > x^*)$.

Proof: Let

$$f(x) := \frac{dPV_A(x)}{d\sigma} = \frac{(1-x)b}{\sqrt{2\pi}\exp(\mu)} \int_{-\infty}^{+\infty} \frac{y\exp(-y^2/2)\exp(-\sigma y)}{(x+(1-x)b\exp(-\mu-\sigma y))^2} dy.$$

Denote the integrand by $g(x,y)$ and let $g_1(x,y) := x + (1 - x)b\exp(-\mu + \sigma y), g_2(x,y) := x + (1-x)b\exp(-\mu - \sigma y)$
Then

$$g(x,y) + g(x,-y) = y\exp(-y^2/2)\{\frac{\exp(-\sigma y)g_1^2(x,y) - exp(\sigma y)g_2^2(x,y)}{g_1^2(x,y)g_2^2(x,y)}\}$$

Then for $y > 0$ it follows

$$g(x,y) + g(x,-y) > 0 \Leftrightarrow g_1^2(x,y) > \exp(2\sigma y)\ g_2^2(x,y)$$

$$\Leftrightarrow x + (1-x)b\exp(-\mu+\sigma y) > x\exp(\sigma y) + (1-x)b\exp(-\mu)$$

$$\Leftrightarrow x(1-\exp(\sigma y)) > (1-x)b\exp(-\mu)(1-\exp(\sigma y)).$$

Because $y > 0$ implies $1 - \exp(\sigma y) > 0$ this is equivalent to $x < x^*$.

Taking into consideration $g(x,0) = 0$ for all $x \in [0.1]$ and

$$f(x) = \frac{(1-x)b}{\sqrt{2\pi}\exp(\mu)} \int_0^{+\infty} (g(-y) + g(y))dy,$$

finally yields

$$f(x) \begin{cases} > 0 & \text{if} \quad x < \bar{x} \\ = 0 & \text{if} \quad x = \bar{x} \\ < 0 & \text{if} \quad x > \bar{x}. \end{cases}$$

Theorem 2: Assume $\mu = \log b$. Then the return-oriented portfolio will be realized for $\bar{x} = 0.5$.

Proof: For $\mu = \log b$

$$PV_A(0.5) = \sqrt{\frac{2}{\pi}} \int_{-\infty}^{+\infty} \frac{\exp(-y^2/2)}{1+\exp(-\sigma y)} dy - 1.$$

Denoting the integrand as $h(y)$ gives $h(y) = \exp(\sigma y) h(-y)$.

Thus

$\int_{-\infty}^{+\infty} h(y)dy = \int_0^{+\infty} (h(y) + h(-y)dy = \int_0^{+\infty} h(y)(1 + \exp(-\sigma y))dy =$
$\int_0^{+\infty} e^{-y^2/2} dy = \sqrt{\frac{\pi}{2}}$. As a result $PV_A(0.5) = 0$.

References

[1] Cox, J.C., Ross, S.A., Rubinstein, M. (1979): *Option Pricing: A Simplified Approach*,, Journal of Financial Economics, 229 - 263.

[2] Feller, W. (1968): *An Introduction to Probability Theory and its Applications*, Wiley and Sons, New York.

[3] Hellwig, K. (1987): *Bewertung von Ressourcen*, Heidelberg.

[4] Ingersoll Jr., J.E. (1987): *Theory of Financial Decision Making*, Rowman & Littlefield, Savage, Maryland.

[5] Jarrow, R., Rudd, A. (1983): *Option Pricing*, R.D. Irwin, Homewood.

I am indebted to Werner Kratz (University of Ulm) for the Limiting functions (10) and (11). Besides others, I am also indebted to Walter Gruber and Gerhard Speckbacher (both from the University of Ulm).

DISCOUNTING WHEN TAXES ARE PAID ONE YEAR LATER: A FINANCE APPLICATION OF LINEAR PROGRAMMING DUALITY

L. Peter Jennergren
Stockholm School of Economics
Box 6501, S-11383 Stockholm, Sweden

1. Introduction

In connection with financial leases, one frequently ecounters the following valuation rule: Discount the after-tax lease payments and depreciation tax shields displaced by the lease at the company's after-tax borrowing rate. This valuation rule, which assumes simultaneous taxes, was derived by Myers et al. (1976), Franks and Hodges (1978), and Levy and Sarnat (1979). It has since been applied by a number of authors, for instance Benninga (1989, pp. 39-66) and Brick et al. (1987). The same rule, to discount the after-tax amounts at the after-tax borrowing rate, has also been proposed for safe, nominal cash flows by Ruback (1986) and Brealey and Myers (1991, pp. 470-474). This rule follows very easily, if the problem of choosing between leasing or borrowing, or valuing a safe nominal cash flow, is posed as a linear programming (LP) problem (Jennergren 1990).

This paper considers a somewhat more complex problem situation, that of valuing a safe nominal cash flow where the tax consequences occur *one year later*, not simultaneously with the primary cash flows as in the papers cited above. This latter situation, i. e., lagged tax payments, is typical of some European countries, for instance Sweden and the UK (cf. Hodges 1985, p. 69). By means of an LP formulation, it is again possible to derive a discounting rule. That is the purpose of this paper.

The next section formulates an LP problem for the valuation of a safe, nominal cash flow when taxes are paid with a one-year lag. Section 3 considers the dual LP problem and derives a valuation rule for the lagged-taxes situation. That valuation rule implies a slight approximation, as demonstrated in Section 4 by means of a numerical example. The fundamental result in the paper, the interest rate formula (2) below, has already been obtained by Franks and Hodges (1979), although in a rather different fashion. This paper nevertheless represents an extension of the Franks and Hodges analysis, as will be pointed out in the final Section 5.

2. An LP Problem for Valuing a Safe, Nominal Cash Flow with Taxes One Year Later

Suppose that some company pays taxes with a one-year lag. The corporate tax rate is τ. The company will receive a single pre-tax cash flow of X_{S-1} in year S-1. There will thus be a tax payment of $-\tau X_{S-1}$ in year S. The firm can borrow and lend at the interest rate r. The question is now: How much can the company borrow and lend in order to net out the future cash flow X_{S-1} and the associated subsequent tax payment? The borrowing and lending will be rolled over each year at the interest rate r and will be constrained to have non-negative net cash flow consequences in future years. The present value of the amounts X_{S-1} in year S-1 and $-\tau X_{S-1}$ in year S is equal to the maximal amount that can be borrowed right away, subject to the restrictions that the net consequences (net outflows) of the borrowing-lending plan should be less than or equal to X_{S-1} in year S-1, less than or equal to $-\tau X_{S-1}$ in year S, and less than or equal to zero in all other years.

This leads to the following LP formulation:

$$
\begin{array}{lllll}
\text{Max } B_0 & & & & (\text{year } 0 = \text{now}) \\
\text{s. t.:} & & & & \\
 & (1+r)B_0 & - B_1 & \leq 0, & (\text{year } 1) \\
-\tau r B_0 & + (1+r)B_1 & - B_2 & \leq 0, & (\text{year } 2) \\
-\tau r B_1 & + (1+r)B_2 & - B_3 & \leq 0, & (\text{year } 3) \\
\cdot & & & & \\
\cdot & & & & \\
-\tau r B_{S-3} & + (1+r)B_{S-2} & - B_{S-1} & \leq X_{S-1}, & (\text{year } S-1) \\
-\tau r B_{S-2} & + (1+r)B_{S-1} & - B_S & \leq -\tau X_{S-1}, & (\text{year } S) \\
\cdot & & & & \\
\cdot & & & & \\
-\tau r B_{T-3} & + (1+r)B_{T-2} & - B_{T-1} & \leq 0, & (\text{year } T-1) \\
-\tau r B_{T-2} & + B_{T-1} & & \leq 0. & (\text{year } T)
\end{array}
$$

The variables B_0, B_1, B_2, ..., B_S, ..., B_{T-1} denote the closing borrowing-lending balances in years 0, 1, 2, ..., S, ..., T-1. Positive values represent borrowing, negative values lending. The structure of the optimal borrowing-lending policy will be to borrow until year S-1, with the outstanding loan balance increasing each year until year S-2. In year S-1, the company lends at the interest rate r, in order to net out the tax amount $-\tau X_{S-1}$ in year S. However, lending from year S-1 to year S leads to a further tax consequence in year S+1. In order to net out that amount, the company lends from year S to year S+1, which in turn leads to a further tax consequence in year S+2, and so on. In order to put an end to this cycle, the company transfers an amount *in cash* (i. e., lends at zero interest rate) between years T-1 and T. It is apparently assumed that $S \geq 2$, $T \geq 3$, and $T > S$.

The objective is to maximize B_0, the amount borrowed immediately. B_0 is hence the present value of the pre-tax riskless cash flow X_{S-1} in year S-1 and its associated tax outflow $-\tau X_{S-1}$ in the subsequent year S.

3. The Dual Variables: Discount Factors

It is easy to solve the above LP problem and hence to determine the optimal borrowing-lending policy using, e. g., a spreadsheet (cf. Benninga 1989, pp. 39-66). That is, the simplex method is not necessary for solving the LP problem in this case. However, the solution method which is of interest here proceeds by way of the dual problem, i. e., discounting the amounts X_{S-1} in year S-1 and $-\tau X_{S-1}$ in year S to a present value. For that purpose, one needs the discount factors, i. e., the dual variables, associated with years S-1 and S. The dual variables for the above LP problem can be calculated as follows. Define:

$$
\begin{aligned}
D_1 &= 1, \\
D_2 &= (1+r) - \tau r, \\
D_3 &= (1+r)D_2 - \tau r D_1, \\
D_4 &= (1+r)D_3 - \tau r D_2, \\
&\;\;\vdots \\
D_S &= (1+r)D_{S-1} - \tau r D_{S-2}, \\
&\;\;\vdots \\
D_T &= (1+r)D_{T-1} - \tau r D_{T-2}.
\end{aligned}
$$

Under the obvious assumption that the interest rate r is positive and the corporate tax rate τ less than 100 percent, the solution to this homogeneous linear second-order difference equation with constant coefficients is the following: D_i equals

$$\frac{1-0.5(1+r)+\sqrt{[0.25(1+r)(1+r)-\tau r]}}{2\sqrt{[0.25(1+r)(1+r)-\tau r]}} \cdot$$

$$\{0.5(1+r)+\sqrt{[0.25(1+r)(1+r)-\tau r]}\}^{i}$$

$$+$$

$$\frac{-1+0.5(1+r)+\sqrt{[0.25(1+r)(1+r)-\tau r]}}{2\sqrt{[0.25(1+r)(1+r)-\tau r]}} \cdot$$

$$\{0.5(1+r)-\sqrt{[0.25(1+r)(1+r)-\tau r]}\}^{i} . \qquad (1)$$

The discount factors depend on the cut-off horizon T and are therefore denoted d_{iT}, for i = 1, 2, ..., S, ..., T. It is easy to verify that

$$d_{iT} = D_{T-i}/D_T \quad \text{for } i = 1, \ldots, S, \ldots, T-1,$$
$$d_{TT} = 1/D_T.$$

The second term in (1) goes rapidly to zero with increasing i. This means that the discount factors d_{iT} are nearly independent of T for i = 1, 2, ..., S, if T-S is sufficiently large (for instance, T-S = 3). Under that assumption, the discount factors are denoted d_i and are equal to

$$d_i = (1+r^\circ)^{-i} \quad \text{for } i = 1, 2, \ldots, S,$$

where

$$r^\circ = 0.5(r-1) + \sqrt{[0.25(1+r)(1+r)-\tau r]}. \qquad (2)$$

That is, the *approximate* valuation rule for safe, nominal cash flows with a one-year tax lag is to discount at the interest rate $r°$. In the above example, the value of the cash flow X_{S-1} in year S-1 and the tax payment $-\tau X_{S-1}$ in year S is thus

$$X_{S-1} \cdot (1+r°)^{-(S-1)} \quad + \quad -\tau X_{S-1} \cdot (1+r°)^{-S},$$

with $r°$ defined as in (2).

4. *An Example*

More generally, a safe, nominal after-tax cash flow of X_1, X_2, ..., X_S in years 1, 2, ..., S can be valued by discounting at the interest rate $r°$ defined in (2), if there is a one-year tax lag. The assumption implicit in this procedure is that the tax effects will be carried forward for at least a few years after the final year S of the cash flow under consideration (i. e., the cut-off horizon T should be something like two or three years after year S). To see the approximation involved, consider again the previous example with $r = 0.10$, $\tau = 0.3$, and $S = 4$. The safe, nominal cash flow to be obtained in year 3 is 100, and the tax consequence in year 4 is thus -30. The approximate discount factors d_i and the exact ones d_{iT} for $T = 5$ and $T = 6$ are given in Table 1.

Table 1. Discount factors in example problem

i	d_i	d_{i5}	d_{i6}
1	0.9328	0.9328	0.9328
2	0.8702	0.8702	0.8702
3	0.8117	0.8117	0.8117
4	0.7572	0.7586	0.7572
5	0.7063	0.7586	0.7077
6	0.6589		0.7077

Using the discount factors d_i, the present value of the cash flow and its subsequent tax consequence is 58.45. The same value is evidently obtained, if one uses the discount factors d_{i6}. However, a slightly different value, 58.41, is obtained when using the discount factors d_{i5}. The conclusion from this example (and other similar examples as well) is that the discount factors d_i are very good approximations, indeed.

5. *Conclusion*

As already mentioned, the formula (2) for the approximate discount rate with a one-year tax lag has been derived in a previous paper by Franks and Hodges (1979, p. 30). They argue as follows: The after-tax interest rate on a loan is obtained by discounting the tax effect and subtracting it from the pre-tax interest rate. This gives the equation

$$r^\circ = r - \{\tau r/(1+r^\circ)\},$$

which can be solved to obtain (2). Their argument evidently assumes away the effect of the cut-off horizon T, i. e., presupposes a sort of steady-state situation. This paper has extended the analysis by Franks and Hodges by deriving the approximate discount factors as limits of the exact ones and demonstrating the degree of approximation involved.

More generally, this paper has provided yet another example how linear programming can be used for valuation problems in finance in some situations. Those situations mainly refer to cash flows where uncertainty plays no essential role, e. g., leasing and bond portfolio management; cf. earlier discussions by Hodges and Schaefer (1977) and Jennergren (1990). In certain cases, simple discounting rules can be derived by means of LP formulations, as shown in this paper. Although the same discounting rules can be derived by other lines of argument as well, the LP formulations are nevertheless instructive, in that they bring out the underlying assumptions very clearly, assumptions which are not always explicitly stated in finance theory discussions.

In the case discussed here, of taxes with a one-year lag, the assumption was that the company could borrow at the interest rate r in each future year, in fact that the outstanding loan balance could be *increased* from one year to the next at that interest rate. This type of arrangement is evidently less plausible than one where the company takes out a loan at a fixed interest rate r over S years, and where the company is allowed to *reduce* (but not increase) the outstanding loan balance prior to year S. Moreover, the additional assumption was made that the company could *lend* at that same interest rate r in future years. Also, the company was assumed to be in a permanent tax-paying situation.

If these assumptions are not satisfied, then the simple discounting rule discussed in this paper is no longer valid. However, more complex LP problems can be formulated for such valuation situations, taking into account the financial instruments which actually do exist in the capital market (including actually existing borrowing and lending alternatives) and the actual tax situation of the company in question (cf. also Dermody and Rockafellar 1991). More complex formulations of this kind are typically not reducible to simple discounting rules. Linear programming is thus a more general method for valuation than discounting in some situations.

References

Benninga, S., 1989, *Numerical Techniques in Finance* (MIT Press, Cambridge, Massachusetts).

Brealey, R. A. and S. C. Myers, 1991, *Principles of Corporate Finance*, 4th edition (McGraw-Hill, New York).

Brick, I. E., W. Fung, and M. Subrahmanyam, 1987, Leasing and financial intermediation: Comparative tax advantages, *Financial Management* 16, Spring 1987, 55-59.

Dermody, J. C. and R. T. Rockafellar, 1991, Cash stream valuation in the face of transaction costs and taxes, *Mathematical Finance* 1, 31-54.

Franks, J. R. and S. D. Hodges, 1978, Valuation of financial lease contracts: A note, *Journal of Finance* 33, 657-669.

Franks, J. R. and S. D. Hodges, 1979, The role of leasing in capital investment, *National Westminster Bank Quarterly Review*, August 1979, 20-31.

Hodges, S. D., 1985, The valuation of variable rate leases, *Financial Management* 14, Spring 1985, 68-74.

Hodges, S. D. and S. M. Schaefer, 1977, A model for bond portfolio improvement, *Journal of Financial and Quantitative Analysis* 12, 243-260.

Jennergren, L. P., 1990, Valuation by linear programming -- A pedagogical note, *Journal of Business Finance & Accounting* 17, 751-756.

Levy, H. and M. Sarnat, 1979, Leasing, borrowing and financial risk, *Financial Management* 8, Winter 1979, 47-54.

Myers, S. C., D. A. Dill, and A. J. Bautista, 1976, Valuation of financial lease contracts, *Journal of Finance* 31, 799-819.

Ruback, R. S., 1986, Calculating the market value of riskless cash flows, *Journal of Financial Economics* 15, 323-339.

Acknowledgement: The author is indebted to Ken Angelin for discussions and comments.

The Asset Transformation Function of Financial Intermediaries

Wolfgang Kürsten
University of Passau

1. Introduction

Financial intermediaries like commercial banks, savings banks, or savings and loan associations – we call them *banks* for short in the following – perform various kinds of intermediation functions in the capital market, e.g. pooling of supply and demand, providing market participants with arbitrarily sized loan or deposit volumes, supply of perfectly liquid investments, risk sharing, and asset maturity transformation. This paper focuses on the last issue, i.e. the transformation of market rate sensitive, short term liabilities (deposits) into fixed–rate, long term assets (loans). In the case of a normal (rising) yield curve, the usually resulting *positive* gap in the bank's balance sheet – the volume of fixed–rate loan contracts *exceeds* that of fixed–rate liabilities – provides the bank with a positive net interest rate margin which is the main source of profits for most depository financial institutions. Besides this rather "classical" reasoning, more recent contributions ground the intermediaries' asset transformation function on maturity preferences of credit customers (v. Furstenberg

1973), on trade–offs between different kinds of bank risk as, for example, interest rate risk vs. default risk (Santomero 1983, Kürsten 1991), or on stochastic cumulation effects between market rates and future loan demand (Morgan/Smith 1987).

On the other hand, the perhaps most important *consequence* of the asset transformation function is that the induced balance sheet gap exposes the bank to interest rate risk. With a positive gap, for example, the bank's net interest rate margin can become smaller or even negative if interest rates are rising. While this is the common view in the literature (e.g. Schierenbeck 1987, Gardner/Mills 1988), this paper takes a view quite the other way round. It is shown that a risk averse bank facing stochastic asset or liability interest rates will always exhibit a *non–zero* balance sheet gap. Specifically, this gap will be *positive* under reasonable assumptions, i.e. interest rate risk exposure *induces* positive maturity transformation. This is discussed in chapter 2 together with some consequences concerning the measurement of banks' risk exposure. In chapter 3, the impact of Financial Futures engagements on the bank's asset transformation process is analyzed. The procedure used herewith is also contrary to the prevailing view in the existing literature which focusses on the optimal Futures volume with the balance sheet gap as *given* (e.g. Ederington 1979, Koppenhaver 1985a), whereas here *both* the gap *and* the Futures position are assumed to be decision variables. It can be shown that the possibility to engage in Futures positions enlarges the bank's gap and thereby increases asset transformation volumes as well as profit opportunities. We call this the *real production effect* of Financial Futures. Chapter 4 gives some directions for future research.

2. Interest Rate Risk and Asset Transformation

2.1 Assumptions

We use a 2–period framework with an exogenously given total demand volume for two period loans. Borrowers demand these funds to finance a 2–period investment whose return is realized at the end of period two (t=2). A portion $x \in [0,1]$ of total demand consists of roll–over one period (short term) contracts, the remaining part 1–x contains two period (long term) contracts. All interest plus principal is paid in t=2 since borrowers exclusively use the investment's cash–flow to meet their debt obligations. The interest rate of short term loans is given by the product of the (known) one period asset spot rate $R_1^A = 1 + r_1^A$ times the (unknown) one period spot rate $\tilde{R}_1^A$ which prevails at the end of the first period (t=1). From the t=0 point of view, where all loan decisions are made, $\tilde{R}_1^A$ is random. The interest rate of long term loans is given by the squared (known) two period asset spot rate $(R_2^A)^2$. Similarly, a portion $d \in [0,1]$ of the bank's liabilities consists of short term deposits (R_1^L = one period liability spot rate) which are rolled over at the (in t=1) prevailing liability rate $\tilde{R}_1^L$. In t=0, $\tilde{R}_1^L$ is random. The remaining part 1–d contains long term (e.g. time) deposits with the two period liability rate $(R_2^L)^2$. As on the asset side, all liabilities are treated as discount instruments repaid in t=2. The correlation between the asset rate $\tilde{R}_1^A$ and the liability rate $\tilde{R}_1^L$ can be non–perfect. All contracts are fulfilled in t=1, i.e. quantity risks like prepayment risk, deposit withdrawal risk or loan default risk are not taken into account (for an analytical discussion of quantity risks in banking see Batlin 1983b, Koppenhaver 1985b, or Kürsten 1991). Note that, by construction, the bank exclusively uses discount instruments and, thus, will not have to consider any refinancing constraints in t=1.

While this seems to be a rather uncommon case from a practical point of view (usually, interest is paid at the end of the first and second period), it stands in line with other theoretical contributions (e.g. Koppenhaver 1985a) and, more important, exhibits (at least) two major advantages to study the theoretical questions this paper is interested in. First, if interest is also paid in t=1, the bank's t=2 proceeds from *both* variable *and* fixed rate loans are random, whereas this paper focuses on the bank's decision *between* pure fixed rate and variable rate contracts. Second, incorporating interest payment in t=1 needs the cases of a positive or negative (net) refinancing volume to be dealt with separately, and thereby requires further assumptions about *how* the additional net position can be contracted with other participants in the capital market. This, at the end, would result in a combined price *and* quantity risk model (e.g. Morgan/Smith 1987) which is not the subject of this paper.

The decision variable of the model is the short term asset portion x, whereas the liability portion d is taken as given. We thus follow the traditional *asset management* approach which regards the liability side of a bank as market determined (since dependend on interbank competition and depositors' habits, for example), while on the asset side the bank retains some discretionary control. The bank's monetary objective is its equity at the end of period two. If the considered loan engagement exhibits no systematic correlation effects with the bank's remaining activities (as it is commonly assumed in the theory of single loan decisions; see Wilhelm 1982), the relevant monetary objective is the profit π given by

$$\pi = x \cdot R_1^A \cdot \tilde{R}_1^A + (1-x) \cdot (R_2^A)^2 - [d \cdot R_1^L \cdot \tilde{R}_1^L + (1-d) \cdot (R_2^L)^2] \qquad (1)$$

The risk averse bank maximizes the expected utility of profits π (Santomero 1983, Morgan/Shome/Smith 1988) using the preference functional

$$EU(\cdot) = E(\cdot) - \frac{\lambda}{2} Var(\cdot) \tag{2}$$

The final decision problem is thus

$$\max_{x \in [0,1]} \; EU(\pi) = E(\pi) - \frac{\lambda}{2} Var(\pi) , \tag{3}$$

where π is given by equation (1), $\lambda>0$ is the bank's absolute risk aversion parameter, and $E(\cdot)$ or $Var(\cdot)$ denote expected value and variance, respectively.

2.2 Components of Interest Rate Risk

In the present case, interest rate risk is caused by stochastic future spot rates $\tilde{R}_1^A$, $\tilde{R}_1^L$ and implies that the variance of profits

$$Var(\pi) = x^2 \cdot (R_1^A)^2 \cdot Var(\tilde{R}_1^A) + d^2 \cdot (R_1^L)^2 \cdot Var(\tilde{R}_1^L) \tag{4}$$

$$- 2\, x\, d\, R_1^A\, R_1^L \cdot Cov(\tilde{R}_1^A, \tilde{R}_1^L)$$

is positive ($Cov(\cdot,\cdot)$ denotes covariance). Specifically, interest rate risk stems from three distinct sources of uncertainty: the degree of mismatch in the fixed–variable proportions of the balance sheet (i.e. $x\, R_1^A \neq d\, R_1^L$), a possible difference in rate volatilities (i.e. $Var(\tilde{R}_1^A) \neq Var(\tilde{R}_1^L)$), and a possibly non–perfect correlation between asset rate and liability rate (i.e. the correlation coefficient $\mathrm{corr}(\tilde{R}_1^A,\tilde{R}_1^L) =: \gamma<1$). Correspondingly, we call the first interest rate risk component *fixed–rate risk*, the second *elasticity risk*, and the third *basis risk* (cf. Schierenbeck 1987, Bangert 1987).

For an illustration, assume that there is no elasticity risk and no basis risk ($\mathrm{Var}(\tilde{R}_1^A) = \mathrm{Var}(\tilde{R}_1^L), \gamma = 1$). Then isolated fixed rate risk is operationalized by the remaining variance of profits

$$\mathrm{Var}(\pi) = \mathrm{Var}(\tilde{R}_1^A)\cdot[x^2\cdot(R_1^A)^2 + d\cdot(R_1^L)^2 - 2\,x\,d\cdot R_1^A\cdot R_1^L] \tag{5}$$

and becomes minimal (zero) for $x\,R_1^A = d\,R_1^L$ ("value adjusted" *matching*). Elimination of fixed–rate risk, on the other hand, can be achieved by assuming that the bank can always maintain the matching condition $x\,R_1^A = d\,R_1^L$ (see Kürsten (1991) for a similar procedure). Interest rate risk is now completely due to the presence of some elasticity risk and/or basis risk. In either case, the variance of profits

$$\mathrm{Var}(\pi) = (x\cdot R_1^A)^2\cdot \mathrm{Var}(\tilde{R}_1^A-\tilde{R}_1^L) \tag{6}$$

remains positive as long as the variable portion x is positive and there is either an isolated elasticity risk ($\gamma=1$, $\mathrm{Var}(\tilde{R}_1^A) \neq \mathrm{Var}(\tilde{R}_1^L)$) or an isolated basis risk ($\gamma<1$, $\mathrm{Var}(\tilde{R}_1^A) = \mathrm{Var}(\tilde{R}_1^L)$). Therefore, isolated elasticity risk as well as isolated basis risk is minimal (zero) if and only if $x=0$, i.e. the bank grants only fixed rate loans. To demonstrate the main ideas, it will thus be sufficient in the following to assume the presence of some basis risk and fixed rate risk, i.e. that there is no elasticity risk ($\mathrm{Var}(\tilde{R}_1^A) = \mathrm{Var}(\tilde{R}_1^L)$; for a recent empirical study supporting this assumption see Jaenicke/Kirchgässner (1992)). An integration of elasticity risk complicates the interpretation of formulae, but does not affect our results substantially.

2.3 Optimal Asset Transformation

The optimal asset transformation volume x* is the result of the optimization problem (3). Since the objective function is concave, differentiation yields necessary and sufficient conditions for an inner solution (${}_0R^A_{1,2}$ denotes the implied forward rate in the asset market)

$$x^* = \frac{E(\tilde{R}^A_1 - {}_0R^A_{1,2})}{\lambda \cdot R^A_1 \cdot \mathrm{Var}(\tilde{R}^A_1)} + \gamma \cdot \frac{R^L_1}{R^A_1} \cdot d \tag{7}$$

As the liquidity premium (*"speculation"*) term indicates, a speculative oriented bank (ceteris paribus) prefers a greater (smaller) portion of its loan volume to consist of short term contracts if spot rates are expected to rise (fall). The speculative term becomes less significant for higher coefficients of risk aversion λ. If bank management follows the expectation hypothesis of interest rates ($E(\tilde{R}^A_1 - {}_0R^A_{1,2}) = 0$), only the second term which represents the minimum risk position is relevant. Obviously, the variance minimizing asset transformation requires

$$x^* = \gamma \cdot \frac{R^L_1}{R^A_1} \cdot d \leq \gamma \cdot d < d, \text{ or } |x^*-d| > 0 \tag{8a}$$

i.e. the bank's optimal balance sheet gap $|x^*-d|$ is non-zero.

Specifically, as long as the bank's interest rate margin remains non–negative, the intermediary performs some *positive maturity transformation* since the volume of long term assets exceeds that of long term liabilities

$$1-x^* > 1-d . \tag{8b}$$

Note that this is the *result* of an optimal interest rate risk management, while in the existing literature non–zero gaps are commonly regarded as the main *reason* for the interest rate risk exposure of banks. Formally, the result follows from the fact that the bank chooses an optimal *trade–off* between the two interest rate risk components, fixed rate risk and basis risk. While the elimination of isolated fixed–rate risk can be achieved by the matching condition $x = d \cdot R_1^L / R_1^A$ (see (5)), a minimization of isolated basis risk requires $x = 0$ (see (6)). An optimal position is thus reached for some $0 < x^* < d \cdot R_1^L / R_1^A$.

Two economic consequences of this formal result deserve further attention. First, measuring the bank's interest rate risk exposure on the magnitude of its actually taken balance sheet gap (Gardner/Mills 1988, Rolfes 1985) seems to be questionable. This is because – we denote x for the *actually* taken asset position and assume a zero margin $R_1^A = R_1^L$ for simplicity – a part $|x^*-d|$ of the *total gap* $|x-d|$ is already due to risk minimization behaviour. Only the remaining *net gap* $|x-x^*|$ corresponds to an *additional*, voluntarily accepted interest rate risk. We therefore suggest that it is the net gap which should be considered as a theoretically appropriate risk measure. We do not deny, however, that a practical procedure for the estimation of the net gap to be implemented in the real world would probably not be straightforward.

Second, the net gap can differ from the total gap even in sign. In this case, taking the total gap as the basis for an (e.g.) interest rate swap hedging policy could thus further increase the bank's overall risk position. Similar conclusions can be drawn for Financial Futures which are commonly used to hedge a given asset position (Koppenhaver 1990). In the following, an optimization procedure is presented which alleviates those difficulties by optimizing the bank's objective function with respect to both the asset and the Futures position *simultaneously*.

3. Financial Futures and Asset Transformation

3.1 Simultaneously Optimized Asset–Futures Position

The preceding results led to the suggestion that fixing hedging policies on a *given* asset position can induce a suboptimal overall risk position. We thus argue that the bank should try to optimize its risk exposure by a *simultaneous* optimization of its asset and hedging position. While this procedure is quite common in the theory of hedging *real* production risks (Batlin 1983a, Antonovitz/Roe 1986, Spremann 1986), is has nearly never been utilized in the theory of financial hedging (to our best knowledge, the only exception is Kürsten 1991 with a bank model concerning the trade–off between interest rate risk and default risk). In the following, we choose the example of Financial Futures hedging to demonstrate the usefulness of this simultaneous optimization procedure.

To maintain generality, we do not assume that the Futures contract necessarily has to call for delivery of either a bank loan or a bank liability, or that the delivery date T coincides with the point of time (t=1) where all uncertainty concerning interest rates is resolved (though those possibilities are not excluded). Instead, the bank in t=0 enters a delivery date T≥1 Futures contract (at a known futures rate R_f) which is offset in t=1 at a (in t=0) unknown futures rate $\tilde{R}_f$. A possibly non–perfect correlation between $\tilde{R}_f$ and $\tilde{R}_1^A$ (or $\tilde{R}_1^L$, resp.) represents "basis risk" induced by the Futures engagement. For the ease of demonstration – but not necessary for our main results – we assume $Var(\tilde{R}_1^A) = Var(\tilde{R}_1^L) = Var(\tilde{R}_f)$ and $\delta := corr(\tilde{R}_1^A, \tilde{R}_f) = corr(\tilde{R}_1^L, \tilde{R}_f) \neq \pm 1$ holds. The case of perfect hedging $\delta = \pm 1$ is discussed separately below (section 3.3). We further assume that the bank, possibly making use of adequate deferral accounting schemes (see Goodman/Langer 1983), treats any Futures trading profits or losses as being realized in t=2 together with the proceeds from her asset position (since otherwise additional or *ad hoc* assumptions concerning the investment or funding of those profits or losses would be required), and ignore initial or variation margins for simplicity as is common in most Futures hedging models (e.g. Koppenhaver 1985a). The bank's profit from a combined loan–Futures portfolio is now given by

$$\pi_f = \pi + y(R_f - \tilde{R}_f) \,, \tag{9}$$

where y>0 (y<0) indicates a long (short) Futures position. The simultaneous maximization of the concave objective function $EU(\pi_f) = E(\pi_f) - \frac{\lambda}{2} Var(\pi_f)$ w.r.t. the asset variable $x \in [0,1]$ and the Futures volume variable $y \in \mathbb{R}$ yields the linear equation system

$$\begin{aligned} &\frac{\partial}{\partial x} EU(\pi_f(x,y)) = 0 \\ &\frac{\partial}{\partial y} EU(\pi_f(x,y)) = 0 \end{aligned} \tag{10}$$

for an inner solution. The calculations are tedious, but straightforward and need not be made explicit here. We thus give the results and sketch some implications.

3.2 Real Production Effect of Financial Futures Hedging

Solving the linear system (10) yields explicit expressions for the optimal asset–Futures portfolio (x_f^*, y_f^*)

$$x_f^* = \frac{E(\tilde{R}_1^A - {}_oR_{1,2}^A) - \delta \cdot E(\tilde{R}_f - R_f)}{\lambda \cdot R_1^A \cdot Var(\tilde{R}_1^A) \cdot (1-\delta^2)} + \tag{11a}$$

$$+ \frac{\gamma - \delta^2}{1-\delta^2} \cdot \frac{R_1^L}{R_1^A} \cdot d \qquad (\delta \neq 1)$$

$$y_f^* = \frac{\delta \cdot E(\tilde{R}_1^A - {}_oR_{1,2}^A) - E(\tilde{R}_f - R_f)}{\lambda \cdot Var(\tilde{R}_1^A) \cdot (1-\delta^2)} \tag{11b}$$

$$+ \frac{\delta(\gamma-1)}{1-\delta^2} \cdot R_1^L \cdot d$$

Clearly, we cannot discuss the whole myriad of (ceteris paribus) parameter impacts, so only some selective remarks are given. First, both the optimal asset and Futures position split up into a speculation oriented term and a risk minimizing term. The corresponding terms in (11a) and (11b), resp., exhibit several mutual cross impact effects. Therefore, confronting (11a) with the mere asset optimization results in (7) clarifies how an additional Futures engagement affects the previously optimal asset position. If, for example, we set $E(\tilde{R}^A_1 - {}_0R^A_{1,2}) = 0$, and assume that futures rates are expected to fall ($E(\tilde{R}_f - R_f) \leq 0$) and are positively correlated with the spot rates ($\delta > 0$), the resulting speculative Futures position is long since offsetting by selling Futures promises speculative profits. This, as a *secondary* effect, raises the portion x of roll–over loans (compare (11a) with (7)) since the bank has to accept more basis risk in order to make use of the positive correlation between spot and futures rates, and thereby balances the additional speculative Futures risk.

Second, and more interesting in the context of modelling risk averse bank behaviour, there is also a cross impact between the risk minimizing terms in (11a,b). To isolate this effect, we assume the *sum* of the two expectation differences in (11) to be zero, so that the speculation terms vanish (assuming martingale efficiency for both implied forward rates and futures rates would be another possibility but requires caution since, in arbitrage–free markets, correlation effects between the stochastic discount factors have to be taken into account. A sufficient condition for both hypothesis to hold simultaneously is mutual independence of discount factors; for details see Cox/Ingersoll/Ross 1981 and Wilhelm 1985). A comparison of the risk minimizing asset–Futures position(x^*_f, y^*_f) from (11) with the corresponding minimal asset risk position x^* from (8a)

$$(x^*_f, y^*_f) = \left(\frac{\gamma - \delta^2}{1-\delta^2} \cdot \frac{R^L_1}{R^A_1} \cdot d \, , \, \delta \cdot \frac{\gamma - 1}{1-\delta^2} \cdot R^L_1 \cdot d \right) \quad , \delta \neq 1 \tag{12a}$$

$$x^* = \gamma \cdot \frac{R^L_1}{R^A_1} \cdot d \tag{12b}$$

now exhibits a change in the previously optimal asset position ($x^* \neq x_f^*$) which is exclusively due to the simultaneously optimized asset–Futures procedure. This *real production effect* of Financial Futures has not been analyzed in the existing literature which takes the bank's asset position as given (e.g. Batlin 1983b, Koppenhaver 1985a,b, Goldfarb 1987). Specifically, a short calculation shows

$$x_f^* < x^* \quad , \text{or } d - x_f^* > d - x^* \ , \tag{13}$$

that is, the bank's balance sheet gap has *increased*. Analytically, this is not surprising since the Futures position is short (long) for a positive (negative) correlation δ and thus hedges a part of fixed–rate risk which, in order to maintain the total risk position to be balanced, forces the intermediary to take a greater position in fixed–rate risk, i.e. to largen the balance sheet gap. From an economic point of view, however, this result is interesting because Financial Futures not only can be used as a (well–known) risk reduction device, but also allow the bank to *widen its asset transformation functions*. With a normal yield curve, this implies improved interest income opportunities for the bank which are solely due to a portfolio oriented simultaneity in the treatment of asset and Futures positions as equivalent decision variables of the bank.

Note further that the usefulness of Futures should vanish as soon as the second interest rate risk component, basis risk, is no longer present (γ=1). This is because fixed–rate risk can now be eliminated by a value adjusted matching $x = d \cdot R_1^L / R_1^A$ (see (5)) without using any Futures contracts at all. Specifiying formula (12a) for γ=1 confirms this conjecture analytically.

3.3 Perfect Hedging and Elimination of Interest Rate Risk

As a final case we consider a situation where a perfect hedging instrument is available, i.e. the absolute value of the correlation coefficient between futures and spot rate $|\delta|$ approaches one. As an example, one may think of a forward contract which calls for delivery of a one–period bank loan and matures at the time point t=1. In this case, applying appropriate limiting arguments to the equation system (10) yields for the risk minimizing asset–Futures position

$$(x^*_{f,p}, y^*_{f,p}) = (0\ ,\ \mp dR^L_1)\quad , \text{if } \delta = \pm 1\ . \tag{14}$$

As a result, the balance sheet gap with perfect hedging $|x^*_{f,p}-d|$ has further increased (compare (14) with (12a)) and reaches its maximum possible value

$$|x^*_{f,p}-d| = d = \max\{|x-d|,\ 0 \leq x \leq d\cdot R^L_1/R^A_1\} \tag{15}$$

The intuition behind (15) is that fixed–rate risk is now completely hedged in the Futures market and can thus be accepted at its maximum which, on the other hand, allows the bank to take a zero position in basis risk : $x^*_{f,p} = 0$. Perfect Futures hedging, therefore, not only accomplishes the *elimination* of *both* interest rate risk components simultaneously, but also provides the bank with the opportunity to *maximize* her asset transformation volume or, consequently, her source of interest rate income. To some respect, this result exhibits an analogy to the simultaneous elimination of both interest rate risk and default risk with Financial Futures as has been recently demonstrated elsewhere (Kürsten 1991).

4. Conclusions

The preceding analysis suggests that a theoretically founded modelling of bank's financial policies requires the relevant risk components as well as the different decision variables to be simultaneously taken into account in a portfolio oriented way. This has been demonstrated by the example of a risk averse bank which faces two kinds of interest rate risk (fixed rate risk or basis risk) and has the opportunity to engage in Financial Futures contracts to alleviate its interest rate risk exposure.

A couple of questions, however, are still waiting for future research. One of them shall be briefly sketched here. Recent empirical studies indicate that the use of Financial Futures by banks is still underdeveloped compared with the theoretically predicted volume which, as has been mentioned above, takes the bank's risk position (gap) as *given* (Koppenhaver 1990). The corresponding *sequentially optimized*, risk minimal Futures volume $y^*(x^*)$ is the solution of the problem

$$\min_{y \in \mathbb{R}} \quad \mathrm{Var}(\pi(x^*) + y(R_f - \tilde{R}_f)) \qquad (16)$$

$$\text{with} \quad x^* = \arg \min_{x \in [0,1]} \mathrm{Var}(\pi(x)) \qquad \text{(see (7), (8a))}$$

whereas the simultaneously optimized, risk minimal Futures volume y_f^* propounded above is calculated from (see (10))

$$\min_{\substack{x \in [0,1] \\ y \in \mathbb{R}}} \quad \mathrm{Var}(\pi(x) + y(R_f - \tilde{R}_f)) \qquad (17)$$

However, the sequentially optimized Futures volume from (16) with the gap $|x^*-d|$ as given is always *smaller* than the simultaneously optimized volume from (17):

$$|y^*(x^*)| = d \cdot R_1^L \cdot |\delta(\gamma-1)| \tag{18}$$

$$< d \cdot R_1^L \cdot \frac{|\delta(\gamma-1)|}{1-\delta^2} = |y_f^*| \qquad (\delta \neq 1)$$

The empirical shortcome in Financial Futures use is thus even *greater than reported*, if we agree that the simultaneously optimized asset–Futures position (12) should be the correct theoretical benchmark. Therefore, it seems to be evident that financial intermediaries could take considerably better risk positions by more theoretically guided Futures engagements. The estimation of the scope of this risk reduction potential could be an interesting task for further empirical research.

References

Antonovitz, F. and T. Roe (1986): "Effects of Expected Cash and Futures Prices on Hedging and Production", The Journal of Futures Markets, 6, 187–205.

Bangert, M. (1987): Zinsrisiko–Management in Banken, Wiesbaden.

Batlin, C.A. (1983a): "Production under Price Uncertainty with Imperfect Time Hedging Opportunities in Futures Markets", Southern Economic Journal, 49, 681–692.

Batlin, C.A. (1983b): "Interest Rate Risk, Prepayment Risk, and the Futures Market Hedging Strategies of Financial Intermediaries", The Journal of Futures Markets, 3, 177–184.

Cox, J., Ingersoll, J. and S. Ross (1981): "A Re–examination of Traditional Hypothesis about the Term Structure of Interest Rates", Journal of Finance, 36, 769–799.

Ederington, L.H. (1979): "The Hedging Performance of the New Futures Markets", The Journal of Finance, 34, 157–170.

v. Furstenberg, G.M. (1973): "The Equilibrium Spread Between Variable Rates and Fixed Rates on Long–Term Financing

Instruments", Journal of Financial and Quantitative Analysis, Dec., 807–819.

Gardner, M.J. and D.L. Mills (1988): Managing Financial Institutions: An Asset/Liability Approach, Chicago et al.

Goldfarb, D.R. (1987): "Hedging Interest Rate Risk in Banking", The Journal of Futures Markets, 7, 35–47.

Goodman, L.S. and M.J. Langer (1983): "Accounting for Interest Rate Futures in Bank Asset–Liability Management", The Journal of Futures Markets, 3, 415–427.

Jaenicke, J. und G. Kirchgässner (1992): "Asymmetrie im Zinsanpassungsverhalten der Banken?", Bank und Markt, 21, 29–34.

Koppenhaver, G.D. (1985a): "Bank Funding Risks, Risk Aversion, and the Choice of Futures Hedging Instrument", The Journal of Finance, 40, 241–255.

Koppenhaver, G.D. (1985b): "Variable–Rate Loan Commitments, Deposit Withdrawal Risk, and Anticipatory Hedging", The Journal of Futures Markets, 5, 317–330.

Koppenhaver, G.D. (1990): "An Empirical Analysis of Bank Hedging in Futures Markets", The Journal of Futures Markets, 10, 1–12.

Kürsten, W. (1991): "Optimale fix–variable Kreditkontrakte: Zinsänderungsrisiko, Kreditausfallrisiko und Financial Futures Hedging, Zeitschrift für betriebswirtschaftliche Forschung, 10, 867–891.

Morgan, G.E., Shome, D.K. and S.D. Smith (1988): "Optimal Futures Positions for Large Banking Firms", The Journal of Finance, 43, 175–195.

Morgan, G.E. and S.D. Smith (1987): "Maturity Intermediation and Intertemporal Lending Policies of Financial Intermediaries", The Journal of Finance, 42, 1023–1034.

Rolfes, B. (1985): "Ansätze zur Steuerung von Zinsänderungsrisiken", Kredit und Kapital, 18, 529–552.

Santomero, A.M. (1983): "Fixed Versus Variable Rate Loans", The Journal of Finance, 38, 1363–1380.

Spremann, K. (1986): "Produktion, Hedging, Spekulation – Zu den Funktionen von Futures–Märkten", Zeitschrift für betriebswirtschaftliche Forschung, 38, 443–464.

Schierenbeck, H. (1987): Ertragsorientiertes Bankmanagement, 2., vollst. überarbeitete und erweiterte Auflage, Wiesbaden.

Wilhelm, J. (1982): "Die Bereitschaft der Banken zur Risikoübernahme im Kreditgeschäft", Kredit und Kapital, 15, 572–601.

Wilhelm, J. (1985): Arbitrage Theory, Introductory Lectures on Arbitrage–Based Financial Asset Pricing, Berlin et al.

MANAGEMENT OF THE INTEREST RATE SWAPS PORTFOLIO UNDER THE NEW CAPITAL ADEQUACY GUIDELINES

Mario Levis and Victor Suchar
City University Business School

I. Introduction

The notional principal of interest rate swaps has exceeded $3 trillion by the end of 1990. The massive explosion of this market over the recent years was inevitable to attract the attention of bank regulators and highlight the risks and formidable organisational and technical challenges encountered by banks engaged in the intermediation of interest rate swaps. The academic literature, however, has been dominated by issues concerning the underlying rationale of interest rate swap transactions and the complexities of pricing and hedging such transactions. With the notable exceptions of a recent paper by Cooper and Mello (1991) the issues related to the default risk of swaps still remain largely unexplored in the academic literature.

Swap intermediaries must contend with two major kinds of risk: credit risk and price risk. Credit risk is the risk that a swap counterparty might fail to perform after the contract has commenced, thus subjecting the intermediary to a possible loss. The magnitude of such loss depends on the cost of re-establishing the swap's flow of interest payments at current interest rates. Exposure to price risk may arise without the occurrence of a default if a swap counterparty chooses not to hedge an open position swap and interest rates change from the day the contract was originated. The intermediary may fully hedge the potential price risk by entering into a pair of perfectly matched swaps, causing interest receipts to match interest payments.

To safeguard financial institutions against credit risk the Bank of International Settlements (BIS) has now issued definitive guidelines on bank capital adequacy requirements. They came into force in March 1989 but the recommended supervisory ratios in their final form become effective by the end of 1992 following gradual adjustments during the intermediate transition period. Although there is a widespread consensus in the market that these guidelines will eventually have far reaching implications on currency and interest rate swaps it is still not clear how and what extent the management of the swaps' portfolio by intermediating banks would be affected by the new regulatory framework.

The purpose of this paper is twofold: First, to assess the impact of the new capital adequacy guidelines on the profitability of interest rate swaps. We provide stylized estimates of the level of intermediation fees needed, for medium and long-term interest rate swaps, for banks to achieve their required rates of return on equity. Second, to investigate the potential impact of the guidelines on the functioning of the swap market in general and the operations and strategies of interbank swap traders in particular. Using a unique dataset of daily swap spreads we demonstrate that plain interbank swap trading is unlikely to generate an adequate level of profitability.

The rest of the paper is organised as follows. Section II provides an outline of the credit risk evaluation problem and a brief description of the BIS guidelines related to interest swaps. Section III, examines the implications of the requlatory framework on the return on equity of financial intermediaries. Section IV, outlines the problem of interest rate swap management under current market conditions while section V provides descriptive statistics of the stochastic process of interest rate swap spreads. Section VI uses historical and simulated data to assess the potential profitability of three warehouse management strategies. The conclusions and wider implications of this study are presented in section VII.

II. Credit Risk and the Capital Adequacy Guidelines

A. Credit Risk

The market value of a swap contract, $V(t)$, at any time during its maturity may be calculated as the difference between the present value of the cash flow expected to be received and the cash flow expected to be paid.

$$V(t) = PV(Receive) - PV(Pay) \qquad (1)$$

Default of the counterparty will result in a loss to the intermediary if the contract's market value is positive and in a profit if its is negative. In effect the loss to the financial institution is the cost of replacing the cash flows of the swap. This replacement cost would equal the discounted value of the differential between the original swap rate and the new rate on the replacement swap. However, although in theory a counterparty's default could result in a profit to the financial intermediary in practice such profits are unlikely to materialise. The rules of enforcement in such cases are quite complex[1] and depend on the specific clauses contained in the master agreement covering the swap transaction. On the assumption that a financial intermediary cannot realise a gain from a counterparty's default, its exposure on the swap at time t can be expressed as:

$$max[0, V(t)] \qquad (2)$$

The nature of this exposure may be thought of as equivalent to the payoff from writing a call option on the swap with zero exercise price. If there is no default, the call option never crystallizes. If a default takes place, the call option matures at the time of the default. The utilisation of an option type framework to the estimation of the value of the default option enables the intermediary to apply a systematic procedure - credit risk model - in determining expected exposures for different credit risk counterparties. Such a model, however, still depends on the subjective estimation of the probability of default for each individual counterparty. Hull (1989a) and Whittaker (1987) employed the option approach to provide stylized estimates of the value of the default option for currency and interest rate swaps respectively.

An alternative approach that has been extensively used for quantifying the swap credit risk is based on the Monte Carlo simulation technique. The purpose of the simulation is to assess

---

1 Price and Henderson (1988) point out that "the solvent party may find itself in a dilemma. Its right to terminate is not enforceable; it is required to make payments to the debtor while rates are against it; and when rates move in favour of the solvent party, the debtor ceases to perform and rejects the contract, leaving the solvent party with a claim of damages" (p. 143).

the average replacement cost of a matched pair of swaps, in case of a counterparty's default, under randomly generated interest rate scenarios. Assuming that default may occur at any time during the life of the swap, exposure is defined in terms of the distribution of average replacement cost on a matched pair of swaps. Thus, under certain assumptions about the stochastic processes underlying the market value of a swap, credit conversion factors can be obtained using a Monte Carlo simulation to sample the market value of the swap:

$$\alpha = \frac{E[\max(0, V(t))]}{H} \qquad (3)$$

α	-	credit conversion factor
H	-	principal amount of swap
$V(t)$	-	market value of swap at time t

The credit conversion factor describes the cost of replacing the contract, on the assumption that theoretical profits on default are not realizable, as a percentage of the notional principal of the swap. The simulation approach has been employed by the Federal Reserve and the Bank of England (1987) for devising the credit conversion factors incorporated in the BIS guidelines. Ferron and Handjinicolaou (1990) and Hull (1989b) have also estimated average credit conversion factors for interest rate swaps using a broadly similar simulation approach but different assumptions about the volatility of interest rates and the stochastic process of interest rate movements. Table 1 summarises the estimates of three simulation based studies and those of an option based approach.

Table 1
Estimates of Credit Conversion Factors for Interest Rate Swaps *

	Interest Rate Volatility	Maturity of the Swap in years: 1	5	10
Whittaker	22%	0.43%	3.15%	6.74%
Hull	15%	na	0.90%	2.50%
	20%	na	1.20%	3.30%
Ferron & Handjinicolau	15%	0.09%	1.12%	2.37%
	20%	0.12%	1.49%	3.13%
Fed/BoE:				
Average estimates	18.2%	0.10%	1.70%	4.20%
95% Confidence level	18.2%	0.30%	3.60%	9.10%

* Whittaker's (1987) estimates are based on an option valuation approach. Hall (1989b), Ferron and Handjinicolau (1990) and Fed/Bank of England (1987) estimates are based on a simulation approach.

B. Capital Adequacy Guidelines

The BIS guidelines for a common framework of credit risk assessment differ from previous regulations in two fundamental ways. First, they distinguish among different types of assets according to their degree of risk. Second, they explicitly bring into the regulatory framework all off-balance sheet items, like interest rate and currency swaps.

The classification of assets into different risk categories has risen out of regulators' concern that the traditional simple capital to asset ratio provides opportunities to some banks for circumventing existing regulations by portfolio realignment -i.e. increasing the proportion of their assets on high risk-high return assets. By establishing a direct link between the quality of assets and the bank's required capital, a shift towards higher risk business increases directly the required capital resources. On the other hand, the incorporation of off-balance sheet items into the capital adequacy framework reflects the increasing importance and risks inherent in this type of banking activities.

The new framework assesses capital adequacy for interest rate and currency swaps by relating the sum of the following two components to the level of capital.

1. The mark-to-market value of each contract (current credit exposure).
2. An estimate of the potential future credit exposure

The estimation of potential future credit exposure for an off-balance sheet item involves a two step process. First, the nominal amount of such an item is converted into a "credit equivalent" by multiplying it by the appropriate "credit conversion factor", as follows:

Credit Conversion Factors for Potential Future Credit Exposure of Interest Rate Swaps	
Remaining Maturity:	
One Year or less	0.0%
Over one year	0.5%

Second, the resulting credit equivalent is multiplied by a risk-weight (in the same way as on-balance sheet instruments) to produce the "risk adjusted credit equivalent". The recommended risk-weighted scheme reflects the degree of credit risk associated with the relevant category of the counterparty. According to the guidelines, assets have been assigned to five arbitrary risk categories using a simple 5, 10, 20, 50 and 100% weighting scheme. An overall weight of 50% has been suggested for corporate interest rate swap counterparties and a 20% for bank equivalents.

The new framework also defines a minimum Risk Asset Ratio of 8% (total capital over total risk adjusted credit equivalent) as a yardstick against which the capital adequacy of individual institutions would be monitored. The guidelines, however, distinguish between two components of capital: Tier 1 capital is the sum of paid up ordinary shares, general reserves, retained earnings, non-cumulative irredeemable preference shares and equity minority interests. This must represent at least 50% of the qualifying total capital. Thus, the minimum overall risk-asset ratio of 8% should include 4 percentage points in the form of Tier 1 capital elements. Tier 2 capital consists of general provisions for doubtful debts, asset revaluation reserves, cumulative irredeemable preference shares, mandatory convertible notes, perpetual subordinated debt, redeemable preference shares and term subordinated debt.

The mechanics of the BIS guidelines for estimating future potential exposure for an interest rate are best illustrated by the following numerical example:

Nominal Principal on a 3-year interest rate swap	$1,000,000
Credit Conversion Factor	0.5%
Credit Equivalent Amount	$50,000
Risk Weight	50%
Risk Adjusted Credit	$25,000
Total Capital Required	$2,000

III. The Implications of BIS guidelines

The main concern of the regulatory authorities in introducing the BIS guidelines is the strengthening of financial institutions' capital positions as a safeguard against credit risk. Financial institutions, however, have to ensure that they charge sufficient intermediation fees to achieve the required level of return on the equity capital tied up in the swap operations under the new guidelines. Such fees have to be set at the inception of the swap contract in such a way as to cover the intermediary bank for the *total exposure* during the entire swap's life. When current exposure is estimated by marking-to-market, its magnitude changes continuously in line with the movements of interest rates and time to maturity. It is zero at the specific moment of the origination of the swap but changes at each reporting date (usually twice a year). Thus, the actual capital employed over the life of a particular swap is only known at the maturity or termination of the contract. Swap intermediaries, however, need to have an estimate of the magnitude of the required capital right at the origination of the contract if they are to set intermediation fees to achieve a certain return on capital. The simulation and option based approaches, described in the previous section, provide a convenient technology for obtaining appropriate estimates of total exposure and capital required under the BIS guidelines.

To estimate the return on equity (RoE) and the level of intermediation fees[2] that a bank needs to charge to achieve a

---

2 Throughout this paper we refer to the *swap rate* as the fixed rate paid/received by the buyer/seller of the swap to/from the intermediating bank. The *swap spread* is the difference between the yield on the bench-mark Treasury security and the swap rate. The bid/offer spread in swap spreads is referred as the *intermediation fee*.

certain rate of return on equity we use the following equation.[3]

$$RoE = \frac{IF}{RAR \times T1 \times RW \times CV} \qquad (4)$$

IF - Basis points intermediation fee charged

RAR - Risk asset ratio

T1 - Proportion of Tier 1 capital

RW - Risk weight

CV - Conversion factor

To obtain RoE and intermediation fee estimates covering total exposure over the life of the swap, we use conversion factors derived from the simulation analysis by the Bank of England (1987).[4] The estimates for 3, 5, 7 and 10 year interest rate swaps

---

3 It could be argued that equation (4) underestimates the true return on equity since it assumes that the underlying Tier 1 capital is invested in a non-interest earning asset. Thus, a more precise estimate of the rate of return on equity should include a second term (*RF*) - the Risk-free rate earned on invested capital - in the nominator of equation (4). Depending on the particular capital structure - Tier 1 vs Tier 2 capital - of the bank this adjustment may have a material effect on the rate of return estimates. It should be noted, however, that any interest earned on the equity portion of capital may be more than offset by the interest payments by the bank on Tier 2 capital. At a 50-50 capital structure the above adjustment is practically immaterial.

4 The Bank of England simulation analysis assumes that interest rates and currencies follow a lognormal distribution and the term structure is flat. To account for changes in volatility over time, the estimates of standard deviations in the simulations are taken from the upper end (90% quantile) of observed annual volatilities for the five-year intervals ending 1981-86. The underlying rationale of this approach is to introduce an additional element of safety caution on the estimated conversion factors.

are shown at the bottom line of Table 1.

The various estimates of credit conversion factors shown in Table 1, clearly demonstrate that they depend not only on the interest rate volatility assumptions and the adopted methodological approach - simulation vs option valuation - but on the level of confidence that the swap intermediary requires in assessing the degree of total credit exposure. For the purposes of this study and in line with the Bank of England implicit recommendations we adopt a cautious view and calculate rates of return on equity based on a 95% confidence level. Thus, a credit conversion factor of 3.6%, for a 3-year swap, with a confidence limit of 95% would indicate that there is a 95% chance that the exposure on the swap would be less than 3.6% of the principal when a default occurs. The choice of the appropriate level of confidence is of course a matter of judgement but is equivalent to an explicit credit assessment of the swap counterparty. The higher the parameter of the probability distribution (confidence level) the higher the implied probability of default.[5]

Table 2 shows the rates of return on equity obtained on dollar[6] interest rate swaps of three to ten years maturities and intermediation fees between 1 and 15 basis points under two alternative, 20 and 50%, risk weights. Table 3, shows the basis points of intermediation fees per annum required to achieve gross

---

5 A similar simulation approach for the derivation of credit conversion factors is discussed in Hull (1989b). Instead of assuming a random probability of default during the life of the swap he introduces an arbitrary functional form describing the probability of default by a counterparty.

6 As the credit conversion factors used in (4) are based on volatility estimates for US interest rates, the estimates in Table 2 are applicable to dollar interest rate swaps only.

rates of return on equity between 20% to 55%.[7] Both sets of figures assume that the intermediating bank operates at the 8% minimum risk asset ratio required by the BIS guidelines and its capital structure consists of 50% Tier 1 capital. BIS guidelines stipulate that the minimum overall risk-asset ratio of 8% should include at least 4 percentage points in the form of Tier 1 capital elements. Thus, the estimates in Tables 2 show the maximum rates of return on equity that can be achieved under the BIS guidelines. In practice, most banks will find that their returns on equity at the different levels of intermediation fees are materially lower than those shown in this table since their capital structures include a higher than 50% Tier 1 capital. For the same reason, the basis points of intermediation fees to achieve a certain return on equity, in Table 3, represent minimum estimates. Reading down the third column in Table 2, for example, one finds the return on equity at 1 basis point intermediation fee for maturities 3 to 10 years for risk weights of 20 and 50%. If the intermediation fee is 1 basis point, then a swap of 5 years, for example, provides a return of 13.9% if the counterparty falls within the 50% risk weight category and 34.7% return on equity if the applied risk weight is 20%. It is important to note that the return on equity estimated here are before tax and gross of all operating expenses. Thus, if a financial institution requires a net after tax return on equity of say 20%, this would probably imply a rate of return on equity of about 50% gross.

A bank intermediating, for example, in a five year interest rate swap between another bank and a government entity may charge an intermediation fee of, say, 2 basis points per annum. According to the guidelines, the risk weight is 20% and the risk asset ratio 8%.

---

7 Both tables are based on the conversion factors of the Bank of England simulation at the 95% confidence level.

Table 2

% Rate of return on equity for an interest rate swap *

	% Risk	Basis points intermediation fee				
Years	Weight	1	5	9	11	15
3	20%	73.5	367.6	661.8	808.8	1102.9
	50%	29.4	147.1	264.7	323.5	441.2
5	20%	34.7	173.6	312.5	381.9	520.8
	50%	13.9	69.4	125.0	152.8	208.3
7	20%	21.9	109.6	197.4	241.2	328.9
	50%	8.8	43.9	78.9	96.5	131.6
10	20%	13.7	68.7	123.6	151.1	206.0
	50%	5.5	27.5	49.5	60.4	82.4

* Estimates are based on equation (4) and assume a Risk Asset Ratio of 8% and 50% Tier 1 capital.

Table 3

Basis points intermediation fee required for an interest rate swap *

	%Risk	% Return on equity				
Years	Weight	20	30	40	50	55
3	20%	0.3	0.4	0.5	0.7	0.7
	50%	0.7	1.0	1.4	1.7	1.9
5	20%	0.6	0.9	1.2	1.4	1.6
	50%	1.4	2.2	2.9	3.6	4.0
7	20%	0.9	1.4	1.8	2.3	2.5
	50%	2.3	3.4	4.6	5.7	6.3
10	20%	1.5	2.2	2.9	3.6	4.0
	50%	3.6	5.5	7.3	9.1	10.0

* Estimates are based on equation (4) and assume a Risk Asset Ratio of 8% and 50% Tier 1 capital.

Assuming that the intermediary operates at the 50% capital ratio and taking into account the conversion factor corresponding to a 95% confidence level, in Bank of England's simulation, the equity required per $1 million of nominal value is $288; this transaction provides a gross return on equity equal to 69.4%.[8] If, however, one of the counterparties in the swap is an AAA rated corporate, the intermediary may charge a fee of, say, 3 basis points per annum; in this case the resulting gross return on equity is only 41.6% Furthermore, if the corporate counterparty is BBB rated and the intermediary charges 5 basis points per annum (a premium of just 2 basis points over the AAA corporate) the resulting return on equity is 69.4%. The BIS guidelines only allow for a single risk weight for all corporate counterparties irrespective of their credit quality rating. Thus, strict adherence to the guidelines may be considered by some as an incentive to build portfolios of lower quality credits in order to achieve the required levels of return. Such an outcome, however, would be totally inconsistent with the overall objectives of the new regulatory framework.

Finally, it is important to note two critical issues which may affect the implications of the above analysis. First, is the question of the impact of capital structure on market value. Although, the implications of capital structure on the value of financial institutions awaits a rigourous theoretical analysis there are, nevertheless, some forceful arguments suggesting that the irrelevance proposition may not be applicable for such institutions. In addition to the complications arising from the explicit or implicit deposit insurance provided by governments to commercial banks, Sealey

8 Equity Required = Nominal Value of Asset x Risk Asset Ratio x Proportion of Tier 1 Capital x Risk Weight x Conversion Factor, -i.e. $288 = $1,000,000 x 0.08 x 0.5 x 0.2 x 0.036. Profit = $1,000,000 x 0.0002 = $200.

(1983) argues that the debt/equity analysis applied to corporate financial decisions independently of their operating activities is not appropriate in the case of banks because of the inter-related nature of their business and financing decisions. If capital structure matters, as the above arguments suggest then the imposition of the BIS guidelines may affect the required rate of return on equity and the overall cost of funds for interest rate swap activities. If, for example, the BIS guidelines prove binding on a financial intermediary then the required increase in equity may produce some reduction in the required on equity. Second, the analysis in this section assesses the implications of the BIS guidelines on interest rate swaps in isolation from the bank's other activities. It could be argued, therefore, that the above conclusions are valid in so far as the guidelines do not alter significantly the expected risk-return trade-off of the bank's portfolio of products and its utility preferences. To the extent that either of these assumptions is markedly violated then the financial institution would have to reconsider its portfolio of activities. In practice such analysis requires not only estimates of the expected risk and return of individual activities but calculation of their variance-covariance matrix as well. Such an assessment, however, is beyond the scope of this paper and for all practical purposes probably attainable only for specific institutions.

IV. Price Risk

In the early days of the swap market intermediaries merely brought together the two swap parties. The initial purpose in setting such transactions was to provide access by lower quality credits to the pool of fixed rate capital raised by top rated entities. The intermediary performed, in effect, a bridging (credit arbitrage) function between the easily accessible floating rate interbank market (the source of loans for lower but still respectable credits) and the relatively small quality oriented public markets tapped by highly rated entities. The simultaneous existence of the two swap parties resulted in a perfect match of swap inflows and outflows; in this case the intermediary was practically fully hedged; its income was equal to the difference between the interest paid and the interest received, the bid/offer spread.

Today the structure of this market is rather different. At least at a conceptual level, it can be regarded as two-layers market. The top layer is occupied by investment houses with a strong corporate basis. The majority of their swap transactions follows the traditional pattern of tailored-made swaps for individual clients seeking to reduce their cost of borrowing. Such swaps are matched either by counterparties aiming to fix their floating liabilities or other swap intermediaries prepared to commit capital to participate in the swap market. The nature and underlying rationale of the transaction itself ensures an adequate spread for the swap intermediary. The second layer of the market (interbank) consists almost entirely of swap intermediaries with very limited or nonexistent corporate basis. They concentrate on the high-volume, low margin products attempting to generate profits on the bid/offer spread, -i.e. they will take one side of an interest swap with one interbank participant and try to match it with another interbank counterparty earning a narrow spread.

Before the introduction of the BIS guidelines, an intermediary could run, at least in theory, the entire swap book without any equity or long-term capital. The guidelines, however, force an explicit consideration of the credit risk by imposing a capital requirement against the nominal value of the swap. Thus, interbank market participants will have now to earn, according to our estimates in Table 2, intermediation fees ranging from 1 to 4 basis points per annum, depending on maturity, if they were to achieve a gross return on equity of 50 percent. On the basis of recent market experience (4 to 6 basis points of intermediation fees for short to medium term swaps) such level of profitability appears plausible. In the interbank market, however, intermediation fees are in effect considerably tighter. If, for example, an interbank participant bids, say for 50 basis points, it is rather unlikely that a potential interbank counterparty would be prepared to bid for anything significantly higher at the same point in time. Although it is difficult to obtain an adequate intermediation fee at the same point in time, it is, nevertheless, feasible to secure the required fee at some later stage due to a subsequent favourable movement of swap spreads. If the attainment of an adequate intermediation fee, either instantaneously or within a short time is considered unfeasible, the swap intermediary may choose to unload the original swap transaction to the market for a very narrow margin. Consider, for example, the case of a swap intermediary (A) who entered into a swap agreement with another interbank player (B) and simultaneously hedged the transaction with treasury securities; intermediary (A) concluded that this swap cannot be closed profitably in the interbank market and decided to sell it to another swap intermediary (C) for 0.5 basis point. In this case, of course, the capital adequacy guidelines do not apply and there is no need for capital maintenance. It should be noted, however, that even this latter type of operation creates problems. The new counterparty (C) to whom the swap was sold to may be unacceptable to the original counterparty (B), either due to credit quality considerations or current credit lines availability.

The strategy adopted by a number of swap players, as a means of generating adequate intermediation fees, is active "warehouse" management, -i.e. buying and selling each swap independently. A swap may be originated before the offsetting side has been arranged, kept for a certain time period and closed when a suitable counterparty is found. Thus, while the warehouse was originally set to sort out the logistical problems of marketing the transaction to suitable counterparties, it has now acquired an entirely new dimension. The length of time intermediaries are prepared to carry an open position varies across institutions. Some intermediaries seek to close their book by the end of the day while others are willing to carry an open swap for weeks. Banks, however, may also use their swap warehouses to facilitate the generation of profits by attempting to close the second swap at a better rate than the initial one. With the introduction of BIS guidelines active warehouse management may emerge as the prime vehicle for profit generation for swap participants in the interbank market.

During the period that a swap is in the warehouse (unmatched) it is always at least partially hedged. The hedging can be done using either future contracts or the Treasury bond market. In the latter case, for example, the intermediary paying the fixed rate in an interest rate swap, buys the current five-year Treasury note to hedge itself, creating a long position to hedge its short position in the swap. This hedging strategy is based on duration analysis of the Treasury bond and the fixed rate paying swap. The amount of the Treasury hedge should be such as to equate the sensitivity to changes in the term structure of the total values of the fixed side of the swap to the Treasury hedge instrument.

Suppose the intermediary enters into a three-year swap with a corporation when the yield (T) on three-year US Treasuries is 10%. It pays 10% plus 40 basis points in exchange for six-month LIBOR and hedges the swap temporarily with Treasury notes. A few days later, the dealer closes the swap. In the interim the spread has remained constant at T+40 (bid), T+45 (offer), but the yield on three-year US Treasuries has fallen to 9%. In this case the intermediary losses 95 basis points on the notional principal at every payment date. This loss, however, is offset by the gain on the Treasury holdings. Thus, the Treasury hedge covers the dealer against movements in interest rate levels during the warehousing period.

Assuming parallel shifts in the term structure the duration based treasury hedge provides full cover against interest rate movements during the warehousing period. The bank, however, is still exposed to a certain degree of risk due to fluctuations of the swap spreads over treasuries. If there was a strong correlation between swap spreads and treasury yields the warehouse manager could hedge the swap spread exposure by topping-up the amount of the treasury hedge. Alternatively, the spread exposure could be hedged by maintaining a balanced portfolio of fixed paying and receiving swaps. Assuming in this case parallel shifts in the term structure of spreads a balanced warehouse portfolio of unmatched swap maturities can be regarded as self-hedging.

Thus, the efficacy of the immunization approach to warehouse management depends on the empirical behaviour of three factors. First, the correlation of treasury yields across the term structure. Second, the relation of swap spread and treasury yields. Third, the correlation of swap spreads across different maturities (the swap spreads term structure).

V. The Behaviour of Swap Spreads

Data for daily interest rate swap spreads has been provided by Barclays Bank plc. They are swap spreads used by Barclays in their 'indication pricing schedules'. Such schedules assume transactions of a standard type; in practice transactions may differ in a number of ways depending on commencement dates, transaction size, spreads above or below the floating rate index, various mis-matches, premium or discounts or reimbursement of issue fees and expenses. Spread adjustments are usually necessary to accommodate these variations. Nevertheless, the spreads from indication pricing schedules form the basis of all such possible subsequent adjustments.

Table 4 shows descriptive statistics for the levels of swap spreads of different maturities during the period December 11, 1986 to May 16, 1989 (628 daily observations). The average swap spreads ranged from 78 basis points for 3 year swaps to 90 basis points for the long 10 year swap indicating an average positively sloping term structure for swap spreads during the period under consideration. An examination of the daily percentage changes in swap spreads, in Table 5, suggests that 3 year swap spreads are markedly more volatile than their longer counterparts. As the short end of this market is predominated by the funding and hedging activities of banks this pattern of volatilities is not surprising.

Table 4

Descriptive statistics for swap spreads levels (basis points) *

	3-Years	5-Years	7-Years	10-Years
Mean	78	84	87	90
Standard deviation	11.6	12.9	13.6	14.9
Minimum	53	53	57	58
Maximum	128	122	118	124
Skewness	0.392	0.017	-0.265	0.160

* Daily data over the period December 11, 1986 to May 16, 1989 (628 observations). The swap spread is defined as the difference between the yield on the bencmark Treasury security and the swap rate of the same maturity.

The autocorrelations and partial autocorrelation coefficients of the daily changes in swap spreads reveal noticeable departures from the serial independence assumption. Significant positive autocorrelations of first, second or third order are apparent in the daily movements of swap spreads for all four maturities. The presence of serial dependence patterns are important if they lend themselves to effective utilisation in devising profitable warehouse management techniques.

Table 5
Descriptive statistics of daily swap spread percentage changes

	3-Years	5-Years	7-Years	10-Years
Mean	-0.02	-0.06	-0.06	-0.06
Stand. deviation	2.37	1.50	1.34	1.26
Minimum	-9.26	-8.06	-6.56	-8.82
Maximum	12.67	11.58	11.11	9.90
Skewness	1.25	1.03	1.11	0.78
Autocorrelations:				
r_1	0.097*	0.235*	0.216*	0.101*
r_2	0.016	0.183*	0.119*	0.115*
r_3	0.042	0.149*	0.079	0.066
Partials:				
p_1	0.097*	0.235*	0.216*	0.101*
p_2	0.008	0.135*	0.076	0.106*
p_3	0.041	0.086*	0.041	0.049

* significant at 5%

The discussion in section III suggests that the effectiveness of the immunization approach to price risk critically depends on the pattern of shifts of the treasury yields term structure, the relationship of swap spreads movements to changes in the term structure and the correlation of swap spreads at different maturities. Table 6, panel A, shows significant correlations among daily swap spread changes at different maturities. The correlation coefficients range from 0.304 to 0.616; the short end of the market appears again to behave markedly differently from the longer maturities. In spite of the positive and often significant correlations it is doubtful whether they are sufficient to provide a reliable hedge on a duratîon based strategy. It is also worth noticing that the relationships of swap spread changes across the four maturities are also remarkably weaker than the equivalent relationships across the Treasury yield changes (panel B) for the same ladder of maturities.

Table 6

Correlation coefficients for daily swap spread changes and Treasury yield changes

A. Swap spreads changes across different maturities

	3-Years	5-Years	7-Years
5-Years	0.408		
7-Years	0.304	0.605	
10-Years	0.324	0.515	0.616

B. Treasury yields changes across different maturities

	3-Years	5-Years	7-Years
5-Years	0.784		
7-Years	0.779	0.883	
10-Years	0.740	0.866	0.840

C. Cross correlations of swap spreads and treasuries changes

	Swap spreads			
Treasuries	3-years	5-years	7-years	10-years
3-years	0.092	-0.052	-0.044	-0.045
5-years	0.156	-0.005	-0.028	-0.045
7-years	0.120	-0.002	-0.017	-0.074
10-years	0.139	-0.011	-0.018	-0.052

The non-significant correlation coefficients between daily swap spread changes and equivalent changes in Treasuries' yields (panel C) casts even further doubts to the efficacy of the immunization approach on hedging price risk. It is clear that the swap spread risk cannot be hedged with treasuries only; immunization of this type of risk requires an instrument whose rate movements are positively correlated with swap spread changes. Cornell (1986) suggests a broad correlation between the swaps spread between the 3 month T-bill and LIBOR rates. This suggests that the swap spread could be potentially hedged using a "TED" spread in the T-bill and Eurodollar futures markets. Our analysis, for the period under consideration in this study, failed to detect any material correlation between the above variables. In this context it is also worth noting that there is a strong positive relation (about 0.7) between swap spreads and the term structure of treasury yields. This is consistent with the notion that swap spreads widen when future interest rates are expected to rise. The demand to buy interest rate swaps stems mainly from medium rated entities wishing to fix the cost of their liabilities. If interest rates are expected to rise, such borrowers would prefer to be fixed-rate payers locking-in the current, relatively low, interest rate. This increased demand for interest rate swaps exerts upward pressure on swap spreads.

VI. The Profitability of the Warehouse

The potential profitability of swap warehousing is evaluated using both historical and simulated data of interest rate swap spreads. The historical analysis provides an exact assessment of warehouse profitability for the period December 1986 to May 1989. The purpose of the simulation model is to evaluate the same trading strategies under a wider set of market conditions than those prevailed during this specific period. Both types of analyses depend on:

1. The maximum acceptable length of the warehousing period.
2. The loss tolerance of the swap manager.
3. The swap trading strategy in operation.

The simulation model, however, also depends on the assumed stochastic process of swap spreads. Based on the evidence presented in section IV, daily strings of swap spreads are generated by a simulation model utilising the autoregressive patterns shown in Table 5. Thus, the swap spread (S_t) of a certain maturity at day t is given by:

$$S_t = S_{t-1} + \phi_1(S_{t-1} - S_{t-2}) + \phi_2(S_{t-2} - S_{t-3}) + \ldots + \phi_p(S_{t-p} - S_{t-p-1}) + \epsilon_t$$

where: $\phi_1 \ldots \phi_p$ - p_{th} order autoregressive parameter
ϵ_t - error term

The length of the warehousing period varies markedly among financial institutions. If a swap intermediary is to benefit from warehousing swaps the transaction has to be closed at a better rate than the one entered at the inception of the swap. Swap intermediaries may choose to close transactions as soon as a suitable counterparty becomes available or at some point when it is considered profitable to do so depending on the expected movements of spreads. Of course as warehousing incurs carry-costs a swap will have to be closed at some point even if such closure means taking a loss. If, for example, the maximum allowed length of warehousing is 25 days the intermediary will close at day 25 even if at an unfavourable rate. Alternatively the warehouse manager may decide to cut losses and close a transaction before the end of the full warehousing period (stop-loss limit) if it is perceived that there is nothing to be gained by extending the warehousing of a particular swap. For the purposes of the analysis in this study two arbitrary warehousing periods - 25 and 50 days - and a stop-loss limit of 5 basis points are assumed.

Based on these fundamental underlying considerations both historical data and a simulation model are used to assess the swap manager's potential of attaining a target intermediation fee during the warehousing period. For the purposes of this analysis three alternative trading strategies are considered:[9]

1. A naive strategy assumes that the warehouse manager has no knowledge of the autoregressive pattern of swap spreads and thus no attempt is made to exploit this pattern. Thus, a swap is closed at the first day of the warehousing period when spreads have moved above the spread of the original swap; if no such opportunity arises during the whole of the warehousing the swap is closed at whatever loss is incurred at the last assumed day of warehousing. The maintenance of an open position over the entire duration of the assumed warehousing period may result in substantial losses when swap spreads are constantly moving against the swap intermediary. This strategy is clearly inefficient since it aims to lock-in a certain level of profit regardless of the future path of swap spread movements. Thus, swap positions may be closed (maintained) sooner (longer) than is optimal.
2. A naive strategy with a stop-loss is similar to the above strategy but assumes that the swap manager will close a position and cut losses as soon as such losses exceed 5 basis points.
3. A autoregressive strategy with a stop-loss aims to exploit the known historical pattern of swap spread movements. Thus on a daily basis the swap manager observes the prevailing swap spreads and makes a decision between: (1) closing the swap

9 The trading strategies under consideration in this paper are adopted as useful benchmarks to judge the level of skill required to generate adequate intermediation fees under the new capital adequacy guidelines. It is indeed possible that other trading strategies, not tested in this paper and not known to us, may indeed prove more profitable.

immediately, to lock-in a potential profit, or (2) postponing the swap-closure for one more day. The decision as to whether to maintain the open position for another day depends on the expected market value of the swap, which in turn is a function of the movement of swap spreads during the previous day. If, for example, the intermediary is paying the fixed rate, in the original swap, it will keep the position open so far as the spread movement in the previous day is positive. A positive daily change in swap spreads implies that spreads will continue on an upward trend, thus maximising the profit to the swap intermediary. Chen and Millon (1989) demonstrate that the optimal decision rule for the swap manager is to close the swap immediately if the current market value of the swap is higher than its expected value and postpone the swap-closure if the reverse is the case. Thus, a rise in daily swap spread is a necessary but not a sufficient condition for the swap warehouse manager to close the swap.

Testing of the three trading strategies requires utilisation of 25 (50) consecutive days swap spreads data. In the first instance, for example, the historical analysis assumes that the original swap is entered at spreads prevailing on December 11th, 1986 and kept open for the next 25 (50) days. The difference between the spread in the original and closing swap constitutes the annual profit (loss) over this first trial period. Using rolling 25 (50) days windows, equivalent profits (losses) are estimated for a subsequent 602 (for 25 days warehousing periods) or 577 (for 50 days warehousing periods) trial periods. Profits and losses for all trials are assembled to provide the cumulative distribution results reported in the following tables. The simulation model operates in a similar fashion but the equivalent strings of daily swap spreads for each trial period are generated by equation (2) and the autocorrelation coefficients in Table 5. The reported simulation results are based on 10,000 independent trials.

Table 7 summarises the results of the historical analysis while Table 8 reports similar results for the simulated swap spreads data. They show the probabilities of achieving more than a certain number of basis points per annum for warehousing periods of 25 and 50 days. Panels A, B and C of each table, present the results for the naive, naive with a stop-loss and autoregressive with a stop-loss strategies respectively.

A cursory inspection of Table 7 is sufficient to indicate that none of the three trading strategies for either 25 or 50 days of maximum warehousing period, is capable of generating the level of profitability imposed by the capital adequacy guidelines if the gross required return on equity is 50%. Our estimates in Table 3 suggested that to achieve a gross 50% return on equity, financial institutions in the interbank market will have to charge intermediation fees on interest rate swaps ranging from 0.7 to 3.6 basis points per annum. The results based on the historical data demonstrate that even under the autoregressive strategy with 50 days maximum warehousing period the probability of attaining more than 1 basis point profit from warehousing activities is only 44.3% for 3 year swaps. The probability of achieving the 3.6 basis points required for a ten year swap is below 20.3% under the autoregressive strategy and less than 6.6% under either one of the naive strategies.

The implementation of a stop-loss strategy has only a marginal negative effect on the probability of achieving positive returns but reduces markedly the probability of large losses. It is worth noting, however, that the operational stop-loss has to be set at a level considerably lower than the actual loss that the intermediary is in effect prepared to sustain. In other words, if todays' loss is say 4 basis points (below the assumed operational of 5 basis points) and the position is left open, swap spreads could move over the next day well outside the operational limit. Given the

Table 7

Warehouse profitability ofthree alternative strategies based on historical swap spreads data *

	Maturity of interest rate swap							
	3 Years		5 Years		7 Years		10 Years	
	Warehousing period (Days)							
	25	50	25	50	25	50	25	50
Basis Points	Probability of achieving more than a number of basis points							
A. Naive strategy								
3	13.0	13.7	4.2	5.4	5.1	6.5	5.1	6.6
2	24.5	23.8	8.1	11.6	9.0	10.5	7.8	9.3
1	40.3	39.2	19.3	24.2	19.6	21.9	17.9	20.1
0	76.6	80.7	65.3	76.2	65.5	73.2	66.8	76.9
-12	92.4	89.3	94.6	88.6	96.1	91.6	97.5	92.3
B. Naive strategy with a Stop-Loss								
3	12.5	12.3	3.9	4.0	4.7	5.6	5.7	5.8
2	23.7	22.4	6.9	7.4	7.6	8.8	9.0	8.8
1	36.4	37.6	19.1	20.1	17.8	16.3	18.3	18.9
0	69.4	72.7	66.3	69.3	61.8	65.0	65.5	69.9
-12	97.3	98.2	99.5	99.6	99.8	99.1	99.5	99.5
C. Autoregressive strategy with a Stop-Loss								
3	26.7	25.6	22.7	23.3	21.8	17.8	16.2	20.3
2	34.3	34.8	31.3	29.9	27.7	23.1	21.7	26.3
1	41.8	44.3	42.8	43.6	36.5	34.5	32.1	35.2
0	55.2	58.0	58.5	61.3	52.1	48.7	51.9	61.8
-12	95.6	96.5	99.9	99.6	99.7	99.6	99.3	99.5

* Probability estimates are based on actual swap spreads during the period December 11, 1986 to May 16, 1989. For definitions of the three trading strategies see text.

historical volatility of swap spread changes a strategy with a 5 basis points stop-loss limit it can still result in losses of twice than level.

Extending the length of the warehousing period is not always beneficial to the swap manager. Given the pattern of daily swap spread movements it appears that only in about 50% of the cases a profit opportunity will arise for closing a swap after day 25 from its origination. In fact, results not reported in this paper, suggest that under the first two trading strategies less than 2% of the swaps are closed after day 25. The average period of holding a position open with either one of the naive strategies is about 5 days.

The simulation results in Table 8 confirm the conclusions drawn from the historical analysis. The overall pattern of probability distributions is very similar to that emerged from the historical analysis, although the actual probabilities of achieving positive returns are marginally higher. In spite, however, of the overall "optimistic" nature of the simulated results it is still apparent that none of the trading strategies under consideration is capable of generating the intermediation fees implied by the Basle guidelines. Thus, swap intermediaries actively managing a warehoused swap portfolio cannot expect to generate consistent profits by pure screen trading without superior predictive ability on the daily movements of swap spreads. Forecasts based entirely on the historical data alone are undoubtedly of some value, in comparison to naive strategies, but they still cannot be relied on to generate consistent profits. In that sense, additional insight on the fundamental pattern of swap spreads movements could be of considerable value in designing effective warehouse management strategies.

Table 8

Warehouse profitability under three alternative strategies based on simulated swap spreads data *

	Maturity of interest rate swap							
	3 Years		5 Years		7 Years		10 Years	
	Warehousing period (Days)							
	25	50	25	50	25	50	25	50
Basis Points	Probability of achieving more than a number of basis points							
A. Naive strategy								
3	15.3	15.3	3.1	3.3	1.7	1.7	1.2	1.0
2	31.3	32.5	13.6	14.7	10.3	10.7	7.8	8.1
1	54.2	59.1	40.7	41.3	35.5	38.7	33.1	35.2
0	88.1	91.0	85.7	89.7	87.3	90.4	88.9	90.6
-12	93.1	92.7	92.8	92.8	96.3	95.6	97.7	95.2
B. Naive strategy with a Stop-Loss								
3	13.2	13.1	3.6	3.2	1.7	1.7	0.9	1.3
2	27.6	27.2	13.0	12.9	9.6	9.7	7.0	7.2
1	49.1	48.8	36.2	36.3	33.7	34.2	31.3	31.2
0	77.7	76.5	78.4	78.6	83.1	82.8	84.1	83.6
-12	99.9	99.9	99.9	99.9	99.9	99.9	99.9	99.9
C. Autoregressive strategy with a Stop-Loss								
3	30.5	33.1	34.5	35.2	30.3	31.4	29.9	29.6
2	38.8	41.2	41.3	41.7	38.2	40.0	38.2	38.6
1	48.4	49.8	50.3	50.7	49.6	51.1	48.1	49.0
0	60.3	61.3	62.5	62.5	64.6	66.7	63.0	65.1
-12	99.9	99.9	99.9	99.9	99.9	99.9	99.9	99.9

* Probability estimates are based on 10,000 independent trials of simulated swap spreads. For definitions of the three trading strategies see text.

VII. Conclusions

In this paper we investigated some of the implications of the BIS guidelines on interest rate swaps. First, it is argued that the method proposed by BIS for estimating the amount of capital required to comply with the guidelines is not suitable for estimating the level of intermediation fees that an institution has to charge on an interest rate swap to achieve a target return on equity. Since intermediation fees are set at the inception of a swap transaction, and remain fixed over its entire maturity, while the amount of capital required against such a transaction changes during the swap's life, financial institutions have to address the estimation of capital required and swap pricing as two separate issues. Using a simple methodological framework we provide stylized estimates of the likely rates of return on equity on interest rate swap transactions under different assumptions of intermediation fees, risk weights and swap maturities.

Second, our empirical investigation of daily swap spreads suggests some departures from serial independence. Moreover, the absence of any significant relations between swap spreads and treasury yields casts doubts to the effectiveness of an immunization approach to price risk. The results of our simulation analysis demonstrate that simple trading strategies on interest rate swaps in the interbank market are not capable of generating the level of intermediation fees implied by the BIS guidelines.

Finally, it is worth noting that from a practioner's point of view our evidence tends to suggest that swap activities conducted only within the interbank market and with highly rated counterparties is unlikely to be profitable. The intermediary operating under these circumstances cannot earn a sufficient return on the capital required under the BIS guidelines since it depends only on a favourable movement of swap spreads while the transaction is warehoused.

References

Bank of England, 1987, Potential Credit Exposure on Interest Rate and Foreign Exchange Rate Related Instruments, Bank of England.

Beidleman, C., 1985, Financial Swaps, Dow Jones-Irwin.

Chen, A. and M. Millon, 1989, The Secondary Market and Dynamic Swap Management, Recent Developments in International Banking and Finance, S. J. Khoury and A. Ghosh (eds.), McGraw-Hill Company.

Cooper, I. and A. Mello, 1991, The Default Risk of Swaps, The Journal of Finance, pp. 597-620.

Cornell, B., 1986, Pricing Interest Rate Swaps: Theory and Empirical Evidence," Working Paper presented at the New York University Conference on Swaps and Hedges.

Ferron, M. and G. Handjinicolaou, 1990, Understanding Swap Credit Risk: The Simulation Approach, The Handbook of Currency and Interest Rate Risk Management, R.J. Schwartz and C. W. Smith, New York Institute of Finance.

Hull, J., 1989a, Assessing Credit Risk in a Financial Institution's Off-Balance Sheet Commitments, Journal of Financial and Quantitative Analysis, pp. 489-501.

Hull, J., 1989b, An Analysis of the Credit Risks in Interest Rate Swaps and Currency Swaps, Recent Developments in International Banking and Finance, S. J. Khoury and A. Ghosh, McGraw-Hill Company.

Price, J. and S. Henderson, 1988, Currency and Interest Rate Swaps, Butterworths.

Sealey, C.W., 1983, Valuation, Capital Structure and Shareholder Unanimity for Depository Financial Intermediaries, Journal of Finance, pp. 857-872.

Whittaker, G. 1987, Interest Rate Swaps: Risk and Regulation, Economic Review, Federal Reserve Bank of Kansas City, pp. 3-13.

DEVELOPING A MULTINATIONAL INDEX FUND

Nigel Meade, The Management School, Imperial College

Two approaches to portfolio selection from a multinational universe are described. The problem is addressed in the context of selecting a fund to track a multinational equity index such as Eurotrack 100. However, the results are general and can be applied whatever the objective of fund selection.

The additional dimension that a multinational universe brings to the portfolio selection problem is that of foreign exchange risk coupled with the differing economic performance of the nations considered.

The recently introduced Eurotrack 100 index considers eleven countries in mainland Europe (i.e. not including the United Kingdom). The constituents of this index are used to define the universe that is examined here.

The essence of quantitative portfolio selection is the estimation of the covariance matrix of returns of the assets considered; thus the main theme of the paper is the parsimonious modelling of the structure of this matrix. The approaches considered are an arbitrage pricing model and a multi-index model using national equity indices.

1. Introduction

The recent introduction of two European index options on the FTSE Eurotrack 100 and the Eurotop 100 is evidence of a demand from investors to hedge pan-European risk. The FTSE Eurotrack 100 was designed to closely resemble the longer established and widely quoted Morgan Stanley European index.

The Eurotrack 100 covers a hundred companies in eleven countries in continental Europe. The index is denominated in DM and a breakdown by value into the different countries covered is given in figure 1.

Figure 1

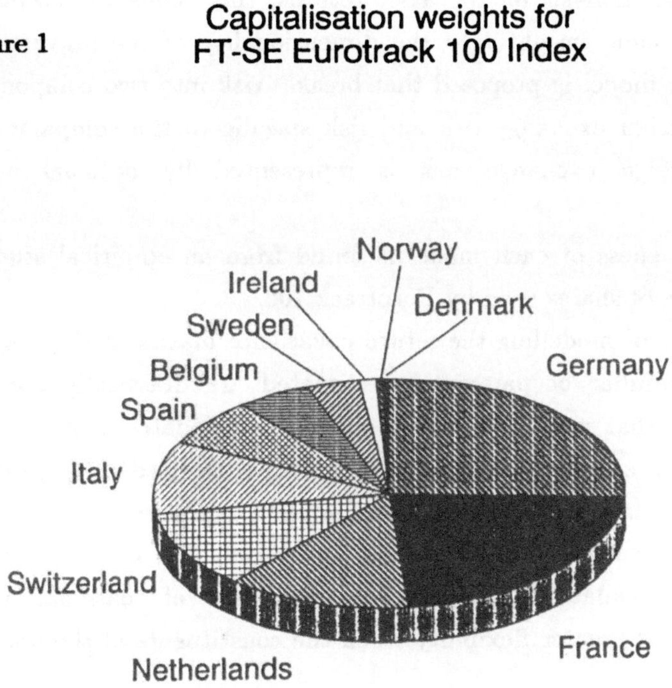

Another recently introduced European index is the Eurotop 100 index denominated in ECUs, this index contains twenty two UK companies which represent 27% by value of this index.

The attraction of investments in these indices is that they provide a basis for weighted exposure to Europe, investors can then build on this basis by investment in individual countries.

The multinational context of the universe of shares defined by this index raises some new questions for the selection of portfolios, whether the portfolios are chosen for absolute performance or to track the index. Various possible objectives of portfolio selection will be discussed, in all cases the crucial role of the covariance matrix of returns is clear.

The extra source of risk present in a multinational portfolio is the combination of country risk coupled with foreign exchange risk. Two models of the return covariance matrix are proposed and examined.

The arbitrage pricing model of Ross(1976) is used, this involves the use of factor analysis on the asset returns; this yields the useful by-product of some insight into the dimensionality of the universe. A multi-index model is proposed that breaks risk into two components: country/foreign exchange risk and risk specific to the company. The country/foreign exchange risk is represented by national equity indices.

The effectiveness of each model is found from an empirical study of the universe of shares used by Eurotrack 100.

The benefits of modelling the return covariance matrix in this way are that the number of parameters estimated are drastically reduced. This means that portfolios can be created and updated more quickly, the overall size of the optimisation problem is reduced calling for less resources of time and computing equipment. There are particular advantages associated with the multi-index model in terms of greater simplicity, availability of external forecasts of national index behaviour and greater flexibility when the constituents of the universe change.

2. Modelling the covariance matrix

Consider a universe of N shares from which a portfolio is to be selected. The return on share i at time t is modelled below:

$$X_{i,t} = \mu_{i,t} + v_{i,t} \quad \text{for } i=1,\ldots\ldots,N \tag{1}$$

The covariance matrix of returns is Σ_t where

$\text{Cov}(X_{i,t}, X_{j,t}) = \text{Cov}(v_{i,t}, v_{j,t}) = \Sigma_{i,j,t}$ for $i=1,\ldots,N$ and $j=1,\ldots,N$

and

$\text{Cov}(v_{i,t}, v_{j,t+k}) = 0$ for all $k \neq 0$

and

$E(v_{i,t}) = 0$.

The investor's decision variables are ϕ_i (i=1,...,N), the proportions of the initial capital available to be invested in share i, where $\phi_i \geq 0$ and

$$\sum_{i=1}^{N} \phi_i = 1$$

The aims of the investor, the fund manager, range from risk minimisation to index tracking. There are many ways of formulating the objective function, a selection of rational objective functions are given in appendix 1.

2i) The arbitrage pricing model: Ross(1976) put forward the Arbitrage Pricing Theory (APT) of capital asset pricing. The return on an asset is determined by a number, J, of orthogonal factors $F_{j,t}$ where $E(F_{j,t}) = 0$.

$$X_{k,t} = \mu_{k,t} + \sum_{j=1}^{J} \pi_{k,j,t} F_{j,t} + \epsilon^{a}_{k,t}$$

The factors are derived from an analysis of the past history of the returns on the N assets, no other information is used. The covariance of returns, Σ, can be written as follows:

$$\underset{(NxN)}{\Sigma} = \underset{(NxJ)(JxJ)(JxN)}{\Pi \quad \Lambda \quad \Pi'} + \underset{(NxN)}{D} \tag{2}$$

where $\Pi_{k,j} = \pi_{k,j,t}$ and Λ is the covariance matrix of the factors. The factors are chosen to be orthogonal so that the off-diagonal elements are zero. D is the "own" variance matrix with the kth diagonal element $V(\epsilon^a_{k,t})$ and the off-diagonal elements zero. The determination of J, the number of factors is a subjective part of the factor analysis procedure; (Roll and Ross (1980) use a χ^2 criterion).
The APT can be summarised as an explicit attempt to condense the covariance structure of returns as far as practicable without significant loss of information.

2ii) The multi-index model: the capital asset pricing model (CAPM) of Sharpe(1963,1964), Mossin(1966) and Lintner(1965) is the best known model of the covariance matrix. It assumes that all the pairwise relationships measured in the covariance matrix can be described in terms of market risk, the relationship between the share and the market index, and specific company risk.
In simplified terms, the return on share i is

$$X_i = \beta_i I + \epsilon_i$$

and the covariance matrix is

$$\Sigma = \beta' V(I) \beta + \mathrm{diag}(V(\epsilon_i)).$$

Multi-index models have been devised for single nation portfolios, see Elton and Gruber(1987) for examples. However they have not been shown to be demonstrably better than the CAPM.
The model proposed below exploits the multinational nature of the

universe of shares:

$$X_{i,c,t} = \alpha_{0ic} + \alpha_{1ic} C_{c,t} + \epsilon_{i,t} \qquad (3)$$

where share i is quoted in country c. $C_{c,t}$ is the return on a quoted market index in country c at time t (c=1,..,M). $\epsilon_{i,t}$ is the residual variation specific to share i.

This means that the covariance matrix Σ can be represented thus:

$$\underset{(NxN)}{\Sigma} = \underset{(NxM)}{\alpha} \underset{(MxM)}{\Sigma_c} \underset{(MxN)}{\alpha}' + \underset{(NxN)}{\sigma} \qquad (4)$$

Σ_c is the covariance matrix of the returns on the national equity indices,

α is an (NxM) matrix with one non-zero element in each row α_{1ic} and

σ is diag($V(\epsilon_i)$).

3) Empirical analysis

The data used for this analysis run from 1 January 1986 to 16 October 1991, they are the prices of the shares of the companies forming Eurotrack 100 as at 15 July 1991. The data, which are weekly, were taken from Datastream, the number of companies for which data were available decreases as time goes back to 1986.

Other data necessary for the analysis were the foreign exchange rates to convert all prices to DM (Eurotrack is denominated in DM); the values of the national equity indices for each of the eleven countries in Eurotrack were collected. The names of the companies and of the indices are listed in appendix 2.

The data were converted to series of weekly returns and broken down into three two year blocks to examine the stability of the models over time.

3i) Factor analysis of the returns data: Factor analysis is the statistical technique underlying the APT. The statistical package SAS was used.

Firstly the correlation matrix of returns, R, is calculated. Then a spectral decomposition of the correlation matrix is carried out, this identifies the principle factors of the data. These are linear combinations of the returns on the companies, chosen in descending order of their power to explain the generalised variance of the data set, $|R|$. It is this exercise that yields insight in to the dimensionality of the data. The results of this part of the analysis are shown in table 1.

Table 1 Dimensionality of the return data

	1986-7	1988-9	1990-1
% variation explained by 10 factors	71.6	59.0	68.7
% variation explained by 20 factors	84.5	75.2	82.0
No. of factors to explain >60% of $\|R\|$	5	11	7
No. of factors to explain >70% of $\|R\|$	10	17	11
No. of factors to explain >80% of $\|R\|$	16	25	19
No. of factors to explain >90% of $\|R\|$	28	38	31

The first and third data sets from 1986-7 and 1990-1 exhibit the same level of dimensionality, the middle set requires more factors to explain a given level of variation. An explanation possibly lies in the differing rates of recovery after the October 1987 slump.

The choice of the number of factors to be used in the subsequent analysis to represent the correlation matrix is mainly subjective. The choice is helped by being able to label the different factors in an intuitively satisfactory manner. A reasonable choice in each case was eleven factors, the same number in each time period was chosen to aid comparability.

After the number of factors has been decided they can then be rotated to aid their interpretation. The Varimax criterion was used, this puts either very high or very low weightings on the loading of each company on the factors, the similarities between the heavily loaded companies on each factor suggest a name for the factor.

The naming of the factors for the three time periods is given in table 2. There are six or seven clear national factors in each time period. The placings of the German, Italian and French companies in the first three positions, in terms of variation explained, are maintained throughout. Belgian, Irish, Swiss and Swedish companies group together consistently but their ranking in terms of variation explained changes over time. The only industrial sector that appears is oil, represented by Total, Elf and Royal Dutch Shell, Petrofina stayed within the Belgian factor. Although the Dutch companies rank third in terms of market value, a Dutch factor never appeared. This is because there are only five companies including Royal Dutch Shell, the highest weighted company in Eurotrack (7.7%) and Unilever (2.3%), their business is international and any common national influence is comparatively weak.

3ii) A multi-index model of the returns data: the model defined in (3) was fitted to the data over thc same three time periods. The correlations associated with these regressions were averaged for each country, in order to give a rough impression of how well the variations of company returns were modelled by the national equity indices. The results are shown in table 3.

The values for Norway and Denmark are each based on one company, thus the variance unexplained by the index is captured in the company's own variance term. Belgium and Ireland maintain a stable level above 0.7. The Dutch companies exhibit a weak correlation with their national index (this is consistent with the lack of a Dutch factor).

Using the estimated regression coefficients the covariance matrix was reconstructed using (4).

Table 2 Description of factors - extraction of 11 factors followed by varimax rotation (% variation explained shown in brackets)

Time period	1986-7	1988-9	1990-1
No. of companies	74	89	92
Factor 1	All German co.s + Philips (Neth) (12.1)	All German co.s + Philips (Neth) (9.9)	All German co.s +EuroDisney (Fr) (11.7)
Factor 2	13 Italian co.s (9.1)	All Italian co.s (9.4)	16 Italian co.s (11.0)
Factor 3	10 French co.s (7.6)	10 French co.s (7.7)	15 French co.s + Iberdrola(Spain) (10.3)
Factor 4	9 Belgian co.s (5.6)	8 Swiss co.s (5.2)	11 Swiss co.s (8.9)
Factor 5	11 Swiss co.s (5.2)	9 Belgian co.s (4.7)	9 Belgian co.s (4.8)
Factor 6	5 Swedish co.s + 1 Norwegian co. (4.7)	5 Swedish co.s + 1 Norwegian co. (4.0)	4 Irish co.s (3.9)
Factor 7	4 Irish co.s (3.4)	5 Spanish co.s + Swedish Elec + 3 oil co.s (3.6)	7 Swedish co.s (3.8)
Factor 8	3 Oil co.s (2.0)	4 Irish co.s (3.3)	2 Italian telecom co.s(2.8)
Factor 9	2 Italian banks (1.8)	3 Swiss co.s (2.5)	3 Spanish co.s (2.8)
Factor 10	unclear (1.5)	unclear (2.2)	3 oil co.s+Norsk H (2.7)
Factor 11	unclear (1.4)	unclear (1.9)	unclear (2.1)
Total	(73.4)	(61.1)	(70.4)

Table 3 Average correlations between company returns and national index returns

Country	1986-7	1988-9	1990-1
Belgium	.79	.74	.80
Denmark	.18	.37	.52
France	.73	.54	.65
Germany	.69	.60	.65
Ireland	.79	.72	.82
Italy	.70	.66	.75
Netherlands	.66	.53	.42
Norway	.81	.81	.72
Spain		.57	.70
Sweden	.79	.57	.68
Switzerland	.79	.63	.78

3iii) Comparison of models: Although the covariance matrix is used in portfolio selection it is more convenient to use the correlation matrix for comparisons. There is no loss of generality since

$$R = \text{diag}\left(\frac{1}{\sqrt{V(X_i)}}\right) \Sigma \, \text{diag}\left(\frac{1}{\sqrt{V(X_i)}}\right)$$

and the terms $V(X_i)$ are common to both models. R is the observed correlation matrix, the model of the correlation matrix based on factor analysis is $\hat{\rho}_1$, that based on the multi-index model is $\hat{\rho}_2$.
The differences $R - \hat{\rho}_1$ and $R - \hat{\rho}_2$ were computed. The number of separate correlations in an n variable correlation matrix is $\frac{n(n-1)}{2}$, thus there are too many to examine in detail. Figure 2 shows the relative performance of the two models by plotting the frequency of errors in correlation against the size of the error.
R fits the factor analysis model $\hat{\rho}_1$ very well, although there is evidence that the proportion of deviations above 0.05 increases

overtime (possibly due to more companies entering the universe). The multi-index model does less well, however only about 5% of correlations have errors greater than 0.2 . A point worthy of emphasis is that the multi-index model approaches the estimation of the correlation matrix from below, using the indices as external data sources; factor analysis starts with the correlation matrix and then simplifies its structure.

Figure 2

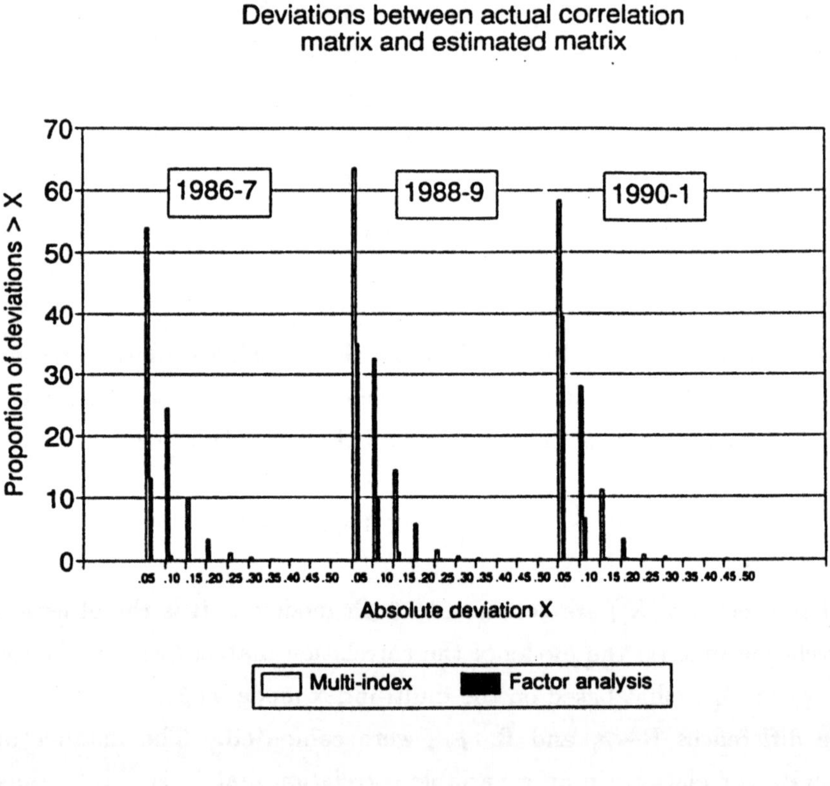

4) Conclusions and suggestions for further work

The comparisons between the two approaches have been based on modelling the historical covariance matrix. They have shown that the APT (factor analysis) model is superior to the multi-index model in terms of explaining historical correlations. It is difficult to assess the practical significance of this superiority without using the models for portfolio selection.

A more powerful test and more relevant test in practice would be to build an index tracking portfolio using both models. The advantage of using index tracking rather than a performance based objective is that there is a clear target (the returns on the Eurotrack index) and the tracking error is measure of comparative performance. Some minor practical difficulties, such as the absence of a published index before October 1990, need to be overcome before this can be achieved.

References

Elton, J.E. and M.J. Gruber, 1987, "Modern portfolio theory and investment analysis" (Third Edition), Wiley, New York.

Lintner, J., 1965, "Valuation of risk assets and the selection of risky investments in stock portfolios and capital budgets", *Review of Economics and Statistics*,47,13-37.

Mossin J., 1966, "Equilibrium in a Capital Asset Market", *Econometrica*, 34,768-783.

Roll, R. and S.A. Ross, 1980, "An empirical investigation of the Arbitrage Pricing Theory", *Journal of Finance*,35,1073-1103.

Ross S.A., 1976, "The Arbitrage Pricing Theory of Capital Asset Pricing", *Journal of Economic Theory*,12, 341-360.

Sharpe, W.F., 1963, "A simplified model for portfolio analysis", *Management Science,* 9,277-293.

Sharpe, W.F., 1964, "Capital asset prices: a theory of market equilibrium under conditions of risk", *Journal of Finance*,19,425-442.

Appendix 1: Objective functions for portfolio selection

The conventional objective in portfolio selection is the minimisation of a weighted sum of risk and return;

i.e. minimise [− Expected return on the portfolio + λ(Variance of portfolio return)]

where λ is a parameter reflecting the investor's risk averseness.
In the above notation, this objective is:

$$\text{minimise} \ \left[-\phi'\mu + \lambda(\phi' \, \Sigma \, \phi) \right],$$

varying λ between 0 and ∞ generates the efficient frontier of portfolios. This familiar objective is used in the selection of portfolios for multinational tactical asset allocation.

For an index fund, the accepted measure of its performance is the tracking error, this is usually a root mean square error measure of the difference in returns between the portfolio and the index.

$$\text{T.E.} \ = \ \sqrt{\frac{\sum_{t=1}^{T} (F_t \ - \ I_t)^2}{T}}$$

where, at time t, the return on the chosen market index is I_t where

$$I_t \ = \ \mu^I{}_t + v^I{}_t$$

and the return on the index fund is F_t, where

$$F_t = \sum_{i=1}^{N} \phi_i X_{i,t}$$

and T is some time horizon. The covariance between the index and share i is

$$\mathrm{Cov}(X_{i,t},I_t) = \mathrm{Cov}(v_{i,t},v^I_t) = \psi_{i,t} \quad \text{for } i=1,\ldots.,N \ .$$

An index fund is selected to minimise the expected tracking error, this objective can be expressed as

$$\text{minimise} \quad \phi' (\Sigma + \mu\mu') \phi \ - \ 2\phi' (\psi + \mu\mu^I)$$

(constant terms in the mean and variance of the index returns are dropped) .

In some situations, the objective is to track an index where the index weights are considered fixed over the relevant time horizon. If the benchmark weight on share i is b_i , then

$$I_t = \sum_{i=1}^{N} b_i X_{i,t}$$

and the objective becomes

$$\text{minimise} \quad (\phi - b)' (\Sigma + \mu\mu')(\phi - b) \ .$$

A hybrid approach between index tracking and tactical asset allocation is to maximise excess return (return on fund - return on index) subject to a risk correction defined by the tracking error. The resultant objective is:

$$\text{minimise} \quad -(\phi - b)'\mu \ + \ \lambda(\phi - b)' (\Sigma + \mu\mu')(\phi - b) \ ,$$

where λ is a risk aversion parameter as above.

Appendix 2 The membership of Eurotrack 100 (with % weights) and the national equity indices

Belgium
Brussels-SE General

Delhaize	0.398
Electrabel	0.840
G.I.B.	0.225
G.B.L.	0.175
Kredietbank	0.246
Petrofina	1.267
SGB	0.663
Solvay	0.528
Tractebel	0.466
Total	4.811

Denmark
Copenhagen S.E.

Novo ADR	0.400

France
Paris CAC General

Accor	0.491
Havas	0.524
Alcatel Al.	1.853
Elf Aquitaine	2.510
AXA	0.862
BSN	1.452
F N Suez Cie	1.429
Canal Plus	0.562
Carrefour	0.724
Euro Disney	0.609
Gen. Des Eaux	1.366
L'Air Liquide	1.008
Larfarge	0.556
L'Oreal	0.962
LVMH	1.689
L.E.D.	0.749
Paribas	1.071
Peugeot	0.857
St.Gobain	0.883
Soc. Generale	0.863
Total (Oil)	0.889
Total	21.919

Germany
Frankfurt-FAZ Gen.

Allianz	4.021
BMW	0.841
BASF	1.402
Bayer	1.804
Commerzbank	0.641
Deutsche bank	2.724
Daimler Benz	3.550
Dresdner	1.255
Hoechst	1.468
Mannesmann	0.864
RWE	1.180
Siemens	3.366
Thyssen	0.732
Veba	1.555
Volkswagen	1.037
Total	26.447

Ireland
Irish S.E. ISEQ

Allied Irish Bk.	0.309
Bank of Ireland	0.160
CRH	0.190
Smurfit (JFSN.)	0.358
Total	1.018

Italy
Milan Banca Comm.Ital.

BCI	0.499
Benetton	0.241
Credito Italno.	0.465
Fer Fin	0.335
Fiat SPA	1.235
Fiat RISP	0.213
Fiat PRIV	0.367
Gemina	0.320
Generali	2.498
Ital Gas	0.233
Mediobanca	0.699
Montedison SPA	0.408
Olivetti	0.254
Pirelli SPA	0.242
SIP	0.610
SIP RISP	0.190
Stet RISP	0.358
Stet	0.870
Total	10.044

Netherlands
CBS-Tendency General

ABN Amro Hlds.	0.862
Intl.Nederlanden	1.065
Phillips Elect.	0.815
Royal Dutch	7.711
Unilever	2.284
Total	12.739

Norway
Oslo Stock Exchange

Norsk Hydro	0.449

Spain
Madrid Stock Exchange

Bnco.Blbao.Vzcya	1.178
Banco Central SA	0.728
Endesa ADR	0.968
Iberduero	0.503
Repsol SA	1.275
Telefonica ADR	1.437
Total	6.092

Sweden
Veckans Affarer Weighted

Asea B Free	0.168
Astra A Free	0.287
Astra B	0.282
Electrolux	0.589
Ericsson	1.032
Procordia "B" Free	0.190
S.C.A. "B"	0.224
Skandia Free	0.384
Volvo B	0.255
Total	3.415

Switzerland
SBC General

BBC BR.	0.573
Ciba-Geigy REG	1.382
C.S.Hldgs.Br.	0.867
Nestle Br.	1.130
Nestle Reg.	2.378
Roche Hldgs.	1.951
Sandoz P/CT	0.375
Sandoz (REG.)	1.556
Swiss Bank BR.	0.536
Swiss Bank P/CT.	0.317
UBS BR.	1.589
Total	12.660

DIRECTIONAL JUDGEMENTAL FINANCIAL FORECASTING: TRENDS AND RANDOM WALKS

Andrew C Pollock
Department of Mathematics, Glasgow Polytechnic

Mary E Wilkie
Department of Psychology, Glasgow Polytechnic

1 INTRODUCTION

In the volatile and rapidly changing financial environment human judgement is an essential ingredient in decision-making. Effective exchange rate and stock price forecasting not only require quantitative models but also the personal beliefs and views of a forecaster formed according to some subjective procedure. It is important, then, to understand how people involved in the financial world make judgements on currency or stock price movements. This paper reports an exploratory investigation of this issue undertaken with a sample of delegates at the 9th. Meeting of the Euro-Working Group on Financial Modelling at Curacao, Netherlands Antilles, in April 1991.

While forecasting financial time series has been subject to extensive research using time series, econometric and technical analysis techniques, very little research has examined the judgemental accuracy of individuals with financial expertise. This lack of interest is rather surprising since 'eyeballing' (i.e. reaching a cognitive understanding of time series behaviour and then extrapolating it forward) appears to be a commonly used approach in many real world forecasting situations. Indeed, classical chartist forecasting techniques are significantly based on this principle.

To gain an understanding of judgemental forecasting, a starting point is to examine the way individuals look at simple graphical and numerical data. Although in practical forecasting situations individuals usually have additional information available to them, to understand time series extrapolative judgement (specifically) it is necessary to control this information. When information is not controlled judgement is likely to be based on both time series and non-time series information such that little can be said about the possible causes of judgemental bias that may exist. For instance, it would be impossible to determine whether poor judgement was the result of poor memory recall, the salience of recent events or a failure to appreciate signals or noise in the series.

The present study examined the overall judgemental accuracy of individuals with financial expertise using time series data in a controlled framework. Specifically, the present study investigated an extremely important issue in financial forecasting: 'Can individuals distinguish between a random walk series with no drift and a random walk series with drift?' In other words, can financial professionals distinguish between situations when a deterministic trend is present from when it is not? This issue gave rise to further questions that are extremely pertinent to judgemental forecasting. These were as follows: i) Can individuals make accurate directional forecasts? ii) Can individuals provide a reliable measure of the confidence they have in their predictions? iii) Is the reliability of these predictions influenced by an individuals perceived expertise on financial markets and statistical concepts? iv) How does the perceived uncertainty that abounds in currency and stock markets modify the individuals interpretation of the series? v) Does combining judgemental forecasts from individuals improve accuracy?

2 METHODOLOGY

2.1 Subjects

A group of eighteen delegates (of both sexes) attending the 9th Meeting of the Euro-Working Group on Financial Modelling in April 1991 participated in the study. The sample was comprised of academics and practitioners from a number of different countries including Denmark, Italy, Netherlands, Netherlands Antilles, Spain, UK, USA and Yugoslavia. All individuals who took part in the inquiry had considerable expertise in the field of finance, although their areas of interest were not necessarily directed towards currency or stock markets. The subjects, however, all had some knowledge of these markets as well as a sufficient understanding of the statistical analytical techniques essential for this study. That is, all the subjects who participated in the study had a relatively high degree of both substantive and normative 'goodness' in forecasting.

2.2 Materials

Constructed data for the time paths of 36 series were presented numerically and graphically to the subjects. The subjects were not told how the data were constructed, only that it was data obtained through a statistical procedure to simulate currency or stock price series. These series were presented for a 60 month period (months were numbered from 1 to 60) and indexed with the initial value in month 0 set at 1000.

The data were based on 6 randomly generated series from a standard normal distribution. Cumulative values were then obtained and the series were given a starting value of 1000. To these 6 series linear trends of varying gradients were added. The gradients could be categorised as: i) mild: which gave an expected probability for an increase or decrease, as appropriate, of 0.6; ii) medium: which gave an expected probability of 0.7; iii) strong: which gave an expected probability of 0.8; iv) very strong: which gave an expected probability of 0.9; and v) dominant: which gave an expected probability of almost 1. For each of these expected probabilities 3 positive and 3 negative trends were obtained. This resulted in 36 series, of which 6 were random walks and 30 were random walks with varying degrees of constant drift (15 positive and 15 negative). The data were rounded to the nearest whole number and were presented to the subjects in a random fashion.

The use of constructed random walk series with varying degrees of drift were chosen for two reasons. First, random walk series with varying degrees of drift reasonably approximate monthly financial time series behaviour (Autoregressive Conditional Heteroscedastic [ARCH] models are, arguably, more appropriate for daily series than for monthly series). Certainly, Pollock and Wilkie (1992) found on a time series probabilistic forecasting task with actual monthly currency series that the random walk with drift model performed relatively well in comparison to more complex models and much better than the time series extrapolations of a group of professional forecasters. Second, the data contains only one signal (drift) that individuals need to identify. When actual data is used a variety of signals may or may not be present. It is, therefore, almost impossible to distinguish when an individual makes a valid from an invalid interpretation of the data.

The subjects were given numerical and graphical data together with an instruction sheet and a booklet to indicate judgements and levels of confidence. They were requested to complete the booklet independently from the other subjects. This booklet contained various questions and was set out as follows:

i) **Preliminary Questions.** These basically involved questions on age, sex, type of employment and country of employment. The answers from these questions were not used directly in the analyses. However, they did provide information on the composition and diversity of the subjects.

ii) **Questions on the familiarity of subjects with financial data.** These questions were designed to obtain information from the subjects as to how they viewed their level of expertise in this area. In particular, subjects were asked whether they found it easier to view the data as exchange rate series, stock price series or whether they were indifferent between the two. Subjects, after given this choice, were then asked to rate their understanding of the markets and their ability to predict future values on a 7 point scale. They were also asked to rate the ability of analysts to do this on a similar scale. This provided an measure of how the subjects perceived their own expertise and that of specialised experts in the field.

iii) **Questions on statistical understanding.** A minimum level of statistical understanding is essential in probability judgement forecasting. These questions asked the subject to rate their understanding of probability, arithmetic mean, standard deviation and normal distribution on a 7 point scale. This provided an indication as to whether or not the reliability of the subjects forecasts were directly related to statistical understanding.

iv) Questions on the application of statistics to financial series. These questions were designed to obtain the views of the subjects on the usefulness of techniques frequently used in currency and stock market forecasting: time series, econometric and chartist techniques. Subjects provided their answers on an 7 point scale.

v) Directional forecasts. These questions, which related to the 36 series of data, were designed to examine if subjects could give reliable probabilities for a directional change in the series. Subjects were requested to indicate whether the series would, in month 61, rise or fall and express the likelihood of this by assigning a probability (expressed as a percentage) to this prediction.

2.3 Procedure

The subjects were instructed to answer these questions at their own pace and convenience. In addition, each subject studied each series and made directional forecasts for the subsequent one month period. They were also asked to indicate how certain they were about their choices by assigning probabilities between .5 and 1.

On completion of the task a statistical analysis of the results was undertaken.

2.4 Techniques for the Statistical Analysis of the Results

A comparison of subjects' predictions with expected probabilities were made using a range of statistical procedures. These essentially follow the lines of the covariance decomposition approach, set out in Yates (1982, 1988), but with modifications to take into account that the expected outcome indices for the correct forecast range from .5 to 1 in increments of .1 .

The response probabilities for each forecast (x_i) (adjusted to the expected direction) were compared with the expected probabilities (e_i) by probability judgement accuracy measures. The first of these measures was the mean probability score (MPS) given in equation (1):

$$MPS = \{ \sum_{i=1}^{n} (x_i - e_i)^2 / n \} \qquad (1)$$

where n denotes the number of values.

The MPS was obtained for all subjects using all the series. It was also obtained for particular expected probabilities of .5, .6, .7, .8, .9 and 0.9995 to detect if this measure varies with the strength of the trend. The MPS was also obtained using the mean probability for each series from all subjects to examine if the composite measure is better than individual measures. Furthermore, the MPS was decomposed to examine the multidimensional aspect of judgemental accuracy following broadly the lines of Yates (1982, 1988). This decomposition can give important insights into the strengths and weaknesses of an individual forecaster. The MPS was decomposed for each subject and the composite forecaster as defined in equation (2).

$$MPS = V(e) + b^2 V(e) + V(u) + (M(x) - M(e))^2 - 2 b V(e) \qquad (2)$$

Where b is the slope coefficient of a regression line of form x=a+be+u, with a the constant and u the error term. M(x) and M(c) denote the respective means and V(x) and V(c) the respective variances.

In this study as 36 series were equally divided into expected probabilities of .5, .6, .7, .8, .9 and 0.9995, the value of V(e) is 0.0292.

The term $b^2V(e)$ reflects the minimum variance of x or the total variance expected in an individuals responses that are explained by variation arising from the rises and falls in the series: the variation in x accounted for by the variation in e.

The term V(u) reflects noisiness or scatter which is the variation due to forecast errors that are independent of rises and falls in the series. Noisiness is important in financial forecasting as it can reflect a weakness in the forecaster's assessment procedure. If the causes of this noise can be identified, forecast performance can be improved. There are numerous instances when noisiness can occur in forecasting. It can occur when the forecaster is inconsistent such that the interpretation of similar situations results in differing forecasts. It can also arise when a forecast is made using only partial information as would be the case when the forecaster relies on inefficient heuristics that are not closely related to the behaviour of the series. For example, a forecaster subject to 'illusory correlation' who incorrectly considers factors which are unimportant to be important in determining the future path of the series. The higher the value of the scatter statistic the greater the noise.

The term $(M(x)-M(e))^2$ reflects the square of the bias. Bias or under/overconfidence over a range of forecasts is defined as the difference between the mean response and the mean probability expected. If the square value is omitted, the term $(M(x)-M(e))$ can be used to detect the direction of bias. It is positive in the case where the forecaster is overconfident and negative in the case where the forecaster is underconfident. It is zero for perfect confidence.

The last term $(-2bV(e))$ is essentially the covariance between the forecast and expected probabilities. The covariance is directly related to the degree of association between the two variables. The covariance is close to zero when no relationship exists. As this term is multiplied by (-2), it implies that the closer the association between the two sets of probabilities the lower will be the probability score.

The slope coefficient, b, reflects resolution or discrimination. Resolution reflects the ability of the individual to distinguish occasions when a rise or fall is likely to occur from when it is not. The closer the value of b to unity the better the resolution. A value of zero indicates that a forecaster cannot discriminate between situations where the series is likely to change (that is, either rise or fall) from when it is not. Resolution is an important concept in currency and stock price forecasting especially where buy and sell decisions are being based on the forecasts.

3 RESULTS

3.1 Understanding, Prediction and Application of Techniques

The questions in the first part of the booklet provided useful information on the subjects views as to their: (i) understanding of exchange rate and stock price behaviour; (ii) understanding of statistical techniques; (iii) perception of their ability to forecast; (iv) perception of analysts ability to forecast; and (v) assessment of the value of common quantitative techniques to exchange rate and stock price forecasting.

The subjects as a whole rated their understanding of exchange rate and stock price series as just above basic (i.e., mean of 4.4 on a 7 point scale). The subjects tended to be conservative in their answers to this question as they realised that foreign exchange and stock markets are very complex and not easy to understand.

When subjects were asked to rate their own ability and that of analysts, they, on average, rated their own ability as, in between not possible and possible (mean of 4.1 on seven point scale). Analysts where only rated 0.5 of a point higher. It appears that the subjects were not only unsure as their ability to predict movements in foreign exchange and stock prices but also not sure experts could do this either. Only 7 out of 16 (2 non-responses to these questions) indicated that analysts were more able to predict these movements than themselves.

The subjects, on the whole, perceived that they had a reasonably good understanding of probability, the arithmetic mean, the standard deviation and the normal distribution. This is important as the probability judgement analysis used in this study required a basic knowledge of these concepts.

The subjects, on the whole, viewed time series and econometric techniques as being useful, especially the latter, and chartist techniques to be of some use. The subjects, therefore, viewed these analytical techniques as having some value but appreciated their limitations.

3.2 Probability Judgement Accuracy

A comparison of the forecast probabilities from each subject with expected probabilities was undertaken using the MPS statistic defined in the previous section. In addition, the average of individual forecast probabilities was also compared with the expected probabilities using this statistic. The results are set out in Table 1.

The table illustrates that the combined MPS from the group gave much better results than the individual subjects. Only one subject obtained a MPS value better than the group value.This might be due to the fact that more information was included in the evaluation of probabilities (from a number of subjects rather than only one subject) and that symmetric errors between individuals tended to cancel themselves out.

TABLE 1

Mean Probability Score Measures Using Expected Probability Groupings and Components.

	MPS							Bias	Resol.	Scat.
	All	.5	.6	.7	.8	.9	1	M(x)-M(e)	b	V(c)
n	36	6	6	6	6	6	6	36	36	36
Subject										
1	.006	.003	.000	.002	.014	.008	.012	-.049	.727	.002
2	.016	.007	.010	.027	.029	.025	.001	-.076	.998	.013
3	.017	.008	.020	.029	.017	.033	.000	.023	1.001	.017
4	.021	.023	.029	.038	.017	.022	.010	-.053	.843	.018
5	.023	.008	.007	.046	.014	.022	.040	-.119	.714	.006
6	.026	.021	.008	.041	.028	.029	.028	-.111	.691	.011
7	.005	.004	.005	.003	.003	.003	.010	-.019	.824	.003
8	.025	.010	.057	.052	.013	.005	.010	-.057	.964	.021
9	.037	.097	.053	.044	.018	.004	.004	-.040	.817	.034
10	.024	.025	.003	.060	.033	.013	.010	-.075	.727	.016
11	.009	.027	.008	.008	.003	.003	.004	-.015	.936	.009
12	.007	.005	.013	.007	.005	.002	.013	-.004	.745	.005
13	.053	.037	.037	.028	.072	.108	.038	-.117	.419	.030
14	.006	.003	.007	.009	.010	.005	.001	.002	.941	.005
15	.045	.014	.045	.094	.045	.042	.013	-.115	.841	.031
16	.016	.004	.049	.022	.014	.002	.005	.061	.795	.011
17	.037	.033	.023	.027	.050	.027	.063	-.072	.438	.023
18	.033	.000	.008	.013	.030	.108	.038	-.136	.491	.007
Composite										
	.006	.001	.002	.008	.006	.009	.011	-.053	.773	.002
Perfect										
	.000	.000	.000	.000	.000	.000	.000	.000	1.000	.000
Uniform										
	.092	.000	.010	.040	.090	.160	.250	-.250	.000	.000

The MPS values for expected probabilities of .5, .6, .7, .8, .9 and .9995 show that for low probabilities (.8 and below), the combined probabilities clearly produce more accurate forecasts. For high probabilities (above .8) there did not appear to be much difference. Underconfidence was shown where a very strong or dominant trend existed. This underconfidence was probably due to the subjects, who had familiarity with these markets, exercising caution when faced with strong trends. That is, the subjects included what is in effect an uncertainty modification to their interpretation of the data. Overall, the bias statistic illustrates that underconfidence was shown for 16 out of the 18 subjects.

The above results are most easily appreciated when compared to a couple of hypothetical forecasters often used as standards of comparison: the 'perfect' subject and the 'uniform' subject.

The perfect subject is one who knows exactly how the data is constructed and uses this information in his or her assessments of probability. This subject would give assessed probabilities that exactly match the expected probabilities. Hence, this subject would have an MPS of zero with bias and scatter components also zero and resolution of unity.

The uniform subject refers to someone who is unable to anticipate a target event's occurrence and assigns the same probabilities to all possibilities. In the context of the present study, the uniform subject would select answers at random and assign a probability of .5 to each answer. In financial forecasting this has a particular significance as a forecaster viewing all series as a random walk would do just this.

The results for the uniform subject show an overall MPS value greater than or equal to all the subjects. In other words, nearly all the subjects had a better performance than a person who considered all the series to be random walks. The uniform subject performed relatively well for low probabilities, but relatively poorly for high probabilities, as would be expected. One reason for the underconfidence for the high probabilities is that the subjects took the view that currency and stock price series tended to follow a quasi-random walk such that drift was underestimated.

The series with expected probabilities of .5 provided a very interesting set of MPS values as these series were all random walks. Only one of the subjects correctly spotted this and gave a value of .5 to all six random walk series. The average number of .5 values (rounded to the nearest .05) was approximately 2 per subject. This indicates that random walks are not easy to spot and that even individuals with expertise in finance can be subject to 'illusory correlation' - that is, they make associations that are not statistically present. Forecasters should be aware of this and recognise the distinction between deterministic and stochastic movements. It is often not very easy to distinguish between the two. This is a very important factor for those who use chartist techniques to consider: they too, can be fooled by a random walk. This, and other psychological biases in relation to currency forecasting are discussed in Pollock and Wilkie (1991) .

The results, however, implied that using the mean of the aggregate probabilities for the .5 expected probabilities gave a MPS statistic value closer to zero than the 17 subjects who did not spot the random walk series in all cases. This tends to suggest that the subjects inability to recognise the random walk series was a factor of their own perception of the data rather than the data itself. This view is further supported by the fact that in all 6 cases the mean value for the probability of a rise for all 18 subjects was within a range .05 of the .5 value.

The resolution statistic shows substantial variation between subjects with a range of values from 0.42 to 1.00. An individuals who had no resolution (as is the case of the uniform subject) would have had a score of zero on this measure. The higher the value the better the resolution. A value close to unity implies good resolution. The results show that 10 subjects had higher resolution values than the combined results of all subjects. This implies that perhaps the most important aspect of currency and stock market forecasting (resolution) is unlikely to be achieved by aggregating the results from individuals.

The scatter statistics show substantial variation between subjects with values ranging from .002 to .034. The closer the value of this statistic to zero the better. Scatter arises from a subjects misinterpretation information. The uniform subject was consistent and had zero scatter as no information from the series was used, hence it could not be misinterpreted.

The three statistics (bias, resolution and scatter) contribute to the MPS decomposition set out in equation (2). Scatter and the absolute value of bias positively influence the MPS, whereas resolution negatively influences the MPS. The three statistics allow us to see the sources of the weakness in forecasters who have relatively high MPS values and the strengths of forecasters who have relatively low MPS values. The results show that a high MPS value can be due to poor performance in one or more of the components. Identification of the source of poor judgemental accuracy is the first stage in the development of a procedures to correct it.

It must be pointed out, however, that the components of the MPS are not independent of each other. A product moment correlation coefficient of -0.589 illustrated clearly that a highly significant negative correlation existed between the bias squared and resolution values (a significant positive correlation of 0.501 between bias and resolution). That is, the greater the underconfidence, the poorer the resolution. In other words, subjects whose views were closely related to the random walk forecaster showed high bias and low resolution, whereas those whose views were to interpret the data at face value showed low bias and high resolution.

3.3 Probability Judgement Accuracy and the Understanding, Prediction and Application of Techniques

Rank correlation coefficients (not presented) did not appear to show that probability judgement accuracy was influenced by the subjects views as to their understanding of exchange rate and stock price behaviour, understanding of statistical concepts, their perception of their own and analysts ability to forecast the series and their assessment of the value of common quantitative techniques used in financial forecasting.

4 CONCLUSION

This exploratory investigation set out to determine how people involved in the financial world make judgements on currency and stock price movements using constructed data. Some very revealing and interesting results were obtained which are of considerable use in the examination of judgemental financial forecasting.

These can be examined in relation to the key questions set out in the introduction. That is:

i) Can individuals make accurate directional forecasts? The results suggest that individuals can usually pick up a general deterministic trend in a series. They may, however, be fooled by a stochastic trend in a random walk series.

ii) Can people provide a reliable measure of the confidence they have in their predictions? The results suggest that underconfidence is a problem with directional predictions using this type of data. This may be attributed to the fact that the subjects used in the study did not accept strong and dominant trends in the series.

iii) Is the reliability of the predictions influenced by the perceived expertise that individuals have on financial markets and statistical concepts? The results did not show this to be the case. The subjects, however, all had some expertise in this area which is essential for this type of forecasting. It would appear that all subjects had a level of expertise above the minimum required such that differences between subjects probably had only a marginal influence.

iv) How does the perceived uncertainty that abounds in currency and stock markets modify the individuals interpretation of a series? It appears that individuals were very reluctant to expect very strong and dominant trends in these series. Probabilities above 0.85

were not used as often as would have been justified by the nature of the data.

v) Does combining judgemental forecasts from individuals improve accuracy? The results show that the combined individual forecasts for each series resulted in probability judgements that generally had better overall accuracy with less bias and scatter than the individual forecasts. Aggregating the individual forecasts did, therefore, appear to give more reliable results. Resolution, however, was relatively poor for the aggregate forecasts. It appears that aggregating the results did not improve resolution. In fact it made it worse. This is important as averaged forecasts are often used in practical forecasting situations, (for example, in 'The Currency Forecasters' Digest' published by Alan Teck). Such averaging does not appear to improve on what is perhaps the more important aspect of forecasting in financial markets: resolution. It is this that often distinguishes the good forecaster from the poor forecaster. Statistical aggregation cannot be used to create expertise.

To sum up, this study highlights a number of areas that require further research. In particular, the general applicability of the results and the psychological factors underlying the points i) to v). In judgemental currency and stock price forecasting it is important not only to know the strengths and weaknesses of forecasters but also the factors that cause them. When these questions are answered then we are on the way to obtaining improved judgemental financial forecasts.

REFERENCES

Pollock A.C. and Wilkie M.E. (1991). Briefing - Forex Forecasting, Euromoney, June, 123-124.

Pollock A.C. and Wilkie M.E. (1992). Currency Forecasting: Human Judgement or Models? VBA-Journaal, (forthcoming).

Teck A. (Publisher). The Currency Forecaster's Digest. (Monthly Periodical). White Plains, New York.

Yates J.F. (1982). External Correspondence: Decompositions of the Mean Probability Score. Organisational Behavior and Human Performance, **30**:132-156.

Yates J.F. (1988). Analyzing the Accuracy of Probability Judgements for Multiple Events: An Extension of Covariance Decomposition. Organisational Behavior and Human Decision Processes, **41**:281-299.

FORECASTING THE BEHAVIOUR OF BANKRUPTCIES[1]

Christian Starck
Dr. Econ.
Bank of Finland
Central Bank Policy Department

P.O. Box 160, SF-00101 Helsinki, FINLAND

and

Matti Virén
Professor of Economics
University of Turku
Department of Economics

SF-20500 Turku, FINLAND

Abstract

This paper explores the determinate of corporate failures in Finland. The analysis makes use of aggregate monthly time series for some financial and non-financial variables covering the period 1922-1990. It is partly based on some recent Finnish micro evidence on bankruptcies and partly on recent literature on the role of financial intermediation in the propagation of aggregate economic shocks. The empirical analyses indicate that bankruptcies constitute an important

---

[1] We would like to thank Anneli Majava and Huang Shumin for research assistance and an anonymous referee for useful comments. Financial support from the Cooperative Banks' Research Foundation is also gratefully acknowledged.

ingredient in terms of the determination of other variables. In particular, it turns out that overall liquidity and firm failures are closely related. We also find the basic relationships strikingly stable over long periods. Finally, we find some, although not very strong, evidence of non-linearities in the financial and non-financial time series.

Keywords: Bankruptcy, financial intermediation, time series models

Contents

1 Introduction

This paper explores the determinants of corporate failures in Finland. The analysis makes use of aggregate time series for some financial and non-financial variables. As a starting point we have some recent findings which suggest that financial – or, more precisely, financial intermediation – variables play an important role in the propagation mechanism determining the behaviour of bankruptcies and some key macroeconomic variables.

Obviously, the role of bankruptcies has two sides: the determination of bankruptcies and the effects of bankruptcies. Thus, basically, we need a more general model in which both channels are taken into account. One framework which can be utilized in this context is the theory of financial intermediation (see e.g. Williamson (1987) for an overview on this literature). The theory of financial intermediation has many obvious applications. For instance, one might argue that the propagation mechanism of the Great Depression can be seen as an application of this theory (see Bernanke (1983), who vigorously demonstrates the importance of the credit allocation process and corporate failures in aggravating the severity of a depression). The role of bankruptcies can also be analyzed in the "equilibrium credit rationing" framework (see e.g. the seminal paper by Stiglitz and Weiss (1981) in which the credit supply is affected by the riskiness of the banks' customers). Lastly, the analysis can be carried out in the modern version of the credit rationing framework (see e.g. Gertler and Gilchrist (1991)). There is a growing body of evidence suggesting that particularly small firms face liquidity constraints and these constraints affect at least their investment activity (see e.g. Morgan (1991)).

Our empirical analysis examines the importance of different financial and non-financial variables in explaining the behaviour of bankruptcies over time. Thus, we are concerned with the question of whether bankruptcies are only a real phenomenon, i.e. dependent only on demand conditions, profitability and so on, or whether they are also affected by financial variables such as (aggregate) liquidity, interest rates and the stock market. This kind of question cannot really be analyzed using standard structural models. Thus we make use of an unrestricted Vector Autoregressive (VAR) model.

The model is estimated from monthly Finnish data covering the period 1922M1–1990M12. This very long period also includes the Great Depression and it is used to examine whether the basic relationships are invariant with respect to different institutional settings and policy regimes. Secondly, the large data sample is required to analyze the potential nonlinearities in the financial and non-financial times series. If such nonlinearities were to exist, they would, of course, completely change the way in which bankruptcies can be predicted.

We start by presenting the analytical framework for the empirical analysis in Section 2. Empirical results are presented in Section 3 and some concluding remarks follow in Section 4.

2 Analytical framework for the time series analysis

We start by briefly reviewing the aggregate bankruptcy behaviour of Finnish firms (see Figure 1 for the graph of the corresponding time series).[1] As one can see, the bankruptcy series are rather volatile, particularly during periods when the capital market was not regulated.[2] We are interested here in evaluating the performance of various macro variables in predicting bankruptcies. Our analysis is, however, also motivated by regime changes in the Finnish capital market, particularly in terms of credit rationing (see again Figure 1). Thus, we are interested in seeing whether these regime changes are reflected in the bankruptcy behaviour which is implied by our model. In addition to scrutinizing the determinants of bankruptcies, we briefly examine the role of bankruptcies in the transmission mechanisms of aggregate economic fluctuations in Finland.

Our analysis makes use of the VAR model framework mainly because it is far from obvious how the structural equations linking bankruptcies to the other variables should be specified. Another reason is the fact we have an exceptionally large body of data available, running from January 1922 to December 1990. Thus, altogether there are 828 observations. These data make it possible to have a very general dynamic specification in terms of all variables. A priori, it is precisely the dynamic adjustment path which seems important when considering the role of bankruptcies in an economy.

The set of variables used here is the following:

- number of bankruptcies, b
- (real) industrial production, y^r
- the consumer price index, p
- the (real) exchange rate, e^r
- the money supply (m1, or alternatively m2)
- the UNITAS stock index for the Helsinki stock exchange, s

Because of data availability issues we have to use seasonally adjusted data. More precisely, this means that the time series of b, y^r and m1 (m2) are seasonally adjusted using the conventional X-11 adjustment procedure. In the subsequent empirical analysis all variables are expressed in logarithmic level form (see Virén (1992) for other details of the data).

As far as the bankruptcy series are concerned, we also used two alternative measures for bankruptcies: 1) total debt of bankrupt firms (at constant prices) and 2) bankruptcies in relation to all companies. Unfortunately, there are some serious data problems with these latter definitions. The series for debt and number of companies are available on an annual basis only and even then the data are to some extent deficient. Still, if one compares, for instance, the time series of the number of bankruptcies and the total debt of bankrupt firms, the difference is relatively small (cf. Figure 1). This suggests that the size distribution of bankruptcies has not changed very much over time.

One may ask why level form data are used. It is quite clear that none of the series are stationary, and some or all of them may have unit roots. The conventional way to proceed would be to formulate an error-correction type model where the system is estimated in first differences and where the error-correction structure corresponds to the long-run restrictions of the model which are derived from the co-integration analysis. We did not, however, follow this route. This is partly because with monthly data the first differences are highly noisy, with some outlier-type observations dominating the variability. Another reason, which is perhaps more important, is the fact that given our exceptionally large data set we can still obtain consistent results both in terms of the parameter estimators and the t and F tests – including the Granger causality test (with some caveats, however). This has been pointed out in the recent paper by Sims, Stock and Watson (1990). Moreover, the possible cointegration constraints among our variables will be satisfied (cf. Engle and Granger (1987)).

The empirical analysis follows some steps which are more or less regularly taken in the course of a VAR model analysis. Thus, the model is first estimated in the autoregressive form and then a Cholesky decomposition is carried out in order to examine the variance decompositions and impulse responses of the model (see e.g. Hakkio and Morris (1984) for an exposition of the VAR model analysis). In this connection, we also pay attention to the stability properties of the model, recalling the regime changes which have taken place in the capital market (and also in the determination of exchange rates, and presumably in the determination of prices and wages).

This stability analysis can also be extended to examine the existence of possible nonlinearities in the set of variables. To be more precise, one may examine whether the time irreversibility property applies to the data. Quite recently, it has been argued in several studies that this property may not hold in all economic and financial data. If this is indeed the case, one might argue that the time series reflect some chaotic (bubble) behaviour. If this is so we should approach the forecasting issue from a completely different angle (see e.g. Ramsey (1990) for further details of this irreversibility issue).

The variance decompositions give us a concrete measure of the importance of each variable in explaining the variability of these variables over different time horizons. The impulse responses serve the same purpose but they also provide information on the qualitative nature of the results. In essence, this means the sign pattern of effects.

3 Empirical results with aggregate bankruptcy data

Let us now turn to the empirical results. Table 1 contains the multivariate causality test statistics for the six variables in the VAR model (as far as the R2's and autocorrelation test statistics are concerned, we may refer to Table 4b). Table 2 contains the variance decompositions for a VAR model with the variable ordering {e^r, p, y^r, m1, b, s}.[3] Table 3 contains the long-run impulse responses for the six variables. The whole impulse response path is reported only for the bankruptcy variable, see Figure 2. In this figure, the impulse responses show how a (positive) innovation (of the size of one standard deviation) in the respective shocked variable affects bankruptcies. Results from the stability analysis are presented in Table 4. This analysis is carried out by adding step-wise one (or two) decade(s) to the sample period starting from 1950 (or backwards starting from 1939). Finally, the results for the non-linearity (time irreversibility tests) are presented in Figure 3.

We start from Table 1, which contains multivariate causality test statistics for the six variables included in the model. The model is estimated using a constant and 12 lags for each variables and, in addition, 5 dummies for the war years 1939–1944. The test statistics indicate that the real exchange rate, the price level, money and bankruptcies are essential ingredients of the model while industrial output and the stock index are of somewhat marginal importance. This result is reinforced by the variance decompositions reported in Table 2.

TABLE 1. **Multivariate causality tests for a VAR model for the vector $\underset{\sim}{y}=(e_t^r\ p_t\ y_t^r\ ml_t\ b_t\ s_t)'$**

	e^r	p	y^r	ml	b	s
Marginal significance level	0.011	0.000	0.098	0.001	0.001	0.124

Multivariate Granger-Sims causality tests are employed. The null hypothesis for these tests is that the lags of one variable do not enter into equations of the remaining variables.

The variance decompositions are in general intuitively appealing. Thus, the strong link between the real exchange rate and industrial output can be discerned, it can be seen that money is not impotent in terms of other variables (including real variables) and, finally, it can be seen that stock market prices are related to other variables in a reasonable way (even though the stock market is not a very important causal factor in our model).

As far as bankruptcies are concerned, there seem to be several important interactions between this variable and the other five variables. Perhaps this is the reason why our empirical model is not dichotomous as it has been in many similar models (but which do not include the bankruptcy variable). Thus, the nominal and real variables are not independent of each other, nor are the financial

TABLE 2. **Variance decomposition for a VAR model for the vector $\underset{\sim}{y}_t = (e_t^r\ p_t\ y_t^r\ m1_t\ b_t\ s_t)'$**

		Innovation in					
	k	e^r	p	y^r	m1	b	s
e^r	1	100.0	0.0	0.0	0.0	0.0	0.0
	3	98.3	0.1	0.3	0.3	0.1	1.0
	6	97.4	0.3	0.5	0.7	0.1	1.0
	12	90.9	3.4	1.3	0.9	1.6	2.0
	24	72.2	9.6	1.2	2.0	7.5	7.6
	60	54.4	13.1	6.2	2.6	14.2	9.6
	120	46.2	11.6	10.6	4.7	18.9	8.0
p	1	0.0	100.0	0.0	0.0	0.0	0.0
	3	1.7	97.4	0.0	0.1	0.4	0.4
	6	5.1	90.6	0.2	0.1	1.6	2.5
	12	7.4	80.4	0.3	0.6	6.3	5.0
	24	9.6	65.1	1.1	4.7	14.3	5.2
	60	9.4	27.1	1.2	29.8	30.2	2.3
	120	9.3	9.0	0.5	44.7	35.1	1.3
y^r	1	0.0	0.0	100.0	0.0	0.0	0.0
	3	0.2	0.0	99.5	0.0	0.1	0.2
	6	1.0	0.7	96.1	0.2	0.1	1.8
	12	2.5	3.9	86.5	0.5	1.2	5.3
	24	14.7	3.8	70.3	1.0	3.0	7.2
	60	34.8	2.0	46.5	8.9	2.4	5.4
	120	36.7	1.5	34.5	18.5	4.0	4.8
m1	1	0.0	0.0	0.0	100.0	0.0	0.0
	3	0.3	0.3	0.0	98.7	0.2	0.5
	6	0.9	0.2	0.1	97.5	0.6	0.7
	12	1.6	0.2	0.0	91.2	4.4	2.5
	24	3.8	0.2	0.1	72.1	15.9	7.8
	60	11.9	0.1	0.2	56.4	27.0	4.4
	120	11.7	0.1	1.4	53.1	28.4	2.3
b	1	0.0	0.0	0.0	0.0	100.0	0.0
	3	0.3	0.9	0.6	0.2	97.7	0.3
	6	0.7	1.3	0.7	0.7	96.0	0.7
	12	1.3	1.2	1.2	1.6	93.8	0.8
	24	2.0	1.3	1.2	4.8	89.6	1.1
	60	2.2	2.3	1.0	12.2	72.8	9.5
	120	2.3	2.5	1.2	13.6	69.0	11.4
s	1	0.0	0.0	0.0	0.0	0.0	100.0
	3	2.3	1.8	0.0	0.8	0.6	94.5
	6	2.5	1.7	0.1	1.3	2.4	92.0
	12	1.5	6.3	1.1	2.0	3.9	85.1
	24	2.0	15.1	1.2	2.5	3.0	76.2
	60	2.9	21.4	1.2	7.4	3.8	63.4
	120	7.7	17.3	2.1	14.8	5.4	52.6

k denotes the prediction horizon in months.

and non-financial variables. In particular, bankruptcies seem to have a strong effect on the real exchange rate, the price level and the money supply. On the other hand, bankruptcies are affected by money and stock prices (the latter probably serving as a leading indicator). By contrast, there seems to be only a very weak link between industrial production and bankruptcies, which suggests that the latter variable is not determined solely by demand considerations.

In order to gain more insight into the qualitative nature of various effects we have to scrutinize the impulse responses. They are reported in Table 3 and Figure 2 together with the standard errors (Table 3) and the confidence intervals (i.e. ±2· standard errors; Figure 2). The standard errors are so small that the impulse responses are in almost all cases different from zero at the conventional 5 per cent level of significance. As the number of observations is so large this is not very surprising. Perhaps, one should, in a case like this, have a more conservative interpretation of the proper level of statistical significance. In our case, this would not, however, make much difference.

When the response estimates are scrutinized it turns out that, except for a few cases, the corresponding values clearly make sense. Thus, for instance, bankruptcies have a positive effect on the real exchange rate (i.e., ceteris paribus, the Finnish Markka is devalued), a negative effect on the price level and industrial output, and a negative effect on money supply and stock prices. Thus, bankruptcy innovations seem to contribute to some sort of "credit crunch", which means that banks' credit supply and the overall liquidity in the economy decrease. This, in turn, adds to the adverse direct effects of bankruptcy innovations on output and rates of return. Altogether, this suggests that, for instance, in the case of an economic depression, corporate failures may constitute a more serious problem than merely a loss of equity wealth.

TABLE 3. **Eventual impulse responses for a VAR model for the vector $y_t = (e_t^r\ p_t\ y_t^r\ m1_t\ b_t\ s_t)'$**

	Innovation in					
	e^r	p	y^r	m1	b	s
e^r	0.065	-0.016	0.107	-0.107	0.151	-0.003
	(0.002)	(0.002)	(0.002)	(0.001)	(0.002)	(0.002)
p	0.811	-0.185	0.313	2.154	-1.737	-0.405
	(0.007)	(0.006)	(0.006)	(0.006)	(0.007)	(0.007)
y^r	0.214	-0.054	0.183	0.217	-0.099	-0.090
	(0.005)	(0.004)	(0.004)	(0.004)	(0.005)	(0.004)
m1	0.684	-0.160	0.383	1.378	-1.020	-0.298
	(0.009)	(0.008)	(0.008)	(0.008)	(0.010)	(0.009)
b	-0.010	0.011	-0.017	-0.022	0.018	0.034
	(0.008)	(0.006)	(0.008)	(0.006)	(0.009)	(0.008)
s	0.289	-0.042	0.160	0.443	-0.261	-0.026
	(0.006)	(0.005)	(0.005)	(0.005)	(0.006)	(0.006)

Positive one standard deviation shocks are used. Responses are in terms of fractions of standard deviations; the response of a variable is divided by the standard deviation of its residual variance. The prediction horizon is 120 months. Standard errors for the point estimates are presented in parentheses. They are computed using Bayesian methods and Monte Carlo integration (see Klock and Van Dijk (1978)). The number of drawings is 1000.

On the other hand, both the real exchange rate, industrial output and money have a negative long-run effect on bankruptcies while the price level effect is positive. In the same way, the stock price effect is also positive, which is some sort of perverse effect. Notice, however, that the magnitude of the effect is small and, moreover, the corresponding short-run effect is clearly negative, suggesting that positive stock market news has a negative effect on corporate failures. The short and long-run effects also clearly differ in the case of prices. Thus, the immediate effect of a price level shock is negative while in the long run the effect becomes positive. This may be due to the fact that the price level reflects conflicting cost and revenue elements.

Our data sample covers an exceptionally long period and thus one might doubt that the estimated relationships are stable over time. If some important variables were left out of our model, this would moreover show up in inconstancies. This does not seem to be too much of a problem, however. As can be seen from Table 4, there are only very few changes in the long-run variance decompositions when the model is estimated from various subperiods. (Also, the explanatory power of the models seems to be quite invariant over different estimation periods.) This result is not very surprising given the fact that the size distribution of bankrupt firms is apparently constant over time (cf. again Figure 1).[4] This does not, however, mean that the changes in estimation results are totally unimportant. In the case of bankruptcies, it can be seen that there has been some sort of change in causation. During the prewar

TABLE 4. **Long-run decompositions of variance for a VAR model for the vector $\underset{\sim}{y}_t=(e^r_t\ p_t\ y^r_t\ m1_t\ b_t\ s_t)'$ using data from different periods**

	Estimation period	Innovation in					
		e^r	p	y^r	m1	b	s
e^r	1922–1949	43.1	8.1	11.4	2.1	16.5	18.7
	1922–1959	45.8	11.2	12.7	4.6	20.8	4.9
	1922–1969	48.3	13.7	11.4	4.5	18.8	3.2
	1922–1979	47.6	11.6	11.5	5.9	17.0	6.5
	1922–1990	46.2	11.6	10.6	4.7	18.9	8.0
	1939–1990	56.4	16.9	6.7	2.6	9.1	8.3
p	1922–1949	4.4	17.6	5.8	43.4	21.1	7.7
	1922–1959	7.9	9.3	2.2	29.9	47.5	3.3
	1922–1969	9.1	11.0	1.2	31.7	45.2	1.7
	1922–1979	14.4	9.7	0.8	38.9	34.0	2.2
	1922–1990	9.3	9.0	0.5	44.7	35.1	1.3
	1939–1990	22.7	13.1	0.4	27.9	34.6	1.2
y^r	1922–1949	42.1	0.8	18.9	24.9	2.6	10.7
	1922–1959	30.6	2.7	38.3	20.6	5.0	2.8
	1922–1969	42.9	2.8	29.6	20.4	2.7	1.5
	1922–1979	45.0	1.7	29.3	16.7	2.8	4.6
	1922–1990	36.7	1.5	34.5	18.5	4.0	4.8
	1939–1990	51.0	3.1	32.2	8.8	2.0	2.9
m1	1922–1949	21.0	3.7	4.4	62.3	3.5	5.1
	1922–1959	17.5	0.7	3.0	44.2	33.1	1.6
	1922–1969	19.7	0.4	0.9	44.1	33.8	1.1
	1922–1979	24.5	0.4	1.5	45.4	26.0	2.3
	1922–1990	11.7	0.1	1.4	53.1	28.4	2.3
	1939–1990	29.9	0.3	0.5	40.8	25.6	2.9
b	1922–1949	11.7	9.5	7.1	19.2	40.7	11.8
	1922–1959	8.8	5.1	3.8	15.5	58.2	8.6
	1922–1969	5.6	5.9	1.5	13.5	67.6	5.9
	1922–1979	5.0	4.9	1.3	12.0	67.6	9.1
	1922–1990	2.3	2.5	1.2	13.6	69.0	11.4
	1939–1990	5.6	4.7	2.5	3.3	75.7	8.3
s	1922–1949	21.1	9.2	8.9	24.7	10.3	25.8
	1922–1959	16.7	8.0	11.3	29.0	12.6	21.8
	1922–1969	18.2	10.8	4.7	29.1	11.9	25.3
	1922–1979	18.9	11.6	4.4	24.1	8.2	32.7
	1922–1990	7.7	17.3	2.1	14.8	5.4	52.6
	1939–1990	6.2	19.6	2.0	13.6	6.5	52.1

The prediction horizon is 120 months.

period, causation seems to run from money to bankruptcies while the opposite seems to be true during the postwar period. Unfortunately, there is no undisputed way of splitting the sample period so that subsamples would exactly correspond to some well-defined regimes (assuming, of course, that such regimes exist).

Finally, a few words about the nonlinearity test results which were already discussed in Section 2. The plots of the G irreversibility statistics suggested by Ramsey (1990) are presented in Figure 3.[5] Comparing these test statistics with the computed standard deviations (not displayed) indicates that there are some, although not very strong, signs of nonlinearities in terms of time irreversibility in univariate models. In particular, this concerns prices with k equalling 20–30 months and bankruptcies, share prices and money with k equalling 1–2 months. In the case of prices, the alarming test values may be explained by stationarity problems while otherwise the problems may be due to some abnormal observations and/or data compilation procedures.[6] Finally, notice that our univariate time series results do not, of course, exclude the possibility that nonlinearities also exist in the relationships between different variables. To examine this possibility is, however, a task for further study.

4 Concluding remarks

This study has demonstrated that bankruptcies play a very important role in the determination of key (macro)economic variables, both financial and non-financial. The importance must at least partially be due to the effects firm failures have on banks' behaviour and thus on the supply of credit and liquidity. Moreover, it seems that liquidity itself has an impact on bankruptcies. An interesting question is how important is this link and what are the channels via which the liquidity effect operates? This is a problem which seems to require somewhat different data, i.e. micro panel data covering different liquidity regimes.

If such kind of data were used, one could also explain the discrepancies which seem to exist between empirical analyses using either cross-section micro data or aggregate time-series data (cf. fn. 1). Obviously, this kind of analysis would require somewhat more sophisticated variable specifications, at least in terms of financial factors, but this would also produce more concrete and intuitive results.

Footnotes

1 There are several microeconomic studies which deal with the causes of bankruptcies in Finland. Practically all then apply the ZETA-model by Altman et al. (1977) as a frame of reference. Thus, the analyses have made use of discriminant analysis, where a set of (financial ratio) variables is used to classify firms according to the bankrupty risk. Finnish studies include Prihti (1975), Laitinen (1990) and Sundgren (1991).

The results from these Finnish studies can be summarized in the following way: they imply that insolvency problems and bankruptcies are strongly related to firms profitability and indebtedness but not so much in terms of liquidity and the structure of earnings and costs. Clearly, we might now expect the behaviour of the total number of bankruptcies to be highly dependent on macro variables which correspond to aggregate demand. It is interesting to check whether this link is actually operative. It is also of considerable interest to check whether the liquidity, or monetary, phenomena in general, really are unimportant for the determination of bankruptcies. In this connection, very little evidence has been available on firms' other characteristics, for instance in terms of quality of management and accounting, which have been stressed e.g. by Argenti (1976). See also Keasey and Watson (1987) for further evidence of the importance of these non-financial symptoms.

2 Immediately after the outbreak of WWII, various regulatory measures were put into effect in the capital market. This marked the start of a 40-year period of market regulation, which was evident in strict control of banks' (average) lending rates and in non-price rationing of credit. Credit rationing obviously had an adverse effect on the borrowing opportunities of more risky firms, which, in turn, might explain why the level of bankruptcies stayed at a relatively low level during the whole 40-year period, including the 1976–1977 recession.

3 Results with the broad money concept, m2, were qualitatively similar to the reported results, except that the explanatory power decreased somewhat when this alternative measure was used. Because of this, and also because of lack of space, these results are not displayed here. As far as the variable ordering is concerned, we experimented with some alternative orderings. The residuals did not turn out to be uncorrelated and therefore the results were slightly sensitive to the ordering of variables. Thus, the following correlation coefficients were obtained for the residuals: e^r;p -.223, e^r;y^r .002, e^r;m1 .034, e^r;b -.030, e^r;s .042, p;y^r .025, p;m1 .049, p;b -.001, p;s .144, y^r;m1 .009, y^r;b .071, y^r;s -.015, m1;b .023, m1;s .097, b;s -.062 (the asymptotic standard deviation of the correlation coefficients is .035). We cannot defend our choice very firmly, but the chosen ordering seems to be the most obvious in terms of the so called "small open economy" model.

4 This constancy finding is obviously at variance with the hypothesis mentioned earlier according to which financial constraints affect small firms disproportionately (see e.g. Gertler and Gilchrist (1991)).

5 The G statistic for variable x is defined as

$$G_{ij}^{k} = \sum_{t=1}^{n}\left(\frac{1}{n}\right)[(x_t)^i(x_{t-k})^j - (x_t)^j(x_{t-k})^i], \quad k=1,2,\ldots,K.$$

Here, following Ramsey (1990), we assume that i=2 and j=1. The (maximum) lag length K is set at 120. For all the time series in Figure 3, the log difference transformation is used to induce stationarity. As far as testing for the significance of the G statistic is concerned, see Ramsey and Rothman (1988).

6 The price level is a somewhat difficult case because it is not at all clear how to make it stationary. In the prewar period, the price level was stationary while in the postwar period the inflation rate has been roughly stationary.

References

Altman, E.I, Haldeman, R.G. and Naraynan, P. (1977) ZETA Analysis: A New Model to Identify Bankruptcy Risk of Corporations, Journal of Banking and Finance 1, 29-54.

Argenti, J. (1976) Corporate Collapse. The Causes and Symptoms, McGraw-Hill, London.

Bernanke, B. (1983) Nonmonetary Effects of the Financial Crisis in the Propagation of the Great Depression, American Economic Review 73, 257-276.

Engle, R. and Granger, C. (1987) Co-Integration and Error Correction: Representation, Estimation, and Testing, Econometrica 55, 251-276.

Gertler, M. and Gilchrist, S. (1991) Monetary Policy, Business Cycles and the Behavior of Small Manufacturing Firms, National Bureau of Economic Research, Working Paper 3892.

Hakkio, G. and Morris, C. (1984) Vector Autoregressions: A User's Manual, Federal Reserve Bank of Kansas City Working Paper RWP 10/84.

Keasey, K. and Watson, R. (1987) Non-Financial Symptoms and the Prediction of Small Company Failure: A Test for Argenti's Hypothesis, Journal of Business Finance and Accounting, 335-354.

Kloek, T. and Van Dijk, H.K. (1978) Bayesian Estimates of Equations System Parameters: An Application of Integration by Monte Carlo, Econometrica 46, 1-19.

Morgan, D.P. (1991) New Evidence Firms are Financially Constrained, Federal Reserve Bank of Kansas City, Economic Review, September/october, 37-45.

Laitinen, E. (1990) Predicting Bankruptcies (in Finnish), Vaasan Yritysinformaatio Oy, Vaasa.

Prihti, A. (1975) Predicting Bankruptcies with the Help of Firms' Balance Sheet Information, Helsinki School of Economics, Acta Academiae Oeconomicae Helsingiensis A:13, Helsinki.

Ramsey, J.B. (1990) Economic and Financial Data as Nonlinear Processes, in G. Dwyer and R. Hafer (eds.) The Stock Market: Bubbles, Volatility, and Chaos, Kluwer Academic Publishers, Dordrecht.

Ramsey, J.B. and Rothman, P. (1988) Characterization of the Irreversibility of Economic Time Series: Estimators and Test Statistics, Economic Research Reports 88-39, C.V. Starr Center for Applied Economics, New York University, New York.

Sims, C., Stock, J. and Watson, M. (1990) Inference in Linear Time Series Models with Some Unit Roots, Econometrica 58, 113-144.

Stiglitz, J. and Weiss, A. (1981) Credit Rationing in Markets with Imperfect Information, American Economic Review 71, 393-410.

Sundgren, S. (1991) Predicting Bankruptcies and Insolvency Problems with Financial Ratios (in Finnish), Velkakierre 5/91.

Virén, M. (1992) Some Long-Run Trends in Finnish Financial Variables, University of Turku, Department of Economics, Research Reports 16.

Williamson, S. (1987) Recent Developments in Modeling Financial Intermediation, Federal Reserve Bank of Minneapolis Quarterly Review, Summer 1987, 19-29.

Figure 1. Bankruptcies (12-month moving sum), left scale [1] ———
Total debt of bankrupt firms, right scale -----

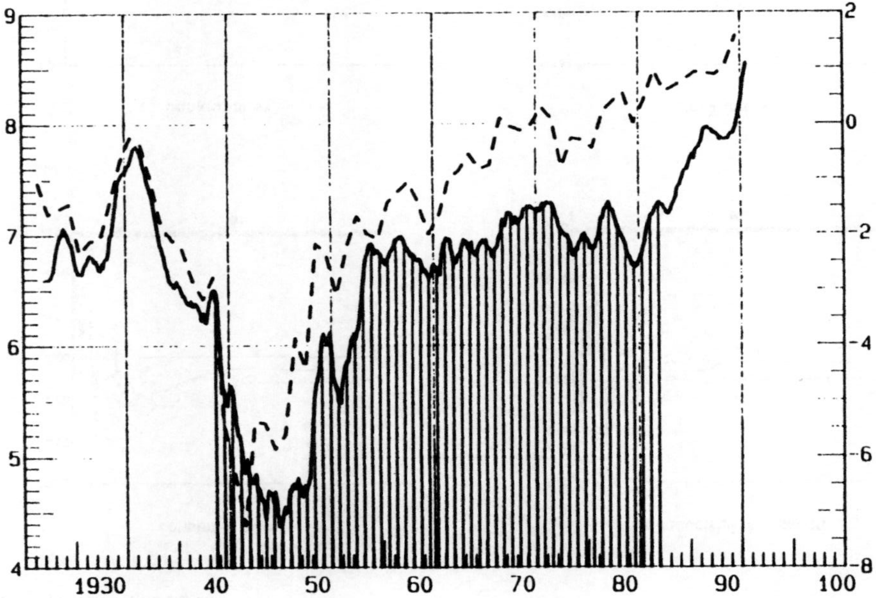

1) The credit rationing period has been marked

Figure 2. Impulse responses for bankruptcies

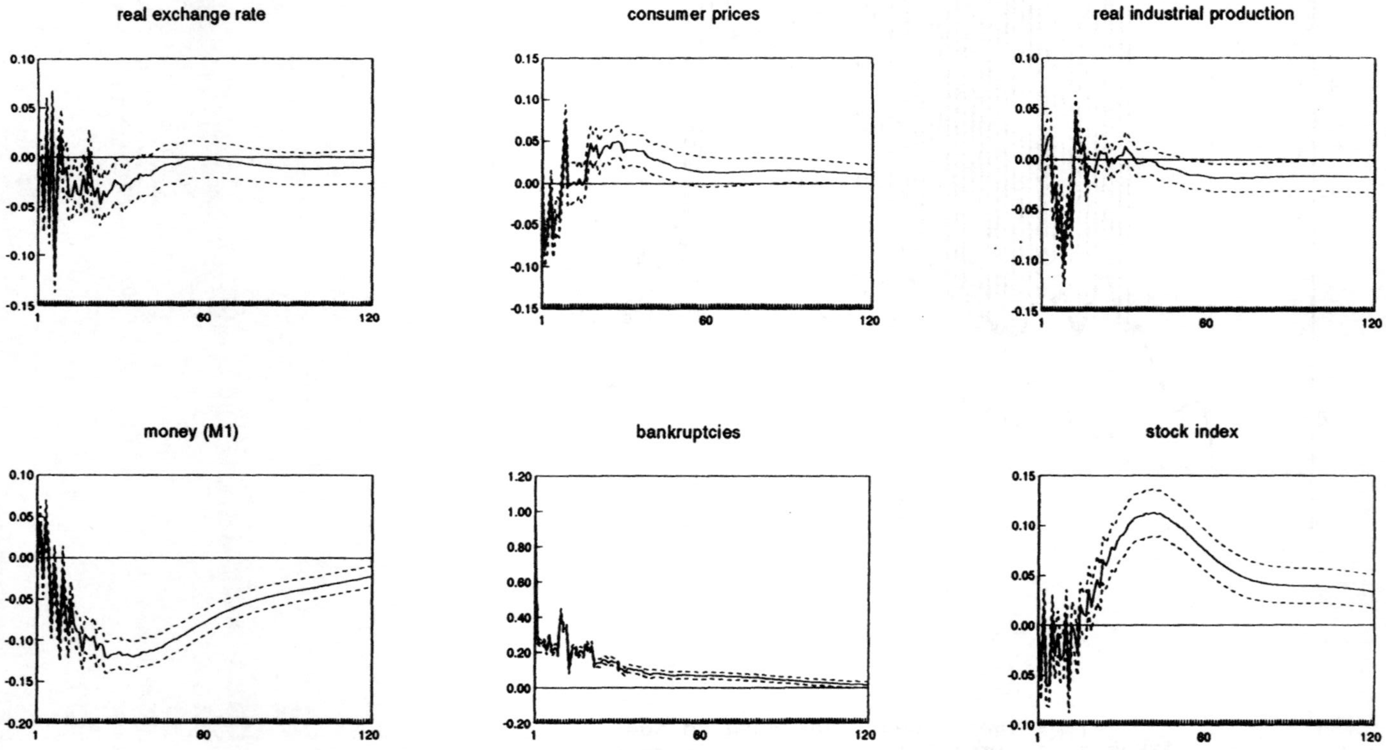

Figure 3. Plot of the irreversibility test coefficients

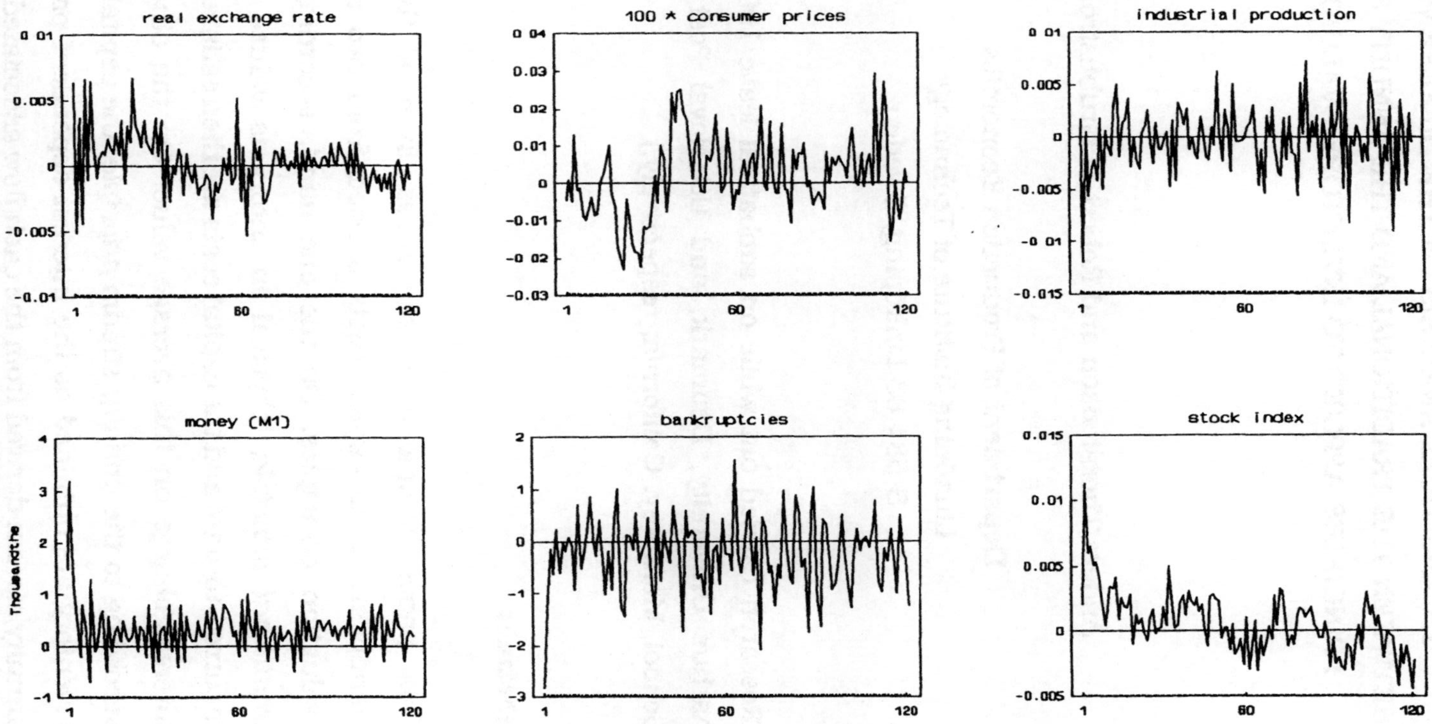

THEORETICAL ANALYSIS OF THE DIFFERENCE BETWEEN THE TRADITIONAL AND THE ANNUITY STREAM PRINCIPLES APPLIED TO INVENTORY EVALUATION

Anders Thorstenson and Robert W Grubbström

Department of Production Economics
Linköping Institute of Technology
S-581 83 Linköping, Sweden

(Research carried out while on sabbatical leave 1991/92 at Aarhus University, Denmark, and US Naval Postgraduate School, Monterey, California, respectively.)

Abstract

This paper compares consequences from a theoretical standpoint as to capital costs derived from two inventory evaluation principles. On the one hand, according to the *traditional principle*, physical inventory is valued at cost-incurred-to-date and the capital costs are then estimated as an interest charge on this average value. On the other hand, according to the *annuity stream principle*, the capital costs of inventory are obtained as the interest-dependent part of the annuity stream derived from the cash flow associated with the physical inventory build-up. Whereas the traditional approach attempts at approximating traditional accounting procedures, the annuity stream principle is in agreement with financial theory and it is therefore considered the superior of the two, since it implies that a coherent methodology is applied to the evaluation of capital used in any type of investment, whether it be inventory or other working capital, plant, equipment, or any other type of material or immaterial asset. The present inquiry highlights some theoretical issues concerning the differences between the two evaluation principles. It is shown how the first-order difference in capital costs depends on the fluctuation of profit around its long-run average.

1. Introduction

The valuation principle to be analyzed in this paper takes as its basis the idea that the ultimate consequences of all economic activities in a manufacturing firm are in the form of payments or payment streams. In principle this idea applies to actions taken on strategic and tactical as well as on operational decision levels in a firm. The crucial role that is played by payments of a firm is emphasized by the fact that one of the typical measures taken when facing the acute risk of bankruptcy is the discontinuation of payments. From a theoretical point of view, the valuation of firms and of assets held by firms, i e of the firm's activities, should also be based on payments.

We accentuate the difference between *payments*, on the one

hand, and *cost and revenue measures*, on the other. Payments are the events when cash (or other monetary transactions via accounts etc) actually change hands. These are occurrences of real events which are recorded and can be observed objectively. Cost and revenue measures are more abstract and can be subject to a more or less subjective judgement. These measures may be defined as payments distributed over time according to some convention. Typical examples in which the distinction is emphasized are depreciation charges when some equipment purchase value is distributed over the life-span of the equipment or some prepaid rent for a property which is allocated to the period for which the property may be used by the tenant. Costs and revenues are therefore more abstract than the payments from which they are derived. The modelling of accounting cost procedures thus involves a description of the way in which a process including a mechanism of abstraction already has taken place. This modelling therefore comprises an abstraction operation in (at least) two steps. To model costing procedures is of greater complexity than to model the original payments.

The main objective of this paper is to analyze the relations between the operational activities of a firm, in particular its inventory holding processes, their payment consequences and their valuation with particular reference to the capital costs. In production and inventory control, activities such as determining order quantities, sequencing and scheduling affect both amount and temporal allocation of payments for resources utilized. Inpayments might also be similarly influenced through the effect of lead times, service levels etc on delivery performance and the following payments for finished goods sold. Even if these relations in real life may seem far-fetched or diffuse and in theory may be difficult, complex or impossible to model precisely, the mere awareness of their existence might help intuition in decision-making. Examples of such relations might also contribute to an enhanced understanding of what constitutes optimal decisions in inventory control.

The notion of capital costs is fundamental in inventory theory as well as in practical inventory management. In this context we define capital costs as the costs associated with a production and inventory holding process which depend on the interest rate or the opportunity cost of capital. These costs are determined from the assessed value of capital tied up in the inventory holding process. According to the standard textbook approach and to the usual practical inventory management procedures, this capital amount is determined as a unit price multiplied by the number of units stocked at each point in time. The capital costs are then obtained by calculating the average over time and multiplying this amount by an interest rate, the opportunity cost of capital, or some similar factor serving the same purpose. This method, to use physical inventory levels multiplied by unit prices and by an interest rate, we call the "traditional principle".

The converse principle, regarded as a theoretically superior and more correct point of departure, has been called "the annuity principle". Certainly no economic valuation procedure could be claimed to be universally correct in any sense. Thus the word "correct" is intended to be interpreted according to the same principle as the term "optimal" usually is interpreted, i e with respect to an objective function set forth for mapping some real-world intention. The annuity principle departs from viewing the payment consequences belonging to production and stocking processes. Since the ultimate consequences of all economic activities of any firm are in the form of payment or payment streams, it is argued that all costs and revenues are determined from payments, including inventory holding costs, such as capital costs in this particular context. The capital costs are incurred due to time delays between in- and outpayments in a firm. Therefore an evaluation of inventory capital costs derived directly from payments would be more basic than an evaluation stemming from measured physical inventory levels and per unit costs incurred to date.

If given an original set of payments distributed over time, their net present value (NPV) is first computed. By multiplying this NPV by a certain factor, the annuity factor, the level of a hypothetical constant stream of payments that have the same NPV is obtained. This hypothetical stream we call the annuity stream. The annuity stream may be interpreted as the time average of all profits adjusted by means of the interest rate for their distribution over time. Thus, the annuity stream will include terms corresponding to all capital costs including capital costs for holding inventory. When determining these capital costs, the average unadjusted profits are deducted from the annuity stream. The residue is then interpreted as capital costs, since this difference will depend only on the interest rate applied, i e on the price of capital. Previously a number of inventory models have been analyzed along similar lines, see e g Hadley (1964), Trippi and Lewin (1974), Grubbström (1980), Kim et al (1986) and Thorstenson (1988).

Thus, capital costs may be determined by two different methods. The objective of the research reported in this paper is to investigate how the difference in capital cost evaluations might depend on general characteristics of the production and stocking processes considered. Our analysis is based on models which make use of Laplace transforms and Laurent series. In the Appendix is given a brief introduction of these tools. In Section 2 we characterize the activities of a firm as a set of in- and outpayment flows, and derive expressions for their total value per unit time according to our two evaluation principles. We are then able to show in Section 3 how the (first-order) capital cost difference depends on the fluctuation of profits around their long-run average. We also show how this result can be interpreted if all activities are cyclical with a common cycle time. An example of such a case is presented in Section 4 in which a simple batch production model is investigated. Finally, in Section 5 we summarize our findings and give a suggestion for further analysis.

2. Model formulation of traditional and annuity stream principles

In order to make a comparison between the traditional and annuity stream principles it is necessary to specify a model of each of the two evaluation procedures. As pointed out in the introduction, modelling of the traditional costing procedures is more complex than the modelling of payments. The traditional principle departs from physical stock and its development over time whereas the annuity stream takes the payments over time as its starting point. In the former approach, the value of costs-incurred-to-date is attached to the physical stock.

We will assume that cumulate costs-incurred-to-date (connected with an inventory build-up) are possible to derive from the payments for labour, materials, components, etc, that enter the products as value is added in production and processing. Usually, however, production factors are not paid for immediately in cash; instead there is a credit period. We allow for such an interval between payments and costs to exist. (But in our detailed analysis below, we make this period a constant.)

The foregoing applies to an inventory build-up. On the other hand, when goods are taken out from inventory, its value according to the traditional approach decreases with the cost value of the products or semi-products etc sold (or transferred from inventory to other parts of production). Even if there were a perfect internal pricing system and a detailed profit centre structure, we cannot automatically use revenue inpayments (possibly advanced by some credit period) to describe the inventory decrease, since these payments also contain contributions to profits and for covering fixed costs.

Therefore, in order to model the value outflow from inventory, we let inventory value decrease according to inpayments as long as they do not exceed cumulate costs. If a product is paid for only at one particular point in time, this will be an accurate description of the real-world accounting procedure. On the other hand, if inpayments for some particular item are spread out over time, inventory will decrease according to (possibly advanced) inpayments up to the payback time after which inventory will be valued at zero for the item in question.

Hence, the value of physical stock is assumed to accumulate according to (a possibly advanced) outpayment flow and decrease with (a possibly advanced) inpayment flow as long as net accumulated payments are negative. In this way we can accordingly include credits to customers and credits from vendors. Finally, it is assumed that there is a unique payback time for each item counted from the beginning of the item's production cycle (essentially the time at which the item is delivered to the production system).

The overall activities of the firm we assume to be able to be interpreted as a set of individual activities, each of which we call the production of an "item". In order for the inventory account to be accurately described, an item might be regarded as the smallest entity which is fully paid for at one particular point in time. This corresponds to the usual interpretation of an item. Complications occur for example if prepayments, deposits, etc, exist, as is frequently the case for production related to larger projects. The inpayments are then spread out over time.

To develop comparisons between the two principles, the

following notation is introduced:

$p(t, i) =$ inpayment flow for item i, $i = 1, 2, \ldots,$

$c(t, i) =$ outpayment flow for item i

$z(t, i) =$ release rate of capital tied up in production (and inventory) of item i according to traditional approach

$\tau_i =$ payback time of item i

$p(t) = \sum_{i=1}^{\infty} p(t, i) =$ overall inpayment flow of firm

$c(t) = \sum_{i=1}^{\infty} c(t, i) =$ overall outpayment flow of firm

$z(t) = \sum_{i=1}^{\infty} z(t, i) =$ overall release rate of capital tied up in inventory and production

$r =$ continuous interest rate

It is assumed for the sake of assuring convergence in some later expressions that variables $p(t, i), c(t, i), z(t, i)$ depending on item index i only exist during finite time intervals, that is

$$p(t, i) = c(t, i) = z(t, i) = 0, \quad \textit{for a sufficiently large } t \tag{1}$$

This implies that all Laurent coefficients of their corresponding transforms with negative index values (cf Appendix) are zero.

We shall also assume that the net total cash flow $p(t) - c(t)$ has a finite long-run time average and that the long-run time average of inventory according to the traditional principle also is limited. According to the Appendix, the Laplace transform of the cash flow expanded into a Laurent series is now written:

$$\bar{p}(s) - \bar{c}(s) = \sum_{j=-\infty}^{\infty} (p_j - c_j) s^j \qquad (2)$$

In order for there to be a long-run time average, the limit $\lim_{s \to 0} s[\bar{p}(s) - \bar{c}(s)]$ must exist. From (2) we therefore find the following necessary relations between in- and outflow Laurent coefficients:

$$p_k - c_k = 0, \quad for\ k < -1 \qquad (3)$$

and the long-run average cash flow level will be:

$$\lim_{s \to 0} s[\bar{p}(s) - \bar{c}(s)] = p_{-1} - c_{-1} \qquad (4)$$

That the net total cash flow has a limited long-run level by no means implies that either of the overall in- and outpayment flows does. What is necessary, is that their coefficients for higher-order time powers exactly outbalance each other so that their difference remains limited. Conditions for the long-run limited value of inventory will be formulated below.

Annuity Stream

The *annuity stream* is the constant stream of payments having the same net present value as a given stream of payments. For an infinite horizon using our notations, we obtain

$$A = r \cdot \int_0^\infty [p(t) - c(t)] e^{-rt} dt = r[\tilde{p}(r) - \tilde{c}(r)] \tag{5}$$

Using the Laurent coefficients we find from (2) and (3)

$$A = [s(\tilde{p}(s) - \tilde{c}(s))]_{s=r} = \sum_{j=-1}^{\infty} (p_j - c_j) r^{j+1} = (p_{-1} - c_{-1}) + r(p_0 - c_0) + r^2(p_1 - c_1) + \ldots \tag{6}$$

which is the Maclaurin expansion of the annuity stream. The zeroth-order term, which does not depend on the interest, is interpreted as the long-run average profit flow without consideration of capital costs (with a hypothetical interest rate equal to zero; cf (4)), whereas the remaining terms depending on r are the capital costs. For the sake of comparing this expression with the traditional approach, whose corresponding expression only depends linearly on interest, we usually will only keep the zeroth- and first-order terms in (6) as an approximation of A.

Traditional Approach

As mentioned above, a theoretical description of the traditional approach is more complicated than of the annuity stream principle. To determine the release of capital tied up in item i we observe that the payback time (in physical terms) for item i is determined as the smallest τ_i satisfying:

$$\int_0^{\tau_i} c(t + T_2(i), i) dt \le \int_0^{\tau_i} p(t + T_1(i), i) dt \tag{7}$$

where $T_1(i)$ and $T_2(i)$ are the credit periods for item i on the in- and outpayment sides, respectively. According to our interpretation of the traditional principle above, the release rate is given by

$$z(t,i) = \begin{cases} p(t+T_1(i),i), \quad t < \tau_i \\ \left[\int_0^{\tau_i} c(\alpha+T_2(i),i)\,d\alpha - \int_{\alpha<\tau_i} p(\alpha+T_1(i),i)\,d\alpha\right]\delta(t-\tau_i), \quad t = \tau_i \\ c(t+T_2(i),i), \quad t > \tau_i \end{cases} \tag{8}$$

where $\delta(.)$ is the Dirac impulse (cf Appendix). The middle case takes care of the possibility that inpayments might be discrete at the payback time τ_i. Since cumulate inventory value has decreased to zero at the payback time, it then follows that

$$\int_0^\infty z(t,i)\,dt = \int_0^\infty c(t+T_2(i),i)\,dt \tag{9}$$

which has a limited value by (1). Hence we have the identity

$$\tilde{z}(0,i) = \lim_{s\to 0} \tilde{c}(s,i)e^{sT_2(i)} = \tilde{c}(0,i) \tag{10}$$

where $\tilde{z}(s,i)$ denotes the transform of $z(t,i)$, etc.

Capital $C(t,i)$ tied up by an individual item can now be expressed as

$$C(t,i) = \int_0^t \left[c(\alpha+T_2(i),i) - z(\alpha,i)\right]d\alpha \tag{11}$$

which is zero for $t \geq \tau_i$, and capital $C(t)$ tied up at time t by all items as

$$C(t) = \int_0^t \sum_{i=1}^\infty \left[c(\alpha+T_2(i),i) - z(\alpha,i)\right]d\alpha = \int_0^t \left[c(\alpha+T_2) - z(\alpha)\right]d\alpha \tag{12}$$

where T_2 is an average measure for the credit time on the outpayment side. Average capital $\bar{C}$ tied up in the long run according to the traditional approach is then given by

$$\bar{C} = \lim_{t\to\infty} \frac{1}{t} \int_0^t C(\alpha)d\alpha = \lim_{s\to 0} s\tilde{C}(s) = \lim_{s\to 0} \left[\tilde{c}(s)e^{sT_2} - \tilde{z}(s)\right] \tag{13}$$

where (A8), (A4), (A9) and (12) have been used. Using a Laurent series representation of the right-hand member and developing the exponential function into a Maclaurin series, we obtain:

$$\tilde{c}(s)e^{sT_2} - \tilde{z}(s) = \sum_{j=-\infty}^{\infty} c_j s^j \sum_{k=0}^{\infty} \frac{T_2^k s^k}{k!} - \sum_{j=-\infty}^{\infty} z_j s^j = \sum_{j=-\infty}^{\infty} s^j \left(\sum_{k=0}^{\infty} \frac{c_{j-k} T_2^k}{k!} - z_j \right) \tag{14}$$

In order for $\bar{C}$ to be limited, the following relations must hold between the coefficients in question

$$\sum_{k=0}^{\infty} \frac{c_{j-k} T_2^k}{k!} - z_j = 0, \quad for\ j < 0 \tag{15}$$

and we then obtain the limit

$$\bar{C} = c_0 - z_0 + \sum_{k=1}^{\infty} \frac{c_{-k} T_2^k}{k!} \tag{16}$$

The sum over index values of k greater than zero represents on the one hand the dependence on the average 'vendor' credit time T_2 and, on the other, the dependence on the coefficients of the Laurent expansion of $\tilde{c}(s)$ on first- and higher-order negative powers of s. If a coefficient for an index of k greater than or equal to two is nonzero, this means that there is at least a linear trend in the developments over time of the outpayments etc. If there is no credit time, such trends will have no influence on the average capital tied up.

Note that, although $\tilde{z}(0, i) = \tilde{c}(0, i)$ for an individual item according to (10), in general this will not hold for an infinite sequence, i e $\bar{C} \neq 0$ in the normal case also when there is no credit period T_2. Since

$$\tilde{c}(s)e^{sT_2} - \tilde{z}(s) = \sum_{i=1}^{\infty} \left[\tilde{c}(s,i)e^{sT_2(i)} - \tilde{z}(s,i)\right] \tag{17}$$

this sum will be an infinite sum of zeros when s approaches the limit zero.

Similarly to the derivation of (13)-(16), we now investigate the long-run average profits according to our theoretical interpretation of the traditional approach. Introducing T_1 to represent the average credit period to 'customers', the long-run time average of the profit flow will be:

$$\lim_{t \to \infty} \frac{1}{t} \int_0^t \left[p(\alpha + T_1) - c(\alpha + T_2)\right] d\alpha = \lim_{s \to 0} s\left[\tilde{p}(s)e^{sT_1} - \tilde{c}(s)e^{sT_2}\right] =$$

$$= \lim_{s \to 0} \sum_{j=-\infty}^{\infty} s^{j+1} \sum_{k=0}^{\infty} \frac{p_{j-k}T_1^k - c_{j-k}T_2^k}{k!} = (p_{-1} - c_{-1}) + \sum_{k=1}^{\infty} c_{-1-k} \frac{T_1^k - T_2^k}{k!} \tag{18}$$

where (3) has been used.

The average profit *net of capital costs* in the traditional approach can now be defined as

$$B = (p_{-1} - c_{-1}) + \sum_{k=1}^{\infty} \frac{c_{-1-k}(T_1^k - T_2^k)}{k!} - r\bar{C} =$$

$$= (p_{-1} - c_{-1}) + \sum_{k=1}^{\infty} \frac{c_{-1-k}(T_1^k - T_2^k)}{k!} - r\left(\sum_{k=1}^{\infty} \frac{c_{-k}T_2^k}{k!} + c_0 - z_0\right) \tag{19}$$

where we have deducted capital costs $r\bar{C}$ according to (16) from (18). The two first terms represent average profits before capital costs. In order for these to be non-zero, $\tilde{p}(s) - \tilde{c}(s)$ must have a simple pole at $s = 0$ or there must be a difference between powers of the lengths of the two average credit periods and an expansion of at least t.

3. Comparison of principles

Comparing net profits according to the two principles from (6) and (19) yields the first-order difference

$$\Delta = A - B = -\sum_{k=1}^{\infty} \frac{c_{-1-k}(T_1^k - T_2^k)}{k!} + r\left(p_0 - z_0 + \sum_{k=1}^{\infty} \frac{c_{-k} T_2^k}{k!}\right) \tag{20}$$

We first analyze the difference in the capital cost term, i e the coefficient of r. For this purpose, we define the following *profit function:*

$$\tilde{\Pi}(s) = \tilde{p}(s) - \tilde{c}(s) + \left[\tilde{c}(s)e^{sT_2} - \tilde{z}(s)\right] \tag{21}$$

The first two terms $\tilde{p}(s) - \tilde{c}(s)$ represent the difference between the payment inflow and the payment outflow, i e the net payment flow. The remaining expression represents the difference between the allocation of costs over time $\tilde{c}(s)e^{sT_2}$ (advanced on the average by T_2 compared to payment outflows) and the function $\tilde{z}(s)$ representing the cost of goods sold. In the latter the customer credit period T_1 is implicitly recognized.

According to (21) the long-run average of $\Pi(t)$ will be

$$\bar{\Pi} = \lim_{s\to 0} s\tilde{\Pi}(s) = \Pi_{-1} = p_{-1} - c_{-1} + \sum_{k=0}^{\infty} \frac{c_{-1-k}T_2^k}{k!} - z_{-1} = p_{-1} - c_{-1} \tag{22}$$

where (A8) and (15) have been used. Thus, by (4) $\bar{\Pi}$ also is the long-run cash-flow level. If $\Pi(t)$ has a limit, then $\bar{\Pi}$ will be this limit.

Let us now study the time variation of the profit function $\tilde{\Pi}(s)$ around its long-run average level $\bar{\Pi}$. For this, we form the function:

$$\tilde{\pi}(s) = \tilde{\Pi}(s) - \frac{\bar{\Pi}}{s} \tag{23}$$

By subtracting a step function of the level $\bar{\Pi}$, we have taken away the first-order pole of $\tilde{\Pi}(s)$ and $\tilde{\pi}(s)$ will lack all negative powers of s. The limit of $\tilde{\pi}(s)$ when $s\to 0$, is then interpreted in the following way:

$$\tilde{\pi}(0) = \Pi_0 = \lim_{s\to 0} s\frac{\tilde{\pi}(s)}{s} = \lim_{t\to\infty} \frac{1}{t}\int_0^t\int_0^\beta \pi(\alpha)d\alpha\, d\beta \tag{24}$$

Hence, Π_0 is the long-run average of the integral of the fluctuation of profits around their long-run average. Introducing the Laurent series coefficients for $\tilde{\pi}(s)$ from (22)-(23), we finally obtain:

$$\Pi_0 = \lim_{s\to 0} \sum_{j=0}^{\infty} s^j \left(p_j - z_j - c_j + \sum_{k=0}^{\infty} c_{j-k}\frac{T_2^k}{k!}\right) = p_0 - z_0 + \sum_{k=1}^{\infty} c_{-k}\frac{T_2^k}{k!} \tag{25}$$

We can therefore identify this expression as the coefficient of the first-order difference in the capital cost term in (20):

$$\Delta = -\sum_{k=1}^{\infty} c_{-1-k} \frac{T_1^k - T_2^k}{k!} + r\Pi_0 \tag{26}$$

As regards the zeroth-order difference, this term only includes coefficients c_j, for $j<-1$ (which then equal p_j), and they therefore represent time developments of payment flows of powers t^k for $k>0$. Also, this term is proportional to the difference between powers of the average credit periods on the in- and outpayment sides and vanishes, if their difference can be neglected.

Cyclical case

As an important special case, we consider a *cyclical* process, in which all payment functions, revenue and cost functions and inventory release functions repeat themselves identically at intervals of τ. The transforms of the payment functions, the inventory release function and the profit function may then be written:

$$\begin{cases} \tilde{p}(s) = \tilde{p}(s,1)(1 + e^{-s\tau} + e^{-2s\tau} + \ldots) = \dfrac{\tilde{p}(s,1)}{1 - e^{-s\tau}} \\ \tilde{c}(s) = \dfrac{\tilde{c}(s,1)}{1 - e^{-s\tau}} \\ \tilde{z}(s) = \dfrac{\tilde{z}(s,1)}{1 - e^{-s\tau}} \\ \tilde{\Pi}(s) = \dfrac{\tilde{\Pi}(s,1)}{1 - e^{-s\tau}} \end{cases} \tag{27}$$

where we have defined $\tilde{\Pi}(s,i)$ as the profit function of the i th item. For simplicity , we assume that the first cycle starts at the time $t = 0$. We expand the "chain factor" according to (A14) and obtain:

$$\frac{1}{1-e^{-s\tau}} = \frac{1}{s\tau}\left(1+\frac{s\tau}{2}+\ldots\right) \tag{28}$$

Long-run profits are then obtained as

$$\bar{\Pi} = \Pi_{-1} = \frac{\tilde{\Pi}(0,1)}{\tau} \tag{29}$$

and the profit variation function will be

$$\tilde{\pi}(s) = \tilde{\Pi}(s) - \frac{\bar{\Pi}}{s} = \frac{\tilde{\Pi}(s,1)}{1-e^{-s\tau}} - \frac{\tilde{\Pi}(0,1)}{s\tau} =$$

$$= \left(\frac{1}{s\tau}+\frac{1}{2}+\ldots\right)\left(\tilde{\Pi}(0,1)+s\left[\frac{\partial\tilde{\Pi}(s,1)}{\partial s}\right]_{s=0}+\ldots\right) - \frac{\tilde{\Pi}(0,1)}{s\tau} \tag{30}$$

We introduce $\Pi_j(1)$ for the j th Maclaurin coefficient of $\tilde{\Pi}(s,1)$. Then the limit Π_0 can be written:

$$\tilde{\pi}(0) = \Pi_0 = \tilde{\Pi}(0,1)\left(\frac{1}{2}+\frac{1}{\tau}\frac{\left[\frac{\partial\tilde{\Pi}(s,1)}{\partial s}\right]_{s=0}}{\tilde{\Pi}(0,1)}\right) = \Pi_0(1)\left(\frac{1}{2}+\frac{1}{\tau}\frac{\Pi_1(1)}{\Pi_0(1)}\right) \tag{31}$$

Using the moment-generating property of the Laplace transform (A12), we can now finally interpret Π_0 as:

$$\Pi_0 = \Pi_0(1)\left(\frac{1}{2}-\frac{\bar{t}}{\tau}\right) \tag{32}$$

where $\bar{t}$ is the mean

$$\bar{t} = -\frac{\Pi_1(1)}{\Pi_0(1)} = \frac{\int_0^\infty \Pi(t,1)\,t\,dt}{\int_0^\infty \Pi(t,1)\,dt} \tag{33}$$

This is the mean lead time counted from the beginning of each cycle weighted by the normalized profit function.

If the credit periods T_1 and T_2 are nonnegative (as is the normal real-world case), and if production runs at a profit, then the profit function is a nonnegative function of time. Furthermore, if inpayments only occur at one instant in each cycle (which also is the normal real-world case) and if there is no 'vendor' credit period ($T_2 = 0$, implying that the third term in (21) will be zero), then the normalized profit function only occurs at the payback time as a unit impulse. In such a case $\bar{t}$ will simply be the payback time of the cycle.

Higher-order differences

Hitherto, we have not considered differences due to higher-order terms of r^k, $k>1$. These terms only occur in the annuity stream expression and not in the traditional capital cost expression (which by its very nature is linear in r). Together they are represented by:

$$\sum_{j=1}^{\infty} (p_j - c_j) r^{j+1} \tag{34}$$

Since the coefficients of p_j and c_j here only have positive indices, they correspond to time derivatives of the in- and outpayment streams of successively higher order. Hence this higher-order difference will contribute when the high-frequency variations of the net payment flow are important compared to the interest rate power in question. However, we do not intend to pursue the analysis of this higher-order difference further.

4. A batch production example

As an example we consider a batch production model which includes credit periods. Figure 1 depicts the cumulate cost pattern and the payment pattern. Variations of this example are often used in textbooks for explaining the nature of capital tied-up as working capital.

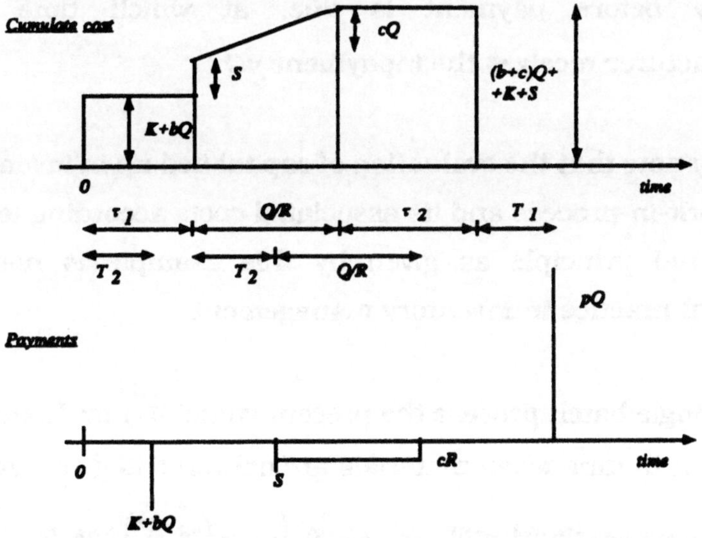

Figure 1 *Cumulate cost and payment patterns in the batch production model.*

Initially, purchased materials are delivered in a batch of Q units into a supply stock. After a credit period T_2, the order is paid for in the amount of $K+bQ$. After τ_1 time units counted from the delivery of materials, production begins and continues at a constant rate R for a period of Q/R. A set-up cost S is incurred at the beginning of production and during production a constant cost per time unit cR is incurred. We assume that the set-up and production costs also are paid for after the credit period T_2. When production is completed the products are kept in an inventory for finished goods on the average τ_2 time units until the whole batch is sold and delivered. The customer is then given a credit period T_1 after delivery before payment is due, at which time the manufacturer receives the inpayment pQ.

We may note that the evaluation of capital tied up in inventory and work-in-process and its associated costs according to the traditional principle as given by this example is not an unusual practice in inventory management.

For a single batch process the present value $V(1)$ evaluated at the point in time when materials are delivered is given by

$$V(1) = pQe^{-r(\tau_1+Q/R+\tau_2+T_1)} - (bQ+K)e^{-rT_2} - \left(S + cR\frac{1-e^{-rQ/R}}{r}\right)e^{-r(\tau_1+T_2)} \qquad (35)$$

Computing the first-order approximation of the annuity stream using (A14), we obtain

$$A = \frac{rV(1)}{1-e^{-r\tau}} = \frac{1}{\tau}\left(1+\frac{r\tau}{2}+...\right)V(1) = \frac{pQ-(bQ+K+S+cQ)}{\tau} + r\left[\frac{pQ-(bQ+K+S+cQ)}{2} - \frac{pQ(\tau_1+Q/R+\tau_2+T_1)-(bQ+K)T_2-(S+cQ)(\tau_1+T_2)-cQ^2/(2R)}{\tau}\right] \tag{36}$$

For the first batch (item) produced we have the functions:

$$\begin{cases} \tilde{p}(s,1) = pQe^{-s(\tau_1+Q/R+\tau_2+T_1)} \\ \tilde{c}(s,1) = (bQ+K)e^{-sT_2} + \left(S+cR\dfrac{1-e^{-sQ/R}}{s}\right)e^{-s(\tau_1+T_2)} \\ \tilde{z}(s,1) = (bQ+K+cQ+S)e^{-s(\tau_1+Q/R+\tau_2)} \\ \tilde{\Pi}(s,1) = \tilde{p}(s,1) - \tilde{z}(s,1) + \tilde{c}(s,1)\left(e^{sT_2}-1\right) \end{cases} \tag{37}$$

The corresponding total functions are obtained by dividing these functions by $(1-e^{-s\tau})$. Computing traditional average capital, we obtain

$$\bar{C} = \lim_{s\to 0}\frac{\tilde{c}(s,1)e^{sT_2}-\tilde{z}(s,1)}{1-e^{-s\tau}} = \frac{(bQ+K)(\tau_1+Q/R+\tau_2)+cQ(Q/(2R)+\tau_2)+S(Q/R+\tau_2)}{\tau} \tag{38}$$

From (37) the following Laurent coefficients will be of interest to us

$$\begin{cases} \Pi_0(1) = pQ - c_{tot} \\ \Pi_1(1) = -(pQ-c_{tot})(\tau_1+Q/R+\tau_2) - pQT_1 + c_{tot}T_2 \end{cases} \tag{39}$$

$$\begin{cases} p_{-1} = \dfrac{pQ}{\tau} \\ c_{-1} = z_{-1} = \dfrac{c_{tot}}{\tau} \\ \Pi_{-1} = p_{-1} - c_{-1} = \dfrac{pQ-c_{tot}}{\tau} \end{cases} \tag{40}$$

$$\begin{cases} p_0 = pQ\left(\frac{1}{2} - \frac{\tau_1 + Q/R + \tau_2 + T_1}{\tau}\right) \\ c_0 = \frac{c_{tot}}{2} - \frac{(S + cQ)\tau_1 + cQ^2/(2R) + c_{tot}T_2}{\tau} \\ z_0 = c_{tot}\left(\frac{1}{2} - \frac{\tau_1 + Q/R + \tau_2}{\tau}\right) \\ \Pi_0 = \frac{pQ - c_{tot}}{2} - \frac{(pQ - c_{tot})(\tau_1 + Q/R + \tau_2) + pQT_1 - c_{tot}T_2}{\tau} \end{cases} \tag{41}$$

where we have used the following abbreviation for the total costs of a batch

$$c_{tot} = (bQ + K + S + cQ) \tag{42}$$

From (41), or from (39) taking the quotient $-\Pi_1(1)/\Pi_0(1)$, we obtain the mean lead time $\bar{t}$

$$\bar{t} = \tau_1 + Q/R + \tau_2 + \frac{pQT_1 - c_{tot}T_2}{pQ - c_{tot}} \tag{43}$$

The capital cost difference between the two evaluation principles in this example is thus given by $r\Pi_0$ and is obtained from (41). If the profit marginal $pQ - c_{tot}$ is positive, capital costs will be underestimated by the traditional principle if the mean lead time $\bar{t}$ is greater than half the time between batches τ. If the lead time is shorter, then capital costs would be overestimated. In the special case when $\tau = \bar{t}$, the underestimation amounts to half of the profit marginal multiplied by the interest rate. This is in complete agreement with our previous findings.

5. Conclusions and a suggestion for further analysis

Our general conclusion from above is that in general there will be a difference between the annuity stream approach and the traditional approach as regards both average profits (the zeroth-order term) and capital costs (the first-order term). The former difference is essentially due to credit periods, i e deviations between outpayments and the costing of inputs. This difference appears only when there is a long-run expansion (poles of the in- and outpayment functions of at least second order). The capital cost difference is a consequence of the traditional approach refusing to take average profit variations into account which also tie up capital in the process and which the annuity stream principle stipulates have to be included. The annuity stream principle thus requires average profit variations to be added to the capital tied-up on which interest is to be charged.

It is the sign of Π_0 that determines whether or not the traditional accounting approach over- or underestimates capital costs (which are more correctly determined by the annuity stream principle). When Π_0 is negative, the traditional principle will provide an underestimation and vice versa. In the cyclical case, if there are profits, then an underestimation will occur if $\bar{t} > \tau/2$. This means that the mean lead time $\bar{t}$ for the profit function exceeds half of the interval between two consecutive cycles. This would be the probable real-world case when demand is reasonably stable over time, whereas one might expect the frequency of setting up batches to be low (a long τ) for the production of more slowly moving items.

As regards future research, it might also be of interest to deal with cases when allowing for the possibility that long-run averages are not limited. In such cases there exist poles of higher order in the net payment flow. This would introduce a possibility to generalize our results in this paper.

6. References

Grubbström, R.W. (1980), A Principle for Determining the Correct Capital Costs of Work-in-Progress and Inventory, *International Journal of Production Research*, Vol 18, No 2, pp 259-271

Grubbström, R.W. (1991), The z-Transform of t^k, *Mathematical Scientist*, Vol 16, pp 118--129

Hadley, G. (1963), A Comparison of Order Quantities Using the Average Annual Cost and the Discounted Cost, *Management Science*, Vol 10, No 3, pp 472-476

Kim, Y.H., Philippatos, G.C. and Chung, K.H. (1986), Evaluating Investment in Inventory Policy: A Net Present Value Framework, *Engineering Economist*, Vol 31, No 2, pp 119-136

Richardson, C.H. (1954), *An Introduction to the Calculus of Finite Differences*, Van Nostrand, New York

Thorstenson, A. (1988), *Capital Costs in Inventory Models - A Discounted Cash Flow Approach*, Production-Economic Research in Linköping (PROFIL), Linköping

Trippi, R.R. and Lewin, D.E. (1974), A Present Value Formulation of the Classical EOQ Problem, *Decision Sciences*, Vol 5, pp 30-35

Appendix: Mathematical preliminaries

In this Appendix we include some basic mathematical formulas from Laplace transform analysis used in our main developments. The Laplace transform of a function of time $x(t)$ is defined as the integral:

$$\mathcal{L}\{x(t)\} = \int_0^\infty e^{-st} x(t) dt \tag{A1}$$

where s is the complex frequency. In order for the transform to exist, the time function can increase at most exponentially when t tends towards infinity. Repeatedly we use the following short-hand notation:

$$\bar{x}(s) = \mathcal{L}\{x(t)\} \tag{A2}$$

indicating the transform being a function of s. There is a one-to-one correspondence between each $x(t)$ and its transform $\bar{x}(s)$.

The following often-used relations are valid (assuming the limits in (A5) to exist):

$$\mathcal{L}\{\dot{x}(t)\} = s\bar{x}(s) - x(0) \tag{A3}$$

$$\mathcal{L}\left\{\int_0^t x(\alpha) d\alpha\right\} = \frac{\bar{x}(s)}{s} \tag{A4}$$

$$\lim_{s \to 0} s\bar{x}(s) = \lim_{t \to \infty} x(t) \tag{A5}$$

where $\dot{x}(t)$ is the time derivative of $x(t)$. The first two relations are derived using partial integration and the third from (A3) and the definition (A1). A further relation, important for our applications, is the following formula for the transform of a time average, which we develop as follows:

$$\mathcal{L}\left\{\frac{1}{t}\int_0^t x(\alpha)d\alpha\right\} = \int_0^\infty \frac{e^{-st}}{t}\int_0^t x(\alpha)d\alpha\, dt = -\int_0^\infty\left(\int_s^\infty e^{-\sigma t}d\sigma\right)\int_0^t x(\alpha)d\alpha\, dt =$$

$$= \int_s^\infty\int_0^\infty e^{-\sigma t}\int_0^t x(\alpha)d\alpha\, dt\, d\sigma = \int_s^\infty \frac{\tilde{x}(\sigma)}{\sigma}d\sigma \tag{A6}$$

where we have used (A4). From (A6) we can derive:

$$\lim_{s\to 0} s\,\mathcal{L}\left\{\frac{1}{t}\int_0^t x(\alpha)d\alpha\right\} = \lim_{s\to 0}\frac{\dfrac{\partial}{\partial s}\displaystyle\int_s^\infty \frac{\tilde{x}(\sigma)}{\sigma}d\sigma}{\dfrac{\partial}{\partial s}\dfrac{1}{s}} = \lim_{s\to 0} s\tilde{x}(s) \tag{A7}$$

where l'Hôpital's rule has been applied. By taking the previous final value theorem (A5) into account, we thus obtain the following generalization:

$$\lim_{t\to\infty}\frac{1}{t}\int_0^t x(\alpha)d\alpha = \lim_{s\to 0} s\tilde{x}(s) \tag{A8}$$

Hence, even if the function $x(t)$ does not have a limit value $x(\infty)$, but its long-run time average $\frac{1}{t}\int_0^t x(\alpha)d\alpha$ does, the limit of $s\tilde{x}(s)$ will approach this average. Of course, if there is a limit $x(\infty)$, then the long-run time average also approaches this limit.

When a time function is translated forward in time by a constant delay T, its transform is obtained as:

$$\mathcal{L}\{x(t-T)\} = \tilde{x}(s)e^{-sT} \tag{A9}$$

If it instead were translated backwards in time by T (provided it will not be truncated at $t=0$), the original transform should be multiplied by e^{sT}. The transform of a *Dirac impulse* $\delta(t-T)$ (having a zero value for $t \neq T$, its time integral being unity if the domain of integration covers T) is obtained as e^{-sT}.

When studying limits of the type $\lim_{s \to 0} s\bar{x}(s)$, their behaviour obviously depends on the speed at which $\bar{x}(s)$ approaches infinity when $s \to 0$. The Laplace transform of a unit step function is $1/s$ and its long-run average is accordingly unity, whereas the transform of t is $1/s^2$ and it does not have a long-run average also shown by s/s^2 not converging when $s \to 0$. More generally, the transform of a time power function t^k has the transform $\Gamma(k+1)/s^{k+1}$, where $\Gamma(k+1)$ is the Gamma Function which reduces to $k!$, when k is an integer. Thus, higher powers of time correspond exactly to higher negative powers of the complex frequency.

To study long-run average behaviour it is therefore suitable to expand the transform into a *Laurent* series around $s = 0$. Such a series is a generalization of the Maclaurin series also to include negative powers of s:

$$\bar{x}(s) = \sum_{j=-\infty}^{\infty} x_j s^j \tag{A10}$$

where x_j, for $j = ..., -2, -1, 0, 1, 2, ...$, are the coefficients of this series. The highest negative power present in such a series represents a *pole* at $s = 0$ of that particular order. For a long-run average to exist which is different from zero, $\tilde{x}(s)$ must therefore have a first-order pole at $s=0$ and the long-run average using this categorization is then:

$$\lim_{s\to 0} s\tilde{x}(s) = \lim_{s\to 0} \sum_{j=-\infty}^{\infty} x_j s^{j+1} = x_{-1} \tag{A11}$$

since all other terms either vanish when $s\to 0$ ($j\geq 0$) or are zero to start with ($j\leq -2$). The coefficient x_{-1} is the *residue* at $s=0$.

In many probabilistic applications the Laplace transform is used as a *moment generating function*:

$$\left[\frac{d\tilde{x}(s)}{ds}\right]_{s=0} = -\int_0^{\infty} x(t)\,t\,dt \tag{A12}$$

Thus its derivative at $s=0$ can be interpreted as the negative of the first-order moment of t using $x(t)$ as a weight function. Higher-order moments are similarly obtained from limits of higher-order derivatives, but only the first-order moment is relevant for our purposes.

Two further expressions of importance to be used for approximating the *annuity factor* and the *sinking fund factor*, are the Maclaurin series expansion of the two functions:

$$\frac{x}{e^x-1} = \sum_{j=0}^{\infty} \frac{B_j}{j!} x^j \tag{A13}$$

$$\frac{x}{1-e^{-x}} = \frac{(-x)}{e^{(-x)}-1} = \sum_{j=0}^{\infty} \frac{B_j}{j!}(-1)^j x^j = \sum_{j=0}^{\infty} b_j x^j \tag{A14}$$

where B_j, $j=0, 1, 2, \ldots$ are the *Bernoulli numbers* (Richardson,

1954, Ch.3). The Bernoulli numbers may be computed as (Grubbström, 1991):

$$B_j = \sum_{i=0}^{j} \frac{1}{i+1} \sum_{k=0}^{i} \binom{i}{k} k^j (-1)^k \tag{A15}$$

and they are zero-valued for odd index values $j \geq 3$. The first few nonzero Bernoulli numbers are:

$$B_0 = 1, B_1 = -\frac{1}{2}, B_2 = \frac{1}{6}, B_4 = -\frac{1}{30}, B_6 = \frac{1}{42}, B_8 = -\frac{1}{30}, B_{10} = \frac{5}{66}, B_{12} = -\frac{691}{2730}, B_{14} = \frac{7}{6} \tag{A16}$$

and the coefficients b_j in (A14), $j = 0, 1, 2, \ldots$, are therefore:

$$1, \frac{1}{2}, \frac{1}{12}, 0, -\frac{1}{720}, 0, \frac{1}{30240}, 0, -\frac{1}{1209600}, 0, \frac{1}{47900160}, 0, \ldots \tag{A17}$$

We may note that the two series only differ in the sign of the first-order term and that their difference therefore is exactly $-x$, which also is immediately seen by comparing the original expressions in (A13)-(A14).

A MICRO-SIMULATION MODEL FOR PENSION FUNDS

Paul C. van Aalst and C. Guus E. Boender
Erasmus University Rotterdam
P.O. Box 1738
3000 DR Rotterdam
The Netherlands

1. Introduction

In recent years there is a growing interest in the management of pension funds:

- The population in the developed countries is ageing. In countries where the pension rights are financed by means of a capitalization system, this implies for example that many pension funds, that had a contribution cash inflow that was larger than the current pension benefits, are now in the position that a part of the investment returns has to be used to pay the benefits. As a result a closer look at the contribution and pension benefit cash flows is necessary.
- The pension contributions are an important element of the total costs of the plan sponsor and of the difference between gross and net wage for the employees. They both prefer low and stable contributions. In this field there is a growing role for dynamic contribution systems, that try to smooth the contributions over time.
- Usually pension contributions are tax-deductable and this part of the income of employees is only taxed at the moment of the pension benefit: many years later and at a probably lower tax rate. Especially in countries with a large public debt, governments would like to accelerate this tax-levy.

All these developments lead to the need for a more professional management of (the link between) the assets and liabilities of the pension fund. Besides the definition of risk in an asset context, for example for the performance measurement of the portfolio manager, the risk of the whole fund should be taken into account.

This paper describes a simulation model that can be used to evaluate the relevant uncertainties of a pension fund. Therefore we start from an individual liability model. Both the liabilities and the assets will be modelled in a stochastic way. On the basis of this model and using real life pension fund data we will analyze how the pension fund can handle the uncertainties by simulating a number of scenario's with respect to the asset mix choice and the contribution policy of the fund.

2. Dutch pension system

Although the problem and the model described above are very general, the application in this paper will be embedded in a Dutch context. Therefore it might be useful to give a brief description of the main characteristics of the pension system in the Netherlands.

The Dutch pension system, like in many other countries, consists of three parts:

- Every citizen above the age of 65 receives a state pension. This pension is related to the minimum wage and provides a subsistence level.
- Former employees receive after their retirement an additional pension. In case of death of the (former) male employee the widow is entitled to a widow pension. A growing number of pension schemes contain benefits for the widower and for the unmarried partner. The additional pensions are managed by pension funds.
- If people think that the sum of state pension and additional pension is not enough, for example as a result of a small number of years of service, it is possible to effect a voluntary pension contract with an insurance company.

The combination of an, internationally seen, rather modest state pension and a normal to generous total (= state plus additional) pension[1] form the basis of the important role of the additional pensions and the pension funds in the Netherlands.

The additional pension is mostly based on the last income of the employee before his retirement (*final pay system*) and sometimes on the average

---

1 See for international comparative studies for example Davis [1988], Hannah [1988] and Petersen [1990].

income during his working life (*average pay system*). Very recently there is a tendency from the final pay system to the average pay system plus indexation, where the accumulated rights are not indexed by the individual wage growth of the participant but by the general wage growth. Although pension schemes vary widely between companies and industries a typical Dutch scheme offers a total pension (state plus additional) of 70% of the last income in the case of 40 years of service.

Unique in the Netherlands is the system of indexation of the pension rights of non-actives (former employees that are not yet retired, so called *sleepers*, and pensioners). Most pension funds index the rights of pensioners by the inflation rate (*inflation proof rights*), except in years when this indexation would endanger the financial position of the fund. Some funds even index by the nominal wage growth (*wage proof* or *prosperity proof rights*). In addition the rights of sleepers are frequently indexed. Under a new law the indexation of sleepers' rights must equal the indexation of pensioners' rights. The Algemeen burgerlijk pensioenfonds (Abp), that insures the pension rights of the public servants, offers a final pay system and unconditionally prosperity proof rights to sleepers and pensioners.

The investment portfolios of the Dutch pension funds are very large because of the combination of the considerable level of the additional pensions and the fact that the pension rights have to be financed by means of a fully funded system. By the end of 1990 the total assets of the Dutch pension funds amounted to almost 390 billion Dutch guilders. In absolute terms the Netherlands have the fourth largest amount of pension assets in the world, in terms of assets per capita or as a percentage of GNP they are number one. Table 1 gives a summary of the composition of the portfolios of Dutch pension funds.

	amount (Dfl mln)	perc.
Fixed income assets	287984	74.3
Equity shares	49268	12.7
Real estate	36783	9.5
Other assets	13715	3.5
Total	387750	100.0

Table 1: Asset mixes Dutch pension funds (Source: Central Bureau of Statistics, 1991)

3. The model

3.1. Why simulation?

Pension funds have uncertain future liabilities. Even in a 'sterile' world, with no economic developments, there is the uncertainty of not knowing how long the participants will live, what kind of career the active participants will make until their retirement, whether there will be a widow/widower after the death of the participant or not, etc. Further economic variables like inflation and real wage growth – having an influence on the development of the pension rights of the actives, both in the final pay system and in the average pay system, and the indexation of the rights of the non-actives – affect the liabilities of a pension fund. At the other side of the balance sheet the contributions are invested for a long time at highly uncertain returns until they are needed for the pension benefits.

So, given a pension scheme and a fixed institutional background, the following uncertainties for the total pension fund can be distinguished:

- the course of the lifes and careers of the participants,
- the development of the inflation and the wages and
- the development of the returns on the relevant asset categories.

Concerning the last two uncertainties Kingsland states:

> "The task of developing a closed form solution to evaluate the potential state of a pension plan following a series of stochastic investment and inflation experiences would be extremely difficult, if not impossible."[2]

But beside of this there is the first mentioned uncertainty. The usual actuarial models in the Netherlands[3] only determine the expected value of the liabilities given an economic scenario. These models implicitly assume that the number of participants is large enough to neglect deviations from the expected values. Especially for smaller pension funds and for pension schemes with different indexations of the rights of actives, sleepers and pensioners these deviations can be of considerable size.

---

2 Kingsland [1982], p. 579.

3 Published versions are for example Huyser and Van Loo [1986] and Möhlmann [1988].

More and more individual simulation models are used for pension fund research. Provided that these models are designed carefully, they can give some insight in the magnitude of the mentioned uncertainties. Further they often play a part as a decision support system to estimate the effect of changes in, for example, the pension scheme. In this paper we will follow the line described by Kingsland:

> " In order to develop an accurate assessment of the range of potential uncertainties, it is necessary to repeat this simulation process by generating dozens or hundreds of possible scenario's, consistent with statistical expectations."[4]

3.2. Liability model

The micro-simulation of the participants that is applied in this paper tries to illustrate the uncertain development of the liabilities of a pension fund in a better way than the usual actuarial models do. The participants of the pension scheme are not classified by age and sex, but they are followed individually through time by means of simulation. Starting from the usual life-, promotion- and resignationtables a game of chance determines every year for every participant whether he dies, gets promotion, resigns, etc. By allowing new employees it is possible to control the size of the underlying company. On the basis of the pension scheme and the economic scenario (inflation, real wage growth) the total liabilities[5] of the pension fund can be determined.

For the process of getting promotion in the company two approaches can be distinghuished: the push approach and the pull approach.

- In the *push approach* every year every participant gets promotion with a certain conditional probability. This promotion probability of the active participant can be dependent on his age or his position within the company, but is independent on the positions of the other participants and the existence of vacancies. In this way the process of getting promotion is in fact modelled the same way as the other transitions

---

4 Kingsland [1982], ibidem.

5 Conform the in the Netherlands common method we define the liabilities of a pension fund as the present value of the accumulated rights of the participants applying a fixed discount rate of 4%.

(death, resignation, etc) are modelled: all can be considered as Markov-chain transition probabilities.

- In the *pull approach* firstly the process of leaving the company, because of death, retirement or resignation, is simulated for all individual participants. After that an employee gets promotion (is pulled upwards in the organization) as soon as one of the positions in the organization is vacant. The promotion probabilities are thereforee dependent on the situation of the other active participants.

In this paper we apply the push principle[6]. Compared to the pull-method this method has, besides a time advantage for the simulations, an advantage and a disadvantage. For smaller companies there is the probability that in a simulation-run the company has for example three chairmen, i.e. there are too many employees at a certain function level. This disadvantageous effect on the determination of the total liabilities diminishes as the number of participants in the fund grows. The flexible number of participants at a certain function level can also be seen as an advantage: just as in reality well functioning employees will be promoted even in the case when there is no vacancy at that higher function level.

By simulating the liability model, given a certain pension scheme and a certain file of participants, many times, the uncertainties of the liabilities of the pension fund are illustrated and quantified.

3.3. Investment model

For the simulation of the assets of the pension fund the following asset categories are taken into consideration: fixed income investments, shares and real estate. Fixed income investment are represented by coupon bearing bulletloans with a fixed maturity of 10 years. For shares and real estate we assume investments in index portfolios. We used the following sources for the historic data of the investment categories:

fixed income	interest on long term Dutch state loans
shares	total return Robeco-shares
real estate	priceindex of newly built houses

---

6 An example of a pull model is described in Van Aalst [1990].

The choice of these time series tries to match the way Dutch pension funds form portfolios of the mentioned asset categories. The fixed income portfolio of a typical Dutch pension fund consists mainly of Dutch state loans. The share portfolios have an overweight in the Netherlands and an underweight in the Far East, just as the investment portfolio of Robeco, a Dutch open-end mutual fund. Because of difficulties of getting real estate data we chose the development of the prices of newly built Dutch houses as a proxy.

All assets are valued at marketvalue. For fixed income investments we assume therefore a flat term structure at the level of the interest rate in the concerning year of simulation. The present value of the cash flows of the existing fixed income portfolio is calculated with this interest rate as discount rate. The share-data are total rates of return whereas the real estate data only reflect the capital gains. We assume therefore that the rentals and the maintenance costs cancel out each other. Probably this approximation gives an underestimate of the total return on real estate.
During the simulation period every scenario uses a fixed asset mix. This portfolio distribution of the pension fund is attained every year by buying and selling until the desired portfolio is reached.

'Matching' can be defined as the procedure that leads to an asset mix that links as closely as possible to the characteristics and the expected development of the liabilities of a pension fund. Starting from the liabilities the matching portfolio is in that case a *result*. Further the matching of assets and liabilities is only meaningful when both sides of the balance sheet of the pension fund are calculated using the same valuation method. Because this study examines the way pre-set fixed asset mixes develop under different pension fund scenario's and because we apply the usual, but different valuation methods for assets and liabilities, 'matching' is not the proper term here.

3.4. Simulation of time series

Both for the determination of the liabilities of the pension fund and for the determination of the value of the assets we need time series describing the development of inflation, real wage growth and the rates of return on the considered investment categories during the simulation period. One possibility was to determine a set of fixed scenario's for these time series and to calculate the liabilities under these scenario's. Given the stochastic nature of the liability model these time series will be generated in a stochastic way in this paper. We did not choose a method that expresses a certain vision of the future (although this possibility can be built in), but a method that maintains the characteristics of the historic time series.

The method[7] estimates the means, (co)variances and auto(co)variances of the relevant time series during a certain (historic) period. Starting from the most recent values the method randomly extrapolates the time series such that the random future series converge to stationary time series with the same means, (co)variances and auto(co)variances as the historic estimates.

We will use the following notation: the estimated vector of means is μ, the matrix of estimated (co)variances is V and the matrix of estimated auto(co)variances is W. Define Ω as WV^{-1} and the vector x_t as the random series at (the future) time t. It is possible to prove that the series:

$$(1) \quad x_t = \mu + \Omega(x_{t-1} - \mu) + \varepsilon_t$$

and

$$(2) \quad \varepsilon_t \sim N(0, V - \Omega V \Omega^T)$$

converges to series with the characteristics μ, V and W as described, from each vector with starting value x_0.

The method is not dependent on the vector μ. Assume that one wants to copy the volatility and mutual interdependence of the series from the historic data, but wants to use other expectations on the basis of an own vision. The Markov chain

$$(3) \quad x_t = \xi + \Omega(x_{t-1} - \xi) + \varepsilon_t$$

with ε_t as in (2) converges to the self defined vector ξ preserving the characteristics as summarized in the matrices V and W.

---

7 The method is described in Boender and Romeijn [1991].

Besides this it is possible to simulate different investment scenario's within one simulation run of the liabilities, by using fixed series of inflation and real wage growth. Because of the mutual interdependence, the return series that will be generated, are conditioned on the already used inflation and real wage growth series.

4. Context

4.1 The pension fund

In this study the data of the participants of a real pension fund are used. To make the data of the original pension fund unrecognizable we took a sample from the file of participants. Table 2 characterizes the data:

	actives	sleepers	pensioners
number	842	286	51
average age	34,0	37,5	67,5
average salary	38000	-	-

Table 2: Data pension fund

For this pension fund we consider the following pension scheme: a final pay system with a total pension of 70% of the last income in case of 40 active years. The accumulated rights of sleepers and pensioners are indexed by the inflation rate. Beside this old age pension there is a pension for widows/ widowers of 70% of the old age pension. In case of death of an active employee the widow/widower receives a pension that is based on the number of years of service assuming that the active would have stayed in the company until the age of 65. Analogously a disablement pension is determined for those that get incapable for work during their active years. Further the official Dutch life tables are used for the probability of dying and internal series for the other probabilities.

4.2 Determination of the contributions

In this study we use a very simple contribution system. The contributions are in the first stage determined as the present value of the accumulated rights in the year of simulation. If these contributions lead to the situation that the assets amount to more than 115% of the liabilities on the basis of the fixed discount rate of 4%, in the second stage there is a discount on the original contributions in such a way that the assets are exactly 115% of the liabilities[8]. In another scenario we will investigate whether an asset buffer of 25% above the liabilities will make an investment portfolio with a larger part of shares and real estate acceptable. The results in paragraph 5 will show the average level of the gross and the net contributions, i.e. before and after the discount, both as a percentage of the total salaries.

Because of the described one year vision the contributions vary much from year to year.[9] To give some impression of this volatility of the contributions paragraph 5 will also show the average of the absolute percentage changes of the contributions.

Finally we will present the average level of funding during the simulations and the 'ruin probability', defined as the probability that the pension fund will get in a situation of underfunding in at least one year during the simulation.

4.3 The asset mixes

As mentioned in paragraph 3.3 this simulation study will consider some fixed asset mixes. These are not realistic asset mixes but they are chosen to illustrate some principal effects. Only the last investment strategy describes a long term target portfolio mix as defined by some Dutch pension funds. Table 3 shows the asset mixes:

---

8 The Dutch government has proposed a law that will tax pension assets above a funding level of 115%. Although the valuation rules of assets and liabilities in this tax proposal differ from the rules in this study, the mentioned analysis can give some insight in the possible effects of the tax proposal.

9 The implementation of a dynamic contribution system would smooth these fluctuations considerably. We will investigate this in a future study.

	fixed income inv.	shares	real estate
strategy 1	100	0	0
strategy 2	75	25	0
strategy 3	60	20	20

Table 3: Asset mixes

4.4 The time series

Five economic series are generated for the forecasts according to the principle described in paragraph 3.4. The following data series are used as input for this procedure (in all cases year end figures over the years 1950-1989):

Series	Source	Avg.	St.dev.	Correlation coefficient				
interest	CBS	6,4%	2,2%	1,00				
shares	Datastream	10,5%	16,6%	-0,06	1,00			
real estate	CBS	5,6%	5,1%	0,09	-0,44	1,00		
inflation	CBS	4,4%	3,2%	0,39	-0,28	0,59	1,00	
real wage gr.	CBS	1,9%	3,3%	-0,34	-0,05	0,30	-0,09	1,00

Table 4: Economic series

To give an impression of the applied procedure figure 1 presents the expected values (the solid line) and results of two (of the 50 generated) simulation series of the total rates of return on shares.

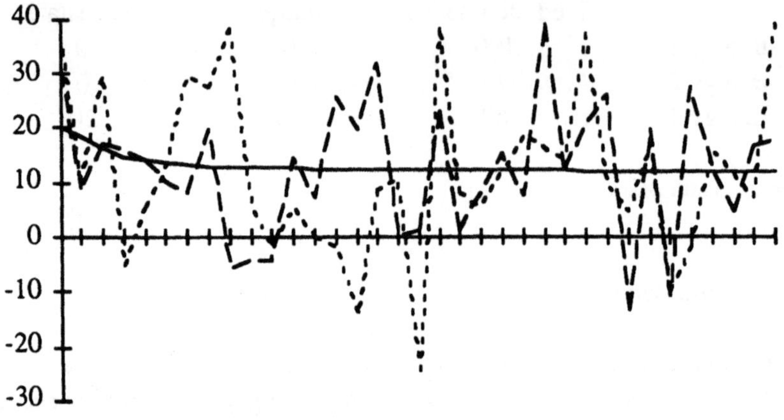

Figure 1: Example results generating rates of return of shares

5. Results

The model, as introduced in paragraph 3, is simulated 50 times[10] during a period of 35 years on the basis of the mentioned pension fund. Table 5 presents the results of the three examined asset mixes and the maximum funding level of 115% and 125% respectively (averages of the results):

	max. funding level 115%			max. funding level 125%		
	100/0/0	75/25/0	60/20/20	100/0/0	75/25/0	60/20/20
gross contribution	28.3	28.3	28.3	28.3	28.3	28.3
net contribution	14.0	7.6	12.6	13.5	6.5	11.9
contr. volatility	12.2	20.1	15.4	12.7	21.3	16.1
funding level	113.2	111.6	112.8	122.6	120.9	122.2
ruin probability	8.0	44.0	16.0	0.0	18.0	2.0

Table 5: Results contribution and funding level

---

10 The number of simulations may seem a bit small but the first and second moment of the distribution of results tend very quickly to the reported values. We checked this using larger simulations.

With the usual reservation the following conclusion can be drawn:

- Adding shares to an investment portfolio purely existing of fixed income assets leads to a significantly larger average contribution discount at the cost of a significantly larger contribution volatility. Research on the implementation of a dynamic contribution system will show how much of these year to year fluctuations can be overcome.
- Adding real estate to the above mentioned portfolio does not lead to results that are very interesting for pension funds. Although the real estate series is positively correlated with inflation and real wage growth and is an interesting asset for diversification from an investment point of view, the average rate of return is so low that it is not able to keep up with the growth of the liabilities.
- Enlarging the asset buffer from 15% to 25% of the liabilities leads to significantly lower ruin probabilities[11]: unexpectedly negative developments of the liabilities or especially the assets of the pension fund can be handled by the buffer in a better way. The larger capital of the fund also makes some larger contribution discounts possible.

Finally we examined how the results of table 5 will change in the case of an ageing pension fund. To illustrate this we decimated the probabilities of resignation. The results are shown in table 6:

	max. funding level 115%			max. funding level 125%		
	100/0/0	75/25/0	60/20/20	100/0/0	75/25/0	60/20/20
gross contribution	30.0	30.0	30.0	30.0	30.0	30.0
net contribution	16.4	9.9	14.9	16.1	9.1	14.5
contr. volatility	12.0	20.2	15.4	12.4	21.2	16.0
funding level	113.3	111.8	112.9	122.7	121.0	122.3
ruin probability	8.0	44.0	18.0	0.0	18.0	4.0

Table 6: Results contribution and funding level for an ageing pension fund

---

11 The magnitude of this ruin probability, defined as the probability that the fund has a funding level blow 100% in at least one year of the simulation, is strongly determined by the simulation period, in this study 35 years.

Summarizing we can say that for this strongly ageing pension fund – at the end of the simulation period the actives are on average 5 year older than in the first variant – the net contribution is about 2.5 percentage points higher.

6. Summary and ideas for future research

In this paper we presented a simulation model that is able to illustrate some risks that are relevant for pension funds. The model uses an individual approach of the participants for the simulation of the liabilities. The investment model examines three asset categories, fixed income investments, shares and real estate. The rates of return of these asset categories and the time series of inflation and real wage growth are simulated in a stochastic way.

To illustrate the model we examined three fixed asset mixes for a real life pension fund file and we checked the effect of the asset mixes on the level of the contributions, the volatility of the contributions and the funding level of the pension fund.

As already mentioned, this last is only meant as an illustration of the model. In future research we will investigate the following subjects.

- An analysis of the total uncertainties of the pension fund in the three categories as described in paragraph 3.1: the course of the lives and careers of the participants, the uncertainty concerning the development of the wages and prices and the uncertainty concerning the rates of return on the investment categories.
- What is the effect of different pension schemes (final pay vs. average pay, different indexations of the rights of non-actives) on the development and the uncertainty of the liabilities of a pension fund?
- The effect of implementation of a dynamic contribution system on the volatility of the contributions will be investigated.
- Finally what is the interaction between these subjects? For example what is the interaction between the different levels of uncertainty and the pension scheme?

Literature:

Aalst, P.C. van, 1990, De verplichtingen van een pensioenfonds: een modelsimulatie, in: P.C. van Aalst, H. Berkman and N.L. van der Sar (eds.), *Financiering en Belegging, Stand van zaken anno 1990*, pp. 105-116.

Boender, C.G.E. en H.E. Romeijn, 1991, The multidimensional Markov chain with prespecified asymptotic means and (auto)covariances, *Communications in Statistics*, 20, pp. 345-359.

Davis, E.P., 1988, *Financial Market Activity of Life Insurance Companies and Pension Funds*, BIS Economic Papers No. 21, Bank for International Settlements, Basle.

Hannah, L. (ed.), 1988, *Pension Asset Management*, Richard D. Irwin, Homewood, Ill.

Huyser, A.P. en P.D. van Loo, 1986, *Vergrijzing, pensioenen en contractuele besparingen*, De Nederlandsche Bank, Amsterdam/Deventer.

Kingsland, L., 1982, Projecting the Financial Condition of a Pension Plan Using Simulation Analysis, *Journal of Finance*, 37, pp. 577-584.

Möhlmann-Bronkhorst, M.J.M., 1988, *Een pensioenfonds op weg naar de volgende eeuw*, academic thesis, University of Twente.

Petersen, C., 1990, Pensioenen in West-Europa, *Economisch Statistische Berichten*, 3-1-1990, pp. 10-13.

ASSET ALLOCATION AND THE INVESTOR'S RELATIVE RISK AVERSION

Nico L. Van der Sar*
Department of Business Finance
Erasmus University Rotterdam
The Netherlands

ABSTRACT

This paper addresses the issue of how an investor allocates his wealth among assets and examines the nature of the dependency of the portfolio selection on the willingness to take on extra risks. We focus on two two-asset allocation models where only the relative risk aversion is needed to establish the investor's risk-return trade-off. A methodological comparison is made between Sharpe's (1987) analysis concerning the two-asset allocation problem and the mean-variance approach, based on the second order Taylor series approximation.

1. INTRODUCTION

This study addresses the issue of how an investor allocates his wealth among assets and examines the nature of the dependency of the portfolio selection on the willingness to take on extra risk. A method to solve the portfolio selection problem involves the use of indifference curves. They represent the investor's preferences with respect to the trade-off between risk and return of the assets and show his degree of risk aversion. The assumption of risk aversion is basic to many decision models in finance. Most investors appear to have a diminishing marginal utility of wealth which leads directly to risk aversion. In this study we focus on two two-

---

* The author wants to thank Winfried Hallerbach and an anonymous referee for their valuable insights. The author is of course responsible for all remaining errors and the opinions expressed.

asset allocation models where only one risk aversion measure appears to be needed to describe the investor's risk attitude.

In an asset allocation model where only two assets are involved, e.g. stocks S and bonds B, Sharpe (1987) derived the relation between the optimal asset mix and the inputs for an expected utility maximizer. It turned out that the optimal amount X_S to be invested in S, as a proportion of total wealth w_0, is given by $X_s / w_0 = \lambda_0 + \lambda_1$ RRT, where the parameters λ_0 and λ_1 are determined by the expected value, variance and covariance of the returns of the assets S and B. RRT denotes the relative risk tolerance, being the reciproke of the relative risk aversion RRA (Pratt (1964)). In order to arrive at this result Sharpe assumed that the rates of return have a (jointly) normal (Gaussian) distribution and that the investor's preferences can be described by a negative exponential utility function of wealth.

The two-asset allocation problem may also be tackled by employing the Taylor series expansion around the amount of wealth to be invested. For the case of truncating after the second order term, i.e. mean-variance approximation, we shall show that the optimal fraction of total wealth to be invested in stocks is given by $X_s / w_0 = \tau_0 + \tau_1$ RRT. The parameters τ_0 and τ_1 are determined by the expected returns, risks and correlation of the two asset classes, but they are not identical to, respectively, λ_0 and λ_1.

Though in both approaches RRA (or RRT) appears to be the only crucial parameter with respect to the investor's preferences, the underlying assumtions as well as the implications differ considerably. In section 2 we shall summarize the most important methodological elements that characterize explicitly and implicitly both approaches and discuss the resulting differences in investment decision making. Section 3 ends not only with some concluding remarks, but it also presents various procedures that can be developed for the identification of the investor's RRA.

2. ASSET ALLOCATION

In this section we make a methodological comparison between Sharpe's framework and the mean-variance approach based on the second order

Taylor series approximation. Throughout our analysis, we assume that individual investors choose their portfolios to maximize the expected utility of terminal wealth. We shall abstract from market imperfections as, for example, transaction costs, taxes and restrictions on short sales. Also, let us suppose that the decision period is relatively short. Actually this study considers only two asset classes and liabilities equal zero. It is self-evident that these assumptions limit the usefulness of the approaches that will be discussed in the following. But we may safely say that these two asset allocation models can be revised and adapted when one (or more) of the assumptions and restrictions is dropped. Before we come to a discussion of some of the strengths and weaknesses, we summarize the most important elements which characterize explicitly and implicitly both approaches, see table 1.

The following observations seem appropriate. A major difference between the two approaches concerns the distribution of the one-period rates of return. In a world of limited liability, normally distributed returns are a poor approximation of actual returns. For it is impossible to lose more than 100% of one's investment, rates of return must be in excess of -100%. However, rates of return greater than 100% are not uncommon. The resulting degree of positive skewness gets smaller as the length of the time-period diminishes, though, e.g., Francis (1975) and also Fama (1976) found a significant skewness in (ex-post) returns measured over periods as short as a month. In a now classic study, Fama (1965) proposed that stock returns conform to a stable Paretion distribution. Also others provided empirical evidence for the common stock returns not to follow a normal distribution. For example, Dowell and Grube (1978) observed daily returns that were predominantly fat-tail, non Gaussian. Although Sharpe (1987) did not give any arguments in support of using normally distributed rates of return, it must be emphasized that in his framework a relatively short decision period is assumed. In the mean-variance approach no hypothesis is made with respect to the returns distribution.

Actually, the first impulse to the development of (modern) portfolio theory was given by Markowitz (1952), who explicitly presupposed investors to make investment choices solely on the basis of mean and standard deviation of the rates of return. Tobin (1958), (1969) showed that the portfolio choices of an expected utility maximizer can be analyzed in terms of the two parameters 'mean' and 'variance' only if (i) the investor has a quadratic

	Sharpe's framework	Mean-variance approximation
r	normally distributed	no assumption
U(wealth)	negative exponential utility function	locally approximated by a second order polynomial
indifference curves	segments of parabolas	segments of circles
ARA	independent of wealth	no assumption
RRA	global risk aversion parameter	local risk aversion parameter
X_s / w_0	$\lambda_0 + \lambda_1 RRT$	$\tau_0 + \tau_1 RRT$
criterion function	$E(r) - \frac{1}{2} RRA\sigma^2(r)$	$E(r) - \frac{1}{2} RRAE(r)^2 - \frac{1}{2} RRA\sigma^2(r)$
$\frac{dE(r)}{d\sigma(r)}$	$RRA\ \sigma(r)$	$\frac{RRA\sigma(r)}{1 - RRA\sigma(r)}$
$\frac{dE(r)}{d\sigma^2(r)}$	$\frac{1}{2} RRA$	$\frac{\frac{1}{2} RRA}{1 - RRA\ E(r)}$
optimal E(r)	$r_f + c^2 RRT$	$\frac{1}{1+c^2} r_f + \frac{c^2}{1+c^2} RRT$
and $\sigma(r)$	$cRRT$	$-\frac{c}{1+c^2} r_f + \frac{c}{1+c^2} RRT$

Table 1. Methodological aspects of the two approaches

utility function of wealth, and/or if (ii) rates of return are normally distributed[1]. In view of this, it doesn't come as a surprise that Sharpe's analysis of the asset allocation problem resulted in a criterion function, viz. $E(r) - \sigma^2(r)/2RRT$, precisely in terms of the two distribution parameters $E(r)$ and $\sigma^2(r)$, since he assumed the rates of return to be (jointly) normally distributed. But what if neighter condition (i) nor condition (ii) holds? In different ways, Samuelson (1970) and Tsiang (1972) arrived at the conclusion that the mean-variance approximation is applicable, i.e. the quadratic solution is approximately identical to the 'true' general solution, when riskiness is relatively limited, viz. risk under consideration is small relative to total wealth. For various utility functions and historical returns distributions, Levy and Markowitz (1979), and Kroll, Levy and Markowitz (1984) showed that an investor, who's objective is to maximize expected utility, could perform very well if his strategy with respect to portfolio choice is based only on the mean and variance or put in other words that the mean-variance approximation fits rather well. The exactness of the mean-variance results appeared to be illustrative of the robustness of the quadratic approximation and was not due to normality of the historical returns (Kroll, Levy and Markowitz (1984)). Therefore, in case the returns are not (jointly) normally distributed and the investor's utility function of wealth is not exactly identical to a quadratic one, one may apply the Taylor series approximation (truncated after the second moment) and fit the investor's utility function as good as possible to a quadratic function around the amount of wealth to be invested when applying the mean-variance approximation of expected utility. However, its approximative and, consequently, local character must be stressed. According to Sharpe, the investor's actual utility function can be adequately approximated by a function displaying a constant absolute risk tolerance ART (being the reciproke of the absolute risk aversion ARA) that is, ART doesn't depend on the amount of wealth to be invested, because the range of the possible values of wealth at the end of a relatively short decision period will be small. Consequently, the investor whose objective is to maximize the (expected) utility of terminal wealth acts consistently with a negative exponential utility function of wealth. Although a relative short time-period is assumed, it remains to be seen whether the investor's actual preferences can indeed be adequately described by this type of utility function.

---

1) Normality is a sufficient but not necessary condition. Chamberlain (1983) and Owen and Rabinovitch (1983) characterize the elliptical distributions, which imply that expected utility is completely specified by its mean and variance.

Of interest is the fact that in Sharpe's framework the RRA can be interpreted as a global relative risk aversion measure, for the subjective risk premium equals 1/2 σ^2 (r) RRA exactly. Under the mean-variance approximation RRA characterizes the investor's risk attitude just locally, since this equation holds only approximately.

In the (E(r), σ(r))-world the investor's attitude with respect to return and risk is completely established by his RRA both in Sharpe's framework and under the mean-variance approximation (cf. also Van der Sar and Antonides (1990)). As a consequence we obtain that for investors with identical RRA values, the optimal portfolio will be similar as well. On a first sight, it seems that the major conclusion of Kallberg and Ziemba (1983), who empirically examined the portfolio choice between a safe asset and a risky asset, is in disagreement with our theoretical result. Their analysis suggested that similar ARA values yield similar optimal portfolios, regardless of the functional forms of the utility functions concerned. However, they didn't focus on the effect of the initial amount of invested wealth on the optimal portfolio mix. Put in other words, their empirical result is not necessarily in contradiction with the outcome of our analysis.

With respect to the most appropriate asset mix, it can be established (see the appendix) that $\tau_0 < \lambda_0$ and $\tau_1 < \lambda_1$. In the case of comparative statics this implies the following. Suppose that there is a general change into more optimism, i.e. E_S and E_B increase, leaving the difference E_S-E_B unaltered as well as the (co)variances σ_S^2, σ_B^2 and σ_{BS}. It can easily be seen that, following Sharpe's line of approach, this growth of optimism does not affect the most appropriate asset mix. However under the mean-variance approximation, more optimism yields a relatively more conservative investment policy, which intuitively seen seems plausible. However, one might, of course, argue that a rising demand for bonds will affect bond prices and the corresponding expected rate of return (at least partly) offsetting the increased relative popularity of bonds.

The criterion function that should be maximized under the mean-variance approximation contains an extra term, viz. $-\frac{1}{2}\text{RRA}\ E(r)^2$, in comparison with the one in Sharpe's analysis. As a consequence we get that the marginal rate of substitution of expected return both for standard deviation and for variance under the mean-variance approximation significantly exceed the corresponding ones in Sharpe's approach. Hence, under the mean-variance approximation the investor's most appropriate asset mix is characterized by less expected return and risk compared to the investor's optimal portfolio in Sharpe's analysis. Notice that in Sharpe's framework, the marginal rate of substitution of expected return for variance appears to be independent of risk=variance, which may be called a somewhat surprising result, since, when moving along an indifference curve, intuitively seen, one would expect the marginal substitution rate to be an increasing function of risk=variance.

In both approaches for asset allocation, RRA appears to be the only crucial parameter with respect to the investor's preferences. If expected returns and (co)variances are given, the RRA provides enough information to be able to determine the optimal asset mix for an expected utility maximizer. This is demonstrated for the case of homogeneous expectations and existence of a risk-free rate of return. Using c to denote the market price of risk, we can write the Capital Market Line as $E(r) = r_f + c\sigma(r)$. Then, for both approaches $E(r)$ and $\sigma(r)$ can be written as a linear function of r_f and RTT. It can easily be established that the asset mix being optimal in Sharpe's framework is characterized by more expected return and risk in comparison with the one under the mean-variance approximation.

For both approaches, albeit in different ways, the expected return and risk characteristics of the most appropriate portfolio mix appear to be directly related to the RRA. Since in general the degree of relative risk aversion is expected to vary among investors, the appropriate asset mix will be subjectively dependent as well. It is of importance to examine whether and, if yes, to which degree RRA correlates with investor-specific characteristics. For, this would provide us information about the dependency of the investor's two-asset allocation on these subjective characteristics. For example, the empirical results of the studies of Cohn, Lewellen, Lease and Schlarbaum (1975), and Van der Sar and Antonides (1990) lead one to suggest that females in comparison with males, on average have a preference for a relatively more conservative investment policy.

3. CONCLUSION

A method of solving the portfolio selection problem involves the use of indifference curves. These curves display the subjective trade-off between return and risk. The measures of the investor's risk attitude, that are used in practice, are (in)directly related to his set of indifference curves. In Sharpe's framework as well as under the mean-variance approximation, the relative risk aversion (RRA) appears to provide enough information about the subjective risk attitude to be able to determine the optimal asset mix, if the expected returns, variances and covariances are given. Thus it is of importance to examine to which degree the RRA correlates with investor-specific characteristics, for it would provide us information on the subjectivity of the investor's two-asset allocation. An intriguing finding regarding investment decision making in practice is that the portfolio mix most appropriate in Sharpe's framework is characterized by a higher level of expected return and risk than under the mean-variance approximation.

However, both approaches, implicitly or explicitly, make use of restrictive assumptions. In order to justify a mean-variance analysis Sharpe adopted the assumption of (jointly) normally distributed returns. Also, he assumed a negative exponential utility function of wealth. The resulting framework may be described as parsimonious but elegant. Still, it remains to be seen whether the asset mix, appropriate in Sharpe's framework, corresponds (by appromation) with the 'true' optimal asset portfolio, even when the decision period is a relatively short one.

The mean-variance approximation is based on the second order Taylor series approximation around the amount of wealth to be invested. Also, this approach has not been sacred from criticism. The mean and variance wouldn't adequately describe the distribution of returns. The third and perhaps even higher order moments should be taken into considerance. For instance, in view of the existence of skewness, Arditti (1967) suggested to include the third moment in portfolio selection analysis. In this case, one could employ the third order Taylor series approximation instead of confining oneself to the one that involves only the first two moments of the return distribution. This leaves us with a wealth utility function that is approximated by a third grade polynom (for the rational of a cubic utility function see, e.g., Levy and Sarnat (1972)). It goes without saying that the inclusion of more moments complicates the analysis. It should be noted that the Taylor series approximation is not necessarily accurate and might even be erroneous (the convergence behavior of the approximation depends on the type of utility-probability combination, cf. Loistl (1976)).

In the foregoing we didn't put our mind to the problem of measuring the investor's risk attitude, among others, because it is not a matter of course. In practice, it usually boils down to (implicity or explicitly) making an estimation of the indifference curves of the investor. Various procedures have been developed for the identification of the investor's trade-off between risk and return. For instance, imagine that the investor is presented with a portfolio. He could be asked to identify the corresponding certainty equivalent CE_r. Assuming the mean-variance approximation, based on the Taylor series expansion, then we can identify the (segment of the) circle with the (expected return, risk)-combination of the presented portfolio and the corresponding CE_r on it. Subsequently, the central point which corresponds with RRT can be found. More formal, $(RRT - CE_r)^2 = (E(r) - RRT)^2 + \sigma^2 (r)$ is solved for RRT. In the case of a negative exponential utility function and (jointly) normally distributed returns, $CE_r = E(r) - \sigma^2(r)/2RTT$ is the relevant equation. Thus, in view of the close relationship between RRT and various other risk aversion measures, one may estimate RRT (indirectly) using a method with which a (to the investor) more familiar concept, e.g. CE_r, can be identified. Another method is to ask the investor to identify two portfolios that, according to him, are equally valued, i.e. their (expected return, risk)-combinations are positioned on the same indifference curve. In the mean-variance framework, based on the Taylor series expansion, as well as under the assumptions of Sharpe's (1987) analysis, RRT can then easily be found. Also one may estimate the investor's utility function of wealth. Then, the subjective risk attitude can be derived from the empirical estimates of the parameters of the wealth utility function. For instance, Van der Sar and Antonides (1990) specified a lognormal wealth utility function and estimated RRA for each member of the sample population (see also Van der Sar (1989)).

In view of our analysis, one may have a preference for applying the mean-variance approximation. Nevertheless we may state that Sharpe's approach also provides a simple but useful framework of how to incorporate subjective investor's preferences into the two-asset allocation problem. However, while the set of investment rules of both approaches can easily be operationalized, it is a mistake to elevate the theories presented to the status of investment law that always reliably operates, or put in other words, yields the true optimal asset mix.

APPENDIX

Assume that the investor's objective is to find the amounts X_S and X_B which maximize the expected utility of terminal wealth. Employing the second order Taylor series expansion around the amount of wealth to be invested yields

$$EU(w) \approx U(w_0) + U'(w_0)E(w - w_0) + \tfrac{1}{2}U''(w_0)E(w - w_0)^2$$

which can be rewritten as

$$\begin{aligned} EU(w) \approx\ & U(w_0) - w_0U'(w_0) + \tfrac{1}{2}U''(w_0)w_0^2 \\ & -U''(w_0)\{E(w)(w_0 + ART) - \tfrac{1}{2}E(w)^2 - \tfrac{1}{2}\sigma^2(w)\} \end{aligned}$$

For a risk averse decision maker, $U''(w_0)<0$ holds. It follows that maximizing expected utility is equivalent to maximizing

$$E(w)(w_0 + ART) - \tfrac{1}{2}E(w)^2 - \tfrac{1}{2}\sigma^2(w)$$

subject to $X_S + X_B = w_0$. First, we introduce some notations. Let r_S and r_B be the rates of return on a stock and bond, resp., and let E_S and E_B represent the corresponding expected values. The variances of r_S and r_B will be denoted by σ_S^2 and σ_B^2 respectively, and σ_{BS} will be used to denote the covariance between r_S and r_B. Our optimalization problem can then be written as

$$\begin{aligned} \max_{X_s, X_b}\quad & \{(1+E_S)X_S + (1+E_B)X_B\}(ART - w_0) \\ & -\frac{1}{2}\{(1+E_S)X_S + (1+E_B)X_B\}^2 \\ & -\frac{1}{2}(X_S^2\sigma_S^2 + 2X_SX_B\sigma_{BS} + X_B^2\sigma_B^2) \end{aligned}$$

subject to $X_S + X_B = w_0$

From the first-order conditions it follows that

$$E_s(ART + w_0) - \{(1 + E_s)X_s + (1 + E_B)X_B\}E_s - (X_s\sigma_s^2 + X_B\sigma_{BS}) =$$

$$=$$

$$E_B(ART + w_0) - \{(1 - E_s)X_s + (1 + E_B)X_B\}E_B - (X_S\sigma_{BS} + X_B\sigma_B^2)$$

with $X_S + X_B = w_0$.

For the optimal amount to be invested in stocks, we obtain

$$X_s = \tau_0 w_0 + \tau_1 ART$$

where

$$\tau_0 = \frac{\sigma_B^2 - \sigma_{BS} - E_B(E_S - E_B)}{\sigma_S^2 + \sigma_B^2 - 2\sigma_{BS} + (E_S - E_B)^2}$$

and

$$\tau_1 = \frac{E_S - E_B}{\sigma_S^2 + \sigma_B^2 - 2\sigma_{BS} + (E_S - E_B)^2}$$

In Sharpe's framework maximizing expected utility is equivalent to maximizing

$$E(w) - \frac{1}{2ART}\sigma^2(w)$$

The optimal amount to be invested in stocks was computed as

$$X_S = \lambda_0 w_0 + \lambda_1 ART$$

where

$$\lambda_0 = \frac{\sigma_B^2 - \sigma_{BS}}{\sigma_S^2 + \sigma_B^2 - 2\sigma_{BS}}$$

and

$$\lambda_1 = \frac{E_S - E_B}{\sigma_S^2 + \sigma_B^2 - 2\sigma_{BS}}$$

Assuming E_S-E_B>0, we can establish the following inequalities: $\tau_0 < \lambda_0$ and $\tau_1 < \lambda_1$.

References

Arditti, F.D., 1967, Risk and the Required Return on Equity, *Journal of Finance*, Vol. 22, 19-36.

Chamberlain, G., 1983, A Characterization of the Distributions that Imply Mean-Variance Utility Functions, *Journal of Economic Theory*, Vol. 29, 185-201.

Cohn, R.A., W.G. Lewellen, R.C. Lease and G.G. Schlarbaum, 1975, Individual Investor Risk Aversion and Investment Portfolio Composition, *Journal of Finance*, Vol. 30, 605-620.

Dowell, C.D. and R.C. Grube, 1978, Common Stock Return Distributions During Homogeneous Activity Periods, *Journal of Financial and Quantitative Analysis*, Vol. 13, 79-92.

Fama, E.F., 1965, The Behavior of Stock Market Prices, *The Journal of Business*, Vol. 38, 34-105.

Fama, E.F., 1976, *Foundations of Finance*, Basic Books, Incl., New York.

Francis, J.C., 1975, Skewness and Investor's Decisions, *Journal of Financial and Quantitative Analysis*, Vol. 10, 163-172.

Kallberg, J.G. and W.T. Ziemba, 1983, Comparison of Alternative Utility Functions in Portfolio Selection Problems, *Management Science*, Vol. 11, 1257-1276.

Kroll, Y., H. Levy and H.M. Markowitz, 1984, Mean-Variance versus Direct Utility Maximalization, *Journal of Finance*, Vol. 39, 47-61.

Levy, H. and M. Sarnat, 1972, *Investment and Portfolio Analysis*, John Wiley and Sons, New York.

Levy, H. and H.M. Markowitz, 1979, Approximating Expected Utility by a Function of Mean and Variance, *American Economic Review*, Vol. 69, 308-317.

Loistl, O., 1976, The Erroneous Approximation of Expected Utility by Means of a Taylor's Series Expansion: Analytic and Computational Results, *American Economic Review*, Vol. 66, 904-910.

Markowitz, H.M., 1952, Portfolio Selection, *Journal of Finance*, Vol. 7, 77-91.

Owen, J. and R. Rabinovitch, 1983, On the Class of Elliptical Distributions and their Applications to the Theory of Portfolio Choices, *Journal of Finance*, Vol. 38, 745-752.

Pratt, J.W., 1964, Risk Aversion in the Small and in the Large, *Econometrica*, Vol. 32, 122-126.

Samuelson, P.A., 1970, The Fundamental Approximation Theorem of Portfolio Analysis in Terms of Means, Variances and Higher Moments, *Review of Economic Studies*, Vol. 37, 537-542.

Sharpe, W.F., 1987, Integrated Asset Allocation, *Financial Analysts Journal*, Vol. 43, 25-32.

Tobin, J., 1958, Liquidity Preference as Behavior towards Risk, *Review of Economic Studies*, Vol. 25, 65-86.

Tobin, J., 1969, Comment on Borch and Feldstein, *Review of Economic Studies*, Vol. 36, 13-14.

Tsiang, S.C., 1972, The Rationale of the Mean-Standard Deviation Analysis, Skewness Preference, and the Demand for Money, *American Economic Review*, Vol. 62, 354-371.

Van der Sar, N.L., 1989, Utility of Wealth and Relative Risk Aversion: Operationalization and Estimation, *Rivista di Matematica per le Scienze Economiche e Sociali*, Vol. 12, 219-228.

Van der Sar, N.L. and G. Antonides, 1990, The Price of Risk Empirically Determined by the Capital Market Line, proceedings of the first *Actuarial Approach for Financial Risks* international colloquium, 163-173.

FINANCING BEHAVIOUR OF SMALL RETAILING FIRMS

D. van der Wijst
Centre for Retail Research
Research Institute for Small Business
P.O.Box 7001, NL-2701 AA Zoetermeer,The Netherlands

1 Introduction

Many financing decisions have effects that stretch well into the future. Long term loans can cover periods of 5 to 10 years and contracts like mortgages may be concluded for periods of 30 years. As a consequence, the amounts presented in a financial statement at any point in time can be regarded as resultants of many decisions in the past. Analysing financial structure expressed in terms of these amounts may, to a certain extent, obscure the behaviour which induces changes in financial structure, i.e. obscure the effects of single decisions or decisions in a short period of time. This is particularly true if the changes are small compared with the observed amounts. Hence, many researchers have focussed on single decisions, like the choice between debt and equity in the issue of new securities [e.g. Baxter and Cragg (1970), Taub (1975), Marsh (1982)].

In this paper, changes in financial structure

are analysed using a database containing the averaged financial data of small retailing firms. This paper extends the results of previous research, in which the same database was used to investigate the determinants of small firm debt ratios [Van der Wijst and Thurik (1992), Van der Wijst and Vermeulen (1991)]. Analysing changes, i.e. percentage first differences between the observed variables, largely removes the effects of decisions made in the past that are still reflected in the present financial statement. For instance, changes in assets only measure new investments or depreciations and not the remaining value of assets that were purchased years ago. Compared with the analysis of amounts or ratios, this procedure may throw additional light on the determinants of financing decisions, i.e. expose behaviour more sharply.

However, an alternative hypothesis is also possible. According to Miller's (1977) neutral mutation hypothesis, changes in financial structure are more or less randomly made around some target value. These changes serve no function, but do no harm too and can therefore persist indefinitely. Additionally, it should be noted that the data only allow the calculation of year-to-year changes in averages, which reflect the effect on balance of all changes in all firms over the period. This may conceal ("average out") the effects of decisions within firms; "average behaviour", if it exists at all, may be hard to explain.

The organization of this paper is as follows. In section 2 the data, variables and hypotheses are discussed. Section 3 contains the empirical analyses and section 4 concludes the paper.

2 Data, variables and hypotheses

The data used in this study refer to the retail trade in Western Germany and are publicly available. The information has been published by the collectors for purposes such as interfirm comparisons and contains detailed financial statements. The data are based on information of individual firms, but the unit of observation used here is the published "industry average", i.e. the averaged data for narrowly defined shoptypes such as supermarkets and shoe shops. The data have a panel character: information on the 27 shoptypes used here is available for 20 different years. Since the data are publicly available and have been described extensively elsewhere [Van der Wijst (1989), Van der Wijst and Thurik (1992)], no further details are provided here. An impression of the financial structure (averaged across shoptypes) of this small business sector is given in Figure 1, where the development of some leverage ratios over time is depicted. Figure 1 shows, that the average financial structure in retailing over the period is largely stable. The share of equity in total assets rises slowly in the fifties, is more or less stable in the sixties and slowly diminishes in the seventies. Total debt shows, of course, the opposite picture but the ratio of long term debt to total

FIG. 1 LEVERAGE RATIOS OVER TIME

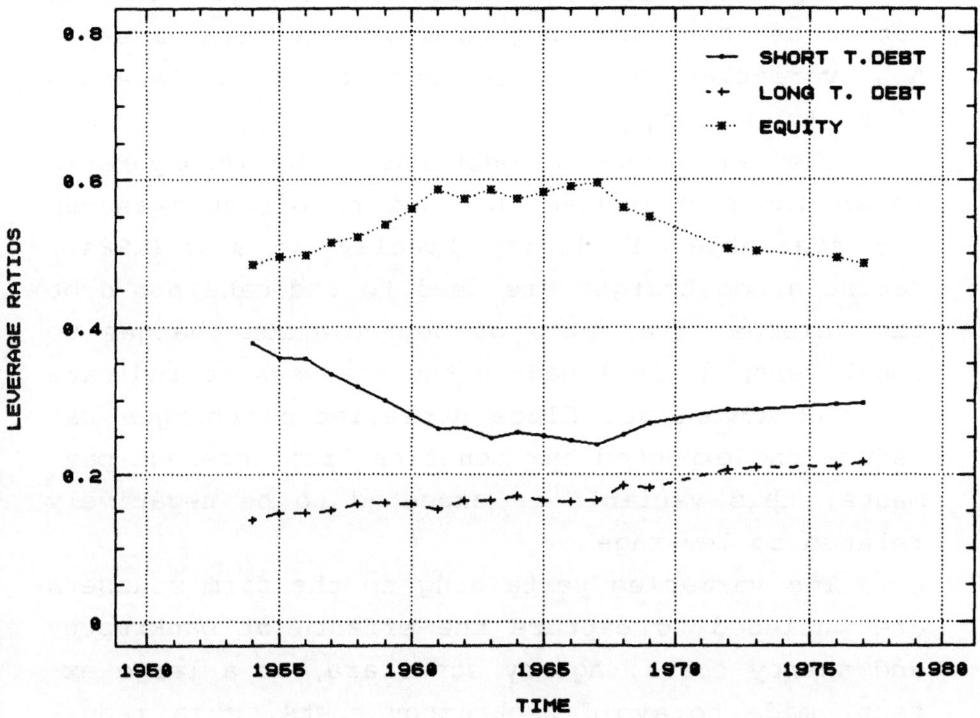

assets slowly increases over almost the entire period. Taken as a whole, however, the year-to-year changes as well as the total development over the period are remarkably small for a time span of almost a quarter of a century.

In this analysis, the determinants of financial structure commonly suggested by the recent theory of finance, are used to explain changes in debt ratios. These determinants include the effects of taxes, bankruptcy- and agency-costs and profitability and they are approximated by the explanatory variables. The variables to be explained (in separate analyses) are the changes in the ratios of short and long term debt to total assets. All variables are percentage first differences (i.e. $(x_t - x_{t-1})/x_{t-1}$).

The tax effect on debt has to be incorporated in an indirect manner, because no direct measures are available. Following Bradley et al. (1984), depreciation charges are used to indicate non-debt tax shields. The ratio of depreciation charges to total costs is included in the analyses to indicate the tax advantage. Since depreciation charges can reduce the expected tax benefits from interest payments, this variable is expected to be negatively related to leverage.

Two variables pertaining to the firm's assets are included to capture the effects of bankruptcy and agency costs. Agency costs are, to a large extent, made to avoid bankruptcy costs, so a reduction in the latter also diminishes the need to incur the former. Hence, both determinants are usually approximated with the same variables. Bankruptcy costs can be thought of as the difference between the firm's operating value and its liquidation value, so a high liquidation value makes debt financing more attractive. Since fixed assets are generally considered to offer more security (i.e. a higher liquidation value) than current assets, asset structure (i.e. the ratio of fixed to total assets) is used to indicate the liquidation value. The second variable to be included, inventory turnover, is not frequently encountered in the literature, but in retailing inventories are a financially (and commercially) important part of the assets. The characteristics of the inventories determine whether or not they are accepted by banks as collateral for loans[1] and this can have a substantial influence on financial structure. Inventory turnover is likely to reflect the liquidity of, and thus, the security offered by the inventories. Both variables are expected to have a positive effect on leverage, but they can also influence the maturity structure of debt, i.e. an increase in the fixed asset component can be associated with a comparatively heavy increase in the long term debt ratio and an increase in inventory turnover with a relatively large increase in the short term debt ratio.

The fourth variable to be included is return on investment, which may have three effects. First of all, highly profitable firms are likely to generate much cash, which can be used to lower debt, especially short term debt. Secondly, ROI reflects the possibilities to retain earnings. The importance of these internally generated funds is stressed by Myers (1984) and Myers and Majluf (1984), following the observation that firms seem to prefer raising capital by retaining earnings in the first place, by borrowing in the second place and by issuing new equity in the last place. An explanation of this "pecking order" in financing alternatives, as Myers calls it, can be based on an asymmetrical distribution of information between potential out-

---

[1]*The inventories of shoptypes selling fast moving consumer goods (e.g. super- markets) typically are accepted as collateral while the inventories of shoptypes selling goods subject to fashion, such as clothes shops, are not.*

side investors and the firm's management. When the investors are less knowledgeable of the firm's prospects than its management, a situation may arise in which firms face the dilemma of either passing by projects with a positive net present value or issuing stock at a price they think is too low. This situation can be avoided if a firm can retain enough internally generated funds to cover its positive NPV opportunities or if it can maintain financial slack in the form of "reserve borrowing power". In this view, observed debt ratios will reflect the cumulative requirement for external financing over an extended period, and will be negatively related to profitability. Thirdly, a high profitability may signal confidence in the future prospects of the firm to the market and a lower risk makes debt financing more attractive by by lowering expected bankruptcy costs.

The fifth variable is total assets, which is included to reflect scale effects in leverage. This variable is split up in four parts to allow for different effects of changes in current and fixed assets and because positive changes in each of these two (i.e. investments) may have different effects than negative changes (i.e. depreciations). The four possible changes in assets are separately included in the analysis, so that minimal restrictions are imposed on the outcomes. In most theories of optimal capital structure, firms differing in size only differ by a scale factor, i.e. the locus of the optimal capital structure is independent of the scale of operations. If this is the case, then changes in asset categories will not be related to changes in leverage. Alternatively, if a relation is found, this could indicate either scale effects in optimal capital structure or a linkage between investment- and financing decisions, which is usually assumed not to exist.

Finally, a variable to capture the effect of rearrangements is included, i.e. the effects of adjustments in the maturity structure of debt. Short term debt can be replaced by long term debt and vice versa. Rearrangements of debt categories can take place under the influence of changes in several variables, e.g. new collateral securities can be given or the relative prices of debt categories may change. Unfortunately, the data comprise neither information on the term structure of interest rates nor on the securities involved. Consequently, rearrangements are accounted for by directly including in the analysis the changes in the complementary debt category, i.e. changes in long term debt are included as an explanatory variable in the analysis of changes in short term debt and vice versa. If both debt categories change independently, the coefficients of these variables will be zero and if rearrangements take place negative coefficients will appear.

3 Empirical analyses

The hypotheses formulated above as a priori expectations are tested in two series of analyses. As a first step, the variables are included in an OLS regression analysis of the pooled cross section and time series data. This should provide a preliminary insight into the relations between the variables and may serve to compare the results obtained here with the results of previous analyses of the same dataset. Whenever appropriate, variables have been deflated with the industry specific price indices included in the data.

Table I Estimated OLS regression coefficients (pooled data, standard errors between parentheses)

	short t. debt		long t. debt	
intercept	-.038	(.007)	-.019*	(.011)
compl.debt cat.	.054*	(.029)	.125*	(.068)
ΔCA+	.511	(.213)	-1.403	(.322)
ΔCA-	.387	(.181)	-1.152	(.273)
ΔFA+	-.366*	(.210)	1.386	(.316)
ΔFA-	-.153*	(.167)	1.073	(.251)
Δasset struct.	.122*	(.205)	-.788	(.312)
ΔROI	-.116	(.036)	-.124	(.056)
Δinvent. turn.	.099*	(.077)	-.001*	(.118)
Δdepr.charges	.008*	(.057)	.001*	(.087)
R^2 (DF adjusted)	.065		.169	

*Note Table I: * means not significantly different from zero at a 5% level of significance.*

Separate regression equations are estimated for changes in long and short term debt ratios; the results are presented in Table I. Table 1 shows that the intercepts, which can be seen as autonomous growth rates, are negative and significantly so in the case of short term debt. No significant rearrangements, i.e. adjustments in the maturity structure of debt, are found: the coefficients of the complementary debt categories are not significantly different from zero. However, both coefficients are positive and positive effects are not anticipated; they may point to a sort of "package deal" in debt financing, but this phenomenon is not mentioned in the literature as a common aspect of the supply of debt.

The results regarding investments and disinvestments in asset categories indicate a linkage between investment and financing decisions rather than scale effects in (optimal) capital structure. Changes in current and fixed assets have opposite effects on long and short term debt and the coefficients of investments and disinvestments pairwise have the same sign (i.e. short term debt is positively related to current assets and negatively to fixed assets and the opposite is true for long term debt). The effects of changes in fixed assets on short term debt are insignificantly negative; the other coefficients are significant. These results are in line with the traditional financing rule of synchronizing the terms of investment and finance. The coefficients of investments are larger than those of disinvestments, although the differences are not large enough to justify the distinction.

The influence of asset structure is, somewhat surprisingly in the light of the above results, contrary to the hypothesis: positive on short term debt and negative on long term debt and significantly so in the latter case. In the earlier analysis of debt ratios (not changes), opposite effects were found. We have no ready explanation for this phenomenon.

The effects of ROI are significantly negative in both cases. Apparently, the negative cash effect and pecking order effect outweigh the positive signal effect. This result is consistent with the earlier analysis. The effects of inventory turnover and depreciation charges are small and insignificant.

The overall picture of the analysis so far is that taking first differences makes the theoretical determinants lose importance and the asset categories gain importance. However, the results obtained above could very well exhibit important industry and/or time commonalities and, more seriously, they can be biassed by industry and time specific omitted variables. In the latter case, the coefficients in Table I would partly reflect the influence of the omitted variables rather than the pure effects of the included variables. This problem is addressed in the next analysis.

In the main analysis of this paper, time and industry effects are introduced. By introducing shoptype and/or time specific variables into the regression equation, it is possible to reduce or avoid the omitted variable bias (see Hsiao, 1986). The panel character of the data permits these variables to be included. Time and industry specific variables can be included in basically two ways. First, since all variables consist of observations per shoptype repeated over time, they can be averaged across shoptypes per period and across periods per shoptype. If these averages would be added to the regression equation, they would provide insight into the cross-sectional (within group) and time series (between group) characteristics of the variables themselves. This procedure would only capture effects of omitted variables in so far as they are related to the fluctuations in the shoptype and period averages of the included variables.

The second way to include time and industry specific effects is based on the more likely assumption that the effects of shoptype specific omitted variables stay constant through time for a given shoptype but vary across shoptypes. Similarly, the effects time specific omitted variables are likely to be the same for all shoptypes, but will vary in time without necessarily showing any pattern. A simple way to take account of these effects is to use variable-intercept models. Given the above assumptions regarding the effects of omitted variables, they can be absorbed into the intercept term of a regression model as a means to explicitly allow for the individual and time heterogeneity contained in the pooled cross section and time series data (see Hsiao, 1986 or Dielman, 1989).

Within the variable-intercept models, the shoptype and period specific effects can be treated as fixed constants (in fixed-effects models) or as random variables (in random-effects models). The 27 shoptypes involved in this study cover a large part of total retailing, so they cannot be considered a small sample from a much larger population of shoptypes. In this situation, the fixed-effects model seems more appropriate than its random-effects counterpart[2]. Hence, time and industry effects are introduced in this study by estimating the coefficients of a fixed-effects model using the least-squares dummy variable (LSDV) approach. For all shoptypes and all but the first period a separate dummy variable is included in the regression equation, replacing the intercept. Note that these dummy variables will not only capture the time and industry specific effects of omitted variables, but also the time and industry commonalities in the included variables[3].

The results of the LSDV regression analyses are reported on in two different ways. First of all, the regression results regarding the non-dummy variables are presented in Table II. The most striking result in this table is that all coefficients in equation for short term debt lose their significance. This is surprising, because in the earlier analysis of debt ratios (not changes), the introduction of time and industry dummies did not alter the sign and significance of the coefficients. In view of these results for short term debt, Miller's neutral mutations hypothesis seems very appealing indeed.

For long term debt, the results are more stable. The only difference between the OLS and LSDV estimates is that the coefficient of ROI is

---

[2]*See Hsiao (1986) p. 41-47, for a discussion of the pros and cons of fixed and random-effects models.*

[3]*Including e.g. both the shoptype dummies and the averages across periods per shoptype would, of course, produce perfect multicollinearity.*

Table II Estimated LSDV regression coefficients (pooled data, standard errors between parentheses)

	short t. debt		long t. debt	
intercept	-		-	
compl.debt cat.	.014*	(.029)	.036*	(.074)
ΔCA+	.308*	(.217)	-1.599	(.337)
ΔCA-	.130*	(.190)	-1.350	(.295)
ΔFA+	-.219*	(.222)	1.690	(.343)
ΔFA-	.074*	(.170)	1.200	(.264)
Δasset struct.	-.034*	(.209)	-1.030	(.328)
ΔROI	-.084*	(.044)	-.115*	(.070)
Δinvent. turn.	.048*	(.082)	-.114*	(.130)
Δdepr.charges	-.000*	(.058)	-.026*	(.092)
R^2 (DF adjusted)	.223		.174	

*Note Table II: * means not significantly different from zero at a 5% level of significance.*

significantly negative in the former and insignificantly so in the latter. Apart from that, the structure of the model (the sign and significance of the coefficients) remains unaffected by the introduction of 27 industry and 18 time dummies. So it can be concluded that the long term debt model is very robust indeed.

The second way in which the results are reported on is presented in Table III, in which the OLS and LSDV analyses are combined to provide a decomposition of the regression analyses results. The differences between the OLS and LSDV estimates spring, of course, from the dummy variables. These differences can be split up (decomposed) into a time specific and an industry specific component by

Table III Decomposition of regression analyses results

	total effect	pure variable effect	time spec. effect	indust. spec. effect
<u>Short term debt</u>				
intercept	-.038	-	.009	-.048
compl.debt cat.	.054*	.014*	.042	-.003*
ΔCA+	.511	.308*	.222	-.019*
ΔCA-	.387	.130*	.201	.057*
ΔFA+	-.366*	-.219*	-.168	.021*
ΔFA-	-.153*	.074*	-.177	-.050*
Δasset struct.	.122*	-.034*	.142	.014*
ΔROI	-.116	-.084*	-.032	.000*
Δinvent. turn.	.099*	.048*	.055	-.003*
Δdepr.charges	.008*	-.000*	.007*	.001*
<u>Long term debt</u>				
intercept	-.019*	-	-.066	.047
compl.debt cat.	.125*	.036*	.096	-.007*
ΔCA+	-1.403	-1.599	.042*	.154
ΔCA-	-1.152	-1.350	.131*	.066*
ΔFA+	1.386	1.690	-.134*	-.170
ΔFA-	1.073	1.200	-.076*	-.051*
Δasset struct.	-.788	-1.030	.114*	.128
ΔROI	-.124	-.115*	-.003*	-.006*
Δinvent. turn.	-.001*	-.114*	.117	-.005*
Δdepr.charges	-.001*	-.026*	.038*	-.013*

*Note Table III * means not significantly different from zero at a 5% level of significance.*

regressing the time and industry dummies (separately) on the same set of explanatory variables that was used in the OLS analyses[4]. The results of these exercises are included in Table III, in which the results add up horizontally. Table III shows that the results found in the analyses of short term debt consist almost entirely of time specific effects. Except for the intercept, all industry specific and pure variable effects are insignificant. Inspection of the time dummies reveals no pattern in their values. Hence, the year-to-year changes in short term debt are found in this analysis to be related to neither changes in asset categories nor to changes in the proxy variables for theoretical determinants.

For long term, debt the few significant time specific effects are cancelled out by opposite industry specific and/or pure variable effects. For most variables, the pure variable effects are large compared with the other effects, so that their influence appears to be rather straightforward.

4 Conclusions

This paper's analyses of changes in debt ratios give rise to mixed conclusions. As regards short term debt, no significant effects (other than time specific effects) were found, so that it must be concluded that the ratio changes more or less ran-

---

[4]*For these analyses it must be assumed that the time dummies are the same for all shoptypes and that the shoptype dummies are the same for all periods.*

domly around some average value. These results are in line with Miller's (1977) neutral mutation hypothesis, according to which the changes in financial structure serve no function, but do no harm too and can therefore be made randomly. Note, however, that earlier research shows that short term debt ratios themselves (i.e. not changes) can be explained by the same variables used here and that those results are robust for the introduction of time and industry specific effects.

As regards the long term debt ratio, changes do not occur randomly but they are related to changes in current assets (negatively) and fixed assets (positively). These results remain unaffected by time and industry specific effects. These results could indicate that rules of thumb, proclaiming that the time span of investments and their financing should be matched (the "golden balance sheet rule" as it is called in The Netherlands), have played an important role in the financial behaviour of small firms over the period, at least as far as long term debt is concerned.

In earlier analyses [Van der Wijst and Thurik (1992), Van der Wijst and Vermeulen (1991)], determinants from the theory of finance were found to be relevant for the maturity structure rather than the overall level of small business debt. This paper's analyses indicate, that theoretical determinants are even less relevant for changes in debt ratios, which seem to follow a random pattern (in the case of short term debt) or seem to follow changes in assets according to rules of thumb. One of the reasons for analysing first differences in this paper is that behaviour may be exposed more sharply by eliminating the effects of decisions in the past from the data. If in this paper behaviour is exposed more sharply at all, it is not the behaviour predicted by the theory of finance.

References

Baxter, N.D. and J.G. Cragg, 1970, Corporate choice among long-term financing instruments, The Review of Economics and Statistics, vol. LII, no. 3, August, 225-235.

Bradley, M., G.A. Jarrell and E.H. Kim, 1984, On the existence of an optimal capital structure: theory and evidence, Journal of Finance, vol. XXXIX, no. 3, July, 857-880.

Dielman, T.E., 1989, Pooled cross-sectional and time series data analysis, (Marcel Dekker inc., New York).

Hsiao, C., 1986, Analysis of panel data, (Cambridge University Press, Cambridge)

Marsh, P., 1982, The choice between equity and debt: an empirical study, Journal of Finance, vol. XXXVII, no. 1, March, 121-144.

Miller, M., 1977, Debt and taxes, Journal of Finance, vol. XXXII, no. 2, 261-275.

Myers, S.C., 1984, The capital structure puzzle, Journal of Finance, vol. XXXIX, no.3, July, 575-592.

Myers, S.C. and N. Majluf, 1984, Corporate financing and investment decisions when firms have information investors do not have, Journal of Financial Economics.

Wijst, D. van der, 1989, Financial structure in small business, theory, tests and applications, (Springer-Verlag, Berlin).

Wijst, Nico van der and Roy Thurik, 1992, Determinants of small firm debt ratios, Small Economics, forthcoming

Wijst, D. van der en E.M. Vermeulen, 1991, Determinanten van financieringsverhoudingen, een analyse van panel data, in: P.C. van Aalst, J. van der Meulen en J. Spronk (eds.), Financiering en belegging, stand van zaken anno 1991, Erasmus Universiteit Rotterdam.

Computing Price Paths of Mortgage-Backed Securities Using Massively Parallel Computing

Stavros A. Zenios and Raymond A. McKendall

HERMES Lab for Financial Modeling and Simulation
Decision Sciences Department, The Wharton School
University of Pennsylvania
Philadelphia, PA 19104

1 Introduction

We consider the problem of pricing fixed-rate mortgage-backed securities (abbreviated: MBS). In particular, we develop a model that tracks the price of MBS across time, but also under different scenarios of the term structure. Central to the developments of this paper is the use of massively parallel computing technology. The computational complexities of MBS, and the related pricing model, rendered them intractable on current workstations or large mainframes. The paper also develops practical procedures for the computation of the pricing model on massively parallel systems, like the Connection Machine CM–2.

Our view of pricing MBS differs from the view common in the literature. Our motivation is twofold: First, building dynamic, multi-stage portfolio-optimization models requires evaluating quantities heretofore unnecessary. Second, recent developments in massively parallel computing allow us to advance the state of what is computationally feasible. Specific references to these motivations are made later.

The pricing model is consistent with the practicalities of MBS:

1. It uses the expectations hypothesis to price the cashflows of MBS, based on the short-term, risk free rate of return. The cashflows of the MBS are related to the prevailing mortgage refinancing rates, since homeowners are prone to refinance their loans as the mortgage refinancing rates drop. In turn, refinancing rates are driven by the rate of return of a long-term, risk free bond. The pricing model is, therefore, consistent with term-structure models.

2. The well-known behavior of homeowners to exercise the mortgage refinancing option in a non-optimal fashion is explicitly captured in the pricing process through the prepayment model of Kang and Zenios [15]. The level of prepayments is dependent on the history of mortgage refinancing rates since the origination of the loan. The prepayment model is dynamic to capture changes in homeowners preferences as their loans age, and is responsive to the prevailing mortgage refinancing rates.

3. The market's assessment that MBS bear higher risk than Government bonds of comparable maturity is captured via the use of an *option adjusted premium.* Current market prices are used to calibrate this risk premium.

Several models have been proposed for the valuation of fixed-rate mortgages. To various degrees they take into account the stylized facts associated with MBS. In particular, the models of Schwartz and Torous [20] and McConell and Singh [17] use two-factor models for the term structure, and include the homeowners' prepayment activity in the form of *conditional prepayment probabilities.* That is, at each point in time these models estimate a probability of prepayment which depends on the prevailing state of the economy. The dependence of prepayments on the history of refinancing rates is captured through the averaging device of Ramaswamy and Sundaresan [19][1]. With this simplifying assumption on the path-dependence of prepayments these studies develop the partial differential equations for the value of MBS and derivative products: IOs (interest only), POs (principal only) and CMOs (collateralized mortgage obligations). To handle the substantial additional complexities of adjustable-rate mortgages, Kau *et al.* [16] use a single factor model of the term structure, but, more importantly, they assume financially rational exercise of the prepayment option.

The most important limitation of the above models, however, is their assumption that the MBS market has the same risk as the Government bond market and hence the instantaneous risk-free rate is the appropriate stochastic process for driving the valuation model. Of course, this assumption does not hold in practice. In particular, default and illiquidity as well as modeling errors create additional risks for MBS holders. Hence, the empirically observed prices of MBS imply a higher rate of return than Government bonds of comparable maturities. To capture this discrepancy the notion of *option adjusted spread* has been

[1] In particular, it is assumed that the state variable that captures the history of refinancing rates is an exponential average of past refinancing rates

developed by analysts in the industry; see Hayer [9]. This is the spread over the short term risk-free rates that investors are charging in order to assume the higher risk of the MBS. The models we propose here incorporate a measure of this risk premium into the pricing equations.

The most important contribution of our models, compared to previous works, is that they track the price of MBS across time and under different interest rate scenarios. The results from these pricing models are very important in the context of portfolio management, where one wishes to place a value on the outstanding balance of a mortgage pool at the end of the portfolio planning horizon. Indeed, Hiller and Eckstein [10] study the mortgage portfolio management problem over a 30-year planning horizon without interim rebalancing decisions and thus avoid the difficulty of having to price their portfolio at intermediate points in time. Zenios [23] proposed a two-stage, stochastic programming model for managing mortgage portfolios with shorter time horizons, and allowing rebalancing. However, he did not report any numerical results, since key pricing information was not available. The pricing models developed here allow the implementation of the latter model, and is the topic of the current phase of this project. The results of the pricing model have been used in the context of a mortgage-indexation model with very encouraging results; see Worzel and Zenios [22].

A second contribution of this paper is the development of procedures to implement the models on data-level, massively parallel computer architectures. The computational requirements of the simulation-based models are enormous. Hence, we use a Connection Machine CM-2a with 4096 processors to execute the model. Details of the implementation are reported. Finally, we discuss observations based on numerical results for the valuation of IO, PO and pass-through securities.

Section 2 describes the models, section 3 their implementations on the CM–2a, and section 4 reports numerical results.

2 Pricing Models

The pricing models are based on Monte Carlo simulation of the term structure. In particular, following Cox, Ingersoll and Ross [6], we obtain the equilibrium value of the MBS as its expected discounted value, with discounting at the risk-free rate. Any suitable term-structure model can be used to drive the Monte Carlo simulations. (See Boyle [4] for Monte Carlo applications to pricing.) Examples include Monte Carlo simulation of a diffusion process — see, e.g., Cox, Ingersoll and Ross [6] — or binomial lattice models, like that of Black, Derman and Toy [2].

We are interested in particular to value the security at some future time period, τ. This might be the planning horizon for a portfolio management problem. Possible states σ of the economy at time period τ are obtained using the term-structure model. From each state of the economy at instance τ we can observe the possible evolution of interest rates until the end of the horizon, $\mathcal{T}$. The time horizon for 30-year mortgages is 360 months. The price of the MBS is the expected discounted value of its cashflow, with expectation computed over the interest rate paths that are *emanating* from that particular state.

In our work we use the binomial lattice model of Black, Derman and Toy [2]. A binomial lattice of the term structure can be described as a series of *base* rates $\{r_t^0 \, , \, t = 0, 1, \ldots, \mathcal{T}\}$, and *volatilities* $\{k_t \, , \, t = 0, 1, \ldots, \mathcal{T}\}$. The short-term rate at any state σ of the binomial lattice at some point t is

$$r_t^\sigma = r_t^0 (k_t)^\sigma .$$

The base rate and volatility parameters are estimated according to the procedure developed by Black, Derman and Toy, in a way that is consistent with the current observations of the term structure and short-term rate volatilities. Long term rates can also be obtained using the binomial lattice. Those are used in driving the prepayment activity of MBS. We point out that a two-factor model would be more appropriate in pricing MBS. Our pricing models — and the associated massively parallel algorithms — can use any other term structure. To keep our development simple we concentrate here only on binomial lattices.

To make the idea of the pricing model precise, let $\mathcal{S}_\sigma = \{1, 2, 3, \ldots\}$ denote a set of interest rate scenarios that emanate from state σ of the binomial lattice at some future time period τ. Let also r_t^s be the short term discount rate at time period t ($\tau \leq t \leq \mathcal{T}$) associated with scenario $s \in \mathcal{S}_\sigma$, and C_t^s be the cashflow generated by the security at period t under the same scenario s. Then, the expectations hypothesis dictates that a fair price for the security at period τ and conditioned on the state σ is

$$P_\tau^\sigma = \frac{1}{\mid \mathcal{S}_\sigma \mid} \sum_{s=1}^{|\mathcal{S}_\sigma|} \sum_{t=\tau}^{\mathcal{T}} \frac{C_t^s}{\prod_{i=\tau}^{t} (1 + r_i^s)} . \tag{1}$$

This procedure is illustrated in figure 1.

Mortgage-backed securities, however, cannot be priced using the same discount rates implied by the treasuries' curve. In particular, the price of the MBS has to reflect the credit, liquidity and default risks associated with this instrument. To value the risks associated with MBS

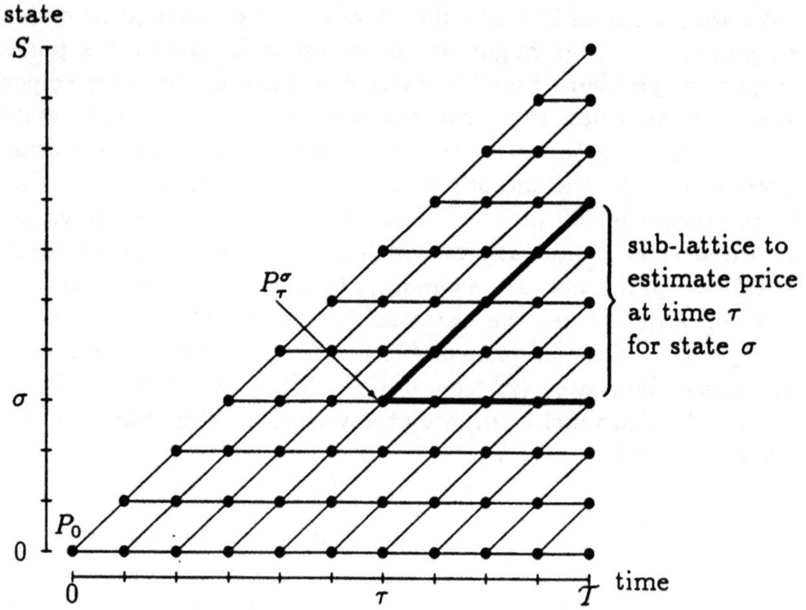

Figure 1: Estimating state-dependent prices of an MBS from a binomial lattice model of the term structure.

we compute an *option adjusted premium* (OAP). The OAP methodology estimates the multiplicative adjustment factor for the treasuries rates that will equate today's (observed) market price with the "fair" price obtained by applying the expectations hypothesis[2]. The discrepancy between the market price and the theoretical price is due to the various risks that are present in MBS, but are not present in the treasuries market. Hence, this analysis will price the risks.

The OAP for a given security is estimated based on the current market price, P_0. In particular, it is the solution ρ_0 of the following nonlinear equation in ρ:

$$P_0 = \frac{1}{|\mathcal{S}_0|} \sum_{s=1}^{|\mathcal{S}_0|} \sum_{t=0}^{T} \frac{C_t^s}{\prod_{i=0}^{t}(1 + \rho \cdot r_i^s)} \qquad (2)$$

Here, $\mathcal{S}_0$ is the set of scenarios emanating from the root of the lattice.

Now that we have priced the various risks associated with an MBS we can proceed to price the security at some future time period. Con-

[2] The use of a multiplicative OAP instead of the standard additive OAS is suggested by Holmer [13]. Its advantages compared to the additive spread are given in Babbel and Zenios [1].

sider once more the price of the security at state σ during time period τ. Then the *option adjusted price* P_τ^σ assuming a premium ρ_0 is

$$P_\tau^\sigma = \frac{1}{|S_\sigma|} \sum_{s=1}^{|S_\sigma|} \sum_{t=\tau}^{T} \frac{C_t^s}{\prod_{i=\tau}^{t}(1+\rho_0 \cdot r_i^s)} . \tag{3}$$

We point out, however, that the price P_τ^σ depends not only on the state σ but also on the history of interest rates from $t = 0$ to $t = \tau$ that pass through this state[3]. This difficulty can be easily resolved by sampling paths from $t = 0$ that pass through state σ at $t = \tau$. Let $\mathcal{S}^{0,\sigma}$ denote the set of such paths, and let $P_\tau^{s(\sigma)}$, $s(\sigma) \in \mathcal{S}^{0,\sigma}$, be the price of the security at state σ obtained by applying equation (3), conditioned on the fact that interest rate scenarios s in $\mathcal{S}_\sigma$ originate from scenarios $s(\sigma)$ in $\mathcal{S}^{0,\sigma}$. Then the price of the security at σ is this:

$$P_\tau^\sigma = \frac{1}{|\mathcal{S}^{0,\sigma}|} \sum_{s(\sigma)\in\mathcal{S}^{0,\sigma}} P_\tau^{s(\sigma)} \tag{4}$$

Figure 2 illustrates estimation of $P_\tau^{s(\sigma)}$ for two scenarios $s(\sigma) \in \mathcal{S}^{0,\sigma}$.

2.1 Option Adjusted Premium

An assumption underlying the use of equation (3) is that the option adjusted premium for the security will remain constant over time. In particular, it will be equal to ρ_0 obtained by solving equation (2). We point out that the OAS methodology assumes that this premium is indeed constant, and hence it estimates a single additive spread. However, the assumption is not realistic. Babbel and Zenios [1] point out that the OAP of a security will change over time and with changes in the level of interest rates. In particular, it should approach 1.0 as the security approaches maturity. Just prior to maturity there are no prepayment risks, and hence the price of the security is precisely the price implied by the expected present value of its cashflows, discounted at the treasury rates. Furthermore, the OAP of a security will depend on the level and volatility of interest rates. Unfortunately, the precise form of these variations is presently unknown.

[3] In particular, the cashflows generated by the MBS at periods after τ will depend on the prepayment activity experienced prior to τ. If the security has experienced periods of low refinancing rates prior to τ then most prepayments have already taken place, and subsequent drops of the mortgage rate will have less impact. Although the short-term rates prior to τ do not appear explicitly in the pricing equations, the mortgage refinancing rates prior to τ are used in the estimation of the cashflows C_t^s after τ.

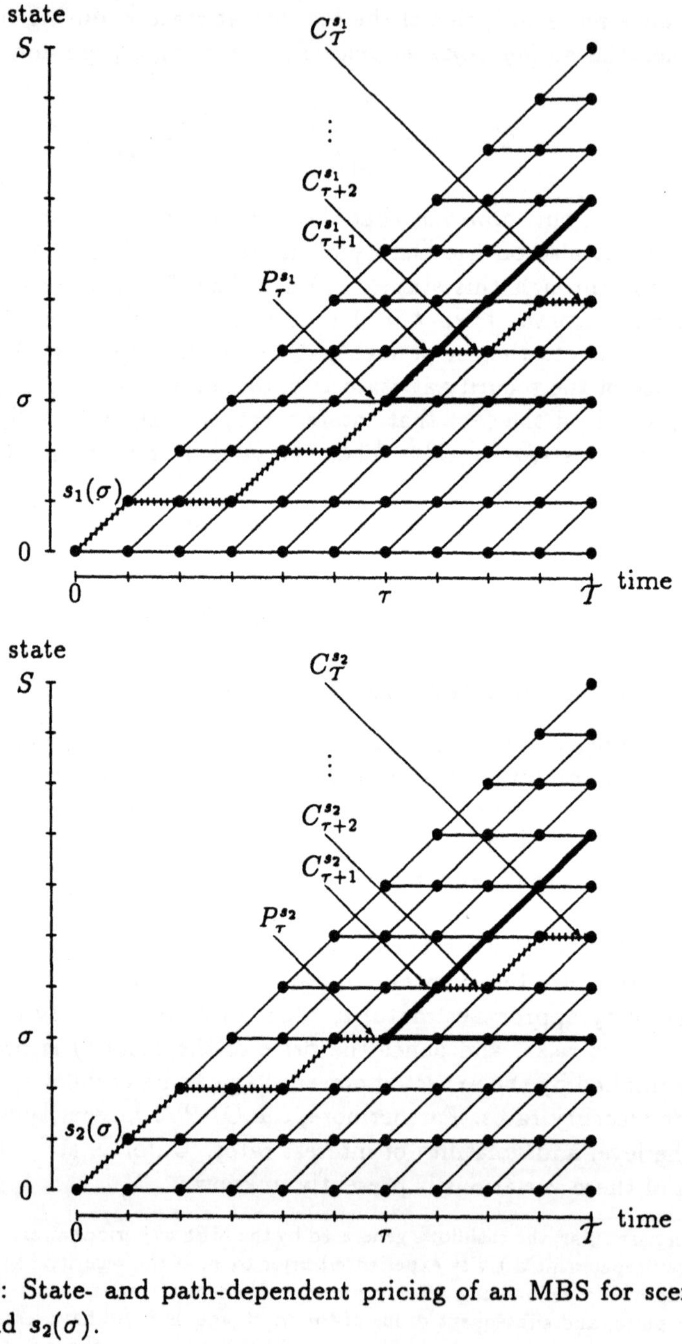

Figure 2: State- and path-dependent pricing of an MBS for scenarios $s_1(\sigma)$ and $s_2(\sigma)$.

There are several ways to estimate option adjusted premia that vary with time over the investment horizon:

1. Use as an approximation the constant OAP obtained by solving equation (2). This is the simplest approximation. We use this approach in our numerical experiments.

2. Use an OAP that changes with the *duration* of the security. It starts with ρ_0 and tends to 1.0 as the security approaches its maturity, and hence its duration is decreased to zero. The fact that the price of the embedded option changes with the duration of the instrument — suggested by Golub [8] — is consistent with options pricing theory. At present we have no formal model to capture the varying nature of OAP.

3. Use historical data to relate the OAP of different groups of securities (e.g., FNMA, GNMA, etc.) to their duration. This approach is followed, for example, by Fannie Mae in estimating OAP for broad sectors of securities in its portfolio.

In summary, however, the precise temporal variation of OAP is an area that requires additional research. Nevertheless, once a reasonable model — or empirical study — becomes available on this topic it can be directly integrated into our pricing models. Section 4.2.5 reports some empirical observations on this topic.

3 Parallel Implementation

We turn now our attention to the computing requirements of the models. It should be clear that deriving the price of a security for a given state σ at period τ requires nested simulations. First, sample scenarios from $t = 0$ to the target period τ that go through the specific state σ. From that point scenarios bifurcate into the future, and further sampling is required. In order to carry out these computationally intensive simulations we used a massively parallel computer, the Connection Machine CM–2a, with 4096 processing elements. The use of massively parallel computing for the Monte Carlo simulation of pricing models was introduced by Hutchinson and Zenios [14]. Subsequent applications were reported in Hiller and Eckstein [10] and by the ACTION program [18]. In this section we illustrate some of the key components of the mapping of our pricing models to the Connection Machine architecture. Expanded introductions to the Connection Machine and to data-parallel computing are given in Hillis [12], Hutchinson and Zenios [14] and [21]. Appendix B introduces concepts of data-parallel computing that are relevant to our discussion.

3.1 General Design

The framework for the massively parallel computation of the pricing models is a two-dimensional rectangular grid of processing elements, called the *simulation grid.* One axis of this grid corresponds to time, and the other axis corresponds to scenario. Each coordinate along the time axis represents one month in the lifetime of an MBS. Each coordinate along the scenario axis comprises an independent simulation of the MBS. The methodology of the simulation is to generate a different scenario of term structure for each coordinate along this axis. The time axis typically has length 360 (for a 30 year MBS), and the scenario axis typically has length 1024.

The data in each *cell* (t, s) of the grid describe the state of the MBS at time t under scenario s. The basic unit of these parallel data is a *field*, which is an allocation of memory in the cells. There are fields for all aspects of the calculations, such as interest rate, prepayment, and cashflow. Thus, for example, the value of the prepayment field in cell (t, s) is the prepayment generated at time t under scenario s. All cells have the same fields, but the contents of a field may differ among cells because the scenarios and time instances differ. For example, the values of the prepayment field in two cells (t, s_1) and (t, s_2) at the same time t may differ since scenarios s_1 and s_2 differ.

The paradigm underlying this framework is *data-parallel* computation: Every cell in the simulation grid has its own *virtual processor* to perform its computations. A virtual processor is a software emulation of a physical processor. Each physical processor in the Connection Machine can be configured to emulate multiple processors transparently to the programmer. The advantages of this model include the one-to-one correspondence of a cell with a virtual processor and the resulting scalability to larger problems or to larger machines. The disadvantages of the paradigm are decreases in speed and local memory as the ratio of virtual processors to physical processors increases.

The implementation uses three forms of parallelism under the two-dimensional configuration of processors:

1. Parallelism due to independence of scenarios: Executing the calculations across each scenario is an *embarassingly parallel* applications. The scenarios are independent from each other. Hence,

the rows of the two-dimensional grid can proceed concurrently to complete multiple simulations.

2. Parallelism due to independence of time-periods: Computation of statistics across time periods is also embarassingly parallel. For example, we can proceed concurrently across all columns of the grid to determine the maximum, minimum and expected price of an MBS at each time period. However, parallelism of this form is useful only for segments of the model that are trivial compared to the execution of the simulations. It is nevertheless important for data-visualization during model development and validation, and in reporting summary statistics.

3. Parallelism due to model decomposition: We are using computer systems with a number of processors that exceeds the required number of simulations. Hence, exploiting parallelism only due to independence of scenarios is ineffective. We also need to exploit parallelism in completing the calculations for each scenario. However, the calculations for each scenario have data dependencies. For example, the unpaid balance of an MBS at period t depends on the unpaid balance at period $t-1$. The models have also some inhomogeneities that preclude the use of the SIMD (i.e., Single Instruction Multiple Data) architecture. Dependencies and data inhomogeneities can be eliminated with suitable model reformulations. These reformulations are the subject of the next section.

3.2 Model Decompositions

Three key ideas were useful for implementing our models: domain decompositions, reordering computations, and combining computations with communications. We briefly explain and illustrate these ideas.

3.2.1 Domain decompositions

The SIMD architecture restricts the parallel execution of operations to the execution of identical instructions on multiple instances of the problem data. Whenever the operations are different for different problem data, it is necessary to *group* the data into sets that require identical instructions. The model is decomposed into homogeneous domains. Domains are processed serially. Within each domain, however, operations are homogeneous and hence can be executed in parallel. In general we wish to avoid this form of decomposition, since it reduces the level of parallelism, and adds a serial part to the calculations. This procedure is illustrated below in estimating the seasonality effect on prepayments.

3.2.2 Reordering computations

In some parts of the model we perform a series of calculations based on two independent variables. Consider, for example, the calculation of a series of constants c_j, $j = 1, 2, 3, \ldots, J$, as a function of two variables x_i, y_j, $i = 1, 2, 3, \ldots, I$, $j = 1, 2, 3, \ldots, J$, i.e., $c_j = \sum_i \phi(x_i, y_j)$. The "natural" order of calculation, whereby each c_j is computed by estimating the value of $\phi(x_i, y_j)$ for each i and then computing the sum, may lack sufficient parallelism if calculations are not identical for all values of x_i. We need to resort to *domain decomposition* whereby the x_j's are partitioned into sets that require identical operations. However, changing the order of calculations, thereby calculating multiple $\phi(x_i, y_j)$'s simultaneously will increase the level of parallelism. We still decompose the domain of the x_j's into smaller subsets, but for each homogeneous subset we have to repeat identical calculations for different values of j. This procedure is illustrated below in estimating the refinancing effect on prepayments.

3.2.3 Combining computations with communications

We consider the case of time dependent calculations, whereby the results for time period t depend on the results from previous time periods. In these cases it might be possible to formulate the model so that calculations for each time period can be combined with the communication of results from prior time periods, using the *scan* primitive operators of the CM–2a. This procedure is illustrated below in the sampling of a binomial lattice and the calculation of the aging effect on prepayments.

3.3 Calculating Prepayments

The prepayment model in this analysis is that of Kang and Zenios [15]. The model estimates a *constant prepayment rate* (CPR) for each month in the life of the mortgage from the product of three factors that depend on time and economic conditions:

$$\text{CPR} = \text{seasonality factor} \times \text{refinancing factor} \times \text{aging factor}$$

The seasonality factor adjusts the prepayment level for seasonal variations: It captures the tendency of prepayments to be higher in the summer and fall than in the winter and early spring. The refinancing

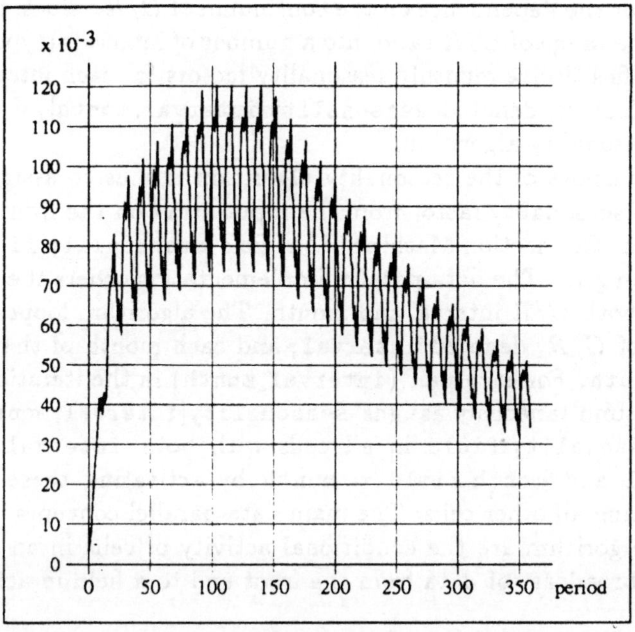

Figure 3: Prepayment of a GNMA-I 9.5 in static 10% refinancing rate.

factor reflects the pure economic incentive of homeowners to refinance their mortgage as market refinancing rates R drop below their mortgage coupon rate C. The aging factor accounts for the temporal variation in prepayment as a mortgage matures. (Figure 3 illustrates a typical projection of prepayments from the model.)

Implementation of this model on the Connection Machine is challenging because of the model's complexity and time dependencies. The framework for the computation is the two-dimensional simulation grid. The purpose of the computations is to assign the CPR corresponding to the state of the security in each cell to the field `cpr_field`. The simulation grid has fields `seasonality_field`, `refinancing_field`, and `aging_field` for the three factors in prepayment. Once the factor fields are assigned, the field `cpr_field` is a simple global product:

$$\texttt{cpr\_field} = \texttt{seasonality\_field} \times \texttt{refinancing\_field} \times \texttt{aging\_field}$$

Summaries of the parallel computation of these three factors follow.

3.3.1 Seasonality factor

The seasonality factor for an MBS at time t depends on the month of the year at time t and on the C/R ratio of the security at time t. To account for the dependence on the continuum of C/R values, the model divides the range of C/R ratio into a number of intervals (typically 20), and specifies twelve monthly seasonality factors for each interval. This array of factors, denoted `seasonality[interval,month]`, is the input to the seasonality algorithm.

The purpose of the seasonality algorithm is thus to assign the appropriate seasonality factor from the input array on the front-end controlling the Connection Machine to the field `seasonality_field` of the simulation grid. The data-parallel implementation orders the computations by both C/R interval and month. The algorithm loops over each interval of C/R, denoted `interval`, and each month of the year, denoted `month`. For each pair `(interval,month)` in the iteration, the algorithm simultaneously assigns `seasonality[interval,month]` to the field `seasonality_field` in all cells with both `interval_field` = `interval` and `month_field` = `month` by activating these cells and deactivating all other cells. The main data-parallel concepts illustrated by this algorithm are the conditional activity of cells in an operation and the broadcast of data from the front-end to a field in active cells.

3.3.2 Refinancing factor

The refinancing factor for an MBS at a period depends only on the C/R ratio at that period. The model first specifies N points ρ_1, ρ_2, …, ρ_N with uniform spacing $\Delta\rho$. It then expresses the refinancing factor $r(\rho)$ for a C/R ratio ρ as a linear combination of basis functions f_1, f_2, …, f_N with weights α_1, α_2, …, α_N:

$$r(\rho) := \sum_{j=1}^{N} \alpha_j \, f_j(\rho)$$

$$f_j(\rho) := \begin{cases} 0 & \text{if} \quad \rho \leq \rho_j \\ (\rho - \rho_j)/\Delta\rho & \text{if} \quad \rho_j \leq \rho < \rho_{j+1} \\ 1 & \text{if} \quad \rho_{j+1} \leq \rho \end{cases} \qquad j = 1, 2, \ldots, N$$

The points ρ_1, ρ_2, …, ρ_N and the weights α_1, α_2, …, α_N are input to the refinancing algorithm.

The purpose of the refinancing algorithm is thus to evaluate the refinancing function r for each C/R ratio field `cr_field` in the simulation grid. The data-parallel implementation orders the computations by basis function: For each $j = 1, 2, \ldots, N$, the algorithm simultaneously computes $\alpha_j \, f_j($`cr_field`$)$ for all cells and adds this to the field `refinancing_field`. The data-parallel concept demonstrated by this algorithm is the organization of calculations to maximize the number of active cells in each operation.

3.3.3 Aging factor

The aging factor for an MBS is itself the product of two factors: the *seasoning* factor and the *burnout* factor. Both the seasoning and burnout factors for an MBS depend on the age τ and the C/R ratio ρ. The models for these two factors are linear combinations of basis functions that depend on time with weights that depend on C/R. The basis functions and weights are different for seasoning and burnout.

The age component of the seasoning model specifies times t_1, t_2, ..., t_{N_t} with uniform spacing Δt and expresses the dependence on age τ through basis functions g_1, g_2, ..., g_{N_t}:

$$g_j(\tau) := \begin{cases} t/t_j & \text{if} \quad 0 \leq \tau < t_j \\ 1 & \text{if} \quad t_j \leq \tau \end{cases} \qquad j = 1, 2, \ldots, N_t$$

The economic component of the seasoning model partitions the domain of C/R values into N intervals $\mathcal{R}_1$, $\mathcal{R}_2$, ..., $\mathcal{R}_N$. To each interval $\mathcal{R}_i$, the model assigns weights γ_{i1}, γ_{i2}, ..., γ_{iN_t}. In summary, the model represents the seasoning factor $s(\tau, \rho)$ of a security with age τ and C/R ratio ρ as

$$s(\tau, \rho) := \sum_{j=1}^{N_t} \gamma_{ij}\, g_j(\tau) \qquad \text{for } \rho \in \mathcal{R}_i.$$

The age component of the burnout model also specifies a set of times t_1, t_2, ..., t_{N_t} and expresses the dependence on age through basis functions h_1, h_2, ..., h_{N_t}:

$$h_j(\tau) := \begin{cases} 1 & \text{if} \quad \tau \leq t_j \\ e^{-\beta(\tau - t_j)} & \text{if} \quad \tau > t_j \end{cases} \qquad j = 1, 2, \ldots, N_t,\ \beta > 0$$

The economic component of the burnout model partitions the domain of C/R values into intervals and assigns a set of weights η_{i1}, η_{i2}, ..., η_{iN_t} to each interval. In summary, the model expresses the burnout factor $b(\tau, \rho)$ of a security with age τ and C/R ratio ρ as

$$b(\tau, \rho) := \sum_{j=1}^{N_t} \eta_{ij}\, h_j(\tau) \qquad \text{for } \rho \in \mathcal{R}_i.$$

The models for seasoning and burnout further specify that these two factors are monotonic with time. For fixed ρ, the seasoning function $s(\cdot, \rho)$ is non-decreasing with age to capture the tendency of increasing prepayment in a new security. The burnout function $b(\cdot, \rho)$

for fixed ρ is non-increasing with age to reflect the tendency of decreasing prepayment in an aged security. Since the ratio ρ may vary with time, however, the aging and burnout functions are not necessarily monotonic with time. To achieve monotonicity for seasoning, the model computes the seasoning for a period t by adding the non-negative slope $\partial s(\tau,\rho)/\partial\tau$ scaled by Δt to the value of seasoning at period $t-1$. The initial value of seasoning is zero. Similarly, to achieve monotonicity for burnout, the model computes the burnout for a period t by adding non-positive $\partial b(\tau,\rho)/\partial\tau \cdot \Delta t$ to the value of burnout at period $t-1$. The initial value of burnout is one.[4]

The tasks of the seasoning and burnout algorithms, then, are first to compute the slopes of the seasoning and burnout functions for each pair (`time_field`, `cr_field`) in the simulation grid, and second to compute the seasoning and burnout levels from these slopes along the time axis for each scenario. The data-parallel implementation for either factor orders the computations of the slopes by C/R interval. The algorithm loops over each interval $\mathcal{R}_i$, denoted `interval`, and simultaneously computes the slope `slope_field` in all cells with `interval_field` = `interval`. Once the slopes for a factor are computed, the field `factor_field` in each cell receives the *scan-addition* over the `slope_field` and along the time axis: $\texttt{factor\_field}_{ts} := \sum_{j=0}^{t} \texttt{slope\_field}_{js}$ for cell (t,s). This scan operation is parallel with respect to scenarios. For burnout, there is next a global addition of 1.0 to `factor_field`. A final computation is a global minimum or maximum on `factor_field` to ensure that the seasoning level is at most one and that the burnout level is at least zero. The important data-parallel concept introduced in these algorithms is scan-addition.

3.4 Sampling a Binomial Lattice

The sampling of binomial lattices using massively parallel SIMD computers is reported in Hutchinson and Zenios[5]. We repeat it here since it illustrates the use of the scan operators in combining computations with communications.

To generate sample paths from a binomial lattice we need to determine the state of each path at each time. Once the sate σ_t of path s at time t in the lattice is specified at virtual processor (s,t) in the simulation grid, the short-term rate is computed simply as $r_t^s = r_t^0(k_t)^{\sigma_t}$.

[4] Seasoning and burnout actually depend on the history of C/R ratios over the lifetime of the security. The formulation described here captures this dependence implicitly through the weights and explicitly through monotonicity.

[5] Patent pending.

The problem in constructing a continuous path is that the state of the lattice at instance t must be attainable by either an "up" or "down" step from the state at instance $t-1$. Such a sequence of states is produced on the CM-2a as follows: A random bit 0 or 1 is first generated at each virtual processor. A scan-addition on these bits along the time axis generates the state index σ_t for each virtual processor. The state at t differs by at most one from the state at $t-1$. Then, calculating short-term rates proceeds in parallel for all time periods.

4 Numerical Results

The models were implemented on a Connection Machine CM–2a with 4096 processors. All programming was done in C/Paris, release 6.02. The models were used to price a variety of pass-through, IO and PO securities. Market prices for April 26, 1991 were provided by BlackRock Financial Management, together with returns on Government bonds of different maturities that were used to build the term-structure models. For the term structure we used the one-factor model of Black, Derman and Toy [2]. The refinancing rates were 150 basis points higher than the long-term rates obtained from the binomial lattice.

We present first results to establish the efficiency of the massively parallel implementation. We then proceed to carry out several experiments to understand the factors that affect the price path of MBS both across time, and at different states of a binomial lattice. In particular:

1. Observe the (nonlinear) dynamics of the price paths of pass-throughs, IOs and POs across time and at different states of the binomial lattice.

2. Observe the effect of increased volatility to the price paths.

3. Observe changes in the convexity of a pass-through as it approaches maturity.

4. Observe the dynamics of the price paths when the prepayment option is exercised optimally.

5. Investigate the impact of the non-constancy of the option adjusted premium on the results of the pricing model.

GNMA Security			
Factor	**Real Time**	**CM Time**	**MFLOPS**
Seasonality	0.07	0.07	—
Refinancing	0.23	0.23	19
Seasoning	0.34	0.33	3
Burnout	1.93	1.57	120
Complete	2.91	2.51	78

FNMA Security			
Factor	**Real Time**	**CM Time**	**MFLOPS**
Seasonality	0.07	0.07	—
Refinancing	0.26	0.26	14
Seasoning	0.39	0.39	2
Burnout	1.01	0.66	44
Complete	2.10	1.70	20

Table 1: Execution times (in seconds) and MFLOPS rates for computing prepayment levels under a VP ratio of 128 ($1024 \times 512 \div 4096$) for a GNMA and a FNMA security at par.

4.1 Performance of the Parallel Implementation

Table 1 reports the MFLOPS rate (i.e., Million Floating Point Operations Per Second) achieved by the various components of our implementation. Results are for the execution of 1024 simulations over a 360 month time horizon, on the CM–2a. These results are merely indicative of the level of parallelism achieved by the different components of the model. It is very encouraging that even the smallest Connection Machine configuration achieves large MFLOPS rates for several components of our model. The achieved MFLOPS rate depends on the type of the security analyzed, and on whether the security is discount, premium or par. This is due to the differences in the basis function evaluations that need to be performed for different securities.

Table 2 compares the times required to execute the various pricing models on a DECstation 5000 workstation with the CM–2a times. Of course the two systems are not comparable in price. Nevertheless, the DECstation times are indicative of the amount of time required for the execution of the models on the latest generation of RISC workstations. Large mainframes would need similar computing times.

Computation	Computer	
	DEC 5000	CM–2a
OAP	45	4–5
Price at $\tau = 0$	17	3–4
Prices at $\tau = 36$ for fixed state	546	3–4
Prices at $\tau = 36$ for all states	NA	256
Price path - yearly	61	13
Price path - monthly	564	127

Table 2: Execution times (in seconds) of pricing models.

4.2 Pricing Mortgage-Backed Securities

We look now at price variations of MBS under various economic conditions. We are interested, in particular, to see how the price of an instrument changes across time, and also how the price changes with the level of the short-term rate. There are two opposing forces that drive prices: prepayment activity and time to maturity. As the MBS approaches maturity the risks associated with prepayment become less important. The price of a pass-through or a PO converges to 100 (par), while the price of an IO converges to 0. As the MBS ages from its issuance date, however, prepayment increases. Also, prepayment burnout is observed as the mortgage ages even further, and homeowners prone to refinancing have already left the pool. (See, for example, figure 3.)

In the following sections we capture some of the complex interactions between these two effects. We use, in most cases, two interest-rate environments: (1) a *static* environment with a constant short-term rate of 8.5 and a constant refinancing rate of 10.0, and (2) a *dynamic* environment based on sampling a binomial lattice calibrated using the term structure of April 1, 1991, with decreasing volatility (figure 4).

4.2.1 Nonlinear dynamics of price paths

Figure 5 illustrates the price path of high premium GNMA-I 11.50 pass-through in the static environment. The price experiences a severe drop during its first year, as prepayment activity increases very rapidly. Following this initial surge, prepayments reach a steady state, whereby the price of the MBS remains constant above par. As the mortgage-pool experiences *burnout* (i.e., prepayment activity subsides) we see an increase of its price: What we have is, in essence, a fully amortizing

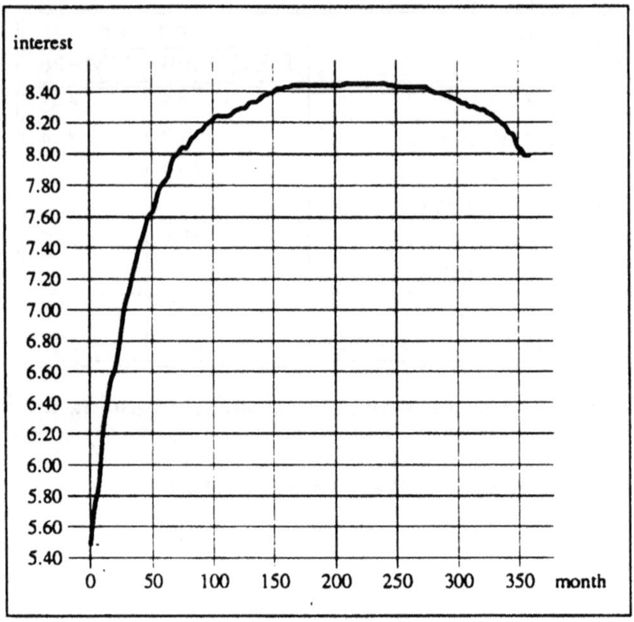

Figure 4: The term structure of April 1, 1991.

high-premium bond. As the security approaches maturity, however, its price slides towards its par value of 100.

Figure 5 also shows the price dynamics of a discount GNMA-I 8.00 in the static environment. Figure 6 illustrates the dynamics of a PO and an IO backed by a FNMA 10.08 security in the static environment. We observe similar behavior as that of the GNMA-I 11.50: rapid change in the price as prepayment increases, and convergence of the price path to that of the bond as the security ages and prepayments subside.

4.2.2 Effect of term-structure changes

We also used the dynamic environment to trace the price path of the same GNMA-I securities; see figure 7. We observe substantial fluctuations of the prices, as both the short-term rates increase (we are using an upward sloping yield curve), while the mortgage ages and the prepayment dynamics change. In particular, the GNMA-I 9.50 moves from above par to below par, and then above par again, before it converges to its limiting par value. These changes are consistent with the price performance of a fully amortizing bond of the same coupon rate and maturity (illustrated on the same figure for comparison), but also account for the complex prepayment dynamics of the mortgage security.

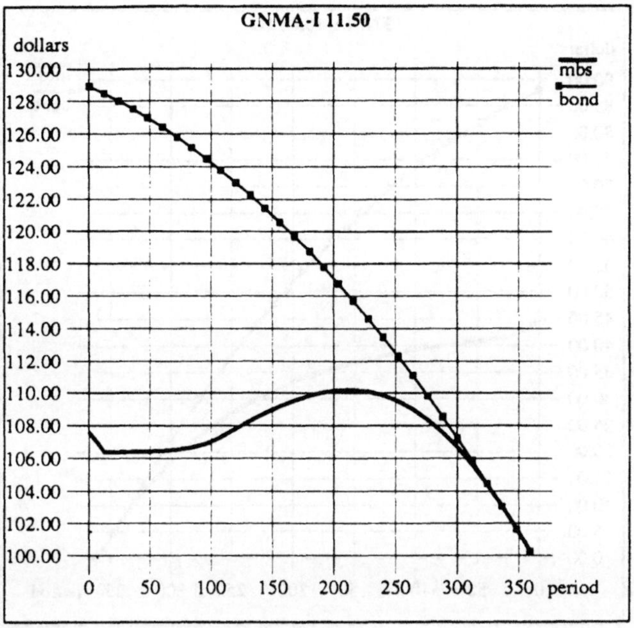

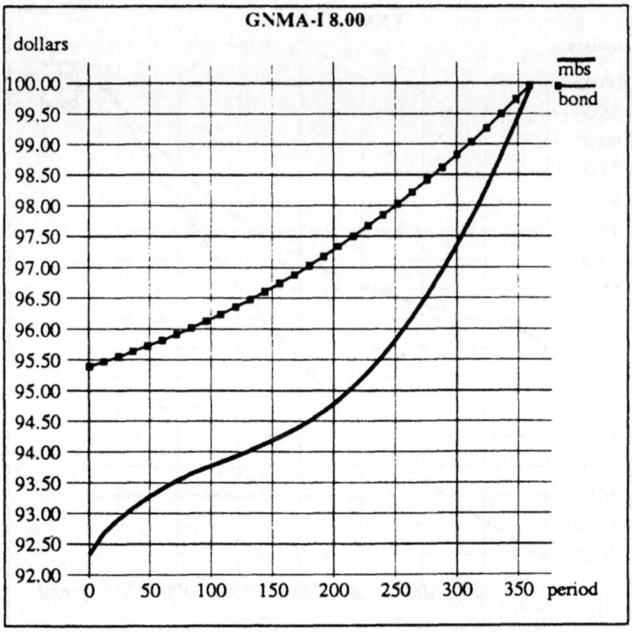

Figure 5: Price paths of premium GNMA-I 11.50 and discount GNMA-I 9.50 in the static environment. The price path of a fully amortizing bond with the same maturity and coupon rates is also shown.

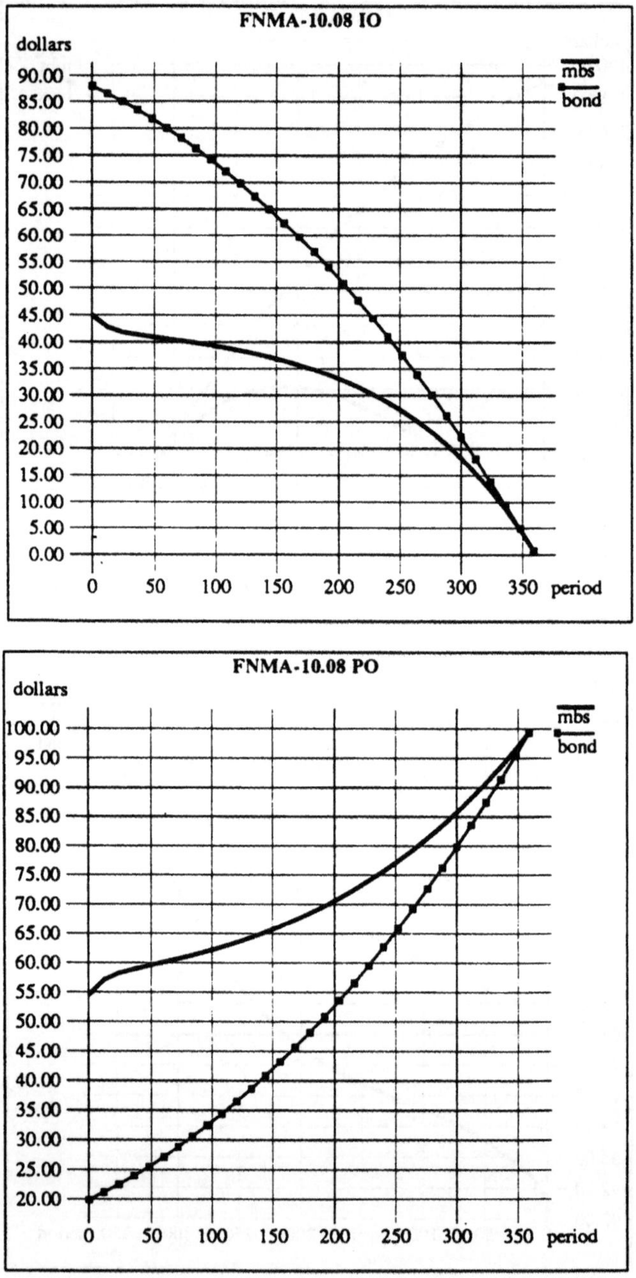

Figure 6: Price paths of an IO and a PO from a premium FNMA 10.08 in the static environment. The price path of a fully amortizing bond with the same maturity and coupon rates is also shown.

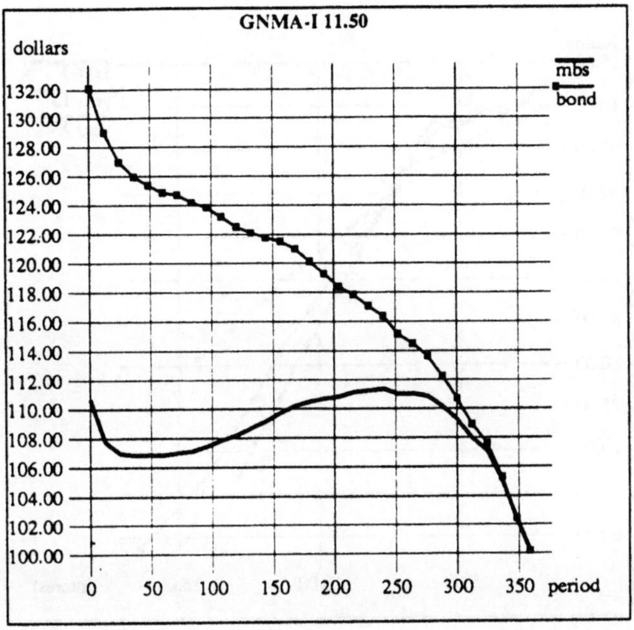

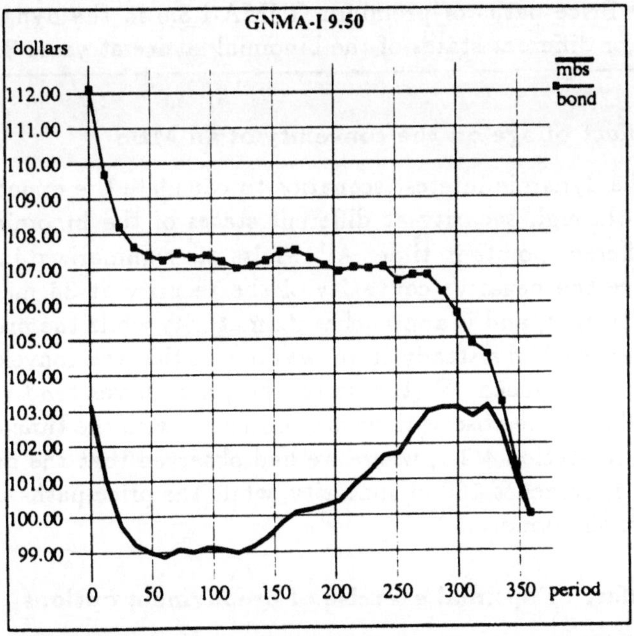

Figure 7: Price paths of premium GNMA-I 11.50 and 9.50 in the dynamic environment. The price path of a fully amortizing bond with the same maturity and coupon rates is also shown.

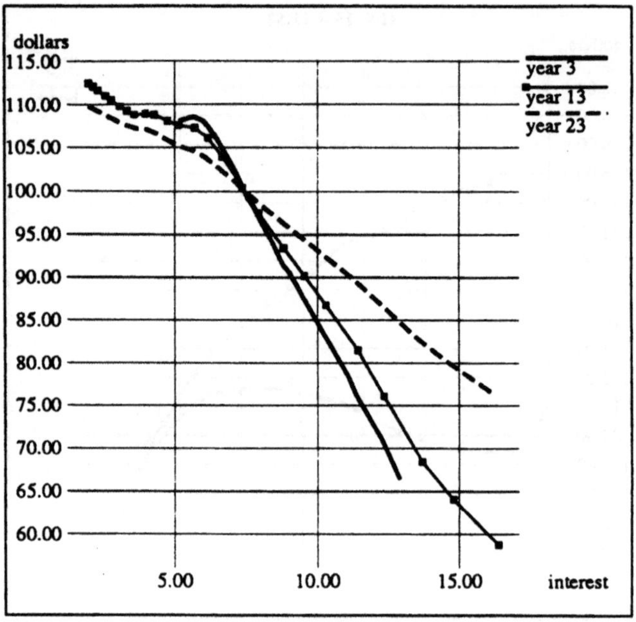

Figure 8: Price paths of premium GNMA-I 8.0 in the dynamic environment for different states of the binomial lattice at years 3, 13, 23.

4.2.3 Effect of age on the convexity of an MBS

We use the dynamic interest scenarios to calculate the expected price of a pass-through security at different states of the binomial lattice, and at different points in time. All results are summarized in figure 8. We observe the negative convexity of the security at 36 months. As the security ages, and it approaches its maturity while the prepayment activity has reached a steady state, we observe that the convexity of the price curve is reduced. Furthermore, the price curves tend to the par value of 100. These observations are consistent with the time-dynamics presented in section 4.2.1, where we had observed that the price of all securities approaches 100 at maturity, while the price paths converged to those of the bond.

4.2.4 Effect of optimal exercise of prepayment options

We consider here the effect of changing levels of prepayment activity to the price paths. This effect is important to study since specific mortgage pools do not prepay at the same rate as generic pools, which are the basis of the prepayment model. In particular, we consider as

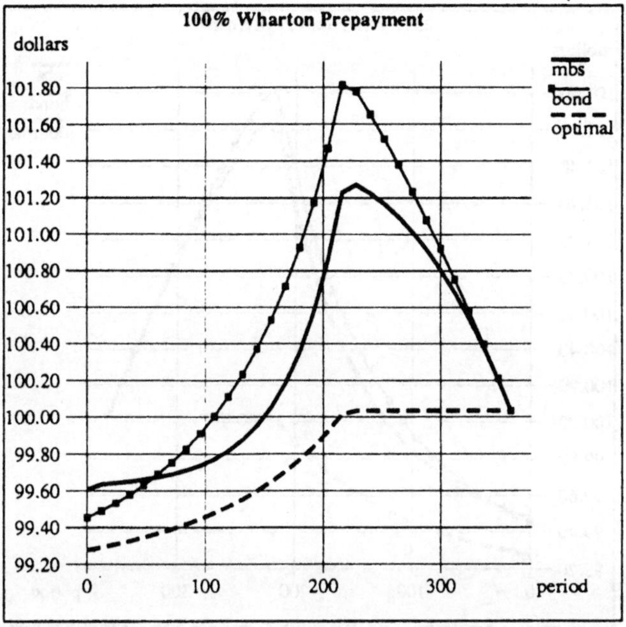

Figure 9: Price path for 100% Wharton-prepayment speed.

extreme cases an MBS with optimal exercise of the prepayment option (i.e., full prepayment of all outstanding balance as soon as mortgage refinancing rates drop below the coupon rate) and a non-prepaying fully amortizing bond. Intermediate cases include MBS that prepay at 25%, 100%, and 250% of the speed of the Wharton prepayment model in Kang and Zenios [15]. Figures 9 and 10 illustrate the price paths for a GNMA 11.4 in an interest-rate environment that is constant at 11.5 until month 224, drops instantaneously to 11.0 at month 224, and remains at 11.0 thereafter.

4.2.5 Effect of varying option adjusted premium

We pointed out that our pricing model assumes that the option adjusted premium will remain constant throughout the life of the mortgage. In practice, however, the premium is expected to change towards a boundary value of 1.0 at maturity. In the implementation of our models we allow a parametric family of curves to capture the changing nature of OAP. In particular, the premium at t, ρ_t, changes according to

$$\rho_t = 1 + (\rho_0 - 1) * (1 - t/360)^p. \tag{5}$$

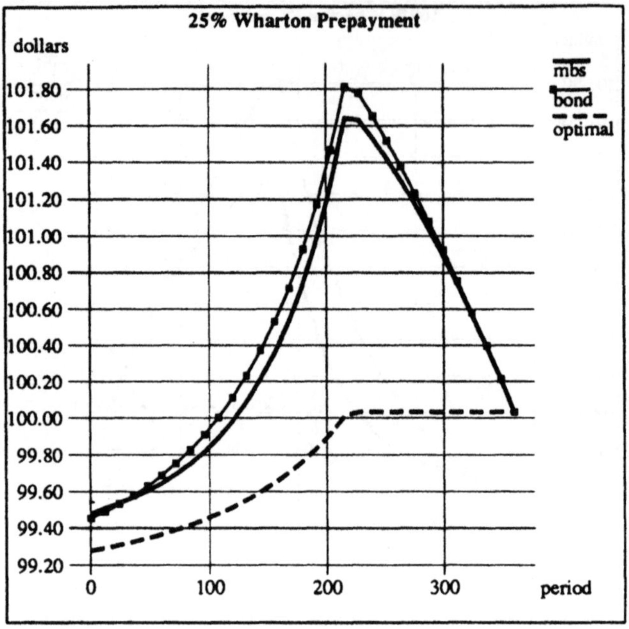

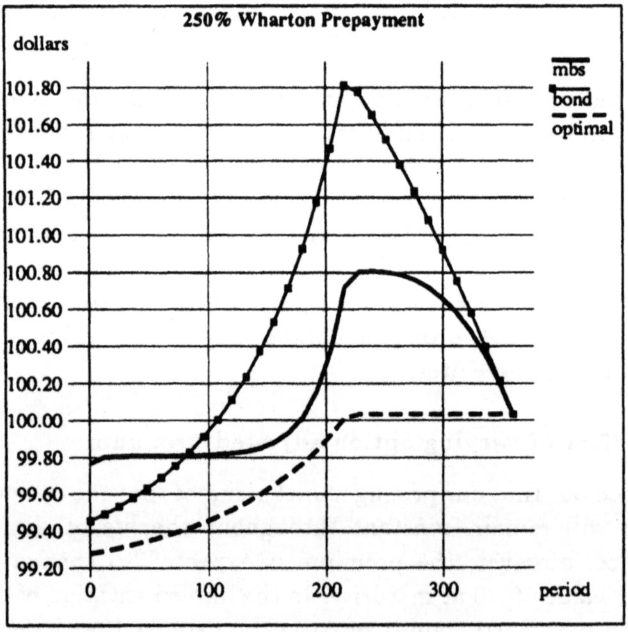

Figure 10: Price paths for 25% and 250% Wharton-prepayment speeds.

For $p = 0$, the option adjusted premium will remain constant. For other values of p it will change towards the boundary value of 1.0, with the rate of change being determined by p. Hence, in the absence of any rigorous model for estimating the temporal variation of the premium, we may resort to sensitivity analysis of the pricing model: "How sensitive are the results of the model to potential temporal variations of the option adjusted premium?". Figures 11 and 12 illustrate the change of the price path for different rates of change of the OAP, i.e., for different values of p. The results are intuitively appealing. Furthermore, we observe that it is only towards the mid-life of the mortgage that the price discrepancies become substantial. For the short, e.g., 3-year, horizon the price discrepancies are small. We point out that the rate of change of the premium used in these experiments is quite high. One would expect slower rate of change in practice. A model that would lead us to a more judicious choice of p is reported in D'Ecclesia and Zenios [7].

4.3 Valuation of a Diverse Portfolio

We used the pricing models of this paper to price a portfolio of 44 securities, that included pass-throughs, IOs and POs. The pass-through securities were both FNMA and GNMA-I with weighted average coupon rates (WACs) ranging from 8.75 to 12.75, and weighted average maturities (WAMs) in the range 265 to 360. IO and POs were backed by both FNMA and GNMA-I collaterals, with range of WACs and WAMs similar to the pass-throughs. The portfolio assumes that all instruments are held in equal amounts of 100. Hence, if all instruments were priced at par the market price would have been 4400. Figures 13 and 14 illustrate the change in the price of the portfolio at different future time periods and for different short-term rates.

5 Conclusions

The models presented in this report provide insights to the performance of MBS and derivative products under widely varying future scenarios. As such they can be used as fundamental decision support tools for portfolio management, in a descriptive capacity. The computational efficiency of the massively parallel implementation makes them particularly attractive. We believe that comparable performance can be achieved with a distributed network of workstations. (See Cagan *et al.* [5].) Such systems are widely available in financial institutions.

These models allow us to develop prescriptive models for active portfolio management. An institutional investor can build portfolios

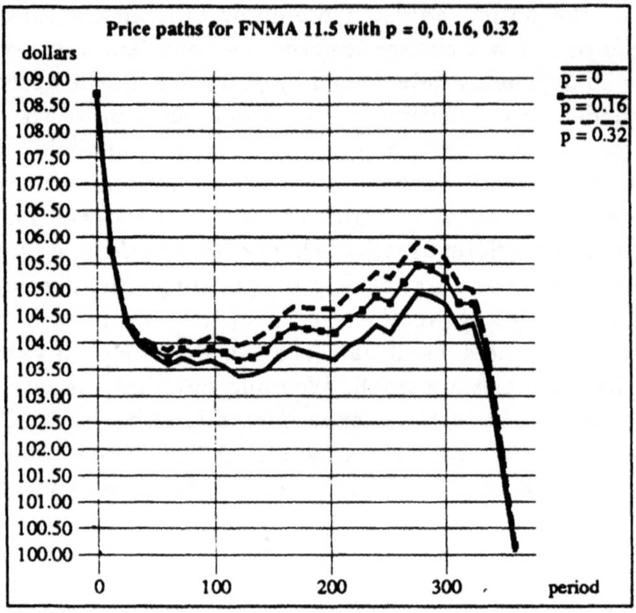

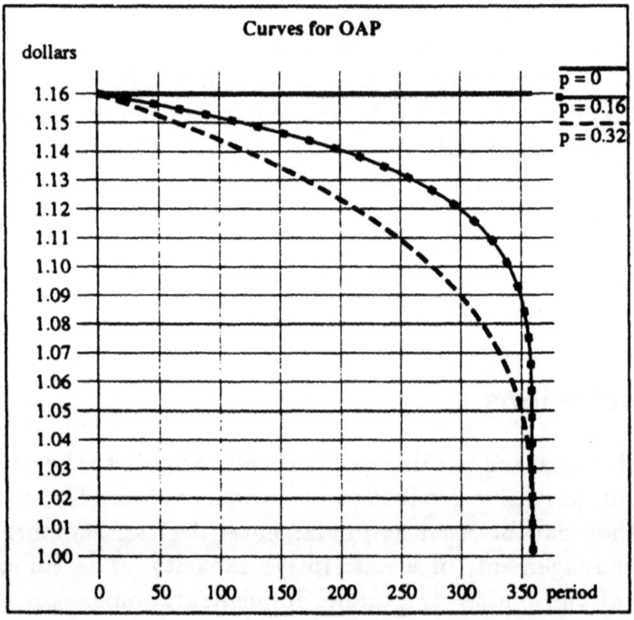

Figure 11: *top:* Effect of varying option adjusted premium on price paths of a FNMA 11.5 with $\rho_0 = 1.16$ and $p = 0, 0.16, 0.32$. *bottom:* Curves of equation 5 for $\rho_0 = 1.16$ and $p = 0, 0.16, 0.32$.

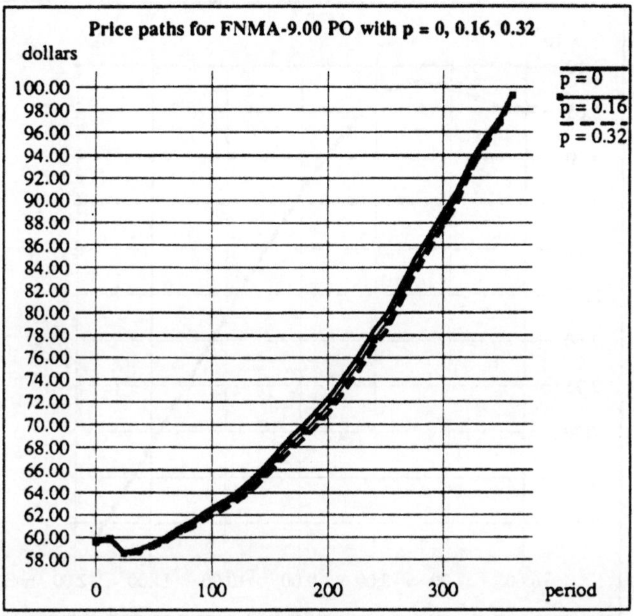

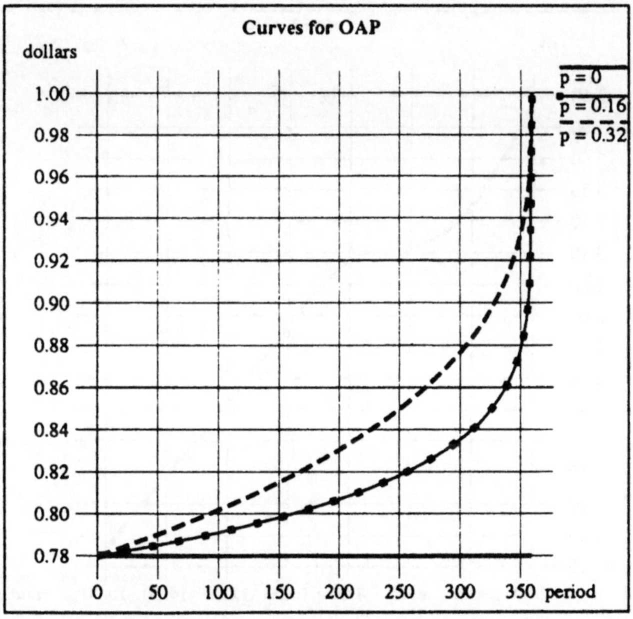

Figure 12: *top:* Effect of varying option adjusted premium on price path of a FNMA 9.00 PO with $\rho_0 = 0.78$ and $p = 0,\ 0.16,\ 0.32$. *bottom:* Curves of equation 5 for $\rho_0 = 0.78$ and $p = 0,\ 0.16,\ 0.32$.

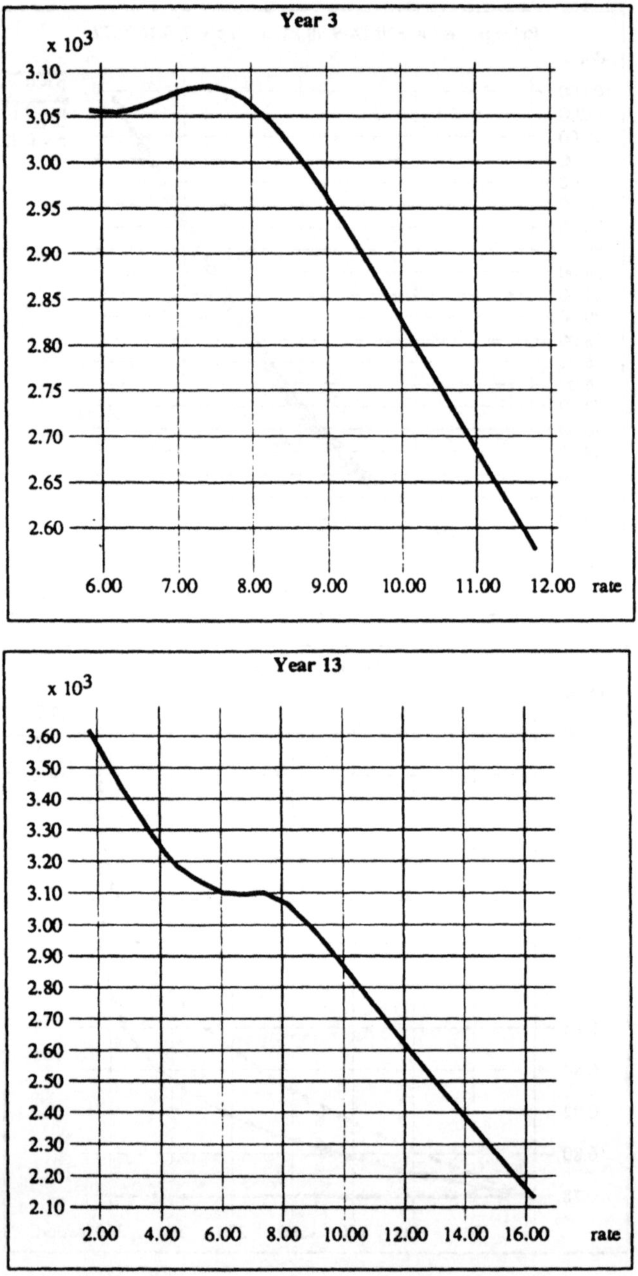

Figure 13: Price paths of a portfolio of MBS in the dynamic environment for different states of the binomial lattice at years 3 and 13.

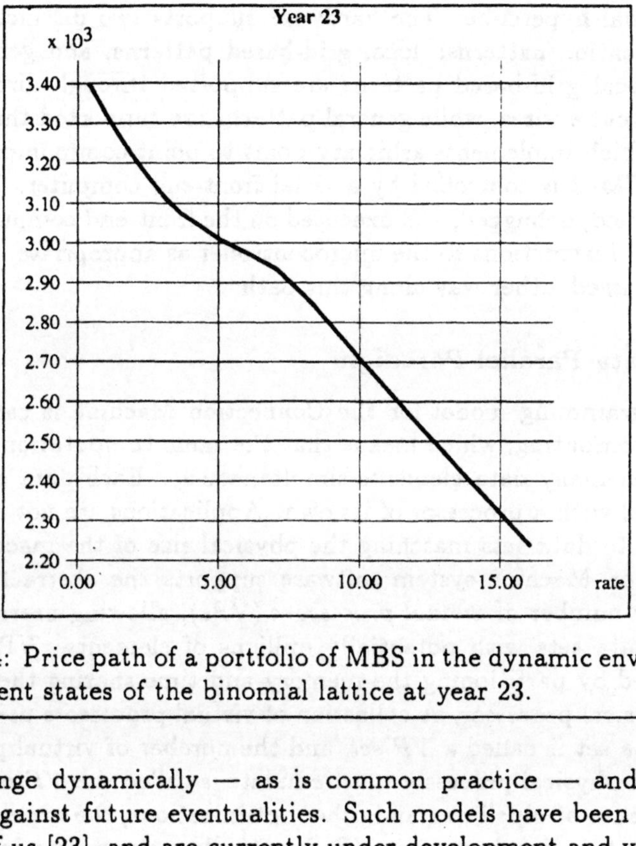

Figure 14: Price path of a portfolio of MBS in the dynamic environment for different states of the binomial lattice at year 23.

that change dynamically — as is common practice — and are well hedged against future eventualities. Such models have been proposed by one of us [23], and are currently under development and validation.

A The Connection Machine CM–2 System

This appendix introduces to the Connection Machine CM–2 system. Expanded discussions include Hillis [11, 12].

A.1 Architecture Overview

The Connection Machine is a fine grain massively parallel supercomputer. It uses a single instruction stream, multiple data stream (SIMD) methodology: each processor executes the same instruction broadcast by a microcontroller on its unique piece of data, or optionally sits out of the computation. The CM–2 has from 4096 to 65536 bit-serial processors, each with local memory of either 8 or 32 Kbytes. Each processor also has access to 32-bit or 64-bit floating point acceleration hardware.

The interconnection scheme for processors in the CM–2 is an N-dimensional hypercube. The hardware supports two distinct types of communication patterns: local grid-based patterns, and general patterns. Local grid-based patterns are supported through direct use of the hypercube wires, while general patterns are supported through the *router*, which implements arbitrary point to point communication.

The CM-2 is controlled by a serial front-end computer. Programs are compiled, debugged, and executed on the front-end computer, passing CM-2 instructions to the microcontroller as appropriate. Data can also be passed either way along this path.

A.2 Data-Parallel Paradigm

The programming model for the Connection Machine is called data-parallel computing, which means that the same computations are performed on many data elements simultaneously. Each data element is associated with a processor of its own. Applications are not restricted, however, to data sets matching the physical size of the machine. The Connection Machine system software supports the abstraction of an arbitrary number of *virtual processors* (VPs), allowing users to easily handle data sets with potentially millions of elements. VPs are implemented by partitioning the memory and time-sharing the cycles of each physical processor. A collection of virtual processors used to handle a data set is called a *VP set*, and the number of virtual processors that each physical processor must emulate is called the *VP ratio*. Note that because of pipelining and other optimizations, the expected linear slowdown from implementing VPs is actually a worst case scenario.

Applications that have no dependencies between data elements are often called *embarassingly parallel*, and are easy to implement efficiently on any parallel computer. Most applications, however, exhibit dependencies between data elements. This gives rise to the need for communications between the processing elements. Furthermore, there is often a natural physical shape to arrange the data, such that dependent elements are laid out close to one another. Weather simulations, for instance, are naturally laid out in a three dimensional grid representing the volume of atmosphere being simulated.

The Connection Machine software allows users to specify the shape of a data set by associating a *geometry* with the VP set of the data. Geometries can be any N-dimensional Cartesian grid. Because an N-dimensional hypercube can be projected onto any lower dimensional Cartesian grid, the software can lay out the grid on the machine so that there is either a hypercube wire between each neighboring grid point, or they are held in the same physical processor (i.e., reside on

VPs that are emulated by the same physical processor), and therefore local communication is fast and efficient. This kind of communication is called NEWS communication, and processors in the grid can be uniquely identified by the N-tuple of Cartesian coordinates called its NEWS address. General router-based communications is performed with a single unique identifier for each VP called its send address.

An important class of Connection Machine instructions that combine computations and communications is the class of parallel prefix operations, Blelloch [3]. These primitives apply associative binary arithmetic to a variable in a binary combining tree along one axis of the geometry. For example, a scan-addition along the first axis of a one-dimensional variable $\{x[0], x[1], \ldots, x[n]\}$ yields $\{y[0], y[1], \ldots, y[n]\}$, where $y[i] = x[0] + x[1] + \cdots + x[i]$ (i.e., the cumulative sum to that point in the axis). Options allow the result to omit a processor's own value for x (e.g., $y[i] = x[0]+x[1]+\cdots+x[i-1]$) or for the operation to proceed in the reverse direction (e.g., $y[i] = x[i] + x[i+1] + \cdots + x[n]$). In contrast, a spread is a scan without directionality. The result of a spread-addition is $y[i] = x[0]+x[1]+\cdots+x[n]$. These primitives extend naturally to multi-dimensional geometries. Furthermore, their execution times are proportional to the logarithm of the number of VPs, and thus scale nicely to large data sets.

Acknowledgments

This research was carried out as part of the University/Private Industry Collaboration initiative of the Decision, Risk and Management Science program of NSF. The industrial sponsors are BlackRock Financial Management of New York and the Federal National Mortgage Association (Fannie Mae) of Washington. We gratefully acknowledge the numerous contributions to this project by Dr. Ben Golub and Dr. Larry Pohlman of BlackRock Financial Management and by Dr. Martin Holmer formerly of Fannie Mae and currently of HR&A, Inc. (Washington office).

This research was partially supported by NSF grant SES–91–00216, NSF grant CCR–9104042, and AFOSR grant 91–0168. Access to the Connection Machine was made available by the General Robotics and Active Sensory Perception (GRASP) Laboratory at the University of Pennsylvania, by the North-East Parallel Architectures Center (NPAC) at Syracuse University, and by the Army High-Performance Computing Research Center (AHPCRC) at the University of Minnesota.

References

[1] D.F. Babbel and S.A. Zenios. Pitfalls in the analysis of option-adjusted spreads. *Financial Analysts Journal*, December 1992.

[2] F. Black, E. Derman, and W. Toy. A one-factor model of interest rates and its application to treasury bond options. *Financial Analysts Journal*, pages 33–39, January–February 1990.

[3] G.E. Blelloch. *Vector Models for Data-Parallel Computing*. The MIT Press, Cambridge, MA, 1990.

[4] P. Boyle. Options: A Monte Carlo approach. *Journal of Financial Economics*, 4:323–338, May 1977.

[5] L.D. Cagan, N.J. Carriero, and S.A. Zenios. Pricing mortgage backed securities with network Linda. *Financial Analysts Journal*, to appear.

[6] J. Cox, J. Ingersoll, and S. Ross. A theory of the term structure of interest rates. *Econometrica*, 53(2):385–407, March 1985.

[7] R. D'Ecclesia and S.A. Zenios. Valuation of the embedded prepayment option of mortgage backed securities. Technical Report 92-07-02, Wharton School of Business, University of Pennsylvania, July 1992.

[8] B. Golub. Private communication. BlackRock Financial Management, NY, 1991.

[9] L.S. Hayre. Understanding option-adjusted spreads and their use. *The Journal of Portfolio Management*, 16:68–71, Summer 1990.

[10] R.S. Hiller and J. Eckstein. Stochastic dedication: Designing fixed income portfolios using massively parallel Benders decomposition. *Management Science*, to appear.

[11] W. D. Hillis. *The Connection Machine*. The MIT Press, Cambridge, MA, 1985.

[12] W. D. Hillis. The Connection Machine. *Scientific American*, June 1987.

[13] M.R. Holmer. The asset/liability management strategy system at Fannie Mae. *Interfaces*, to appear.

[14] J.M. Hutchinson and S.A. Zenios. Financial simulations on a massively parallel Connection Machine. *International Journal of Supercomputer Applications*, 5(2):27–45, 1991.

[15] P. Kang and S.A. Zenios. Complete prepayment models for mortgage backed securities. *Management Sciences*, November 1992.

[16] J.B. Kau, D.C. Keenan, W.J. Muller, and J.F. Epperson. The valuation and analysis of adjustable rate mortgages. *Management Science*, 36(12):1417–1431, 1990.

[17] J.J. McConnel and M.J. Singh. Prepayments and the valuation of adjustable rate mortgage backed securities. Technical report, Krannert School of Management, Purdue University, October 1990.

[18] North East Parallel Architectures Center, Syracuse University, Syracuse, NY. *Parallel Computing News*, August–October 1991.

[19] K. Ramaswamy and S. Sundaresan. The valuation of floating rate instruments: Theory and evidence. *Journal of Financial Economics*, pages 251–272, December 1986.

[20] E.S. Schwartz and W.N. Torous. Prepayment and the valuation of mortgage backed securities. *Journal of Finance*, XLIV:375–392, 1989.

[21] Thinking Machines Corporation, Cambridge, MA. *Connection Machine CM-200 Series Technical Summary*, 1991.

[22] K. Worzel and S.A. Zenios. Tracking a mortgage index: An optimization approach. Technical Report 92-08-01, Wharton School of Business, University of Pennsylvania, August 1992.

[23] S.A. Zenios. Massively parallel computations for financial modeling under uncertainty. In J. Mesirov, editor, *Very Large Scale Computing in the 21-st Century*, pages 273–294. SIAM, Philadelphia, PA, 1991.

GPSR Compliance

The European Union's (EU) General Product Safety Regulation (GPSR) is a set of rules that requires consumer products to be safe and our obligations to ensure this.

If you have any concerns about our products, you can contact us on ProductSafety@springernature.com

In case Publisher is established outside the EU, the EU authorized representative is:

Springer Nature Customer Service Center GmbH
Europaplatz 3
69115 Heidelberg, Germany

Batch number: 10725973

Printed by Printforce, the Netherlands